THE KELLY'S

THE KELLY'S

British J, K and N Class Destroyers of World War II

CHRISTOPHER LANGTREE

Drawings by John Lambert

Colour profiles by John Roberts

CHATHAM PUBLISHING
LONDON

Dedication
To my wife Lulu
Whose life and joy made this all possible

Frontispiece: HMS *Kipling* at Second Battle of Sirte, 22 March 1942.
(IMPERIAL WAR MUSEUM: A8165)

Copyright © Christopher Langtree 2002
Line drawings copyright © John Lambert
Colour profiles copyright © John Roberts

First published in Great Britain in 2002 by Chatham Publishing,
99 High Street, Rochester, Kent ME1 1LX

Distributed by Gerald Duckworth & Co Ltd,
61 Frith Street, London W1D 3JL

British Library Cataloguing in Publication Data
A catalogue record for this book is available from the British Library

ISBN 1 86176 166 X

Designed and typeset by Roger Daniels
Printed in Spain by Grafilur

Contents

Introduction

THE IDEA FOR THIS BOOK arose out of initial research into one member of the 'K' class, *Kingston*. Living near the town of the same name I was curious to find out more about its 'local' destroyer. Research in the local archives turned up ample information on *Kingston*'s launch and relationship with the town but only an incomplete history of the ship. This very incompleteness prompted me to dig further – the history I found had large gaps and I was curious about these. An account written by one of her crew members was also of little help as it concentrated on her later career. If I wanted to fill in the gaps I would have to do a bit of digging. The ideal place for this sort of digging is the United Kingdom's Public Records Office (PRO) at Kew which fortunately I am not too far from. (The PRO represents a marvellous source of Second World War naval information, albeit somewhat disorganised.) By now my research into *Kingston* had expanded to cover all eight destroyers of the 'K' class including Mountbatten's *Kelly*, the most famous member of this group of ships and the only one to have received significant attention. About this time and after a particularly nice bottle of wine the idea of turning this research into a book which would cover these ships arose and I decided to approach someone to publish the book. I must express my thanks to Chatham Publishing who were prepared to look at my proposal and agree to publish what for me is my first attempt at writing a full-length book. They did, though, suggest that I should expand the book to include the two other identical classes of ships, the 'Js' and 'Ns'.

Moving on to the ships themselves, the Kellys (I am using the name 'Kelly' as a convenient shorthand for all twenty-four members of the group) were a radical and innovative break in destroyer design which set the standard for the classes that followed. Introducing many new and innovative features these ships suffered from serious teething problems which had to be overcome before they could realise their full potential. Not all these problems could be overcome, however, particularly the limited elevation of their main armament which created serious difficulties in dealing with air attack. The Kellys had been designed to take a quite heavy – for the time – anti-aircraft armament but this was focused on close-range defence and in the rapidly changing circumstances of the war was quickly outmoded. Improvements and updates to this armament would continue throughout the war but a more innovative policy earlier might have possibly resulted in fewer losses. The Kellys were big ships with a heavy armament and, reflecting the prevailing philosophy at the time, carried a heavy torpedo outfit. However, by the end of the war, requirements had changed and the ideas represented by these ships were no longer relevant and there was no post-war role for them without extensive conversion. Thus they ended up being the ultimate wartime destroyer.

Kellys served in most of the wartime theatres of operation but were particularly active in the Mediterranean for which they proved ideal. They saw hard use and of the ships lost, only two were sunk outside this theatre. Losses were mainly concentrated in 1941 and 1942, reflecting the two hardest years of the war and also emphasising the extensive use these ships were put to. Most were lost to some form of air attack with the next major cause being mines. Whilst a main armament with a high-angle capability might have helped these ships it is unlikely that it would have ensured the survival of any that were lost as only sufficient air cover could have done that. Ships such as cruisers and battleships with far superior high-angle armament also had similar problems in dealing with air attack. By the end of the war most were worn out and some, the 'K' class in particular, were placed in reserve immediately the war with Germany ended.

The Kellys also had the distinction of possessing the only flotilla to be entirely non-British manned. The 'N' class consisted of five Australian, two Dutch and one Polish-manned ship. The Dutch vessels would also prove to be the longest-serving Kellys, surviving until the early 1950s. They were unique in the fact that they were purchased by the Netherlands authorities before completion to serve in the Dutch East Indies though they would not do so until after the end of the war. Surprisingly one Kelly also served on the Atlantic convoy runs, the Polish *Piorun* taking part in several of these during 1941 and 1942. Even though this was well outside the originally envisaged functions of the type, her performance was good enough to earn the praise of her escort commanders, the commander of Escort Group B2 commenting 'She did extremely well throughout and never put a foot wrong … a most efficient ship, whom I hope to have with me again.' *Piorun* would also go on to escort several arctic convoys as well, being 'arcticised' for this role. After the war there were also plans to turn these ships into anti-submarine frigates, but these came to nothing for reasons of economy and the age of their hulls. The needs of the Royal

Navy had changed and there was now no requirement for big fleet destroyers such as the Kellys. Those ships that were not converted were to be scrapped – a sad end for a class of ships that had performed their various functions so well.

In writing this book I have endeavoured to rely on primary sources as much as possible. These include documents such as original reports of proceedings, war diaries and ships' logs. This has not always been possible and I have had to use some secondary sources as well. In using these I have tried to obtain confirmation from two separate sources and where I have been unable to do so, I have mentioned it in the footnotes. Secondary sources have also been useful in filling out or adding detail to dry official accounts as well and I hope the end result is a comprehensive and interesting read. Photographs come from collections of both private individuals and museums around the world and have been selected for their interest and relevance. Thus the reader will see several that are familiar but they will also see many that are previously unpublished. Despite all my efforts though, I have been unable to locate photos of certain ships during their career, I have found no photos of *Khartoum* in service, for example, and likewise the Red Sea Destroyer Force proved a blank. Others I have had trouble with are *Janus* and *Kimberley* after they re-commissioned in 1943 and 1944 respectively though I have some idea of the configuration of both ships.

I have also included a chapter on camouflage, which was extensive on all Kellys. Too many books frequently ignore this aspect of a ship's history but camouflage was a vital part of a ship's later design. For all camouflage information I have restricted myself to photographs and the occasional official report (if it mentions it at all, which the great majority of them did not). I have also included several colour camouflage profiles all of which are based exclusively on photographs. Once again I am faced with gaps in the record and frustratingly have found only partial views of some ships, for example *Jervis* in summer 1944. In these cases I have not attempted to reconstruct the scheme but have referred to it. I have tried to make my list of camouflage schemes as comprehensive as possible but even as I write the Introduction, three more previously unknown schemes turned up. Because of this I cannot say that this is an exhaustive record of the camouflage applied to the Kellys, only that it is the most comprehensive compilation to date.

As a shorthand for the 'J', 'K' and 'N' class I have adopted the term the 'Kellys' based on their most famous member, Lord Mountbatten's ship, *Kelly*. This term is used when I wish to refer to all three classes together, and otherwise I have called them the 'J', 'K' or 'N' class. The actual class name for the 'J' class was the *Javelin* class, the *Kashmir* or *Kelly* class for the 'Ks' and the *Nerissa* or *Napier* class for the 'Ns'. The practice of naming the class by their initial letter was probably more common though. It only remains to say that whilst I have tried to be as accurate and comprehensive as possible there will be mistakes and omissions. These are the responsibility of the author alone.

Acknowledgements
A book like this, especially a first book, does not rest upon a single person's efforts but involves contributions from many quarters. Listed below are many of the people and institutions who have made this volume possible. I should also mention the efforts of several others, too numerous to name, who helped by trying to answer specific questions.

John Lambert provided a magnificent set of drawings for this book and was also an enthusiastic and knowledgeable collaborator. John Roberts provided the wonderful camouflage profiles you see in this volume and for whom, once again, no trouble was too great. I must also mention D K Brown and Marek Twardowski. D K Brown was most generous with his time and knowledge, generously consenting to proof-read several chapters of the book and making clear and incredibly useful suggestions for their improvement. Marek Twardowski allowed me access to his unpublished research on *Piorun* and gave me permission to use it as I wished. Thanks also go to Dimitrios Apostolopoulos who provided much valuable help and information for the sections on camouflage.

Several official institutions were also extremely helpful. Leon Homberg of the Dutch Marinemuseum and Jac van der Avert of the Instituut voor Maritieme Historie were both helpful and very patient with my incessant questions about the two Dutch 'N' class ships. The French Musée de la Marine was particularly helpful in allowing me access to the Le Masson Collection of photographs, taken during the war by a seaman with the French squadron interned at Alexandria. No request was too difficult and their representative M. J M Brunner was particularly helpful. Thanks must also go to Imogen Gibbon and Bob Todd at the National Maritime Museum for their helpfulness and patience. The staff of the photographic archive at the Imperial War Museum were also extremely helpful and understanding.

I would also like to mention the following who all helped in some capacity, Art Nicholson, Mackenzie Gregory, Robert Brown, the Australian War Memorial, Charles Kellam of the Glasgow City Archives and John Sutherland. Finally I would like to thank my wife, Lulu, who supported me throughout the writing of this book and who endured my recounting of my research trials with interest and good humour. Without her this book could not have been written.

The Design Process

AFTER THE FIRST WORLD WAR, Britain had a surplus of well-designed 'V' and 'W' class destroyers. What the war had demonstrated, however, was the unwieldiness of the wartime flotilla with members in double figures. These were reduced in size but no new destroyers were built until the 1920s. In 1924 both the Thornycroft and Yarrow yards produced prototype destroyers, the best features of which were combined to produce the new classes of destroyers. The first of these flotillas set the pattern for the following nine classes of ship which were all very similar. These were identified by the initial letter of their names and ran from 'A' to 'I', except for the class leaders which until the 'D' class had a name beginning with a different letter.[1] Each of these flotillas consisted of one leader, under the command of a full captain, and two divisions of four ships. The leaders were built to a slightly different design to accommodate the flotilla staff and were bigger. Some were also more heavily armed with five 4.7in guns instead of four.[2] With the destroyers of the 1935 Programme (the 'I' class) the number of torpedo tubes increased to ten but they were basically the same ships.

THE 1936 PROGRAMME

Because of the extra torpedo tubes, the 'I' class needed permanent ballast and this affected their performance. The basic 'A' to 'I' design was also thought to have run its course, particularly in comparison to the new designs of other navies. TD Memo 144 laid out the initial requirements for the new destroyer class. These included minesweeping equipment (the Two Speed Destroyer Sweep [TSDS]) and bow protection gear, Asdic, the ability to carry sixty Mk XIV mines and for four ships of the flotilla to be equipped with smoke-laying apparatus. The characteristics of the ships were to be

   a) To carry as heavy a torpedo armament as possible.
   b) To mount a gun armament which will enable them-
      1) To engage enemy destroyers successfully.
      2) To defend themselves against close range air attack.

      3) To contribute in as high a degree as possible to the collective anti-aircraft security of the fleet or ships in company with the destroyers.
   c) Great speed is not of primary importance.
   d) Endurance should be sufficient to give destroyers a reasonable chance of reaching the scene of action.
   e) Good sea keeping qualities.
   f) Good manoeuvring powers.
   g) As small a displacement as possible.

What strikes one immediately about these characteristics is the importance attached to torpedo armament and in fact the rest of the destroyer's functions were subordinated to this function. The destroyer gun was primarily to enable the ship to force its way into a suitable torpedo-firing position and to prevent enemy destroyers from reaching a similar position against the battle fleet.[3] This view did not go unchallenged and there was pressure for a mount with at least 70° elevation which would at least give a good dual-purpose capacity and a 60° mounting (the CPXIII) was tried on the destroyer *Bulldog*.[4] This mounting was considered unsuitable but the angle of elevation for single 4.7in mounts was increased to 40° from the 'E' class destroyers onwards. However, this only gave a very limited improvement in anti-aircraft capability and the Second World War would show it to be totally inadequate. Part of the reluctance to introduce a mount with adequate dual-purpose capability was due to the amount of time the design and construction of new mounts took. It was considered unacceptable to delay the introduction of much-needed destroyers whilst the new mount was developed and the DNO was against any such delay. He was also opposed to the introduction of power mountings though these would be eventually included.

The original plan to build repeat 'I' class ships had also been abandoned though for the time being the nine-ship flotilla was to be kept. What had prompted the change was the new destroyers entering or already in service overseas. The United States *Porter* class and the Japanese *Fubuki* and *Shiratsuyu* classes which carried eight 5in, six 5in and five 5in guns respectively were seen as outmatching the current 'A' to 'I' classes. The 'Tribals' (eight 4.7in, four torpedo tubes) were an effective answer to these ships but too restricted in their scope. Their torpedo armament was too small and they were not really ordinary destroyers but more 'super destroyers' built to challenge their equivalents in other navies. The need was for a well-armed ordinary destroyer to perform all the functions of the earlier classes but also

---

[1] For example the leader of the 'B' class was named *Keith*.
[2] *Keith* ('B' class), *Kempenfelt* ('C' class) and *Duncan* ('D' class) only carried four 4.7in guns.

[3] TD Memo 144, Ships Cover 565.
[4] See TD 58/36 8 May 1936 Ships Cover 565 for a good summary of this debate.

to fulfil the essential torpedo attack requirements that drove destroyer thinking at the time. What is also clear is that with the introduction of the 'Tribals' and the 'J' class important factors outside the Royal Navy's requirements were driving developments. One hesitates to use the term 'keeping up with the Joneses' but effectively that was the result.

A total of nine sketch designs were prepared, JA1-3, JB1-3 and JD1-3, exploring various configurations, The JA designs had one twin turret mounted forward and two singles aft and was for a while the favoured design. JA1 was a two boiler-room variant, JA3 a three boiler-room variant, and JA2 the leader version, but these designs were dropped as the armament layout would interfere with the mounting of TSDS gear. The JB designs were all based on four single gun mounts and these were rejected because of developments with foreign designs. This left the JD designs which carried three twin mounts with the option of three boilers and two funnels or two boilers and one funnel.

The Engineer-in-Chief was very opposed to the introduction of two boilers but seeing that the last substantive discussion on the subject had taken place in 1929 was a bit out of touch. Service opinion, voiced by the fleet Commanders-in-Chief and the Commodore (D) Home Fleet wanted a powerful destroyer with a smaller silhouette and were prepared to accept the claimed disadvantages to achieve this. In the end, war service would show that the number of boilers had no effect on the usefulness of destroyers and either layout was just as vulnerable as the other. What could have improved this aspect was the unit principle which involves grouping together all the machinery needed to drive

one shaft (in the case of the Kellys). This was considered for the Kellys but as it would have complicated the machinery layout significantly was not proceeded with.

Stanley Goodall, the Director of Naval Construction, met the Controller on 10 September 1936[5] to firm up the rear gun mounting arrangement. Part of the problem with installing twin mounts was the time needed to construct them and the need for destroyers to be in service as quickly as possible. Whilst two twin mountings forward had been accepted there was still a question mark about the rear mountings with two singles being considered. The Controller, Admiral Sir Reginald Henderson, wanted twin mounts to match foreign designs and his view prevailed. He also fixed the number of mounts at three, giving the new ships a formidable armament of six 4.7in guns, a choice that was decided also by that fact that it would allow the leader to be the same size as the rest of the flotilla. Due to the delay in constructing the mounts it was planned that the ships would commission with two singles and one twin, the singles being replaced in the first year of the ships' lives. In the event this was unnecessary as there were adequate twin mounts right from the beginning. Goodall notes that the Controller was due to decide on the two boiler/three boiler question the next day. This may have been the case but the first written note of the decision to chose the two-boiler arrangement appears in the minutes of a meeting held on 24 September 1936 and once that decision was taken the design staff were instructed to work out sketch design JD1 in detail.

---

[5] Stanley Goodall, DNC, note 10 September 1936.

A superb photograph of the 'K' class destroyer *Kandahar* taken in Alexandria Harbour on May Day 1941. She is little changed from launch with only a D/F aerial added on top of her foremast and plating round the gun mounts. The markings on her funnel consist of two red bands intersected by a red bar which shows her to be the leader of the 28th Division. Also of interest are the shadows on the hull from the boats and on the superstructure. These suggest camouflage which is not actually there. (NATIONAL MARITIME MUSEUM, LONDON: 31758)

Design studies and proposals for 'J' class fleet destroyers 1936

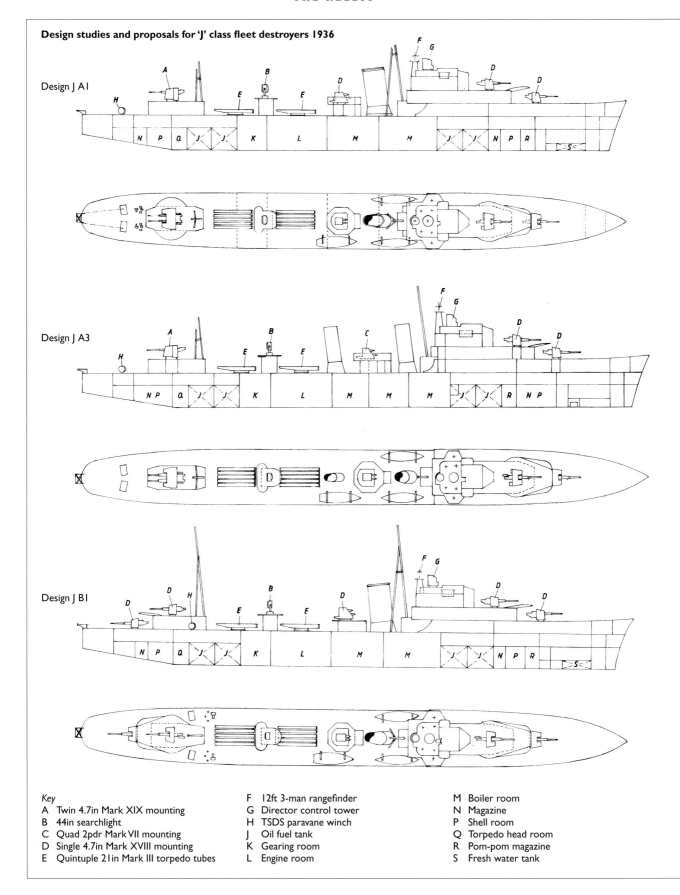

Design J A1

Design J A3

Design J B1

Key
A Twin 4.7in Mark XIX mounting
B 44in searchlight
C Quad 2pdr Mark VII mounting
D Single 4.7in Mark XVIII mounting
E Quintuple 21in Mark III torpedo tubes

F 12ft 3-man rangefinder
G Director control tower
H TSDS paravane winch
J Oil fuel tank
K Gearing room
L Engine room

M Boiler room
N Magazine
P Shell room
Q Torpedo head room
R Pom-pom magazine
S Fresh water tank

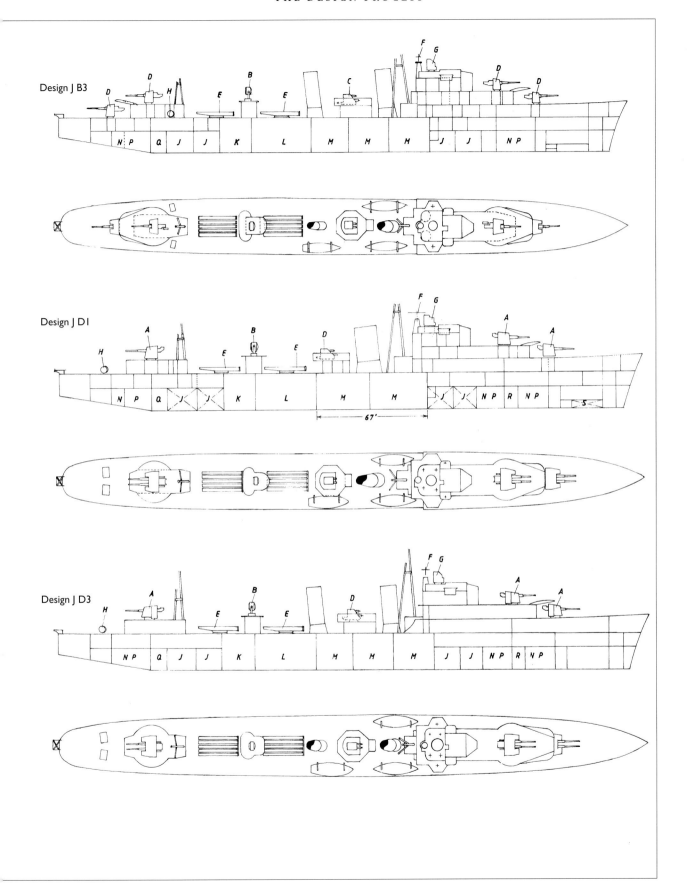

Design J B3

Design J D1

Design J D3

NEW FEATURES

In addition to the twin 4.7in mounting, the Kellys introduced many radical new features to British destroyer design. Their designer A P Cole, wanted to keep the displacement and silhouette as low as possible. For this he needed to consider radical alternatives to the standard practices of the time. The 'A' to 'I' class destroyers were constructed on the transverse system which was traditional and easy to build. With this method of construction the transverse frames were small, closely spaced and were supported by occasional deep longitudinals (often intercostal) attached to them to form the basic structure of the hull. The problem with this method of construction was that the transverse frames did not contribute directly to the overall strength of the hull in bending. The longitudinal system was different, the longitudinal frames being continuous and supported by occasional deep transverse frames. This increased the ship's resistance to buckling, particularly in the deck and the bottom. It also had the effect of making the ship's hull lighter as well but the full benefits of this would only be apparent through the use of welding rather than riveting.[6] As mentioned later longitudinal construction would be opposed by all shipbuilders though they were forced to accept it. However, it did not cause as much trouble as the proposal for two boilers instead of three.

As part of the attempt to reduce the destroyer's silhouette, Cole wanted to restrict the number of boilers to two. The proposal to build destroyers with only two boilers had actually been around since 1928, well before Cole became head of destroyer design but had been resisted. Current design practice was two funnels and three boilers but this made for rather visible destroyers. Both the Americans and

[6] D K Brown, Letter to the author 23 March 2001. Mr Brown gives an excellent explanation of the differences which I have used pretty much as he described.

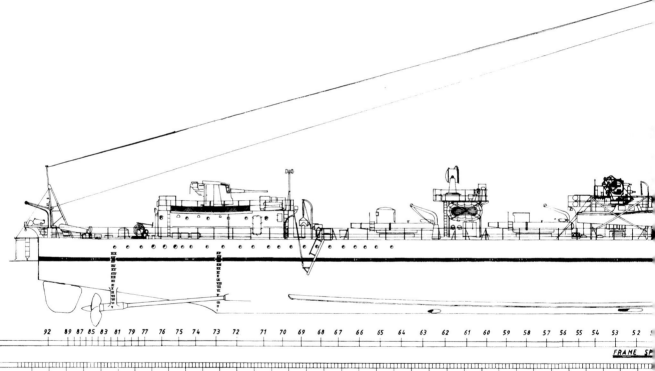

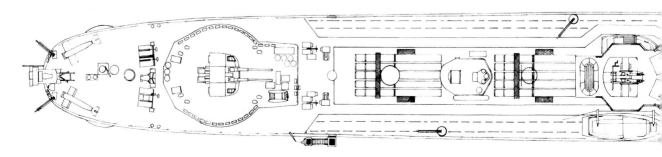

Italians had demonstrated the feasibility of single funnel designs but various objections had been raised.[7] These centred around the changes that would result in watch-keeping practice which would result from having just two boilers. Boiler cleaning in peacetime would also be more difficult as steaming on one boiler would not be safe. Of course, with three boilers a ship would still have two available to use should the need arise. The question of damage also needed to be considered, as with one boiler out of action, there was a considerable reduction in the ship's capabilities. When Cole proposed the two-boiler arrangement he made sure that the sketch designs included three boiler layouts as well. Even so, the Engineer-in-Chief was adamantly opposed to the introduction of the new layout.[8]

[7] The Italian *Dardo* and the American *Bagley* classes, for example.
[8] See TD126A/36 'Revision of staff requirements for destroyers' and D K Brown, *Nelson to Vanguard*, for a summary of the Engineer-in-Chief's arguments.

HMS *Kelvin* (as completed), November 1939

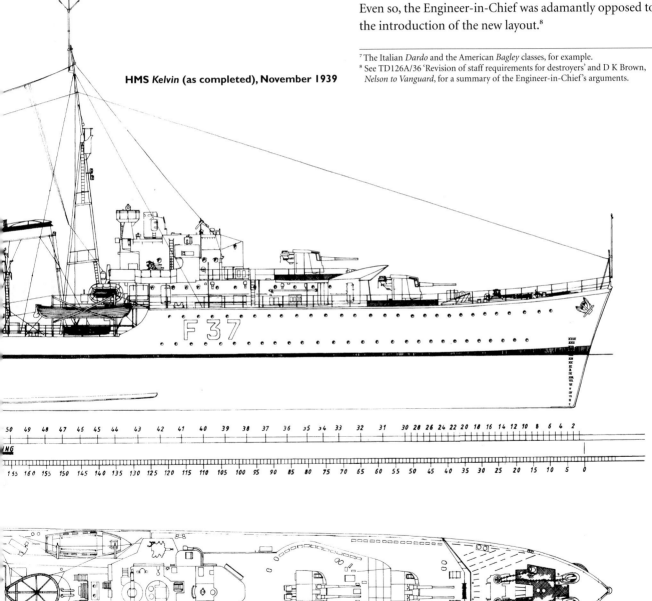

Loading a torpedo onto *Piorun* in early 1941. The Kellys were the first destroyers designed from the outset for the quintuple tube without the need for ballast which was considered a great sin.

(IMPERIAL WAR MUSEUM: 2524)

At the meeting on 24 September 1936, however, the Engineer-in-Chief was overruled by the Controller who considered that the advantages outweighed the disadvantages, particularly with regard to the reduction of silhouette. In this he was supported by the Commodore (D) of the Home Fleet and the Commander-in-Chief Mediterranean whose opinions had been canvassed. Mountbatten also claimed to have had a role: at the time he was serving at the Admiralty and through his friendship with Cole had gotten involved in the design process.[9] He claimed to have visited Henderson and convinced him to accept the two-boiler design. Whilst Mountbatten did play a significant part in the 'J' class design it is unlikely that he was involved in this decision. The Controller, Admiral Henderson, was an innovative and forward-thinking officer who was not averse to new ideas or designs. He had been instrumental in developing early carrier tactics, significantly those to do with dive bombing, and was a forceful character well able to push

through a change if he saw some advantage to it. Furthermore, both the Commanders-in-Chief of the Mediterranean Fleet and the Home Fleet were in favour of the idea and their opinions would have carried considerably more weight than Mountbatten's. So even if Mountbatten had visited Henderson his role in this decision would have been small to non-existent.[10]

Both Commanders-in-Chief had also wanted 70° elevation main gun mounts but these were not possible because of the need to minimise the ships' silhouette. For service purposes, the end-on silhouette was considered more important than the broadside silhouette, and it was considered impossible to achieve a small end-on silhouette with a 70°

[9] See Alan Payne, 'The Introduction of the J Class Destroyers', *Warship 14*.

[10] Mountbatten did sometimes exaggerate his role in matters. Various authors have mentioned this trait, particularly Hough.

mounting.[11] Thus the 70° mounting was dropped from consideration and the 40° mounting as fitted to the 'Tribals' was chosen. Even then the C-in-C Mediterranean suggested stiffening should be included so that the ships could be converted later but this idea was rejected.[12] What was accepted was the introduction of power hoists for the 4.7in mountings. These were electrically operated dredger hoists and two were fitted to each mounting, one for cordite and one for shells. At the same time an electrically operated bollard hoist was installed for raising pom-pom ammunition from the magazine. Also accepted were the move to a flotilla consisting of two divisions of four ships each rather than the previous arrangements,[13] and the installation of TSDS on all ships though the decision would cause problems for divisional leaders.

Two quintuple torpedo mounts were to be fitted, giving the class a formidable torpedo armament. Consideration was given to fitting quadruple mounts instead which would have save 8 tons in weight but this was rejected.

The original requirement for the destroyer to carry sixty mines was dropped. The 'I' class were convertible to minelayers and two of the 'E' class ships had been built specially for this role. New minelayers would be specially-designed fast ships with a significantly larger capacity. The TSDS capacity was retained but with permanent paravane davits as opposed to the demountable ones of earlier classes. A mock-up of the quarterdeck was constructed to ascertain the most appropriate layout for both the TSDS and depth charges.[14] As a result, various recommendations emerged. The TSDS davits were moved outboard and forward of the stern to permit access to the towing slip but at the same time they were to overhang the stern by 6ft 6in. A particular problem was the design of the ensign staff which finally had to be placed 9½ft from the stern. The location of the depth charges was actually decided later. There were to be twelve charges on the quarterdeck of which six would be stored in the rack rather than three as with earlier destroyers. The other six were located, three on each side of the aft superstructure. Firing was controlled from the bridge with an emergency release handle attached to the rack as well.

The close-range anti-aircraft armament was quite advanced for its day but outmoded by the time war arrived. It had been proposed to fit a pom-pom director but this was dropped on grounds of weight and lack of space. Also

included in the initial detail designs were a tripod main mast. This was dropped to allow No 3 mount to train nearer to full ahead and improve the arcs of the pom-pom. To take the radio aerials an aerial spreader would be fitted to the searchlight platform. Radio equipment varied between the leader and ordinary destroyers and whilst both would have had 49A and 51HA (AC) sets the leaders would carry a 60 BLA (AC) as well which was to be located in a second office.

Sir Roger Blackhouse (C-in-C Home Fleet) considered that the sides of the new ships would be too weak.[15] At the time 90 per cent of accidents to destroyers were caused during berthing and as this practice was very common damage would be caused to the new ships. In the event, the Kellys were able to resist berthing damage better than the earlier classes and Sir Roger's concerns were unfounded.

Another request that was not accepted was for a speed of 33kts in deep condition. This would have required an extra 3000hp to achieve and it could not be obtained on two boilers which even with a new design would only develop 20,000hp each. The design deep condition speed was therefore fixed at 32kts which was acceptable given the requirement in section (c) of TD Memo 144 (see above). Extra speed also reduced endurance by increasing fuel consumption and this rose very quickly for each extra knot above 30kts (see Appendix 8). The design for the new boilers was directed by Rear-Admiral Dight with the aim that they would be able to reach 20,000hp. These were to drive a two-shaft arrangement with each shaft driving an HP and LP turbine connected in series. The drive to each propeller shaft would be though a single helical reduction gearing, these being installed in a separate gearing room. The boilers themselves would have a working pressure of 300lbs in² and a temperature of 630° Fahrenheit with superheat of 220° Fahrenheit. Steering was electro-hydraulic with two single rams acting on the tiller located in the tiller flat. A hand pump was installed for emergency use which proved to be a very useful facility to have. Boiler rooms would prove a vulnerable part of the ship, being susceptible to damage but reduction of silhouette had become the overriding principal so any discussion of an alternative arrangement was short-lived. The propellers were to be of 10ft 6in diameter with a pitch of 13ft 2in and a developed surface area of 65 sq ft, compared with propellers of 9ft 6in diameter with a pitch of 13ft and a developed surface area of 53 sq ft for the 'A' class. This was considered sufficient to give the Kellys a propulsive co-efficient of 0.54 in deep condition (defined as 2320 tons) and 0.55 in legend or light condition.

Later changes to the design were mainly internal. On 16

[11] Memo of conversation 29 September 1936 between L D Stanfield (ADNC Destroyers) and DNC.
[12] Memo, 9 October 1936.
[13] Suggested by the C-in-C Home Fleet.
[14] Minutes of conference at Admiralty between DNE, DTM, Vernon, SMD and DNC, 7 January 1938.
[15] Letter 31 October 1936.

May 1939, Captains Mack and Mountbatten, D7 and D5 respectively, met with the Director of Naval Equipment and A P Cole to discuss changes they wanted to the leaders. Both wanted the telegraphic and signal staff reduced by six and replaced by a further eight petty officers. They were to be accommodated in the stoker petty officers' mess and an additional mess would be fitted on the starboard side of the aft lower deck mess for six petty officers. As a result additional access was required and this was arranged via the aft shell room hatch. The other major change was the conversion of the potato store into a coxswain's office. Both captains felt that the omission of such a room was a mistake especially as the coxswain did need somewhere for paperwork and interviews. The decontamination store would become the new potato store, being divided by a longitudinal line middle bulkhead. The port side would then hold bleach powder and the starboard side the potato supply. All these modifications were agreed without problem and would be carried out to *Jervis* on her next refit and *Kelly* before launch.

SUPERSTRUCTURE

The bridge structure of a destroyer was a significant part of its silhouette. The structure of the 'A' to 'G' class was designed to permit the helmsman to see over the top of No 2 mount. With the 'H' class a new bridge design was trialed. This introduced a sloped front which was meant to improve wind flow over the bridge. The helmsman's steering position was raised slightly to allow him to see over the twin 4.7in mounting that was due to be installed in *Hereward*. *Hero* also received the new bridge but not the twin 4.7in. *Hereward* also carried an extended aft deckhouse to test the concept of a leader with the same hull as the rest of a class rather than the then current practice of building separate, slightly larger leaders. These trials showed a need for the deckhouse to be wider.[16] The re-designed bridge which had been introduced for the 'V' class leaders ('Tribals') was installed in the 'I' class and the 'Tribals' themselves before being selected for the Kellys and all subsequent wartime designed destroyers.

---

[16] S V Goodall, Ships Cover No 565a.

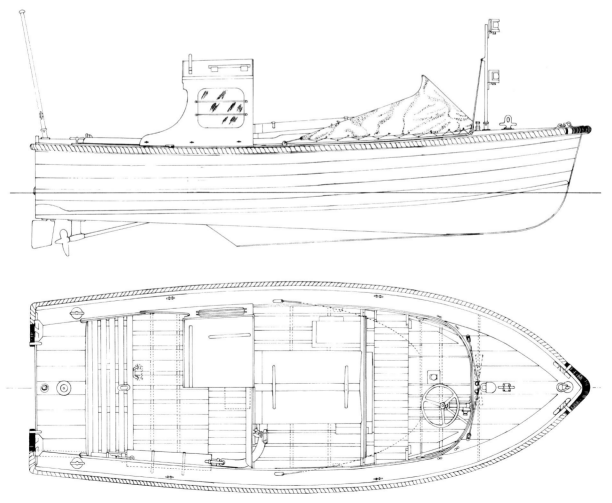

14ft Fast Motor Dinghy (Skimming Dish), 1937-1944

25ft Admiralty Motor Cutter, 1940-1944

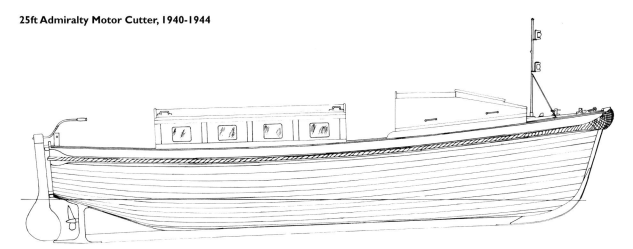

Once again Mountbatten claimed a substantial role in the design but this time with more justification. How much was directly attributable to him is unknown, however. He had returned to London in early 1936 and renewed his acquaintance with A P Cole. Both got on well together and were prepared to discuss each other's areas of expertise. Mountbatten has been credited with suggesting the recessed fore-end which was a result of the need to raise the helmsman's position so he could see over No 2 mount as described above and this is the more plausible explanation for that particular change rather than that of preventing wetness on the bridge.[17] However, the Mountbatten roof, which was intended to keep bridges drier, was not liked and rarely used. It is likely that the general design of the bridge was already settled by very early 1936, before Mountbatten returned to the UK and his role was mainly to do with the layout of the bridge and its facilities. A major change to the actual bridge design by the time Mountbatten returned would have been expensive and unlikely.

The extended rear deckhouse was intended for the accommodation of the flotilla captain's staff and was quite effective for this purpose, although it did bring a weight penalty and took up significantly more of the upper deck than those installed in earlier leaders. This led to the omission of TSDS gear in the leaders of each of the Kelly classes (decided on 14 October 1936) and the sighting of the depth charge throwers on the stern rather than in front of the deckhouse. It had the advantage, though, of eliminating the need for a separate hull for the leader of a flotilla and facilitating repair and maintenance.[18]

STABILITY

The Controller's Board minute of 15 April 1937 for the new design was very specific on the subject of stability for the Kellys;

> The steady growth of top weight carried by destroyers renders the provision of satisfactory stability difficult. In some cases, more particularly foreign destroyers, ballast is carried in certain conditions to satisfy stability requirements. This is considered undesirable. The sizes of the main compartments and the form of the ship have been arranged so that stability should be satisfactory in all conditions without ballast.

The earlier 'I' class had needed permanent ballast and the design intention was that the Kellys could take to the sea without any. This was achieved initially, but later additions would mean that the introduction of ballast would be necessary so that by the end of the war the survivors of the class carried 40 to 50 tons of ballast to compensate. In fact the addition of ballast began as early as December 1939 when 5 tons of pig iron was fitted in the machinery spaces to compensate for the addition of 10lb mild steel protection round the searchlight platform.[19] Throughout their career careful attention would be paid to the amount of top weight on these destroyers. These precautions were perhaps not so necessary in the case of the Kellys which had been designed with adequate stability to start off with, but by taking great care with later additions and subtractions from top weight, the Royal Navy ensured that none of their ships capsized due to extreme weather conditions.

The ultimate vindication of the stability of the Kellys must be the torpedo hits on *Jersey* and *Kelly* where both destroyers

---

[17] Which is an explanation given in several books, see Hough, *Bless our Ship*, for example.

[18] When Fairfield built *Napier* they re-used several drawings originally used for *Juno*.

[19] CAFO 3809/39 issued 7 December 1939.

received damage in their machinery spaces but survived. The desire to keep the silhouette low also helped stability. In the case of *Kelly* this was helped by perceptive damage control on her captain's part. Initially stability would be calculated before being ascertained accurately by inclining the ship. Stability calculations were quite complex and time-consuming and really only gave an idea of what the various factors were likely to be, especially after flooding.[20] Whilst strictly belonging in the chapter on construction and trials, the figures for *Jackal* have been included here to illustrate the difference between the calculated and the actual results.

TABLE 1:
Results of Jackal's *inclining on 28 January 1939* [21]

Item	Light		Deep	
	As calculated	From Inclining	As calculated	From Inclining
Displacement	1720 tons	1724 tons	2320 tons	2332 tons
KG	15.6ft	15.54ft	14.17ft (fluid)	14.11ft (fluid)
GM	2.72ft	2.76ft	2.73ft (fluid)	2.78 (fluid)
Trim by stern	7in	8¾in	8½in	8½in

NOTE: The standard displacement based on inclining was 1710 tons in comparison with 1690 tons as originally reported and 1707 tons as calculated.

These figures, coupled with those from *Javelin* (1 June 1939) and *Jaguar* (22 August 1939) enabled the calculation of the maximum angles when the ship reached her maximum stability and beyond which her righting force diminished. Figures for *Jervis* (20 April 1939) showed that the leaders had slightly more stability and a better set of maximum

---

[20] Ships Cover 565, I have not attempted to explain stability theory but would recommend the interested reader to consult D K Brown, particularly *Warrior to Dreadnought*, *The Grand Fleet* and *Nelson to Vanguard* for discussions about stability, how it is calculated and what factors affect it.
[21] Ships Cover No 565.

angles which was to be expected from the heavier ships. For the two destroyers the angle at which stability vanished came out as over 90° for deep displacement and 67.5° for light or standard displacement. The angle for half oil condition was 83.5°. For *Jervis*, her deep displacement angle was once again over 90° and her light displacement 69°. Her half oil angle was 85° giving an improvement of about 1.5° overall. Thus when *Nizam* was hit by a freak wave in 1945 she heeled at an angle of 30 to 35° which was well within the parameters for all conditions except that of light displacement and it is unlikely that she was in that condition. *Nepal* was also hit by a freak wave and heeled over at least 25° but was able to right herself, once again demonstrating the attention to stability paid in the initial design and after.

BOATS AND ELECTRICS
The Kellys (and the 'Tribals') were designed with more electric appliances than previous classes. Electricity was provided by two 155kW turbo generators and two 50kW diesel generators providing power at 220 volts. The main armament was electro-hydraulic, as was the steering. Torpedo winches and davits were also electrically powered. This increase in electrical power did not come without some drawbacks. Both the 'Tribals' and the Kellys suffered from noise in their transmitting stations, which was traced to inductance between the telephone circuits and other circuits which supplied power to the various motors such as the gyro in the roll recorder, the main gyro of the ship and the motors in the fire control equipment. A further problem was the sheer complexity of the new wiring which caused problems as the number of electrical artificers allowed for in the ship's complement was inadequate to

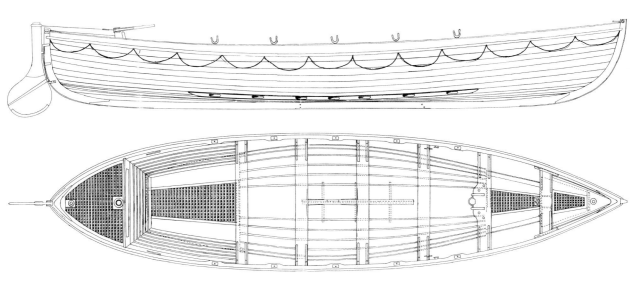

The Standard 27ft Naval Whaler

keep it in order.[22] But this problem disappeared as the crews gradually became familiar with their new ships.

There were five ship's boats included in the final design and a number of Carley floats. This would change as the 'N' class were built as float nets and rafts were added.[23] Initially all 'Js' and 'Ks' carried a 27ft whaler, a 25ft fast motor boat, a 25ft motor cutter, a 16ft motor (or planing) dinghy and a 14ft sailing dinghy. In performance terms this was rather a mixed bag. Service opinion held that the fast motor boat was neither fast and frequently not motorised either. When it did work it could not carry enough men or cargo. The motor cutter on the other hand was highly rated. They had only recently been developed when the Kelly design was being worked out and carried ten men at a speed of 7kts and ten men and 2 tons of cargo at 6½kts, all on a reliable 20hp engine. The 16ft motor dinghy was renowned for getting people sitting in its stern wet.[24] The other two boats, the whaler and the sailing dinghy, were run-of-the-mill unpowered boats which did what was expected of them.

Initially the destroyers carried six Carley floats, with *Jervis* and *Kelly* having seven. These floated but did not prevent those on them getting wet which was a serious hazard in the cold waters of the North Atlantic and the Arctic. Changes to the boat complement happened quite rapidly, The Carley float complement for all ships was increased very early on in the war to seven and eight. This applied to the 'Ns' as they were built but float nets made their appearance with *Nestor*, the first to carry them. Rafts were also introduced, *Nestor* in particular having ten. By 1942 the 14ft sailing dinghy had also been landed, more to do with removing top weight than for any other reason. All 'Ns' completed with two of the motor cutters, the fast motor boat being abandoned, except for *Nepal* which for some reason retained it. When she emerged from refit in 1944, *Kelvin* retained the 14ft sailing dinghy but had lost her 25ft fast motor boat and her Carley float compliment had increased to ten with the addition of several rafts and float nets.

Once war broke out the basic design would continue to be modified and updated to meet changing conditions and requirements, and these modifications are dealt with in other chapters.

---

[22] See Home Fleet War Diary 1939-40 Para 108.
[23] These were considered boats.
[24] As these were usually officers it enjoyed a certain popularity with the lower deck.

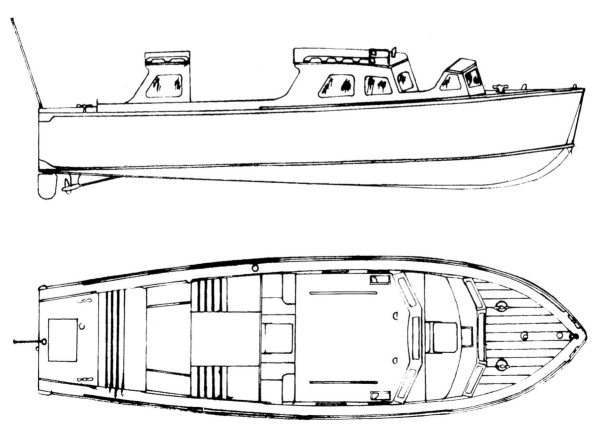

25ft Fast Motor Boat

2

Construction, Trials and Modifications

the Royal Navy to build a number of ships of set types and perform a certain number of functions. For example, when the meetings to decide the 1936 Programme were held there was no provision for destroyers included. This was changed and two flotillas were added (the 'Js' and repeat 'Tribals'). The 'Js' belonged to the 1936 Programme, the 'Ks' to the 1937 Programme and the 'Ns' would come under the 1939 Programme. It is important to realise that allocation to a programme did not result in the immediate commencement of construction. For example, the 'Js' and 'Ks' were not begun until 1937 and 1938 respectively, but the 'Ns' were quicker, being started in 1940.

ORDERS AND CONSTRUCTION

Despite belonging to different programmes, the 'Js' and 'Ks' were in fact ordered together. Eight yards had been invited to tender for the construction of the ships, each yard getting one 'J' and one 'K' class to build. Whites produced the lowest tenders followed by Yarrow, Thornycroft, Fairfield, Swan Hunter, John Brown, Hawthorn Leslie and Denny.

ᴇᴀᴄʜ ʏᴇᴀʀ the Admiralty met with the government of the day to determine what its budget would be for the coming year. With regard to ships, there would be a list of requirements which would then be debated and a compromise agreed. A number of factors would be considered in this compromise such as the international situation and the cost of the proposed programme in line with other budgetary requirements. This compromise would then form part of the overall naval budget and would allow

HMAS *Napier* (flotilla leader) as completed, December 1940

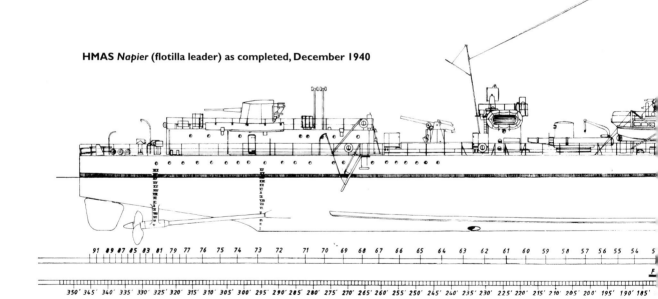

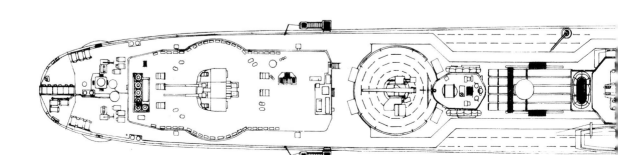

TABLE 2:

Tenders for the 'J' and 'K' class

Shipyard	'J'	Tender (£-s-d)	'K'	Tender (£-s-d)
Hawthorn Leslie	*Jervis*	392,541	*Kelly*	392,226
John Brown	*Jackal*	391,370	*Javelin**	391,570
Denny	*Jaguar*	392,363	*Kandahar*	391,943-10-0
Swan Hunter	*Janus*	392,395	*Khartoum*	392,395
White	*Jersey*	389,204-10-0	*Kingston*	389,204-10-0
Fairfield	*Jamaica*	390,846	*Kelvin*	391,046
Thornycroft	*Kashmir**	390,598	*Kimberley*	390,389-10-0
Yarrow	*Jupiter*	389,911	*Kipling*	389,911

* *Kashmir* and *Javelin* exchanged names leading to two yards building
  two of each class.
† *Jamaica* renamed *Juno* before launch to allow the name to be used
  for a new cruiser.

The costs shown in Table 2 only represent the hull and machinery costs. H B Peebles quotes the actual price of the Denny-built destroyers as £802,598 and calculated the amount that went on profits and overheads as being 31.5 per cent.[1] He suggests that this was due to a degree of price fixing which was tolerated by the Admiralty. With all stores and equipment the final cost of a 'J' or 'K' class destroyer came to £596,197.[2] The rationale behind choosing so many builders was the need to get the ships into service as quickly as possible as well as a desire to prevent shipyards from going bankrupt. However, Whites' yard on the Isle of Wight had not built anything quite as large as *Jersey* and *Kingston* and there were worries that the ships would hit the opposite bank of the river when launched.

Once the decision had been taken to order the new ships, things moved very fast and tenders were invited before enough copies of the drawings had actually been prepared. This meant that representatives of each firm invited to tender had to travel to London to see the drawings. These

[1] *Warship Building on the Clyde* quotes from D K Brown, *Nelson to Vanguard*, p90.
[2] E March, *British Destroyers*. This is an average for the whole class.

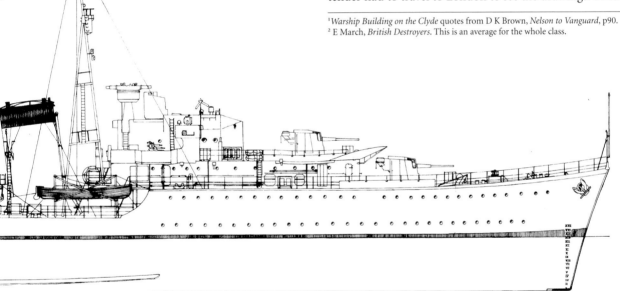

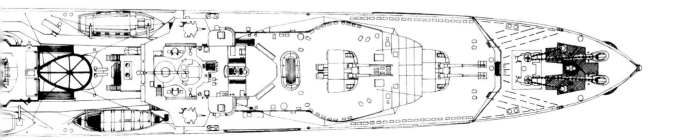

were incomplete and in fact full sets of drawings were only ready by 16 March 1937, the same day the orders were placed! Delivery time for each ship of the 1936 Programme was to be 24 months and for the 1937 Programme, 26 months. These seem mostly to have been achieved, with only *Jaguar* of the 1936 Programme being late. Most of the others were delivered early as were the 'Ks' of the 1937 Programme except for *Khartoum* and *Kipling*.

Despite presenting tenders for the work, most manufacturers were unhappy about the idea of longitudinal construction and a delegation of Clyde shipbuilders did see the Controller, in an attempt to change this and to press for Cole's dismissal.[3] Denny were also unhappy about the use of channels for the stringers and urged the use of angle bulbs instead. This would have reduced the hole in the transverse frames with the added advantage of the bulbs being easier to rivet and work. However, using angle bulbs would have increased the weight of the hull by about 6½ tons which was unacceptable on such a finely-calculated ship.

Whilst some welding was employed, the hulls were to be mainly riveted because the D-quality steel used was not suitable for welding. This added to the weight and was not as strong as welding, but getting the idea of longitudinal construction accepted by the builders was a major triumph and perhaps all-welded hulls were then a step too far. Certainly, later troubles with brittle welds on other ships suggested that this approach was the right one for the time.

Once the design had been worked out, it was easy to re-order another group using the same drawings. The Kelly design was chosen for the 1939 Programme 'N' class because it was cheaper than the later 'Ls' and 'Ms' and because drawings were already available. This time the four lowest tenders were accepted with four yards being chosen, each to construct a pair of destroyers. The lowest tenders came from John Brown, Thornycroft, Denny, and Fairfield which were presumably just for hulls.[4] Each tender also had an additional set amount of £15,800 for fixed auxiliary machinery. Exact figures are shown in Table 3 below.

TABLE 3:
Tenders for 'N' class destroyers

Shipyard	Ship	Tender (£-s-d)	Ship	Tender (£-s-d)
Fairfield	*Napier*	403,960	*Nestor*	398,960
Denny	*Noble**	400,954	*Nonpareil**	400,954
Thornycroft	*Norseman**	402,939	*Norman*	402,939
John Brown	*Nerissa**	400,963-16-0	*Nizam*	400,963-16-0

NOTE: all destroyers marked * were re-named after launch or commissioning.

NAMING

Destroyer names were chosen well before the ships were launched. The leader of each flotilla was named after a famous admiral with the names of the other ships being chosen for a special resonance or tradition behind the name.[5] Once the Admiralty had decided on a particular set of names it was sent to the King for final approval, who could and did occasionally reject names he thought unsuitable but this does not seem to have happened in the case of any of the Kellys. The fact that the King had set his seal of approval on the list of names did not necessarily mean that they were fixed for all time. Several of the 'N' class were renamed after launch but it is unclear as to whether His Majesty was consulted about these changes. Very little detail has survived on the 'Ks' and the 'Ns' but the file for the 'Js' is still extant.[6]

The 'J' class was originally intended to be a repeat of the I class which like the preceding 'A' to 'H' classes was based on a flotilla of nine ships, one leader and two separate divisions of four destroyers each. Thus nine names were originally selected for the class. The leader was chosen from a list of famous admirals whilst a shortlist was drawn up for the eight destroyers. The initial choices were *Jackal*, *Jackdaw*, *Jaguar*, *Jamaica*, *Janus*, *Javelin*, *Jersey* and *Jubilant*. Also considered but not selected were *Jacobin*, *Jed*, *Jewel* and *Juggler*. This was only an initial list and on 28 July 1937 changes were made. The Admiralty were not really happy with the choice of *Jackdaw* or *Jubilant* which to their minds did not sound suitable for destroyers. They also decided that *Jamaica* would be better suited to one of the new 'Colony' class cruisers from the 1938 Programme. As a result, *Jamaica* was renamed *Juno* and *Jackdaw* became *Jupiter*. Both these names were considered much more appropriate. As the new flotilla was going to consist of eight ships including the leader instead of nine, the name *Jubilant* was dropped. The names were presented to the King on 4 September 1936 and approved without alteration.

I could find no files for the 1937 or 1939 Programmes but ships of the 'N' class went through some re-naming after they were launched. The examples of *Piorun*, *Van Galen* and *Tjerk Hiddes* are described elsewhere but *Norseman* was renamed for different reasons. Firstly, there was a need to avoid confusion with a cable-layer of the same name chartered by the Admiralty and secondly there was a wish to acknowledge the part played by the Gurkha regiments in the war. Two ships named *Gurkha* had been sunk by 1942 so giving a third ship the same name was not considered lucky.[7] It was therefore decided to name the ship after the country the regiments came from and so *Norseman* became *Nepal*.

---

[3] D K Brown, conversation with the author, 22 February 2001 and *Nelson to Vanguard*, p98.
[4] See Ships Cover 609 'N class'.

[5] This practice continued until the wartime-built 'Z' class.
[6] PRO, ADM 116/3503, Naming of ships in the 1936 construction programme.
[7] 'Tribal' class, *Gurkha*, lost 9 April 1940 and 'L' class, *Gurkha* – originally *Larne* – lost 17 January 1942.

STRUCTURE[8]

All twenty-four ships were constructed to the longitudinal system which was discussed in the chapter on design. Starting with the keel, this was 54in wide for a length of 185ft before tapering to 48in at the fore end and 42in aft. Vertically it was a uniform 19in deep. Working from the keel on one side only, the first and second longitudinals in the machinery spaces were made up of 15lb plating and connected to the shell plating by angles 3½in by 3½in by 10lb (all attachments for the longitudinals would be different-sized angles). They were thicker in the machinery spaces to take the machinery seatings and gradually decreased in depth until they became 6in by 3in by 3in by 12.41lb continuous channels. No 1 longitudinal was to extend to Bulkhead No 9 and No 2 longitudinal to Station 11. The same process took place aft of the machinery spaces with No 1 longitudinal finishing at Frame 55 and No 2 at the rudder bridge framing. No 3 longitudinal supported the boilers, thrust blocks, overflows and tank sides and consisted of the same type of plate before reducing in thickness to the same channels as Nos 1 and 2. It finished at the forward fresh water tank and bulkhead No 57. The spacing of these longitudinals was not more than 3ft between each.

With the fourth to eighth longitudinals the use of plating ceased and they consisted entirely of channels,[9] gradually decreasing in size. Spacing between these was to be not more than 2ft. The sixth longitudinal stopped at the bilge keel and started again once it had finished. The remaining longitudinals (9 to 15) were similar to 4 to 8 but once again were smaller. Spacing for these was to be as shown in the drawings though if the spacing was greater than 6ft, face bars were to be welded to the free flange of the longitudinals. Forward of No 9 station panting stringers were fitted on top of the frames and to the rear of 57 station around the stern. In general the stringers and longitudinals were to be solid with no lightening holes. The only holes allowed in the longitudinals were those for rivets or pipes. All connections to the stringers were also to be by angles, flanges not being permitted at all.

Transverse frames were fitted intercostally between the vertical keel and the Nos 1, 2 and 3 longitudinals. They consisted of 10lb floor plates with shell bars and reverse bars. The floor plates were connected to the keel and Nos 1, 2 and 3 longitudinals as were the reverse bars. The shell bars took the transverse frames up to the upper deck. The contract specified that they were to be continuous from keel to forecastle or upper deck with double-lapped butt joints fitted where necessary. In the machinery spaces, the frames were slotted over the longitudinals and at the vertical keel their depth was also to be 19in. Between stations 4 to 9 and aft of bulkhead 57, zed bars[10] were used instead. These were specially strengthened in the area of the cut up aft to take the knocks and bangs of docking. The bows were also stiffened.

Bilge keels were 18in deep and extended 2ft forward of frame 19 to about 2ft aft of bulkhead 47. They were connected to the bottom plating by continuous double angles.[11] As previously mentioned they also replaced No 6 longitudinal over their length. The upper deck beams consisted of channel bars[12] worked intercostally between the continuous longitudinal girders. Once again they were of greater strength in the area of the machinery spaces. The hull plating consisted of sheets of steel which were described by weight not dimensions. Each run of plating was known as a strake and the sheer strake had a minimum width of 48in for the whole length of the ship.

TABLE 4:

Shell plating for Kelly class destroyers[13] *(this should be read in conjunction with the shell expansion drawing.)*

		Amidships		Subject to clause below	
		Distance from amidships		Tapering forward to	Tapering aft to
	Poundage	Forward	Aft		
Flat keel	22lb	80ft	102ft	12lb	12lb
Flat keel doubling	22lb	42ft	70ft	20lb for 22ft	20lb for22ft
A strake	22lb	50ft	55ft	17lb for 44ft	17lb for 22ft
B "	17lb	57ft	63ft	10lb	14lb
C "	14lb	46ft	48ft	8lb	12lb
D "	10lb	60ft	67ft	8lb	8lb
E "	12lb	26ft	63ft	8lb	8lb
F "	12lb	40ft	102ft	8lb	7lb
G and sheer strake	18lb	32ft	74ft	7lb	7lb
Above upper deck to forecastle deck					
H	10lb*	at after end of forecastle		7lb	
	12lb			7lb	

*12 lb in 'J' class.

The bridge and deck house were generally constructed of 5lb plate except where they were removed from heavy seas and blast. Then they were reduced to 4lbs plate. Bulkheads and decks were to be watertight but this did not initially work out. When the upper decks were constructed, the plates were joined together with a single row of rivets. These

---

[8] The details for this section derive from the contracts for the ships, which are held by the National Maritime Museum.
[9] 5in by 2½in by 10.22lb.
[10] 4in by 2in by 2in by 6lb.
[11] 3½in by 3½in by 10lb.
[12] 10in by 3in by 3in by 19.28lb.
[13] Table derived from 'JKN' class specification Clause 22.

HMAS *Napier* (Job No 673)

Shell expansion - upper and forecastle decks and hull construction (as fitted), December 1940

Key

Sidelights shown thus:
- Port and starboard
- Port only
- Starboard only
- Emergency escape scuttle 16in dia. clear (P & S)

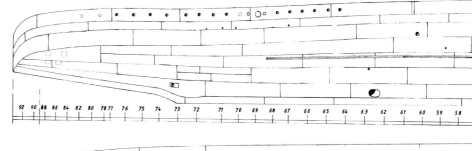

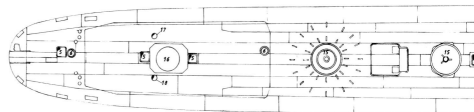

1 Bilge keel	25 No 2 cartridge hoist	48 1¼in blow down valve (P)
2 Circulating inlet	26 4½in distiller pump circulating suction (P)	49 5in storm valve
3 Circulating outlet	27 4⅞in air ejector circulating discharge (P & S)	50 4in storm valve
4 Asdic dome opening	28 1½ turbo generator circulating discharge	51 3in storm valve
5 Watertight hatch	29 1½ diesel generator circulating outlet (P & S)	52 2in storm valve
6 27in dia. watertight scuttle	30 1in refrigerating plant circulating discharge (P)	53 Fresh water tank (P)
7 30in dia. watertight scuttle	31 No 1 cartridge hoist	54 Fresh water tank (S)
8 Steering gear flat	32 No 1 shell hoist	55 Reserve feed tank (P & S)
9 14lbs doubling	33 No 1 gun support	56 Knuckle
10 17lbs doubling	34 Space for shipping asdic unit	57 Heel casting
11 9½in 20-ton bilge pump	35 Fore peak	58 No 2 gun support
12 6⅜in diesel generator circulating inlet (P & S)	36 2ft 6in x 2ft 3in	59 16in dia. emergency escape scuttle
13 12½in x 7in auxiliary circulating pump suction	37 Ladder way - 2ft 6¼in x 2ft 3¼in	60 Duplex pistol room
14 5½in drain cooler circulating discharge	38 Watertight bulkhead	61 1½in storm valve
15 Torpedo tube racer support	39 Rudder stock	62 2in bend
16 No 3 gun support	40 Forecastle deck	63 10in auxiliary condenser circulator discharge (P & S)
17 No 3 cartridge hoist	41 Upper deck	64 6½in lubricating oil cooler discharge (P & S)
18 No 3 shell hoist	42 Lower deck	65 4½in fire and bilge pump sea suction (P & S)
19 24in dia. watertight scuttle	43 Oil fuel tank (P & S)	66 2in evaporator blow down (P)
20 Shipping space for turbo generator	44 1in refrigerating plant circulating inlet (P)	67 3in turbo generator circulating inlet (S)
21 Boiler room ventilator (air intake)	45 3in fire and bilge pump discharge (P)	68 5¾in salt water pump sea suction (P)
22 Funnel gas intake	46 6in seacock	
23 Opening for waste steam pipes	47 1½in air compressor outlet (P & S)	
24 No 2 shell hoist		

Note In the interest of clarity much of the original fine detail such as stringer positions, plating weight – 22lbs, 18lbs, 10lbs etc – has been omitted.

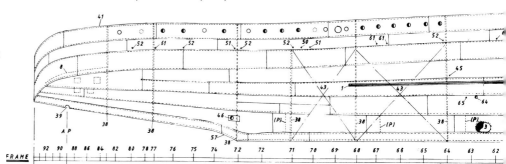

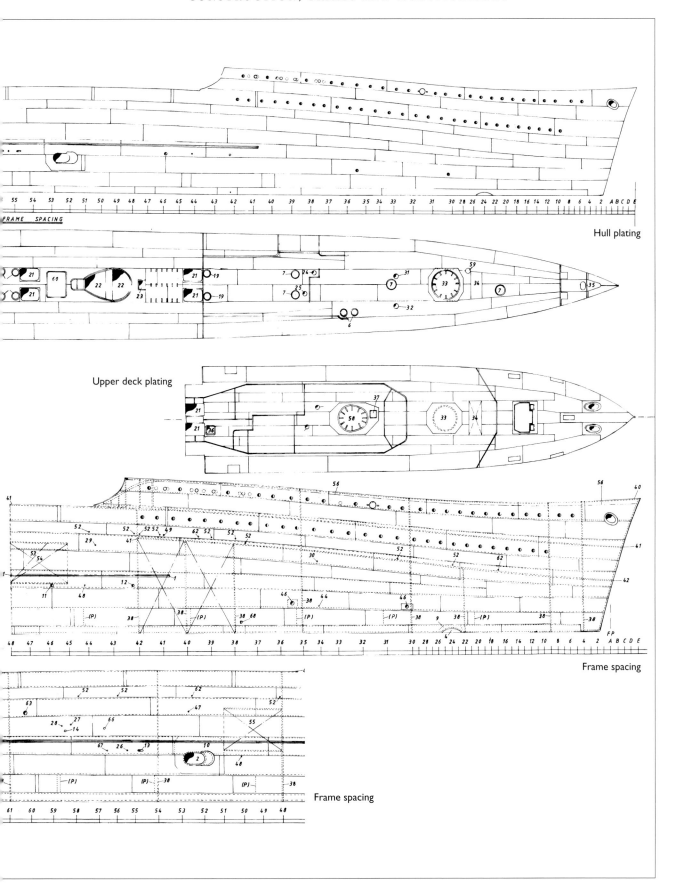

Hull plating

Upper deck plating

Frame spacing

Frame spacing

leaked and made life a misery on the mess decks. The deck beams were also considered rather flimsy by constructors who had to repair the ships.[14] Both problems were eventually cured, the leaking decks by the simple expedient of adding more rivets and the other by strengthening the ships' structure. Watertight subdivision would prove to be very good with watertight doors being effective. These were 5ft 3in by 2ft 2in except that at bulkhead 25 which was 2ft 6in wide. As many wires as possible were put in armoured cables but these could still be damaged by splinters and loss of electrical power would remain a potential hazard for all ships until the installation of auxiliary diesel generators after the loss of *Nestor*.

BUILDING, LAUNCHING AND FITTING OUT

Most Kellys proceeded smoothly from keel laying to launch to fitting out.[15] Several yards tried to get Sir Stanley Goodall, the Director of Naval Construction to attend their ceremonies but without success.[16] By the time the 'N' class was

building, construction time had reduced rapidly, but this increased again as the pressures of war and other construction priorities intervened. *Napier* took 17 months from laying down to commissioning and *Nerissa* was even faster taking just 16 months. By contrast *Noble* took 32 months to complete which is almost certainly due to other factors as *Kandahar* had only taken 19 months at the same yard.

Norseman was also considerably delayed but this was due to enemy action. She was on the stocks at Thornycroft's yard at Southampton when a single aircraft attacked, dropping three bombs on 28 December 1940. One missed, one fell between *Norseman* and the destroyer *Opportune* damaging both and the other hit *Norseman* directly and detonated just under the deck on the starboard side, causing extensive damage. The ship was forced out of alignment on the keel blocks and the bulkheads for the machinery spaces were destroyed. Part of the upper deck was also destroyed and the rest collapsed, crushing and buckling the fresh water tanks. More seriously, the longitudinals in the area of the

---

[14] See F Sutcliffe, letter of 7 February 1940 to A P Cole, Ships Cover 565a.
[15] Dates for all ships can be found in Appendix 5.

[16] Sir Stanley seems not to have attended any launch below cruiser size.

Norman shortly after her launch on 30 October 1940 showing how much work still needed to be done on these ships. The nature of her unusual camouflage is unknown but it was painted over by the time the commissioning photographs were taken.

(NATIONAL MARITIME MUSEUM, LONDON: N11866)

explosion were wrecked. *Norseman*'s launch would be delayed by 4 months as a result of the hit.

Launching ceremonies were fairly straightforward with each ship being launched by someone with a connection to the name of the ship. In the case of *Jersey* and *Kingston* this involved visits by civic officials to launch the ships and presentations of gifts. The ship would be christened with the traditional bottle of champagne and sent down the slipway stern first. She would then be towed to the fitting-out yard. Fitting-out involved a significant amount of work as each ship consisted of just a hull and the deckhouses when launched and all the armament, masts, funnels, director and rangefinder had to be fitted. Later in the war, this included radar as the later ships of the class received radar as standard. They also incorporated D/F offices and 4in guns.

TRIALS

Trials for the Kellys consisted mostly of full-power runs, not necessarily over a measured course. There were several reasons for this, the two major ones being a need to get the new ships into service as quickly as possible and the fact that each ship was built to the same design.[17] *Javelin* and *Jaguar* were

An impressive photograph of *Kipling* on her high-speed trials. This photograph was taken in early summer 1940 after her repairs for bomb damage during the Norwegian campaign. When she re-commissioned *Kipling* still carried the F flag superior but by this time this has changed to G. (IMPERIAL WAR MUSEUM: 1452)

inclined on 1 June and 22 August 1939 respectively and these figures were applied to all twenty-four ships in the three groups. Most of the 'J' and 'K' class underwent 6-hour full-power trials whilst *Kimberley*, *Kelvin* and the 'Ns' underwent a 4-hour trial. Whilst figures are presented below, some points of interest do emerge. *Jackal* was tested at near light displacement (1690 tons) to see whether she would reach the design speed of 36kts. She managed the target and exceeded it by 1.4 knots though this was with 42,000shp suggesting that her engines were forced. Her full speed without forcing and presumably half loaded was actually only 34.3kts[18] which was still fast. The next fastest was *Javelin* followed by *Jaguar* both of which exceeded 35kts.[19] The 'Ks' were slower but as all were tested at half-load displacement or above this is not surprising. The 'Ns' were slower still with *Nepal* not reaching the design speed for deep condition, but this result should be treated with caution as measurement was by fixes and so may not be reliable.

The trials which were held were remarkably successful. The captains liked their new ships and reported back very favourably. Commander Napier, captain of *Jackal* noted that bumping was much reduced and that they rarely needed to reduce speed. However, this did depend on the

---

[17] The ships were so identical that 'J' class drawings were used unmodified for the 'N' class.
[18] *Jackal* Ship's log, August 1939, ADM53/109354.
[19] The problem with the figures in the ships' logs is that they do not give weights. The trial figures in Edgar March do not give dates making comparisons difficult.

amount of fuel in the ship and the emptier the ship the more likely it was that bumping would occur. Spray was a problem being particularly bad at No 2 mounting and on the bridge, especially in a head sea. On turning 10° to port in a head sea, trials on *Nerissa* showed that spray would be thrown across No 2 mount and the bridge. Napier stated that this was worse than in other classes and the Admiralty did go as far at to contact Captain Lockwood, the US naval attaché, to ascertain whether US destroyers had experienced similar problems with their destroyers. Unfortunately he was not able to be of much help.[20] To a certain extent, the spray problem was accepted as the price to pay for such a low silhouette but Napier did consider that it could impede efficiency in certain conditions - at speeds above 20kts and a wind and sea of four to five on the bow.

Jersey's captain, Lieutenant-Commander McKillip, had no complaints about the bridge apart from the Mountbatten roof. This feature was very unpopular and the few photographs which survive show it was only rarely used. Its main problem was that it impeded lookouts, especially those watching for aircraft. It was noted that the bridge was very free of vibration by the standards of the time and even at the critical speed of 20kts it was far from excessive. The ships' manoeuvrability was highly thought of, with captains being impressed by how easy it was to turn rapidly.

[20] Captain C A Lockwood Jr, Letter of 6 October 1941.
[21] These are derived from Edgar March, ships logs and ships covers.

TABLE 5:

Trial figures for the Kelly class[21]

Ship	SHP	Speed (Ships log) (kts)	RPM	Displacement (tons)
Jervis	40,230	33.813 (31.75)	345.1	2045
Javelin	40,183	35.11	351.2	1927
Jackal‡	42,838	37.492	373.1	1700
Jackal‡	40,395	34.083 (34.3)	342.5	2057
Jaguar	39,746	34.785 (35.045)	350.8	2001
Janus	40,361	33.984	354	2041
Jersey	40,674	33.158 (33.66)	342.6	1967
Juno	41,323	33.91	348.4	1989
Jupiter‡	40,797	33.634 (33.3)	343.7	2047
Jupiter‡	40,366	33.045	340.6	2242
Kelly	40,368	34.265 (32.5)	351.6	1978
Kashmir	41,005	33.438	343.4	1972
Kimberley	41,518	-	330.7	-
Kelvin	-	32.926	342.5	2149
Kandahar	40,199	34.134	341.1	2083
Kipling	40,556	33.34	314.8	1993
Kingston	40,566	33.506	343.9	1966
Nestor	-*	33.9	342.5	2000
Nerissa	-*	33.25	331.7	2215
Van Galen	-*	32.58	339.9	2133
Tjerk Hiddes†	-*	32.8	341	2176
Norman	-*	32.7	334.5	2373
Nepal	-*	30.6	325.2	2390

* All given as 40,000 in the records.
† March differs slightly in giving the speed as 33.32kts.
‡ *Jupiter* and *Jackal* underwent a full series of trials but no information exists for *Khartoum*.

Tjerk Hiddes broke down on her trials and had to be repaired before she could continue. *Jupiter* conducted an extensive set of trials with measurements taken at 2000, 5000, 8000, 12,000, 23,000, 32,000 and 40,000shp. These trials did not represent the maximum speed that ships would make in service. Pugsley does talk of the 'Js' reaching 35kts when escorting cruisers of the Humber Force in 1939 but this is unlikely as service speeds tended to be significantly lower than trial speeds.[22] The bottom of a ship got rougher over time, even without fouling. Officially, the top speed of the Kellys would later be fixed at 33kts and this is probably the maximum that they would be able to attain in service.[23] Even so, speeds would normally be significantly lower and on occasions ships were hard put to maintain 30kts especially if they had been out of dock for a long time and were in need of a refit. What the trials did not show were any later problems, and frequently during the working-up period destroyers needed further work to correct defects that arose. These varied from very minor to the major problems that arose with the two Yarrow built ships, *Jupiter* and *Kipling*. Both – surprisingly for that yard – suffered from poorly constructed turbines. The gearing on *Kipling* developed a serious whine and had to be re-cut at Fairfield's. *Jupiter* would suffer from engine and turbine problems until 1941 when she was taken in hand for a major refit. The other ships were largely free of these problems and once the initial defects had been corrected were able to give intensive service. One change that did not arise from defects was the change of the propeller pitch. The Kellys were completed with propellers with a pitch of 13ft 2in. For some reason this was considered insufficient and so in October 1939 *Jaguar* was chosen to conduct trials with propellers with a pitch of 13ft 5in.

Janus on trials in early 1939 showing the 'Js' as originally built and painted. She carries two white bands, the markings of the 7th Flotilla. Also visible is the galley funnel which Sir Stanley Goodall thought marred the fine appearance of these ships. This would be re-located inside the funnel for almost all ships of the 'J' class.

(IMPERIAL WAR MUSEUM: FL3695)

After several tests these were pronounced better and gradually installed on all Kellys. In actual fact the changes produced by such a small alteration in pitch were negligible and would have had no effect on performance at all.[24]

MODIFICATIONS

Modifications to the weapons fit are discussed in the chapter on armament and this section deals mainly with the structural and other changes that were needed throughout the ships' lives. Most modifications were noted in the Admiralty Fleet Orders (AFOs) or the Confidential Admiralty Fleet Orders (CAFOs). The AFOs also covered service practice: for example, AFO 1778/39 specified that boiler cleaning intervals were to be every 750 hours. They also covered hull strengthening and on 14 December 1939 instructions were issued to fit additional stiffening to the shell plating of the Kellys. This consisted of angle bar stiffeners fitted intercostally between the 1st and 3rd and 4th and 6th longitudinals from Frame 30 to 32 and Frame 73 to 76.[25] *Kelvin*, *Kipling* and *Kimberley* were excluded from these instructions as they were able to receive the stiffening before completion. The aim of the strengthening was to prepare ships for Operation 'Catherine' (see Chapter 4) but it was also valuable for other purposes as the original Kelly design did

---

[22] Pugsley, *Destroyer Man*, p30.
[23] Home Fleet Tactical Instructions 1 June 1943, see Appendix 8 for the full table.

[24] D K Brown, conversations with the author. Mr Brown who designed propellers during his long and distinguished career with the Royal Corps of Naval Constructors also mentioned that this was a common belief at the time – that a small change in propeller pitch could induce a significant performance alteration.
[25] The details in my account are simplified.

need strengthening anyway. This instruction was further modified to include fitting angle bars to between the lower deck and the first longitudinal. Panting was also to prove a problem and caused splitting in the shell plating of one ship between stations 14 and 15 above the WT flat.[26] This was considered serious enough for immediate inspections to be arranged and if necessary extra stiffening to be fitted.

Another major concern evinced in the AFOs were the gun mounts. These problems were not major in origin but were significant in their effects. Problems were found with lubrication and the strength of certain fittings. The starter motors for the variable speed gearing tended to open with the shock of firing[27] and the gun shields needed stiffening to deal with the effects of blast and the weather.[28] Weather also affected the fittings on deck, particularly the ready-use lockers and several had to be replaced.[29] The destroyer breakwater also presented problems and needed replacement with a better design.[30] Most modifications came about as a result of service experience with the loss of ships being particularly useful. For example, when *Nestor* was lost part of the reason was the lack of auxiliary power to fight the fires (see Chapter 10). This was due to the dynamos being located close together which led to them being disabled at the same time. Captain Arliss (D7) recommended the installation of diesel generators in widely separate locations, but this was not possible. However, what was possible was the addition of an extra 10kW generator in the gearing room to provide emergency electrical power and this was done for all 'J', 'K', 'N', 'O' and 'P' class destroyers as soon as possible.

---

[26] If they referred to a particular ship the AFOs never named it, see AFO 374/42.
[27] AFOs 3742/40 and 655/41.
[28] AFO 4767/40.
[29] See AFO 4322/40 in particular.
[30] AFO 4762/42.

Radar and other electronic equipment.

The installation of radar on Royal Navy ships was dependent on the theatre the ship operated in and the relative value placed on the ship. Therefore, because of their important role in the battle of the Atlantic, 'Flower' class corvettes would receive radar and HF/DF well before many fleet destroyers. Ships in the Mediterranean theatre also tended to receive radar installations much later than those operating in home waters. The first modification along these lines was the installation of MF/DF equipment which aided navigation and the detection of enemy signals. This began to appear in early 1940 on the Kellys and consisted of a type FM3 diamond shaped aerial fitted either to the foremast or on top of the aft deckhouse. An office to house the receiving equipment was added to the aft deckhouse as well. This was later modified so that all ships carried the aerial on their foremast. Also at a similar time same time ships began to receive the MF/DF installations in front of the bridge. The first ship with this type was *Kelly* which received it shortly after she came out of her last repair. Later in the war the survivors would also receive the FM7 installation either on a pole main mast or on top of the foremast.

Radar was restricted by the size of the ship, destroyers being unable to carry the type of installation that a cruiser could, for example. Initially the only type of radar available for destroyers was the Type 286, based on an RAF set and not of particularly good performance. The first of the Kellys to receive one was *Jackal* whose set was fitted in early August 1940. She sailed with Captain D5 on board to conduct RDF trials on 12 August,[31] and other members of the flotilla also began to be equipped with radar sets, all Type 286. *Javelin*

---

[31] Unfortunately I have not been able to find any records of these trials.

Jackal in the Channel with her Type 286 radar newly installed. The aerial was non-rotating and had a coverage of about 60° each side but added a new dimension to destroyer warfare.

(IMPERIAL WAR MUSEUM: A3605)

was the next to receive a set and was carrying it when she was torpedoed by German destroyers on 29 November 1940 and *Kelly* would receive a set shortly after completion of her refit closely followed by *Kashmir*, *Kelvin* and *Kipling* in early 1941. Of the other members of the flotilla, *Jaguar* joined Force H before she could get a set and *Jupiter* had one installed when she went into dry dock for her refit.[32] When she emerged she was fitted with a 286 which she carried until sunk in the Java Sea. No information could be found for *Jersey*.[33]

The destroyers serving in the Mediterranean received sets much later than the ships in home waters. The first to receive radar sets were *Janus*, *Juno* and *Jaguar*, once again Type 286s. All had received these by 2 May 1941[34] but *Juno* did not have much chance to enjoy her radar as she was sunk on the 23rd of the same month. *Jervis* followed shortly afterwards in June 1941. *Kandahar* and *Khartoum* were sunk before she could be converted and so never received any form of radar. *Kimberley* would be torpedoed before she could be fitted with a Type 286 but when repaired would receive a far more sophisticated outfit. The final Mediterranean destroyer, *Kingston*, was fitted with her set (which was the later 286P) in March 1942 but like *Juno* was damaged and sunk shortly after she received it. The set itself was removed whilst *Kingston* was in dock in Malta, before she was destroyed there (see Chapter 10).

None of the first three 'Ns', *Napier*, *Nizam* and *Piorun*, were commissioned with radar but all received the ubiquitous Type 286 by February 1941. *Nestor*, the fourth 'N', was the first of the Kellys to be commissioned with radar as standard which once again was the Type 286. This was replaced with a Type 291 during her October/November 1941 refit. Thereafter as radar technology improved the four other ships were commissioned with much more sophisticated radar outfits. In 1941 several new and improved types of destroyer radar were introduced, the Type 286P, Type 285, Type 290 and Type 291. The Type 285 was first and was a 50 cm wavelength set used for long range AA gunnery. It was fitted to as many of the surviving Kellys as possible and was always located on the rangefinder tower, behind the rangefinder itself. The Type 286P was an improved version of the Type 286 which was unable to rotate and only had beam coverage of 60° either side of the ship's bow. The 286P could rotate but still suffered from the limited performance of the earlier set. The Types 290 and 291 had a cross-shaped aerial similar to the Type 286P, the Type 291 being a successful gunnery radar with a range of 35 miles. When she

finally completed her repairs in December 1941, *Javelin* would re-commission with a Type 285 and a Type 286P fitted. Three of the four remaining 'Ns', *Norman*, *Nepal* and *Van Galen* would commission with the same radar fit as *Javelin*. Two Kellys received Type 290s, *Piorun* in March 1942 and *Tjerk Hiddes* in June of that year.

For ships fitted with the Type 286 this would gradually be replaced by the Type 286P. Type 285s were also added when they became available. *Nestor* and *Norman* received their sets in November 1941. The ships of the 7th Flotilla left the Mediterranean fleet to join the Eastern fleet with a simple Mediterranean outfit of just a Type 286. They would all have the Type 285 added with the exception of *Napier* which would have her rangefinder tower replaced with a Type 271 in a radar lantern. This sat on a hut which was specially raised to clear the director in front. *Nizam* did not receive her Type 285 until quite late in the war when she also received a Type 291.[35] *Nepal* received a Type 281 in July 1942 which was located on a pole mast on her aft deckhouse. It was removed and replaced in October of that year by a Type 291. As for the surviving 'Js' and 'Ks', several would be lost before they could have new sets or updates installed. *Kipling*, *Jackal* and *Jaguar* would all be sunk with only a Type 286 fitted. The other survivors would receive updates by 1943. *Jervis* would have a Type 286P fitted and take over the Type 285 set first fitted to *Janus* which had departed for extended repair. When *Janus* re-emerged from refit in 1943 her radar equipment was a Type 293X on a lattice mast as well as the Type 285 and Type 242 Interrogator. By 1943 *Kelvin* received a Type 286P but not a Type 285 until after she had emerged from refit in the United Kingdom in April 1944. By then she was also fitted with a lattice mast and a much more superior radar outfit which included the Type 276, a 10cm set.

Besides *Napier*, several Kellys also received a Type 271. CAFO 1161/43 had authorised the fitting of lattice masts to all ships but it had also stipulated that where time did not permit this they were to be fitted with a Type 271. The set was to be fitted in place of the searchlight and aft conning position and four ships received this modification, *Piorun*, *Norman*, *Nepal* and *Jervis*. This was in contrast to *Napier* which as will be recalled carried her Type 271 in lieu of her rangefinder. *Jervis* would lose her Type 271 during the refit in late 1944 and be fitted with a lattice mast similar to those fitted to *Tjerk Hiddes* and *Van Galen*. She would carry her FM7 aerial on top of her lattice mast and her Type 291 on the pole main mast.[36] She would also carry the Type 293 on the lattice mast but the searchlight would not be replaced. *Javelin*

---

[32] Records indicate that this was in place by 19 May 1941, *Pink Lists* for May 1941.
[33] Photographs from early 1941 show her on trials after emerging from refit with no radar in place. They show the diamond MF/DF aerial in place and so it is possible that she never received a radar installation at all.
[34] *Janus* by 6 February 1941.

[35] On 17 September 1943 she is still recorded as being fitted with just a Type 286 and photographs seem to bear this out.
[36] See CAFO 928/44.

The standard location for the Type 271 installation on the Kellys, this time on *Nepal*. The Type 271 needed to be fairly close to its power source which restricted its positioning on the Kellys to two places, either on the bridge (*Napier*) or the searchlight platform (all the rest).

(AUSTRALIAN WAR MEMORIAL: 301077)

received her lattice mast during her 1943/44 refit. This carried a Type 272 and Type 291. She was also equipped with a Type 285 on her rangefinder tower and an FM7 HF/DF installation on a pole main mast. This mast was the same as that carried by *Kelvin* but the latter ship carried a Type 293 instead of a Type 272. Photographs of *Kimberley* during her later career have been very elusive but one taken when she was placed in reserve show her fitted with a Type 272 and 285. A unique feature of *Kimberley*'s fit was she also carried Type 650 missile-jamming aerials located either side of her bridge. She also received a lattice mast but the Australian 'Ns', *Napier*, *Nizam*, *Nepal* and *Norman*, did not. *Nizam* had a Type 293 installed but none of her Australian sisters did. *Piorun* also did not receive the lattice mast. *Tjerk Hiddes* and *Van Galen* did not receive lattice masts until their refits in 1945 when they returned to the UK from the Eastern Fleet.[37] Both received the same radar outfit as *Jervis* using the same locations.[38] *Piorun* followed a slightly different path. As she served in home waters for most of the war, she received radar updates as they became available without having to wait for them to reach her theatre of operations. By 14 June 1944 her outfit consisted of a Type 271, Type 285, Type 291 and Type 252 IFF. Like *Norman* and *Napier* she retained her Type 271 after the war.

The effect of the alterations

As alterations were made the stability of the ship was affected. The Kellys had been designed with very little margin of stability and as discussed in the chapter on design had needed ballast as early as 1939. As their armament and equipment changed so their ballast requirements changed. Partially this was dealt with by removing items of top weight from the ship, for example, the Mountbatten station-keeping equipment and also by adding ballast, usually in the form of pig iron. In the case of *Tjerk Hiddes*, when the 4in HA gun was added an extra 30 tons of ballast was needed. This consisted of 20 tons for general stability requirements and 10 tons to compensate for the loss of the aft torpedo tubes.[39] As the single Oerlikons were replaced by twins, an extra 5 tons of ballast was needed to compensate,[40] and likewise another 5 tons was needed when the Mk VII 2pdr mounting was replaced by a Mk VII*P mounting.[41] It was not just armament that affected the weight of the ship - gunnery control equipment was also liable to have an effect. When instructions were issued for the MkXIV (US) gyro gunsight was authorised to be fitted 15cwt of top weight would need to be landed.[42] By the end of the war the 'Js' and 'Ks' were carrying 50 tons of permanent ballast and the 'Ns' 40 tons.

The effect on crews and stores should also not be neglected. The final war complement of a Kelly class was between 223 and 240 officers and men, an increase of 20 per cent on the complement at the start of the war. These ships were very crowded even with their original complement of 206-208, and space (already reduced by radar offices etc) had to be found for the newcomers, their belongings and the necessary extra supplies.[43] Even flotilla leaders, built to accommodate more personnel, had similar problems. When *Nepal* re-commissioned as a mine trials vessel she only carried a crew of 127, which must have been an extremely pleasant change given the overcrowding of the war years.

[37] *Van Galen* 12 February to 24 June 1945 and *Tjerk Hiddes* 4 April to December 1945.
[38] This was after *Jervis*'s 1944/45 refit.

[39] CAFO 1189/42.
[40] CAFO 1823/42.
[41] CAFO 1603/43. The Mk VII*P was a fully power-operated mounting.
[42] CAFO 640/44.
[43] Both Poolman, *HMS Kelly* and Connell, *Mediterranean Maelstrom* are very good on the kind of overcrowding and conditions that ordinary seamen had to put up with, even in big modern destroyers such as the Kellys.

3
Armament

THE KELLYS were very much multi-purpose vessels, and this is reflected in their armament. As discussed earlier they were an result of the general increase in size of fleet destroyers throughout the 1930s and as such their armament reflected this development. However, gun and torpedo still formed the core of the modern fleet destroyer and this was reflected in the initial requirements for the design. Whilst there was pressure for a high-angle capability, low-angle capability was seen as considerably more important,

> The destroyer's gun is mounted primarily to enable her to force her way into a suitable torpedo position, and to prevent enemy destroyers attaining a like position vis-à-vis our own Battlefleet.[1]

The troubled process of deciding on the type of mount for the main armament was covered in Chapter 1, but close-range AA armament was somewhat easier to settle on. Despite its faults the 2pdr pom-pom was highly thought of by the Navy and considered as a vital component of the Kellys' design and was partly responsible for the single-funnel design being retained. At the time of its introduction it was a very advanced weapon and was easily the best AA system in the world. However, due to a failure to appreciate later developments in aviation and financial stringency it was outdated by the time it was actually installed. The other elements of the close range AA armament were the 0.5in quadruple machine gun mount and the 0.303in Lewis gun.

Torpedoes, the other *raison d'être* of the destroyer, were less problematical still. The design requirement was for the heaviest torpedo armament possible and this was met by fitting two quintuple sets of tubes. These had been tried successfully in the 'I' class though these ships had required compensatory ballast to keep top weight within acceptable bounds. The new destroyers, being larger ships, would need no such additions. No torpedo reloads were carried but this remained the case for all British destroyers and stemmed from the belief that destroyer actions would be short and sharp, not allowing enough time for reloading. In fact, only the Imperial Japanese Navy allowed for reloading of torpedoes into their destroyer tactics but their torpedoes were

[1] TD Memo 144 Paragraph 21.

considerably superior to those possessed by the Royal Navy and enabled them to engage at longer ranges.

Like all fleet destroyers, the Kellys were equipped with an anti-submarine capacity. They would prove quite successful against the submarine menace, losing only *Jaguar* to the *U-652*, though *Kimberley* would be put out of action for a considerable time by *U-77*. All ships were equipped with asdic and depth charges. The numbers carried varied considerably at any one time and capacity was affected by the Royal Navy concern not to overdo top weight. A five-charge pattern was in use initially, two charges fired from throwers to port and starboard, three dropped from the rails on the stern. However, in early attacks (in 1939 and 1940) 'Js' and 'Ks' were prone to use six-charge patterns and five-charge patterns interchangeably. This seems to have been on the particular whim of the captain as officially they were five-charge pattern ships. In an interesting attempt to save space, the rails also formed the storage area for the depressor paravane of the TSDS gear (see below).

The final aspect of the Kellys' armament was their minesweeping equipment. For destroyers and other fleet ships there were three types of sweep available. These were different variants of the paravane, a streamlined tube with an explosive head attached to the ship by a long cable equipped with cutters along its length. Of the three types the Kellys were equipped with the 'Two Speed Destroyer Sweep' (TSDS). TSDS consisted of three paravanes - a left and a right sweeping paravane and a central depressor paravane which could be set for specific depths.

THE MK XII 4.7IN ON THE TWIN CP MK XIX MOUNTING.

The Mk XII 4.7in gun was of all-steel construction and consisted of three parts - an 'A' tube, a jacket and a removable breech ring. The jacket was shrunk onto the tube and the tube itself prevented from moving by a shoulder which locked with a corresponding shoulder on the jacket. The rifling consisted of 38 grooves with a uniform twist of one turn in 30 calibres, the gun being 45 calibres long. Breech-blocks were interchangeable between guns as were most parts of the breech mechanism. Later on these would be modified so that they were interchangeable with the breech-blocks for 4.5in guns as well.

The guns themselves were mounted on a twin shielded CP Mk XIX mounting with a maximum elevation of 40°. The guns could be depressed to -10°. Each mounting was power-operated on an electro-hydraulic system powered by VSG, size 3, Mk3, B-end motors originally developed from the Williams-Janey gear of 1907 by The Variable Speed Gear Limited company. The hydraulic medium used was oil which

Twin 4.7in Mark XII* guns on Mark XIX mounting

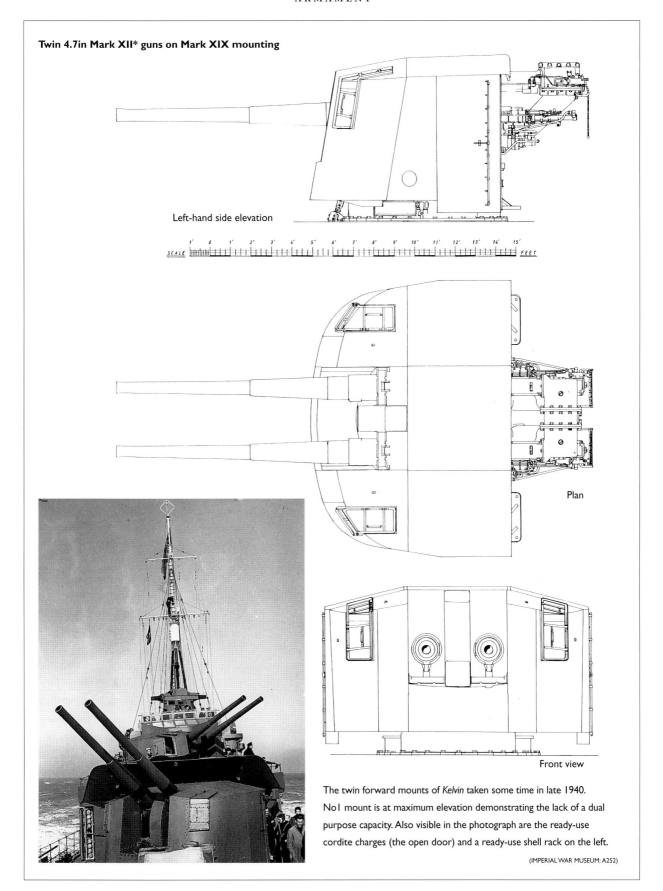

Left-hand side elevation

SCALE 1' 0 1' 2' 3' 4' 5' 6' 7' 8' 9' 10' 11' 12' 13' 14' 15' FEET

Plan

Front view

The twin forward mounts of *Kelvin* taken some time in late 1940.
No1 mount is at maximum elevation demonstrating the lack of a dual
purpose capacity. Also visible in the photograph are the ready-use
cordite charges (the open door) and a ready-use shell rack on the left.

(IMPERIAL WAR MUSEUM: A252)

also helped lubricate the rotating parts of the machinery. Both training and elevating functions used this size of motor.

Under power operation the maximum speed of elevation was 10° per second initiated by turning a handwheel. For training purposes the speed was once again 10° per second with a ½ turn of the training handwheel being needed to move the mount through its entire range. Each mount had a training range of 340° and as No 3 mount normally faced forward this meant that it could not fire directly astern.[2] However, mounts 1 and 2 could not train through their full range. As an emergency feature hand training and elevating handwheels were also included. However, to illustrate the difference between power operation and hand operation, one turn of the elevating handwheel would produce one degree of elevation and one turn of the training handwheel would turn the mount through 1.5°. Power ramming was also used and a pressure supply of 1000lbs per sq in was available for this.

The crew for each mount consisted of a gun layer, trainer, two breech workers, two tray workers, four shell suppliers and a sight setter. The maximum rate of fire for each gun was twelve rounds per minute though seven to eight would be more normal. Useable arcs for Nos 1 and 2 mounts were 280° port and starboard, and 150° port and starboard for No 3 mount. The mount itself had a total arc of 340° but because the guns were originally positioned facing forward(see photographs) it could not actually train directly astern, creating a blind arc of 20°. Later a Confidential Admiralty Fleet Order (CAFO 1998/40 issued on 7 November 1940) would instruct ships to alter the housing from 0° to 180° so that the mount faced directly astern. This would give an arc of 320° which was almost the full effective arc of the mount. This modification was adopted by all Kelly captains who could see an obvious advantage of increasing the arc of No 3 mount even though the guns continued to be trained ahead by some ships throughout the war.

The guns fired a 50lb shell with a muzzle velocity of 2650ft/sec up to maximum range of 23,000 yards. This produced a recoil force of 40 tons if both guns fired together. The upward lift on the front of the mount's base plate amounted to 17 tons and the downward blow was 33 tons, once again with both guns firing. This force, added to the blast effects, shows the considerable pressures that naval ordnance could create, even on smaller vessels. *Kimberley*, for example, suffered significant blast damage around her No 3 mount in her engagement with *Francisco Nullo* in October 1940. Each mount was equipped with its own shell room and magazine. The shells and cordite were carried up to the deck below the mounts on separate electrically-operated dredger hoists. They were then run up chutes to positions fore and aft of the guns. The guns were equipped with sights although director firing was the more usual practice. Like the mounts themselves the director was power-operated and had 340° training.

The ammunition stowage for each gun was 250 rounds. Whilst the type of shell carried remained the same, the proportions per gun also changed as initial ideas about which were best were abandoned. Initially the semi-armoured piercing (SAP) shell had been the favoured type but these were gradually replaced by more and more high-explosive types as it was realised that against destroyers and most other targets that the Kellys would face these were more effective. Interestingly this was also the case with the Fleet Air Arm. SAP bombs were for a long time the preferred weapon for aircraft despite evidence to the contrary that high-explosive weapons were more effective in sinking ships.

TABLE 6:
Changes in 'J', 'K' and 'N' class ammunition allocation.

Year	Type of Shell (per gun)		
	SAP	HETF	HEDA
1939	190	50	10
1941	150	70	20
1944	20	230	-

Initially fifty star shells were allocated per ship but by 1941 this function was taken over by the 4in Mk V HA gun fitted to provide a long-range AA capability. When the 4ins were landed, star shells were once again allocated to the main armament. Practice rounds and blanks were also carried in No 2 shell room.

As discussed above, the main armament was normally controlled by a director tower located high up at the rear of the bridge. Behind the director tower was the 12ft Mk IV rangefinder in a separate tower which also doubled up as a HA director. Type 285 radar would start to appear on the tower in 1941 for anti-aircraft purposes.

As with most new weapons systems, the twin 4.7in had its share of teething troubles. These varied but for the gun itself, the major problem was one of inadequate lubrication affecting various areas. To remedy this, extra channels and grease nipples were added. The mount itself also suffered from this problem and once again extra lubrication points were fitted. Steps also had to be taken to ensure that the mount did not jam if brought suddenly to a stop (as it was initially prone to do). Other modifications included stiffening of the shields to avoid damage by blast and heavy weather and the drilling of channels to allow water to drain

---

[2] As a general rule the mounts on the Kellys were classified as Nos 1, 2 and 3 rather than the practice of A, B and X as for larger ships.

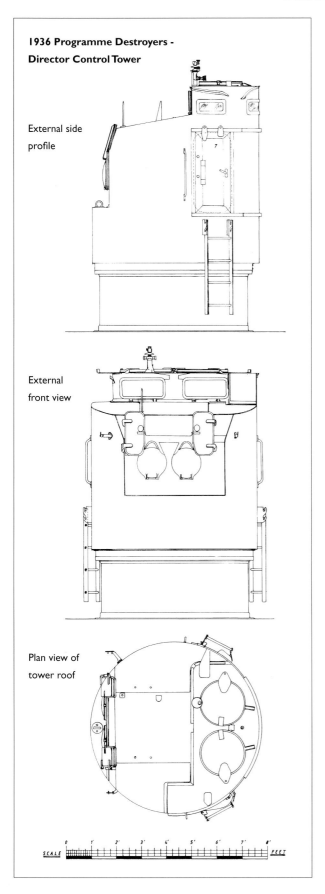

1936 Programme Destroyers - Director Control Tower

External side profile

External front view

Plan view of tower roof

SCALE | 0 1' 2' 3' 4' 5' 6' 7' 8' | FEET

from inside the shield. The variable speed gear was also initially prone to shock effects and the starters needed modification to improve their behaviour. These problems were quickly dealt with and then both the mount and gun proved to be effective and reliable.

ANTI-AIRCRAFT ARMAMENT

Royal Navy philosophy for short range multiple weapons was one of 'hosing an enemy aircraft out of the sky' and the AA weapons chosen for the Kellys reflected that philosophy. At the time they were designed, the multiple pom-poms and machine-guns were innovative and effective but failed to take account of rapid developments in aviation. Anti-aircraft defence had been given a lot of consideration during the initial design phase with a serious debate about whether to wait for a genuine dual-purpose main gun. In this case, conservatism and the need for new destroyers as quickly as possible won out and it was concluded that the twin mount with an elevation of 40° would provide enough AA capacity to be reasonably effective.

For close-range AA protection a multiple pom-pom was considered essential and the weapon was mounted on its own platform just behind the funnel. This gave it a good field of fire but a pom-pom director was not initially mounted and this limited its effectiveness. The original quadruple Mk VII pom-pom fitted to the Kellys was a hand-operated weapon with an elevation of 80° and depression of 10°. It had an arc of 710° though it was not meant to fire forward at less than 36° on the starboard side and 46° on the port side. This restriction was not always observed and led to casualties on the *Kingston* when the pom-pom fired into the transmitting station. Later a power-operated mount (the Mk VII*P) with a training rate of 25° per second would be introduced and this would start to appear on the Kellys in 1943.

The major problems with the pom-pom were its low muzzle velocity, 1920ft/sec, and its rather basic fire control system. Muzzle velocity was increased by the late 1930s but the range of the weapon still remained disappointing. Fire control was gradually improved during the war with the introduction of the Gyro Rate Unit which gave automatic target prediction. These though only really benefited the Kellys when combined with the Mk VII*P mount late in the war but they never received the Type 282 close-range AA set which was installed on larger ships.

The other component of the close-range AA armament was the Mk III quadruple 0.5in machine gun. Two were mounted, one each side of the bridge, on specially-constructed platforms with hinged sides which dropped down to allow the gun to fire, and shields were added during the

Quadruple 2pdr pom-pom

Key
1 Training gear - 1 turn of handles = 4° on guns
2 Elevating gear - 1 turn of handles = 4° on guns
3 Cover plate 7½in x 7½in over 6in dia. hole in
  platform for dismantling post which passes
  through a socket secured to the deck
4 Electric motor 220 volts DC 940 rpm

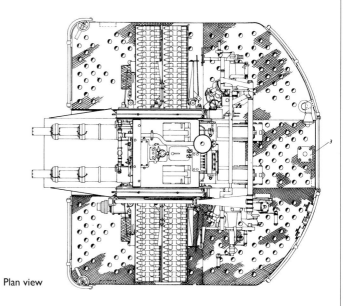

Plan view

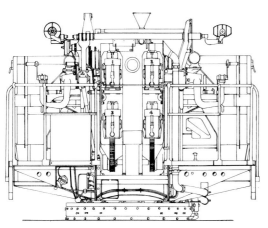

Rear elevation

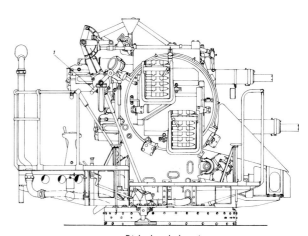

Right-hand elevation

SCALE |0 1' 2' 3' 4' 5' 6' 7'| FEET

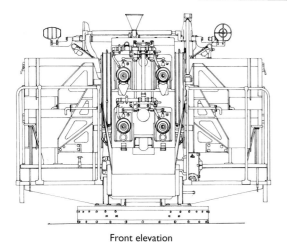

Front elevation

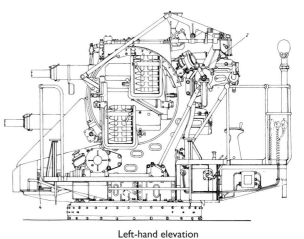

Left-hand elevation

war. The guns elevated to 80° and depressed to 10° and commanded excellent arcs of 180°. The four barrels together could deliver 800 rounds in 20 seconds and were reloaded and firing after another 30. However, it was clear that by 1937 that they would need to be replaced, being extremely short-ranged and firing solid bullets only. The 20mm Oerlikon gun was becoming available but ran into problems being accepted. Whilst Captain Mountbatten was highly impressed by the new weapon and pressed for its introduction,[3] links between Vickers (the builders of the 2pdr and 0.5in machine gun) and the Navy at that time were very strong. Thus Vickers and their adherents were able to delay the introduction of superior weapons such as the 20mm. This led to all the 'Js' and 'Ks' and most of the 'Ns' completing with 0.5in machine guns in place, although they were eventually replaced by Oerlikons (see below).

The 'Js' and 'Ks' also carried a pair of twin 0.303in Lewis guns which were normally carried in the magazine and fitted where needed. For example, at Dunkirk *Jaguar* carried hers mounted on pedestals on the gun deck behind No 2 mount, *Javelin*'s were mounted on the signal projector platforms either side of the bridge when she was torpedoed in November 1940 and *Kingston* completed with hers in place on the searchlight platform. These were even more ineffective than the 0.5in but were useful in that they gave the crew the feeling of being able to fight back.

[3] In 1937 Mountbatten was working at the Admiralty air division and in a position to recommend new AA weapons.

Modifications to AA armament[4]

It is fair to say that the 'J' and 'K' class destroyers started the war with inadequate anti-aircraft armament. This soon became apparent, especially the deficiencies of the 4.7in mounts in the HA role, being unable to deal with high level bombing or dive bombing. The problem affected all pre-war fleet destroyers, which found themselves cruelly exposed in the Norwegian campaign. The immediate response to this was to land torpedo tubes and replace it with a HA gun. In the case of the 'Js' and 'Ks' this was the 4in Mk V HA gun, which replaced the after torpedo tubes.

[4] Full details of all the changes and alterations to the Kellys' AA armament can be found in Appendix 3.

(*Above*) A view of the starboard side of *Javelin*'s 4in HA gun. These began to appear in July 1941 but were not universally popular. This was mainly due to the lack of any HA director. Also visible is the ribbed surface of the gun platform and the netting to catch shell casings.

(IMPERIAL WAR MUSEUM: A289)

(*Left*) A later photograph showing the port side of the gun with further additions (this one is from *Kashmir*). Splinter matting has been added as has bulletproof plating around the base of the mount. Also of interest are the Oerlikon platforms which were installed before the guns themselves were available. The port platform already has a pedestal installed but the gun itself would not be available until April 1941 (the photograph was taken in August/September 1940).

(IMPERIAL WAR MUSEUM: A656)

This was a 45 calibre weapon firing a 31lb shell with a muzzle velocity of 3000ft/sec. It was unable to reach the highest-flying bombers, but these were not much of a threat anyway. Fitting of these started in June/July 1940 on the 'Js' and 'Ks' of the 5th Flotilla operating out of Immingham. The destroyers of the 14th Flotilla in the Mediterranean and Red Sea did not receive them until 1941. The 'Ns' were completed with the 4in in place, while *Khartoum, Kandahar* and *Juno* were lost before they could receive one.

The effectiveness of the 4in was initially limited as no fire control was provided and attempts to link it to the rangefinder tower and take advantage of the installed Type 285 RDF were not successful. The mount, which was not powered, had a horizontal arc of 140° to port and 137° to starboard though at high angles of elevation it of course had a 360° arc. Stowage was available for 384 rounds, 288 in the warhead room and 96 in ready-use lockers. However, normal complement was initially 245 rounds (200 HETF, 34 starshell and 11 practice shells) rising to 345 when the supply of HETF improved. The introduction of the 4in was not universally supported and at a Controller's meeting on 11 December 1940 there was already pressure for it to be removed and the aft tubes replaced. This was resisted by the Controller who said that the HA gun could not be given up. However, by the end of 1942 the aerial threat had abated and the 4in were removed and the aft torpedo tubes were replaced. A Confidential Admiralty Fleet Order was issued on 6 August 1942 and allotted priority to the Eastern Fleet, followed by the 'L' class and the Mediterranean Fleet. *Jervis* had had her 4in installed much later than other ships and consequently she was still carrying it during her service in Operation 'Neptune', the invasion of France, in 1944. *Napier, Nepal, Nizam, Norman* and *Kimberley* had 40mm Bofors guns (see below) fitted instead of the torpedo tubes.

The main improvement in the AA armament of the 'J', 'K' and 'Ns' came about with the introduction of the Mks 1 and 2 20mm Oerlikon. This had been resisted by the Navy until 1939. One reason for this was the fact that during recoil the Oerlikon's breech did not lock. This increased the rate of fire but was considered dangerous. In fact problems with the Oerlikon would mainly occur with the ammunition and magazines, though there was a danger of recoil springs losing their tension. The barrel life of the Mk 1 and 2 Oerlikons was estimated to be 30,000 rounds provided that a limit of eight full magazines was not exceed in full rapid fire.

The Oerlikon fired a 20mm shell at a muzzle velocity of 2725ft/sec to an effective range of 1000 yards. Unlike the 0.5in it fired high explosive and tracer shells and allocation of these was initially 1200 of each per gun (with 300 practice, 300 practice tracer and 240 bulleted blanks). Later this

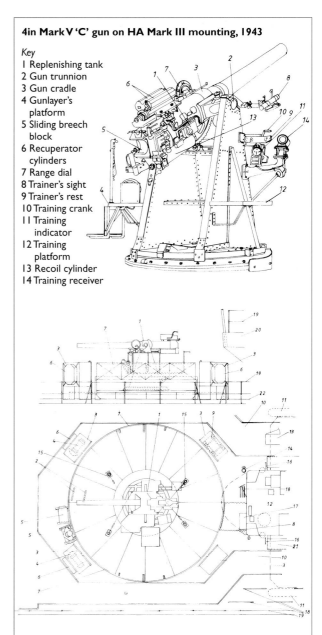

4in Mark V 'C' gun on HA Mark III mounting, 1943

Key
1 Replenishing tank
2 Gun trunnion
3 Gun cradle
4 Gunlayer's platform
5 Sliding breech block
6 Recuperator cylinders
7 Range dial
8 Trainer's sight
9 Trainer's rest
10 Training crank
11 Training indicator
12 Training platform
13 Recoil cylinder
14 Training receiver

Typical 'as fitted' arrangement of 4in HA mounting replacing the after set of torpedo tubes on a fleet destroyer, 1942

Key
1 4in HA mounting
2 Ready-use ammunition on battens
3 4in HA ready-use locker
4 Depth charge carrier stowed under
5 Depth charge stowage
6 Spanner life raft
7 Splinter protection plates (frequently splinter mats were added)
8 Curtained-off gun crew shelter
9 Trolley under for transferring 21in torpedo warheads
10 Semtex walkway
11 Carley float
12 Engine room fan
13 20mm Oerlikon magazine locker
14 Hose connection
15 Ringbolts for securing the mounting
16 Ladder
17 Seat
18 Deck strips
19 Guardrail
20 Searchlight platform
21 Lockers for torpedo chocks and canvas gear
22 Centreline of upper deck

would be changed to a ratio of two-thirds HE/incendiary to one-third HE/tracer. This made it a far more deadly weapon especially with a rate of fire of around 450 rounds per minute. Initially, however, this was restricted by a lack of magazines which meant that empty ones had to be reloaded, a process which took at least two minutes and which could produce dangerous delays in action.

Kelly was the first of the destroyers to receive the Oerlikon, mainly because of Mountbatten's connections. The rest of the ships of the 5th Flotilla received theirs just before sailing for the Mediterranean. Ships of the 14th Flotilla would not receive Oerlikons until much later. Specially-constructed platforms were built just in front of the searchlight platform port and starboard, each to take a single Oerlikon. Initially though, the lack of availability of these guns meant some ships going to sea with no Oerlikons in place. For example, *Piorun* was completed as the previous 'J' and 'K' classes with one pom-pom and two quad 0.5in machine guns as were *Napier*, *Nestor* and *Nizam*. *Norman* was too advanced in her construction and so was completed with 0.5in in her bridge wings and Oerlikons adjacent to her searchlight platform.

Oerlikon allocation gradually increased, the 0.5in being replaced by two single Oerlikons and it was authorised to fit two extra Oerlikons on the quarterdeck. This last decision potentially created a problem as initially the TSDS gear could not be used when these Oerlikons were in place. As a result the mounts were made portable, the guns being lodged in the gunner's store when the TSDS was in use. When the Oerlikons were in use the TSDS davits could be dismounted but this only happened rarely. The leaders did not have enough room for these Oerlikons on the quarterdeck and so they were mounted on the front of the aft deck house. Later twin Oerlikons were introduced and the quarterdeck Oerlikons were surrendered,[5] though the 'Ns' in the Pacific retained theirs. This was the successful Mk V power-operated twin mount which was fitted to the bridge wings of some Australian and British destroyers to replace the manual weapons. It was also installed on the platforms adjacent to the searchlight for several destroyers except *Jervis* which received hand-operated twins. The extra weight of the twin guns meant 5 tons of ballast was needed to compensate.

Not all destroyers received their full complement of Oerlikons. In what seems a local initiative by the Mediterranean

---

[5] Confidential Admiralty Fleet Order 1823/42 issued on 17 September 1942.

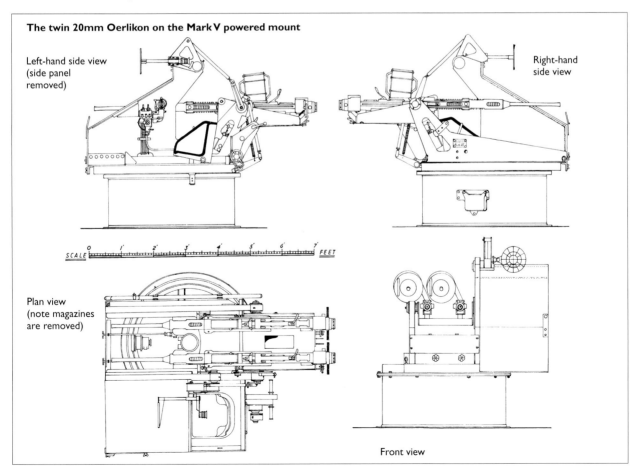

The twin 20mm Oerlikon on the Mark V powered mount

Left-hand side view
(side panel
removed)

Right-hand
side view

SCALE | 0 1' 2' 3' 4' 5' 6' 7' | FEET

Plan view
(note magazines
are removed)

Front view

Fleet in 1942 destroyers of the 14th Flotilla received a single Oerlikon on the quarterdeck between the TSDS winches. Whether this was because of shortages or through local initiative is not known and the extent of the change is also unclear. However, it affected *Kimberley* and *Kipling* and possibly others.

Other alterations to AA armament were specific to certain ships. For example, *Van Galen*, *Tjerk Hiddes*, *Nestor* and *Norman* received a Mk V power-operated twin 0.5in machine-gun tub originally designed for and used by Coastal Forces vessels. This was located between the two TSDS winches on the quarterdeck and quite why a weapon that had proved ineffective as destroyer anti-aircraft armament should be revived is obscure. The other addition was the equipping of the Australian destroyers serving in the Pacific with 40mm Bofors guns. These were of the Mk III variety, a hand-operated army weapon adapted for naval use. It fired a 2lb shell up to an altitude of 18,000ft with a muzzle velocity of 2720ft/sec. *Napier* had one located on her searchlight platform in lieu of the searchlight and the others landed depth charges and throwers and the aft set of torpedo tubes to accommodate it.

TORPEDOES

With the success of the quintuple torpedo tubes in the earlier 'I' class it was decided to retain them for the new design. An advantage of the bigger destroyer was also that there was no need for permanent ballast to counter the top weight of the tubes as there had been in the 'Is'. The Kelly class destroyers were designed to take two PR Mk II mounts located behind the single funnel with the engine room vents and searchlight platform between them. Both mounts were hand-operated and could be fired from the bridge or from the mounts themselves. Each mount could carry five Mk IX or IX** 21in torpedoes. The Kellys used the Mk IX introduced in 1939, which had a maximum range of 11,000 yards at 41kts and 15,000 yards at 35kts. Actual combat ranges were generally lower than this as the chance of obtaining a hit at such long ranges was slight. Initially fitted with a 727lb TNT warhead this was changed during the war to 810lbs of Torpex.

In peacetime the warheads and practice heads were stored in the warhead room with the bodies of the torpedoes remaining in the tubes. In wartime the practice heads were landed and the warheads were permanently attached to the bodies in the tubes. The warhead room was used initially for the stowage of spare depth charge and then for 4in ammunition. This resulted in the addition of pump and spraying arrangements as per a normal magazine.

The air vessel which powered the Mk IX was pressurised to 3100lb/sq in. This high pressure meant that the vessel

needed to be free of flaws. In several vessels this was not the case and several exploded spontaneously, one of these causing the loss of the *Khartoum* (accounts attributing the loss of the *Khartoum* to the action with the Italian submarine *Toricelli* are in error). In *Khartoum*'s case the flaw was near the fore end of the vessel and blew the warhead through the aft deckhouse setting fire to the gravity oil feed tank on No 3 gun deck. The resulting fire set off the aft magazine causing the loss of the ship. Interestingly, the torpedo warhead did not explode, an event which was noted with some satisfaction, especially as the US Navy and French Navy had had troubles with exploding warheads. As a temporary measure pressure in air vessels was reduced to 2900lb/sq in for a few months after the explosion.

The major change to the torpedo outfit was the landing of the aft set of tubes to accommodate the 4in HA gun. This necessitated fitting an extra 10 tons of ballast to compensate. Some destroyers never got their aft tubes back but all the 'Js', 'Ks' and 'Ns' which survived did. In fact, had *Kingston* survived she would have been re-equipped with aft tubes during repairs after the Battle of Sirte. *Jervis* was unusual in that she received the 4in when she departed the United Kingdom for the Mediterranean. There she had a quadruple set of tubes fitted in place of the gun. This was carried into 1943 when the 4in was refitted. Finally her 4in was landed and she emerged from her 1944/45 refit with the quintuple set of tubes restored, which she carried for the rest of her service career. Later, in an attempt to save top weight as to compensate for the increasing weight of the

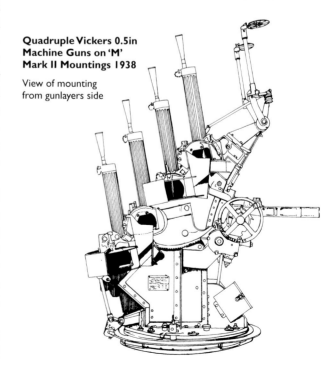

Quadruple Vickers 0.5in Machine Guns on 'M' Mark II Mountings 1938

View of mounting from gunlayers side

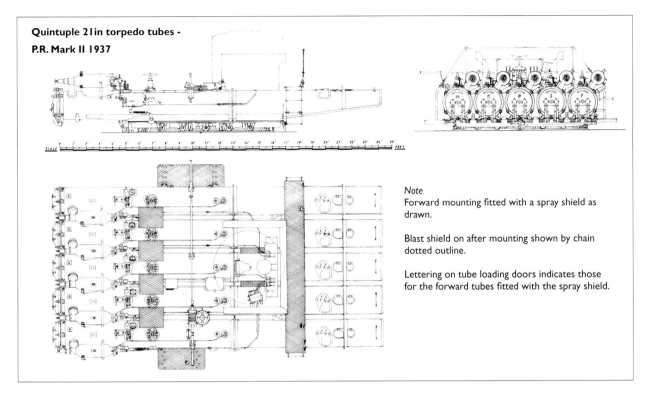

Quintuple 21in torpedo tubes -
P.R. Mark II 1937

Note
Forward mounting fitted with a spray shield as
drawn.

Blast shield on after mounting shown by chain
dotted outline.

Lettering on tube loading doors indicates those
for the forward tubes fitted with the spray shield.

radar equipment, it was authorised to land one torpedo.[6] Also, 60°-0°-60° gyro angling gear and TDS III** torpedo control sights were to be fitted, although it is uncertain as to whether this was done before the war ended.

ANTI-SUBMARINE EQUIPMENT

Standard Royal Navy anti-submarine (A/S) equipment consisted of asdic and depth charges. Asdic was an echo-sounding device which consisted of an oscillator housed in a perspex dome. A sandwich of steel plates and quartz crystals, it emitted a powerful supersonic note when a strong electric current was passed through it. This was controlled by an operator to give a short ping which would be reflected back when it bounced off something and picked up on the operator's headphones. The length of time the echo took to return would be recorded on a chemical recorder and this would give a range to the target. Whilst it was possible to detect differences in echoes returned by fish, wrecks, the seabed etc, it was difficult and operators needed considerable training to do so. Mostly, they looked for the Doppler effect – the echoes caused by moving objects which returned a lower or higher note – but schools of fish could produce the same effect. Another major problem was that of the different density of layers of water which could create blind spots. This was particularly prevalent in the Mediterranean and would cause serious difficulties.

When the asdic had located the target there needed to be a weapon to destroy it and this was the depth charge. The D depth charge was a metal drum 2ft 9in long by 1ft 5½in in diameter, filled with 300lbs of TNT (later Amatol) and fitted with a depth-activated fuse. The Mk VII was slightly larger. The charge was set to a particular depth and fired or dropped over the target. The nearer the target the more effective the charge was and a charge hitting a submarine was usually enough to bring it to the surface or sink it. The Kellys carried two Mk 2 throwers located just in front of the aft deckhouse and one Mk 1 set of depth charge rails located at the stern between the TSDS davits which housed six charges. *Javelin* and *Janus* were altered to carry four throwers, *Javelin*'s forward ones being 57ft 6in from her stern angled at 90° and her aft ones 27ft from her stern angled at 80°. *Janus*'s forward pair were 30ft from her stern angled at 95° and the aft pair 20ft from her stern angled at 90°. The Mk 2 thrower fired one charge at a fixed elevation of 50° with a flight time of 4 seconds. Apart from *Piorun*, *Javelin* and *Janus*, the Kellys were equipped to fire a five-charge pattern of one each from the throwers and three dropped from the rails. However, as mentioned above, during the early stages of the war captains were also dropping six-charge patterns. This practice continued in the Mediterranean but seems to have died out by 1943. During peacetime the complement of charges was ten but at the start of the war this went up to thirty, ten being stowed in the warhead room and twenty on deck.

---

[6] CAFO 928/44. A complete torpedo weighed over 1 ton.

It had rapidly been realised that even thirty depth charges was not enough and that a way needed to be found to increase the number carried. Clearing out the warhead room would provide space for a further twenty-eight charges and another thirty-seven could be accommodated on the quarterdeck if the TSDS equipment was removed. For the leaders (which did not carry TSDS gear anyway) an extra twenty-eight charges could be stored in the warhead room and six on the quarterdeck. Whilst the warhead room was emptied and used for storage of firstly depth charges and then HA ammunition, the TSDS equipment remained in place throughout the war on most of the Kellys. The extra charges tended to be accommodated on deck. Table 7 shows some typical early war depth charge complements for the 'K' class.

Javelin's starboard depth charge thrower and spare charges. The method of attaching the charges to the cradle can also be seen. The crew member to the left is fitting a pistol. (IMPERIAL WAR MUSEUM: A294)

TABLE 7:
Depth charge allocations for 'K' class destroyers

Ship	Date	No of charges	Type
Kingston	29 Nov 1939	30	D.III
Khartoum	19 Dec 1939	30	Mk VII
Khartoum	20 Jan 1940	30	D.III
Kipling	8 Feb 1940	30	D.III
Kingston	25 Feb 1940	30	D.III
Kelly	3 Mar 1940	48	D.II
Kandahar	9 Mar 1940	20	Mk VII
Kelly	10 Mar 1940	48	Mk IV
Kelvin	8 Apr 1940	48	D.III and Mk VII
Kelvin	27 May 1940	48	Mk IV and Mk VII
Khartoum	21 Jun 1940	65	Mk VII
Kingston	26 Jun 1940	75	Mk VII

The extra charges for *Kingston* and *Khartoum* were probably stowed in the warhead room and on deck but TSDS gear was not removed as minesweeping was quite an important role for destroyers operating in the Red Sea. The approved wartime compliment of depth charges was increased to forty-five of the light type in 1940. This remained the standard outfit for the rest of the war. Of these, twenty would be stored on deck and twenty-five below. Consideration was given to including one of the Mk VII heavy depth charges in the complement but priority for these was given to escort vessels of the Western Approaches command and the Kellys never received them. Consideration was also given to adapting the ships to be able to fire the more effective ten-charge pattern but as this would have meant landing the TSDS gear this did not happen until late in the war.

Depth charge attacks needed to be carried out at a certain speed for the firing ship to clear the effects of the explosion. If the speed was too low, damage to the ship's hull could result. For the Kellys the minimum speed was 11kts, though

12kts was more common. In shallow water speed had to be even higher and ships were not supposed to allow their speed to fall below 14kts for a four-charge Amatol pattern. In 1943 the Mk II throwers began to be replaced by the Mk IV version which were more reliable. The Mk II thrower had been vulnerable to water getting into its firing pistol which resulted in it failing to fire, particularly in rough seas. In the early months of the war several ships had suffered from this problem. The depth charge rack remained the Mk I though warnings did have to be issued to discourage crewmembers from using it as an extra storage area and damaging it.

THE TWO SPEED DESTROYER SWEEP
The Kellys had been designed with minesweeping capability from the outset. Initial requirements had included a bow sweeping capability as well as the two speed destroyer sweep (TSDS). The former requirement, where the paravanes were streamed from the ship's bows, was dropped early on but the TSDS, specially designed for destroyers, remained. It had three roles:

1. To carry out a searching sweep to locate any mines that might be in the area.
2. To protect other vessels.
3. To clear minefields.

Two paravanes were trailed from the stern of the vessel, held at a pre-set depth by a third 'depressor paravane' between them. The position of the sweeping paravanes would be marked by a float on either side of the ship. Depending on

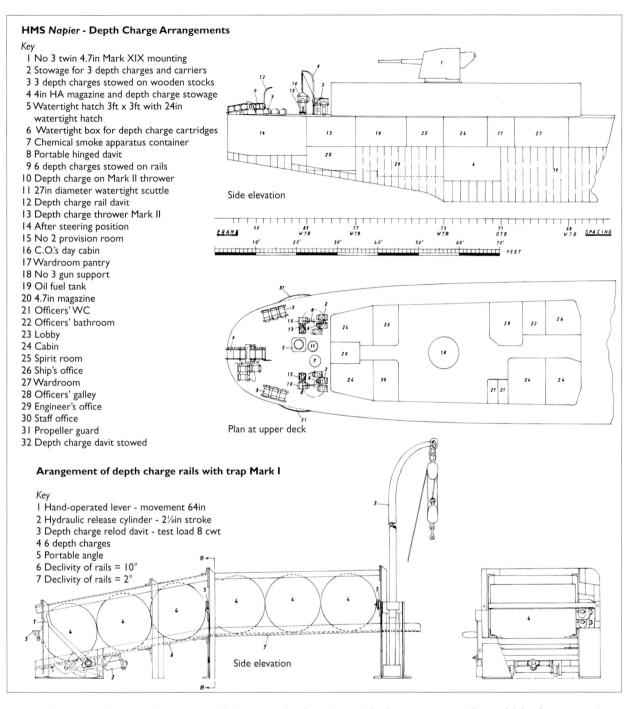

HMS *Napier* - Depth Charge Arrangements

Key
1 No 3 twin 4.7in Mark XIX mounting
2 Stowage for 3 depth charges and carriers
3 3 depth charges stowed on wooden stocks
4 4in HA magazine and depth charge stowage
5 Watertight hatch 3ft x 3ft with 24in
   watertight hatch
6 Watertight box for depth charge cartridges
7 Chemical smoke apparatus container
8 Portable hinged davit
9 6 depth charges stowed on rails
10 Depth charge on Mark II thrower
11 27in diameter watertight scuttle
12 Depth charge rail davit
13 Depth charge thrower Mark II
14 After steering position
15 No 2 provision room
16 C.O.'s day cabin
17 Wardroom pantry
18 No 3 gun support
19 Oil fuel tank
20 4.7in magazine
21 Officers' WC
22 Officers' bathroom
23 Lobby
24 Cabin
25 Spirit room
26 Ship's office
27 Wardroom
28 Officers' galley
29 Engineer's office
30 Staff office
31 Propeller guard
32 Depth charge davit stowed

Side elevation

Plan at upper deck

Arangement of depth charge rails with trap Mark I

Key
1 Hand-operated lever - movement 64in
2 Hydraulic release cylinder - 2⅛in stroke
3 Depth charge relod davit - test load 8 cwt
4 6 depth charges
5 Portable angle
6 Declivity of rails = 10°
7 Declivity of rails = 2°

Side elevation

the speed the vessel was moving at it could clear a path of between 150 and 310 yards (320 yards for the S Mk I* paravane). The faster the vessel, the narrower the path. A detached cutter was used to protect the paravanes but most of the actual cutting was done by the wire itself. The sweep would follow the wake of the vessel provided that no more than moderate rudder (20° maximum) was used. Two speed ranges were used, low speed of around 9½kts which covered role 3 and a high speed of between 16-25kts for role 1. For role 2 the speed range would be 20-25kts for maximum effi-

ciency. The latter was especially useful for fleet protection.

The paravanes themselves were stored on the quarterdeck with the depressor paravane stowed on top of the depth charge rack. They were lowered into the water by fixed davits and trailed using a 2in wire which was supplied in 100-fathom lengths and connected to a 30hp steam winch. There was a winch for each of the port and starboard paravanes. The paravanes (figures that follow are for the S Mk I*) weighed 1070lbs and were 11ft 6in long and 1ft 7in in diameter. They differed from other paravanes in that their tails

Two Speed Destroyer Sweep: general arrangement

Plan view

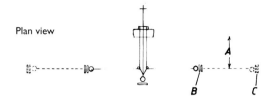

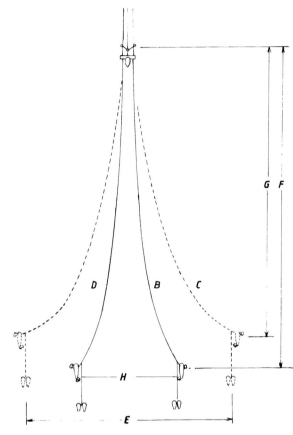

Key
A Depth as ordered
B High speed setting
C Low speed setting
D 200 fathoms (1200ft)
E 310 yards using Sweep Mark I, 320 yards using Sweep Mark I*
F 390 yards
G 340 yards
H 150 yards

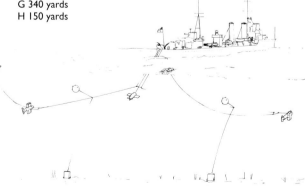

were on the opposite side of the body to the plane. TSDS paravanes were relatively delicate and required careful handling. The plane had to be correctly adjusted otherwise the paravane became unusable. It was also subject to corrosion and needed changing every 6 months. To operate a TSDS sweep the three paravanes would be lowered into the water with the depth normally pre-set to 50ft. Then depending on the width of sweep needed the vessel would accelerate or decelerate as required. Adjustments to the S Mk I* in 1943 were able to produce a sweep of 280 yards at 16kts but these could not be done on board the vessel and were regarded as only temporary. Cutters were increased to nine for sweeps under 40ft in depth in 1943 but the main cutting medium for TSDS continued to be the wire.

As discussed above, when the quarterdeck Oerlikons were installed the TSDS gear could not be used, but there was never any intention to remove it, the Oerlikons being dismounted when it was required. But by 1943 *Janus* and *Kelvin* would be fitted with bow protection gear. It is important to note though, that the leaders did not carry TSDS due to the increased size and weight of their aft deckhouse. *Jervis*, *Kelly* and *Napier* could therefore not be fitted with minesweeping equipment and remain within the stability parameters of the class.

A view of the port TSDS paravane winch, paravane and the depressor paravane on board. The destroyer is moving at some speed and one wonders about the safety of the crew members in the photograph. The cylindrical object on the left of the picture is one of the station-keeping lights.

(IMPERIAL WAR MUSEUM: A2531)

At the start of the war and like all destroyers, the 'J' and 'K' classes were not protected against magnetic mines. Obviously with their minesweeping role this was not satisfactory and so it was quickly decided to fit them with internal degaussing equipment. As the 'J' and 'Ks' were going into dry dock for urgent refits due to their design faults or repairs to damage it was easy to fit degaussing equipment when that happened. Fitting took place from March to May 1940 and

by the time they started to arrive in the Mediterranean both classes had been so fitted. Generally the wires ran along the edge of the ship on the upper deck at its join with the hull side. There was very little external sign of this equipment, unlike some ships where the degaussing coil was visible on the exterior of the hull. *Kipling*, however, did carry her coil around the outside of the hull. The 'Ns' were fitted with internal degaussing equipment while under construction.

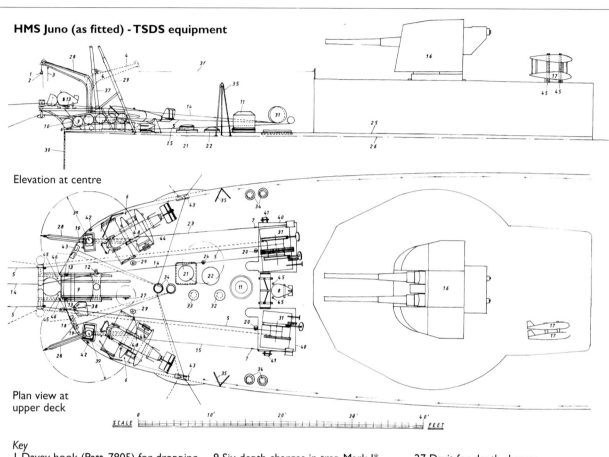

HMS Juno (as fitted) - TSDS equipment

Elevation at centre

Plan view at upper deck

Key

1 Davey hook (Patt. 7805) for dropping paravane
2 Spring hook (Patt. 8816) for recovering paravane
3 1in F.S.W.R. tripping line - length arranged to allow paravane to be tripped about 2ft below the deck
4 Stowed position of davits secured by 1½in F.S.W.R. between davit heads and 1½in F.S.W.R. guy with stretching screw to deck eyeplate
5 Paravane towing wire: Patt. 8868 port, Patt. 8869 starboard (Admiralty supply)
6 ½in eyeplate for taking the receiving guy for paravane davit when in the stored position
7 Pendant out and fitted with thimble and shackle and 2½in white tail cordage with thimble and shackle
8 Depressor peace and war stowage

9 Six depth charges in trap Mark I*
10 Hand lever for depth charge trap – port side
11 Acid container for smoke apparatus
12 Fairlead for depressor towing wire
13 10in cleat for hanging depressor
14 Depressor towing wire Patt. 8827
15 Davit purchase wire 1½in F.S.W.R.
16 No 3 twin 4.7in mounting
17 Stowage for spare floats
18 Fairlead for mooring wire
19 ½in eyeplate for tail line
20 1in eyeplate for chain stopper – Patt. 8819
21 Watertight hatch to steering compartment
22 Watertight scuttle to lower deck
23 Davit purchase wire - 2in F.S.W.R.
24 Portable davit for stores
25 Upper deck at centre
26 Upper deck at side

27 Davit for depth charges
28 Geared paravane davit
29 Stays for ensign staff
30 1½in elm sheathing
31 Steam paravane winch
32 10in mushroom ventilator
33 9in mushroom ventilator
34 Mooring bollard
35 Awning stanchion
36 Awning ridge
37 Ensign staff
38 Towing slip
39 6ft 9in radius
40 Saveall
41 15in cleat
42 Cleat
43 Fairlead
44 2in eyeplate
45 ½in eyeplate
46 ⅜in eyeplate
47 Paravane - S Mark I or S Mark I*

4
Camouflage and Markings

DESTROYER CAMOUFLAGE is a difficult subject because little evidence survives beyond photographs. There was a combined camouflage office which kept records of ship camouflage schemes but the records that survive are incomplete. Scheme cards were supposed to be kept for each ship but these also do not seem to have survived. However, it is doubtful that they would have recorded all camouflage schemes as there were initially several unofficial ones. The researcher is left with photographs and memory or unofficial records though the latter are frequently unreliable. All schemes in this chapter are based only on photographs which constitute the only reliable record of a ship's colour scheme.

Further problems arise with the interpretation of the exact shades of colours in schemes which are not easy to determine from black and white photographs. There is also the question of whether the scheme was the same on both sides, especially if only one photograph exists. For some it is possible to make an educated guess but others are more difficult. There are also schemes for which either only partial or no photographic evidence exists but a contemporary report describes an aspect of it. I have found several such schemes, particularly relating to the period round the invasion of Normandy. The Mediterranean, where almost all the Kellys served, was also a difficult area as initially the C-in-C Admiral Cunningham banned all photography and that which did get taken was desultory. Another problem area was the Red Sea theatre of which only two early photos could be found.

Some camouflage schemes exist only on film but once again there are gaps. Schemes in the Mediterranean changed very rapidly for certain ships in 1941. *Kingston* for example seems to have had four different schemes. Others were not so prolific but still changed significantly. After 1942 things seemed to have settled down and ships retained their schemes for longer periods. Whilst 1943 is fairly well documented 1944 is not and only details exist rather than whole schemes. In late 1944 the Admiralty introduced their standard scheme based on light grey with a blue-grey panel. This was applied on all ships and lasted until the end of the

war when the surviving Kellys in the Mediterranean were painted in overall light grey.

CAMOUFLAGE HISTORY

The first Kellys to be camouflaged were the ships of the 5th Flotilla and this seems to have started in November 1939. Such schemes were based on 'dark hull/light upper works' as illustrated by the profiles of *Kelly* and *Kandahar* but not all the flotilla received camouflage. For example, *Kimberley* was in plain AP507B Medium Grey when she left for the Mediterranean in May 1940. *Kandahar* retained her camouflage in simplified form in the Red Sea at least until late June 1940. Camouflage for the Mediterranean Fleet was ordered under Mediterranean Fleet Order 433/34 issued on 9 August 1940 and is worth quoting in full.

> **Camouflage of HM ships against air and surface attacks.**
> HM ships in the Mediterranean fleet are to be camouflaged in accordance with the following instructions.
> (1) The foundation is to be Mediterranean grey.
> (2) The dazzles are to be of a darker colour as chosen by Commanding Officers, but they should not contrast too strongly with the foundation.
> (3) Decks are not to be scrubbed white but should be stained or darkened at discretion
> (4) Turret tops, etc., are not to be painted black but are to be given a tone in harmony with the ship's general scheme.
> (5) All paint is to have a full surface as far as possible.

Three or four colours figured in most of the early colour schemes which tended to be quite attractive. Another point to note about the Mediterranean schemes is that they tended to be the same for both sides of the ship. *Juno* and *Janus* were the first two 'Js' to be camouflaged, *Janus* sporting an attractive three-colour scheme with white edging (see profile). *Juno* had a false bow wave which was later painted out whilst the rest of her camouflage was retained. False bow waves were initially thought to be quite effective and some were very elaborate but they gradually went out of fashion and the Kellys had all lost theirs by the beginning of 1941. When the three ships of the 28th Division returned to the Mediterranean in April 1941 they were painted in a three-colour scheme of black, AP507B medium grey and AP507C light grey. This may have been applied earlier in the Red Sea but I have been able to find no reliable evidence to support this. The scheme was basically the same with small variations for each ship and would later be simplified or

CAMOUFLAGE SCHEMES

1 *Kandahar* November 1939

Kandahar is shown here in a scheme she carried in November 1939, one of the earliest destroyer camouflage schemes. Very little is known about this scheme except that it consisted of AP507A and AP507C and no photograph has come to light which shows the starboard side of the scheme but it may have been identical. The white bar on her funnel denotes her status as divisional leader for the 5th Flotilla. Normally she would lead the ships of the 10th Division but was also the second in command of the flotilla.

2 *Kelly* cFebruary 1940

The leader of the 5th Flotilla is shown her with AP507B hull and AP507C upper works, a scheme she carried for a short time in early 1940. *Kashmir* also carried this scheme with her pennant numbers in white. *Kelly* carries the broad black band of the flotilla leader at the top of her funnel. It is not known whether other ships of the flotilla received this scheme.

3 *Jupiter* cAugust/September 1940

In late 1940 *Jupiter* was painted in a spectacular three-colour scheme whilst serving on the Humber station, the colours of which were AP507A, AP507B and AP507C. This profile is the first attempt to re-construct the port side of this scheme which differed significantly from the starboard side (see photograph). At the time she wore this scheme, *Jupiter* was acting as 5th Flotilla leader and this is shown by the broad black band on her funnel. The scheme was later simplified and the band painted out but it is likely that it was removed entirely by November 1940 when *Jupiter* joined the Plymouth Command.

4 *Kipling* late 1940

Kipling wore this interesting variant on the dark hull/light upper works scheme whilst serving out of Rosyth. The colours were AP507B and AP507C and the scheme was the same both sides. Of interest is the very elaborate false bow wave in black and white also carried by *Jackal* (but without the black infill). The latter ship remained in overall AP507B. Once again this was probably painted over when the *Kipling* was transferred to the Plymouth Command.

5 *Janus* September 1940

Janus sports a spectacular camouflage scheme made up of AP507C, AP507B and white. The false bow wave was white and quite simple in comparison to those sported by the ships of the 5th Flotilla. This scheme was simplified sometime in early 1941 by the simple expedient of painting over the white lines with AP507B to create a two-colour scheme. The false bow wave was also painted over. The red and black bands denote the 14th Flotilla.

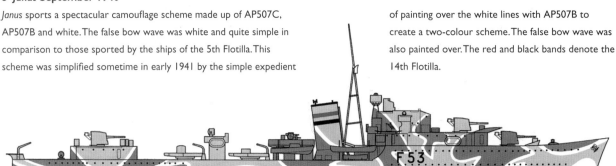

6 *Juno* January 1941

Juno carries what is possibly her first camouflage scheme with a simple false bow wave. The photograph is unclear as to whether this was white but by the time she escorted *Formidable* it had been painted over though the scheme was essentially the same. Colours were AP507A and AP507C and the scheme was identical for both sides, a common feature for Kellys in the Mediterranean.

7 *Kimberley* May 1941

When the three surviving ships of the 28th Division returned to the Mediterranean from the Red Sea they were all given an elaborately conceived camouflage scheme consisting of black, AP507B and AP507C. *Kimberley* and *Kingston* were identical but *Kandahar* was slightly different (see photo p9). The superstructure was not painted but the roofs of the shields, tubes and gun barrels were all camouflaged on *Kimberley* and *Kingston* (not *Kandahar*). It is unknown how long they carried this scheme but it was probably painted out by August 1941. Unusually the three Ks also carried two red bands rather than the normal black and red bands of the 14th and this may have been a divisional indicator. The scheme was identical on both sides.

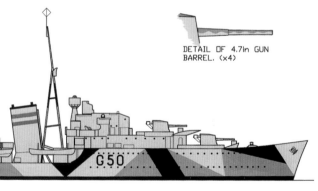

DETAIL OF 4.7in GUN BARREL. (×4)

8 *Kipling* July 1941

Kipling had sailed for the Mediterranean theatre with the other ships of the 5th Flotilla. When this was disbanded the three surviving ships, *Kipling*, *Jackal* and *Kelvin*, were split up between the other two Kelly Flotillas, the 7th and 14th. *Kipling* and *Jackal* were allocated to the 7th Flotilla and were painted in the newly-adopted 7th Flotilla scheme consisting of AP507A hull band with everything above it AP507C. Unusually, *Kipling*'s pennant number was also painted in these colours creating a spectacular effect as they were reversed. She carried this scheme until she was sunk but the pennant numbers and funnel bands did change (see photographs).

9 *Kingston* summer 1941

The elaborate scheme carried by the ships of the 28th Division was difficult to maintain and deteriorated rapidly. By August 1941 they were all painted in either simplified versions of it or new schemes. *Kingston* is shown here in her first scheme after the painting-over of the three-colour scheme. As can be seen this was so rapid that the funnel bands were just painted over rather than being repainted. This scheme would be replaced later in the year by yet another two-colour scheme (see photograph). The colours used were AP507A and AP507C and the scheme was the same for both sides.

10 *Jupiter* October 1941

On arrival in the Mediterranean *Jupiter* was painted in this simple two colour camouflage scheme which once again was the same for both sides and consisted of AP507A and AP507C. It is unknown whether she retained the scheme when she joined the Eastern Fleet.

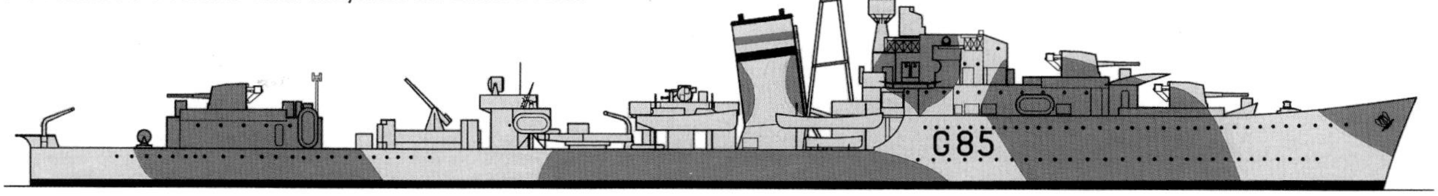

11 *Kelvin* early 1943

Kelvin is shown here in a dark hull/light upper works scheme with an unusual variation. The shield and gun barrels of No.3 mount are also painted AP507A. *Jervis* carried a similar scheme but also had her deckhouse walls painted that colour as well. The other colour is AP507C (soon to be renamed G45) and the pennant numbers are red.

12 *Piorun* mid-1944

Shortly before D-Day, *Piorun* was repainted in this Emergency Special Fleet Scheme. She wore this until at least October 1944 when the Admiralty Standard Schemes were introduced. She was then repainted in Type A.

13 *Kelvin* June 1944

Kelvin is shown in a three colour Admiralty disruptive scheme which was identical on both sides. Other surviving Kellys, *Javelin* and *Jervis* were also painted in Admiralty disruptive schemes. Of interest is the pennant number painted in G10. The colours were G10, G20 and G45.

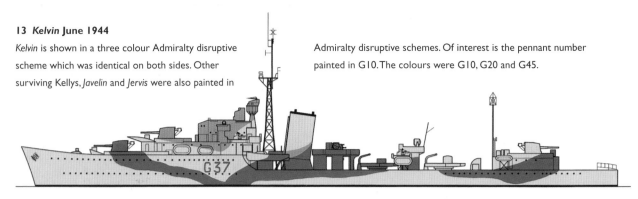

14 *Nepal* July 1945

Nepal is shown in the Admiralty Type A scheme adopted by all ships of the British Pacific Fleet. She also carries her local pennant number in black. These were adopted to avoid confusion and when destroyers left the Pacific Fleet they reverted to their previous numbers. Once again she carries the two white bands of the 7th Flotilla and the colours were B20 and G45. The tops of masts in this scheme were painted white.

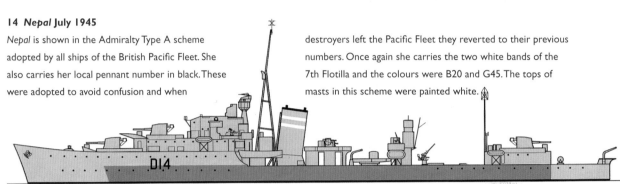

15 *Jervis* April 1946

Jervis in overall Mediterranean grey after the war. She is shown with black markings, her Flotilla now being indicated by its number shown on the funnel. The single black band denotes a divisional leader. *Jervis* wore this scheme until May 1946 when she left the Mediterranean for the United Kingdom and reserve.

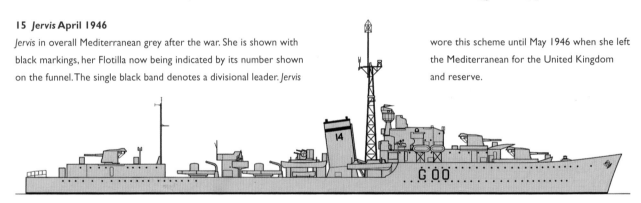

16 *Gadjah Mada* 1951

Very little is known about the career of *Gadjah Mada* apart from what is related in the text. She appears to have been painted light/medium grey with a white '01' on her bows and a red triangle in the position where the pennant number usually was. Her funnel top had a broad black band. The name *Gadjah Mada* is usually reserved for the flagship of the Indonesian Fleet.

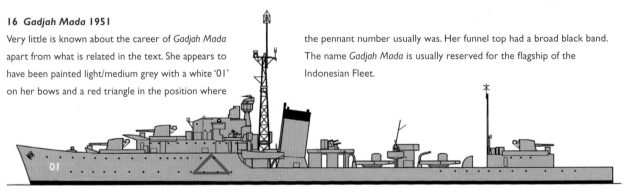

17 False bow waves

(a) *Kashmir* in late 1940. This wave was carried by *Kashmir* during September 1940 and was white. The rest of the ship was overall AP507B with the white mast top.

(b) *Jackal* in late 1940. After the false wave described earlier, *Jackal* carried this rather nice white and black example during the same period *Jupiter* carried the elaborate camouflage. All bow waves and other camouflage seems to have disappeared when the 5th Flotilla served out of Plymouth.

replaced until *Kingston* and *Kimberley* were painted in what was called a 'Tobruk' scheme for the operations to that port in 1941. *Kandahar* would be repainted in a simplified version of her earlier scheme until her loss in December 1941.

By the end of 1941 the Kellys serving in the 14th Flotilla would be painted in various simplified schemes consisting of geometric designs or irregular shapes but the same on both sides. When *Jaguar* arrived from service with Force H she was painted in a geometric design which she wore until her loss. *Janus* and *Juno* would lose their false bow waves and *Janus*'s scheme would be simplified. *Jervis,* funnily enough, kept her more complex schemes for a while longer, these including either a black stern or black stern and bow in addition to whatever other scheme she carried. With the arrival of the reborn 7th Flotilla in the Mediterranean a new concept was introduced, with the whole flotilla carrying the same scheme. *Napier*, *Nestor* and *Nizam* initially carried the dark hull/light upper works scheme before changing to a light Admiralty alternative scheme which involved an AP507A dark grey band round the lower hull with the rest of the ship being painted in AP507C light grey. All ships which joined the flotilla would receive this scheme, including *Kipling* and *Jackal* which joined after the 5th Flotilla was disbanded and would both carry it until their loss. This scheme would continue to be used by the flotilla in the Indian Ocean and when *Nepal* and *Norman* joined they would also eventually be painted in it. Both these ships would arrive in the Indian Ocean in their Home Fleet colour schemes and repaint there.

By 1943 there were only three Kellys in the Mediterranean, *Jervis*, *Javelin* and *Kelvin*. *Kimberley* was reduced to care and maintenance and *Janus* was under repair. *Jervis* and *Kelvin* were in a dark hull/light upper works scheme. *Javelin* had been painted in an elaborate Mediterranean scheme for the June convoy operations but no information exists as to whether she retained this into 1943. However, it is likely that she was still in this scheme when she returned to the UK. With the return of each destroyer to the UK for refit they would emerge upon completion in an Admiralty disruptive scheme, usually a modified light disruptive. The 'Ns' as they completed also received these schemes though *Tjerk Hiddes* did receive a dark disruptive scheme before heading off to the Indian Ocean to join the 7th Flotilla. Once there she and her sister *Van Galen* were painted in the standard 7th Flotilla scheme.

THE KELLYS IN HOME WATERS

The departure of four 'Ks' and two 'Js' to the Mediterranean did not stop the camouflage experiments. All the Kellys in home waters were reorganised under Captain Mountbatten

as part of the 5th Flotilla. Several ships received false bow waves, *Kashmir*, *Kipling* and *Jackal* being the identifiable ones. *Kipling* and *Jackal* had the same style bow wave but *Kashmir*'s was different. *Kipling* combined her bow wave with a false wash and wake and a dark hull/light upperworks scheme (see profile). This was applied around August/September 1940. However, the most elaborate colour scheme to be carried was that of *Jupiter* which consisted of irregular patterns of the three greys available at the time. The profile shows her port side which to the author's knowledge has never previously been reconstructed. This scheme did not last long and was first simplified and then painted over after she arrived in Plymouth in October 1940 with the rest of the flotilla. In fact, most of the other 5th Flotilla schemes were also painted over and the ships received a coat of AP507B medium grey, except *Javelin* which was carrying a dark hull/light upper works scheme when she was torpedoed in December 1940.

One of the persistent stories about camouflage for the 5th Flotilla concerns 'Mountbatten Pink', the colour supposedly invented by Captain Mountbatten. He was escorting a coastal convoy in Autumn 1940 which included a ship from the Union Castle line which was still carrying her pre-war light mauve paint. As the sun rose he noticed that the ship was difficult to see and this was the inspiration for Mountbatten Pink. Mountbatten claimed that it was ideal for conditions of sunrise and sunset, both dangerous periods for destroyers, and that he had it mixed and applied to the whole of the 5th Flotilla. That Mountbatten Pink did exist is unquestioned, but that it was applied to the ships of the 5th is not. No documentary evidence exists to support it and none of the standard accounts mention it at all, apart from Ziegler.[1] Mountbatten was a keen writer of reports so it is puzzling that none detailing his application of the new colour to his ships survives.

Several lists have been drawn up listing the ships which carried the scheme. Most are flawed as they include all eight of the 'K' class though four of these had left the 5th Flotilla for good before Mountbatten Pink was introduced. A problem with Mountbatten Pink is that it is difficult to tell from ordinary grey in a black and white photograph. However, looking at photographs taken before and after the move to Plymouth the contrast on all of them suggests that the ships of the flotilla were all in standard greys. This does not preclude evidence being found to support the 5th Flotilla being painted in Mountbatten Pink but the story seems to have originated with Mountbatten himself who according to

---

[1] Philip Ziegler, *Mountbatten*. It is not mentioned by Poolman, *HMS Kelly* or Hough, *Bless our Ship* both of whom knew Mountbatten. Even Ziegler hints that the colour might not have originated with Mountbatten.

other commentators was not above embellishing his role in things. I have not included any profiles which show a ship in overall Mountbatten Pink for this reason.

When orders were received to transfer to the Mediterranean the 5th Flotilla all repainted in AP507C light grey and sailed in that colour. *Javelin* and *Jupiter* remained behind and whilst *Jupiter* does not seem to have been camouflaged on completion of her refit, *Javelin* received a two-colour scheme. *Jupiter* would receive a Mediterranean scheme when she arrived there in late 1941 and probably retained this until she was sunk at the Battle of the Java Sea. *Piorun* received various schemes throughout her life before being repainted in the final grey/blue panel scheme.

Pennant numbers and funnel markings

All ships of the 'J' and 'K' classes received pennant numbers with the flag superior F. Thus a pennant number would read F (Flag superior), 50 (Pennant number). In 1940 this superior was changed to G. This took some time to come into effect and *Kipling* was still carrying the F superior when she came out of refit in July 1940, as was *Khartoum* when she was sunk. However, by September all Kellys in home waters were carrying the G superior. It took slightly longer for the Mediterranean destroyers. All 'Ns' had the G superior from the beginning but in 1945, the four Australian 'Ns' which served with the Pacific Fleet would receive totally new numbers with the flag superior D, reverting to their previous pennant numbers on their return to the Royal Navy. After the war all destroyers received the flag superior D though this was not implemented for most of the surviving Kellys. The number was also increased with either the addition of 100 or 200 but the only ship to receive its modified number was *Nepal*. Flotilla leaders did not show

their pennant numbers but all other ships did. The table below lists the changes in the superiors and numbers

Pennant numbers were generally white or black though red was also used. In 1942 an attempt was made to specify what colours to use for various camouflage backgrounds.[2] On colours MS1, MS2, AP507A and B5 the pennant numbers would be in either AP507C or MS4. On colours B6, MS3 or MS4 they were to be white. On MS4a, AP507C, light blue or light green they were to be MS3 or equal parts AP507A and AP507C. Black or red was not permitted on any camouflage background though it continued to be used extensively. Reverse-shaded pennant numbers also made an appearance, *Kipling*'s being particularly spectacular.

Funnel markings fell into two different types, the flotilla bands and the markings to indicate the rank of the ship within the flotilla. At the start of the war only the flotilla leader and the divisional leader were so indicated. The Kellys introduced the eight-ship flotilla into the Royal Navy and as such had only two divisions. Prior to this the nine-ship flotilla had consisted of two divisions of four destroyers and a separate leader. For the eight-ship flotilla the leader assumed responsibility for one of the divisions as well as the whole flotilla. Flotilla leaders' funnels were marked with a wide black band at the top and, as mentioned previously, the pennant numbers were not shown. The divisional leader carried a vertical bar on either side of the funnel in the same colours as the flotilla funnel band. Pennant numbers were shown. If funnel bands were carried the bar intersected the bands, level with the top band. This marking fell into disuse during 1941 and was never reinstated. The divisional leaders for the Kellys were, *Kandahar*, 5th and 14th Flotillas;

---

[2] Confidential Admiralty Fleet Order 679/42 issued 9 April 1942.

TABLE 8:
Pennant numbers of the Kellys

Name	As built	Dec 1940	Jul 1945	Jun 1946	Jan 1947	1950
Jervis	F00	G00	G00	G00	G00	–
Jackal	F22	G22	—	—	—	—
Jaguar	F34	G34	—	—	—	—
Juno	F46	G46	—	—	—	—
Janus	F53	G53	—	—	—	—
Javelin	F61	G61	G61	G61	G61	—
Jersey	F72	G72	—	—	—	—
Jupiter	F85	G85	—	—	—	—
Kelly	F01	G01	—	—	—	—
Kashmir	F12	G12	—	—	—	—
Kandahar	F28	G28	—	—	—	—
Kelvin	F37	G37	G37	G37	G37	—
Khartoum	F45	—	—	—	—	—

Name	As built	Dec 1940	Jul 1945	Jun 1946	Jan 1947	1950
Kimberley	F50	G50	G50	G50	G50	—
Kingston	F64	G64	—	—	—	—
Kipling	F91	G91	—	—	—	—
Napier	G97	G97	D13	G97	G97	D297
Nestor	G02	—				
Tjerk Hiddes*	G16	—	G16	J5	JT5	D806
Nepal	G25	—	D14	G25	G25	D125
Nizam	G38	G38	D15	G38	G38	D38
Norman	G49	—	D16	G49	G49	D149
Piorun**	G65	G65	G65	G65	G65	D165
Van Galen	G84	—	G84	J3	JT3	D803

* In Indonesian service *Tjerk Hiddes* carried the pennant number 01
** *Piorun* was named *Noble* when she returned to the Royal Navy in September 1946 as there was another ship named *Nerissa*.

Jackal, original 7th Flotilla and *Nestor,* second 7th Flotilla. Various other ships of the class also served as temporary flotilla leaders and in this capacity they carried the black band but retained their pennant number. In these cases the black band was frequently made from black bunting wrapped around the funnel. However, not all ships carried this marking. When *Javelin* was acting as flotilla leader she did not, but *Kipling, Jupiter, Kelvin* and *Kashmir* all did at one time. *Jackal* also carried the flotilla leader's band when *Napier* was under repair for bomb damage in mid-1941.

The flotilla bands were different-coloured bands round the funnel. Of the three main flotillas involved, the 5th carried no bands. As a result the divisional leaders' marking was a white bar on each side of the funnel. Before the war *Jackal* of the 7th carried a single white band with her divisional leader's marking before switching to two white bands. The 7th in both its incarnations then used two white bands throughout the war. The 14th used a red-over-black band, except for the returning 28th division leader (*Kandahar*) in April 1941 which carried a red bar and two red bands. She later changed to the red-over-black markings. *Janus* and *Kimberley* also carried two red bands at the same time, whilst *Kingston* carried black-over-red bands for a short time before switching to two red bands for the Tobruk run. However, by November 1941 all ships of the 14th Flotilla were carrying red-over-black bands and this would be their flotilla identifier for the rest of the war.

In 1946 markings changed and a new divisional leader's marking was introduced. The leader's black band remained and was to be 4ft wide on the foremost or only funnel. The divisional commander's band was to be black and 2ft wide, starting 3ft from the top of the foremost or only funnel. In place of the funnel bands, each destroyer carried her flotilla number on either side of the foremost or only funnel.[3] *Jervis* carried these markings and also the divisional leader's band during her last tour. *Javelin, Kimberley* and *Kelvin* carried them minus the divisional leader's band in their final days in the Mediterranean as well.

DECKS

Decks were either painted or covered with linoleum and painted. The bridge, signal deck, wheelhouse, chart house, commanding officer's sea cabin, combined signal and plotting office, upper deck forward and lower deck forward and aft were covered with best quality linoleum 4.5mm thick. The weather decks, including the searchlight and gun platforms but excluding the upper deck over the machinery spaces, were covered with an approved non-skid rubber composition which had been tinted to produce a pleasing colour. Strips of rubber matting about 3ft wide were worked into the gangway on each side of the upper deck over the machinery spaces. On the weather decks this colour was mainly dark grey, which was similar in shade to AP507A. Various brands of linoleum were used, Semtex, Corticene and Wundergrip. Wundergrip was the favoured linoleum for external use especially on the gun decks but ran into problems as it became slippery when oil and water mixed on it. It was also too soft and expended cartridge cases tended to cut it badly. It was replaced by coconut matting as a temporary measure before all ships were ordered to install Semtex in August 1940.[4] Semtex had better wearing qualities but did deteriorate more quickly when subject to oil. It was also grey. Semtex was also used internally but was not popular, especially the green variety, because it got dirty very quickly and was difficult to keep clean. *Jackal* installed Corticene on her upper deck in preference. Unusually when she was completed, *Jersey's* deck was coated with a petrol/black lead mixture which was well thought of but for some reason was not used on other ships of the class.

During the war decks were painted in whatever grey or blue-grey was appropriate to the particular camouflage scheme a ship carried. This only became significant in the later panel schemes when B15 was specified for decks. At various times, however, other markings were painted on the decks chiefly to aid aircraft recognition. The eight 'Js' of the 7th Flotilla received the early-war marking of the RAF roundel on the bow whilst serving on the Humber station. In the Mediterranean *Jervis* had a broad red circle painted on her No 3 mount deck[5] and in 1943 her upper decks were painted in red lead[6] which was slow to dry and not popular. This probably also happened to the other ships of the 14th Flotilla but cannot be confirmed.

COLOUR SCHEMES OF THE KELLYS

Presented below is a list of all the Kellys and the colour schemes they wore throughout their service lives. This is not complete and where there are gaps these are noted. More detailed information on the exact nature of the schemes can be obtained from the profiles and the photographs. Definite dates only refer to when the ship went into repair or came out of repair, when it was known to have changed commands or when it was sunk. They do not provide exact details for the application of camouflage but the scheme did change some time after these dates.

---

[3] Dimensions were 4ft deep by 3ft wide for each number which would be in 6in block. Spacing between numbers was to be 1ft 8in. Admiralty SC7/46, BR619(2) issued on 7 February 1946.

[4] Confidential Admiralty Fleet Order 1486/40 issued on 15 August 1940.

[5] See Connell, *Mediterranean Maelstrom.*

[6] See Pugsley, *Destroyer Man,* p141.

Kelly
23 Aug 1939 – 2 Sep 1939: Overall AP507C.[7]
3 Sep 1939 – 6 Nov 1939: overall AP507A.
6 Nov 1939 – 21 Nov 1939: Unknown possibly Overall AP507B.
28 Feb 1940 – 2 Mar 1940: AP507B hull, AP507C upper works.[8]
27 Apr 1940 – 9 May 1940: Overall AP507B.
16 Dec 1940 – 15 Jan 1941: Overall AP507A.
15 Jan 1941 – Apr 1941: Overall AP507B.[9]
Apr 1941 – 23 May 1941: Overall AP507C.

Kashmir
24 Oct 1939 – Feb 1940: Unknown possibly overall AP507B, pennant numbers white.
Feb 1939 – 10 Apr 1940: AP507B hull, AP507C upper works, pennant numbers white.
16 Jun 1940 – 2 Oct 1940 overall AP507B, pennant numbers white, white painted bow wave.[10]
3 Oct 1940 – Apr 1941 overall AP507B, pennant numbers white.[11]
Apr 1941 – 23 May 1941 overall AP507C, pennant numbers black.

Kandahar
10 Oct 1939 – Nov 1939: Unknown possibly overall AP507B or colour scheme shown below, pennant numbers white.
Nov 1939 – 23 May 1940: Elaborate block camouflage scheme using AP507A and AP507C, pennant numbers white.
May 1940 – ?1940: AP507A hull, AP507C upper works.[12]
?1940 – May 1941: Unknown.
1 May 1941 – Sep? 1941: three-tone geometric scheme using black, AP507B and AP507C, pennant numbers black.
Sep? 1940 – 1941: AP507A, AP507C simplified version of

the previous scheme, pennant numbers black.

Kelvin
27 Nov 1939 – 3 Dec 1939: Unknown, possibly overall AP507B, pennant numbers white.
12 Dec 1939 – Apr 1941: Overall AP507B, pennant numbers white.
Apr 1941 - ?1941: Overall AP507C, black pennant numbers.
?1941 – Jun 1943: AP507A hull, AP507C upper works, pennant numbers white then red.[13]
3 Apr 1944 – 10 Nov 1944: Admiralty three-colour light disruptive scheme, G10, G20 and G45, pennant numbers G10.
Nov 1944 – 16 Jul 1945: Admiralty standard scheme A, B20 and G45, pennant numbers black.
17 Jul 1945 – Jun 1949 (when scrapped): Overall medium grey, pennant numbers white.

Khartoum
6 Nov 1939 – 16 May 1940: Unknown, possibly overall AP507B, pennant numbers white.
17 May 1940 – 23 Jun 1940: All that is known is that her upper works and funnel were AP507C.[14]

Kimberley
21 Dec 1939 – 16 May 1940: Overall AP507B, pennant numbers white.
17 May 1940 – Apr 1941: Unknown.
Apr 1941 – Aug 1941: three-tone geometric scheme using black, AP507B and AP507C, pennant numbers black.
Aug 1941 – 12 Jan 1942: Mediterranean disruptive scheme, AP507A and AP507C, pennant numbers black.
24 Apr 1944 – 19 Oct 1944: Unknown.[15]
19 Oct 1944 – 22 Jun 1945: Admiralty standard scheme A, B20 and G45, pennant

numbers black.
23 Jun 1945 – Jun 1949 (when scrapped): Overall medium grey, pennant numbers white.

Kingston
15 Sep 1939 – 16 May 1940: Overall AP507B, pennant numbers white.
17 May 1940 – Apr 1941: Unknown.
Apr 1941 – Jul 1941: three-tone geometric scheme using black, AP507B and AP507C, pennant numbers black.
Jul 1941 – Aug? 1941: two-tone scheme, AP507A and AP507C, pennant numbers black.
Aug 1941 – 23 Mar 1942: two-tone disruptive scheme, AP507A and AP507C, pennant numbers black.
23 Mar 1942 – 11 Apr 1942 (in dock): Overall AP507C, no pennant numbers.

Kipling
20 Dec 1939 – 21 Feb 1940: Unknown, possibly overall AP507B, pennant numbers white.
13 Apr 1940 – 22 Apr 1942: Overall AP507B, pennant numbers white.
20 Jul 1940 – Sep 1940: Overall AP507A, pennant numbers white.
Sep 1940 – Nov? 1940: AP507B hull, AP507C upper works, false bow wave with black centre, false wake and wash, pennant numbers in white.
Nov? 1940 – Apr 1941: Overall AP507B, pennant numbers white.
Apr 1941 – 28 May 1941: Overall AP507C, pennant numbers black.
Jun 1941 – 11 May 1942: Admiralty light intermediate, AP507A band round lower hull with everything above AP507C, pennant numbers reversed AP507A and AP507C.[16]

Jervis
12 May 1939 – 19 Mar 1940: Overall AP507B.
21 Jul 1940 – ?1941: Mediterranean disruptive, AP507A and AP507C.
Sep 1940 – Dec? 1941: Mediterranean disruptive, AP507A and AP507C with black stern section.
Dec? 1941 – late 1942: AP507B hull, AP507C upper works, black bow as far as the

breakwater and black stern.
Late 1942 – Jun 1944: AP507A hull, AP507C upper works, No 3 mount in AP507A.[17]
Jun 1944 – 8 Sep 1944: Admiralty two-colour disruptive scheme, G10 and G45, pennant numbers white.
5 Jun 1945 – 14 Dec 1945: Admiralty standard scheme A B20 and G45, pennant numbers reverse shaded B20 and G45.[18]
14 Dec 1945 – Feb 1946: Admiralty standard scheme A.
Feb 1946 – 5 Jun 1946: Overall light grey, pennant numbers black.
6 Jun 1946 – Jun 1949 (when scrapped): Overall medium grey, pennant numbers black.

Jackal
13 Apr 1939 – Jun 1940: Overall AP507B, pennant numbers white.
Jun 1940 – Nov 1940: Overall AP507B, false bow wave, same pattern as that of *Kipling*, pennant numbers white.
Nov 1940 – Apr 1941: Overall AP507B, pennant numbers white.
Apr 1941 – Jun? 1941: Overall AP507C, pennant numbers black.
Jun? 1941 – 12 May 1942: Admiralty light intermediate, AP507A band round lower hull with everything above AP507C, pennant numbers black.

Jaguar
12 Sep 1939 – 29 Nov 1940: Overall AP507B, pennant numbers white.
30 Nov 1940 – Feb? 1941: Overall AP507A, pennant numbers black.
Feb? 1941 – 26 Mar 1942: Two-tone geometric scheme using AP507A and AP507C, pennant numbers black.

Juno
25 Aug 1939 – ? Sep 1939: Overall AP507A, white pennant numbers.
? Sep 1939 – 16 May 1940: Unknown, possibly overall AP507B, white pennant numbers.
May 1940 – Sep 1940: Overall AP507C, black pennant numbers.
Sep 1940 – Jan 1941: Mediterranean disruptive using AP507A and AP507C with false

---

[7] This is the only occasion I have found where it is possible to be positive about the dates for a colour scheme as they were included in the log.

[8] Dating of this colour scheme is exceptionally difficult as *Kashmir*'s log no longer exists. There is a possibility that it was applied mid-November 1939 but the later date is more likely as *Kelly* has a D/F loop on her foremast at the time and these were introduced after November. *Kelly* only wore it for a very short time.

[9] There is a possibility that *Kelly* was painted in Mountbatten Pink during this period but I have found no evidence to confirm this.

[10] The bow wave was initially a white outline enclosing a black shape but this was replaced by an all-white wave.

[11] *Kashmir* had lost her false bow wave by 17 October.

[12] This simplified scheme was definitely carried on 18 June 1940.

[13] Red pennant numbers were in place by 13 June 1942.

[14] This is all the only photograph of *Khartoum* actually shows. I believe that her colour scheme was the same as *Janus* and *Juno*, overall AP507C with black pennant numbers.

[15] It is possible that the Admiralty standard scheme was applied much earlier but this cannot be confirmed. All other destroyers of the 'J' and 'K' classes received Admiralty disruptive schemes during the Normandy invasion and it may be that *Kimberley* did as well.

[16] On 3 January the 7th Flotilla was transferred to the Indian Ocean. *Kipling* stayed behind and joined the 14th Flotilla, changing her funnel bands to red over black (from two white) and repainting her pennant numbers red. She was wearing these markings when she was sunk.

[17] From January 1944 *Jervis* ceased to be a flotilla leader and lost her leader band. Pennant numbers were painted white for this scheme.

[18] Initially both pennant numbers and the leader band was carried. *Jervis* was the leader of the 14th Flotilla until 12 November 1945 and carried the leader band until she was replaced by *Chequers*. She then became a divisional leader and carried the appropriate band.

bow wave, pennant number black.
Jan 1941 – 21 May 1941: As previous with bow wave painted out.

Janus
5 Aug 1939 – Sep? 1939: Overall AP507A, pennant numbers white.
Sep 1939 – 16 May 1940: Overall AP507B, pennant numbers white.
May 1940 – Sep 1940: Overall AP507C, pennant numbers black.
Sep 1940 – Jan 1941: Mediterranean disruptive involving AP507B and AP507C outlined in white. Pennant numbers black.
Jan 1941 – 9 Jun 1941: previous scheme modified by the removal of white, pennant numbers black.
18 Mar 1942 – 31 Jan 1943: Unknown, possibly same scheme as before.
31 Jul – 25 Jan 1944: Unknown.

Javelin
8 Jun 1939 – Sep? 1939: Overall AP507A, pennant numbers white.
Sep? 1939 – 30 Sep 1940: Overall AP507B, pennant numbers white.
1 Oct 1940 – Nov 1940: Overall AP507C, pennant numbers black.
Nov 1940 – 29 Nov 1940: AP507A hull, AP507C upper works, pennant numbers black.
Jan 1942 – Jun 1942: Two-colour Admiralty disruptive, MS2 and AP507C, pennant numbers reversed MS2 and AP507C.
Jun 1942 – 22 May 1943: Mediterranean disruptive, AP507A and AP507C, pennant numbers black.
6 Mar 1944 – 22 May 1944: Overall, G45 with full hull panel finishing at the breakwater and the rear deck house G20, pennant number MS2.
23 May 1944 – 14 Jul 1944: Admiralty two G10, G45 colour disruptive counter-shaded G45 and G10, pennant numbers.
12 Jun 1945 – 11 Nov 1945: Admiralty standard type A, B15 pennant numbers.
11 Nov 1945 – 17 May 1946: Unknown possibly overall light grey.
May 1946 – Jun 1949 (when scrapped): Overall medium grey, black pennant numbers.

Jersey
28 Apr 1939 – 7 Nov 1939: Overall AP507A, pennant numbers white.
10 Oct 1940 – Apr 1941: Overall

AP507B, pennant numbers white.
Apr 1941 – 2 May 1941: Overall AP507C, pennant numbers black.

Jupiter
22 Jun 1939 – Sep? 1939: Overall AP507A, pennant numbers white.
Sep? 1939 – Aug 1940: Overall AP507B, pennant numbers white.
Aug 1940 - ? 1940: Three-tone disruptive scheme, consisting of AP507A, AP507B and AP507C, pennant numbers white.[19]
? 1940 – 5 Mar 1941: Overall AP507B, pennant numbers white.
23 May 1941 – 9 Aug 1941: Unknown.
10 Aug 1941 – 25 Sep 1941: Overall AP507C, pennant numbers black.
26 Sep 1941 – 19 Nov 1941: Mediterranean disruptive scheme, AP507A and AP507C, pennant numbers black.
20 Nov 1941 – 27 Feb 1942: Unknown but possibly still in her Mediterranean disruptive scheme.

Napier
11 Dec 1940 – 5 Mar 1941: Unknown.
20 Mar 1941 – Jun? 1941: AP507A hull, AP507C upper works.
Jun? 1941 – Dec? 1944: Admiralty light intermediate, AP507A band round lower hull with everything above AP507C.
Dec 1944 – Aug 1945: Admiralty standard type A.
Aug 1945 – 15 Dec 1945: unknown possibly G10 hull G45 upper works.
15 Dec 1945 – Jan 1956 (when scrapped): Overall medium grey, pennant numbers white.

Nestor
3 Feb 1941 – 13 Jul 1941: Unknown.
14 Jul 1941 – ?1941: Overall AP507C, Pennant numbers black.
? 1941 – 30 Nov 1941: AP507A hull, AP507C upper works, Pennant numbers black.
30 Nov 1941 – 15 Jun 1942: Admiralty light intermediate, AP507A band round lower hull with everything above AP507C, pennant numbers black.

Tjerk Hiddes
6 May 1942 – 25 Aug 1942: Admiralty three-colour light disruptive, possibly MS1, B6 and AP507C, pennant numbers white.

26 Aug 1942 – 12 Nov 1944: Admiralty light intermediate, AP507A band round lower hull with everything above AP507C, pennant numbers white.
13 Nov 1944 – Dec? 1944: Unknown.
Dec? 1944 – 20 Apr 1946: Admiralty standard type A, pennant numbers white.
21 Apr 1946 – 2 Mar 1951: Overall light grey, pennant numbers white
3 Mar 1951 – 1961: Overall medium grey, pennant numbers white with shadowing, red triangle on sides.

Nepal
1 May 1942 – Sep 1942: Admiralty two-colour disruptive scheme, MS1 and MS4, pennant numbers white.
Sep 1942 – Nov? 1942: four-colour scheme which could be MS1, MS2, MS4 and AP507C, pennant numbers white.
Nov? 1942 – Mar 1945: Admiralty light intermediate, AP507A band round lower hull with everything above AP507C, pennant numbers black.
Mar 1945 – Aug 1945: Admiralty standard type A, pennant numbers black.
Aug 1945 – 15 Dec 1945: Unknown, possibly G10 hull, G45 upper works, pennant numbers white.
15 Dec 1945 – 13 Oct 1948: Overall medium grey, pennant numbers black.
14 Oct 1948 – 19 Mar 1951: Overall light grey, pennant numbers black.
20 Mar 1951 – Jan 1956 (when scrapped): Overall medium grey, pennant numbers unknown.

Nizam
11 Dec 1940 – 5 Mar 1941: Unknown.
20 Mar 1941 – Jun? 1941: AP507A hull, AP507C upper works, pennant numbers white.
Jun? 1941 – Dec? 1944: Admiralty light intermediate, AP507A band round lower hull with everything above AP507C pennant numbers black.
Dec 1944 – Aug 1945: Admiralty standard type A, pennant numbers black.
Aug 1945 – Dec 1945: G10 hull, G45 upper works, pennant numbers red lined with white.
Dec 1945 – Jan 1956 (when scrapped): Overall medium grey, pennant numbers red edged white.

Norman
15 Sep 1941 – 6 Oct 1941:

Overall MS2, pennant numbers black.
7 Oct 1941 – Feb 1942: Admiralty light disruptive consisting of G55, MS1 and B6, pennant numbers reversed B6 and MS1.
Feb 1942 – Dec? 1944: Admiralty light intermediate, AP507A band round lower hull with everything above AP507C, pennant numbers black.
Dec? 1944 – Aug 1945: Admiralty standard type A, pennant numbers B15 then black.
Aug 1945 – Dec 1945: G10 hull, G45 upper works, pennant numbers white.
Dec 1945 – Apr 1958 (when scrapped): Overall medium grey, pennant numbers white.

Piorun
4 Nov 1940 – ?1942: Overall MS4, pennant numbers white.
?1942 – Sep 1943?: Western Approaches scheme of white and Peter Scott blue, pennant numbers black.[20]
Sep 1943 – Jan? 1944: Admiralty two-colour disruptive, G45 and B30.
Jan? 1944 – Jun 1944: Two-colour scheme with B30 stern and bow. Rest of ship G45, pennant numbers black.
Jun 1944 – Dec? 1944: Home Fleet emergency destroyer scheme, G45, B15 and G20, pennant numbers white.
Dec? 1944 – Feb 1946: Admiralty standard type A, pennant numbers black.
Feb 1946 – 28 Sep 1946: Overall light grey, pennant numbers black.
29 Sep 1946 – Dec 1955 (when scrapped): Overall medium grey, pennant numbers unknown.

Van Galen
23 Mar 1942 – 31 May 1942: Overall AP507B, pennant numbers white.
1 Jun 1942 – 7 Nov 1944: Admiralty light intermediate, AP507A band round lower hull with everything above AP507C, pennant numbers black.
8 Nov 1944 – 3 Aug 1945: Admiralty standard type A, pennant numbers black.
3 Aug 1945 – 14 Jun 1946: Unknown.
15 Jun 1946 – 20 Jan 1947: Medium grey band round hull, rest of hull plus upper works light grey, pennant numbers white.
21 Jan 1947 – 15 Oct 1950: Unknown.
a16 Oct 1950 – Oct 1953: Overall medium grey, pennant numbers white.
Oct 1953 – 1 Feb 1957 (when scrapped): Unknown but probably as previous scheme.

---

[19] This scheme was slightly simplified later on. It does not seem to have lasted long and was probably painted out when *Jupiter* served with the Plymouth command.

[20] The original scheme included blue upperworks and turrets. These were later painted over in white though the hull pattern remained.

5

Pre-War and the Early Months

T HE FIRST OF THE KELLYS into service was *Jackal*, which was accepted by the Royal Navy on 13 April 1939. On the 28th she sailed for Falmouth, the same day her sister *Jersey* commissioned. The third ship of class into service was the leader herself, *Jervis*, which sailed for Chatham from her birthplace on the Tyne on 12 May. These three ships were the nucleus of the 7th Destroyer Flotilla to be commanded by Captain Philip J Mack. However, *Jervis* had to go for repairs at the beginning of June having managed to collide with a tug, a forerunner of the numerous collisions the 'Js' and 'Ks' would be involved in during the early part of the war. *Jervis* eventually sailed to Portland where she joined *Jersey* and *Jackal* for flotilla exercises. These were fairly gentle affairs as at that time they were generally carried out in calm weather. Another interesting feature was that, in order to conserve fuel, speeds were not meant to exceed 16kts and any exception had to be recorded in the ship's logbook.

During this period two more of the flotilla were com-

missioned, *Javelin* on 8 June and *Jupiter* on 22 June. After further exercises *Jervis* and *Jackal* then shut down for seasonal leave. Even the newly commissioned *Javelin* and *Jupiter* followed this ritual. Two of the Kellys, *Jersey* and *Kingston*, had strong links with the places they were named after. *Kingston* had been launched by the then Lady Mayoress of Kingston and the *Jersey* by Mrs A M Coutanche, wife of the Bailiff of Jersey, one of an official party from the island who attended the launch. So it was unsurprising that the *Jersey* would visit her patron island shortly after her commissioning. She arrived at St Helier on 10 July 1939 for a full programme of events and departed on the 15th after the official farewell, returning to Portsmouth.

BUILD-UP TO WAR

These five ships would be joined by *Janus* which commissioned on 5 August. During her torpedo trials on the 9th her steering gear broke down but was fixed that evening. In August most of the flotilla sailed for Rosyth at various intervals, *Jervis* on 30 July, *Jersey* on 2 August, *Janus* the day she commissioned, *Jackal* on 29 July and probably *Javelin* as well, though the relevant log is no longer extant. *Jupiter* remained at Devonport for the whole of the month.

On 11 August, the 7th and 8th Flotillas together with the cruiser *Aurora* sailed for Scapa to take part in the XKO exercises, the last series of full fleet exercises before the war. The exercises were an excuse to send the fleet to its war station (Scapa Flow) and were also an opportunity to refine and develop fleet tactics before war broke out. During the exer-

Jackal on commissioning. Commissioning photographs were often of magnificent quality and these are no exception. Three views were generally taken, two from the bow and stern quarters and one in profile. Generally only one side of the ship was taken. Of interest in

this view is the original position of No 3 mount and the divisional leader's bar which for the 7th Flotilla was white.

(IMPERIAL WAR MUSEUM: FL9784)

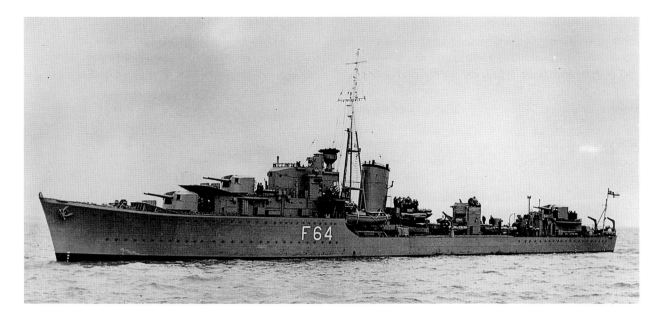

cises *Jersey* achieved 33kts. Surprisingly the ships suffered no defects and after a short period at Rosyth, the flotilla arrived at Dover and commenced patrol duties, apart from *Janus* which sailed for Killinghome at Grimsby to continue her working-up. After visits to Rosyth and Invergordon she would eventually end up at Portland. She would be joined by *Juno* which commissioned on 25 August but which would not have the luxury of an extensive working-up period. The war station for the 7th Flotilla was the Humber estuary.

At the end of August and beginning of September 1939 the 'Js' of the 7th Flotilla began to make their way to Immingham where they would be based. *Jervis, Jersey, Jackal, Javelin* and *Jupiter* all arrived on 1 September, two days before the outbreak of war, and sailed immediately as the anti-submarine screen for the 2nd Cruiser Squadron. On 4 September 1939, as the ships finished their patrol, *Jersey* intercepted the German merchant vessel *Johannes Molkenbuker*, which scuttled herself, and took the forty-two survivors on board. She then sailed for Kirkwall in the Orkneys to disembark her prisoners. *Jervis* joined the Home Fleet bound for Invergordon whilst *Janus* and *Jackal* sailed for Grimsby. *Juno* was also at sea during this time having sailed from Portland to the Humber estuary. On 7 September she was part of the escort force (which included *Jackal* and *Janus*) for the liner *Batavia IV* which had been chartered to bring British embassy staff back from Berlin.

Duties for the rest of September mainly consisted of patrols and convoys. *Janus, Juno* and *Jackal* were based at Plymouth to escort the Channel convoys together with the Polish destroyer *Grom*. The latter was dryer as regards spray than the British ships but extremely short-ranged, lacked asdic, had poor acceleration and was generally unsuitable

Kingston on 15 September 1939. Just visible on the original are her twin Lewis guns mounted on the searchlight platform.

(IMPERIAL WAR MUSEUM: FL 12462)

for convoy duty.[1] On 12 September, *Jaguar*, the final member of the class and flotilla also commissioned. She worked up at Portland before joining the first 'Ks', *Kelly* and *Kingston*.

Enter the *Kellys*

The *Kelly* class started appearing several months after the 'Js'. *Kelly* was the first into service, commissioning on 23 August. The original intention for this class had been for it to become the 3rd Flotilla in the Mediterranean, replacing the 'I' class ship for ship. The leader, *Inglefield* would depart when *Kelly* arrived on station.

Table 9:

Proposed Organisation of 3rd Destroyer Flotilla in the Mediterranean 15 March 1939

Pennant no.	Ship	Expected date of completion	Sub-division	Replacing
Fifth Division				
F01	*Kelly*	23 Aug 1939	9th	*Imogen*
F91	*Kipling*	Early Nov 1939	9th	*Imperial*
F12	*Kashmir*	Jan 1940	10th	*Impulsive*
F64	*Kingston*	Mid-Sep 1939	10th	*Ilex*
Sixth Division				
F28	*Kandahar*	Late Oct 1939	11th	*Isis*
F50	*Kimberley*	Feb 1940	11th	*Icarus*
F45	*Khartoum*	Mid-Sep 1939	12th	*Intrepid*
F37	*Kelvin*	Late Nov 1939	12th	*Ivanhoe*

[1] ADM 199/62.

Kelly was painted in Mediterranean Grey in anticipation of this move but as it was concluded that it would be a better use of resources to keep the 'K' class at home, at least until there were more of them, *Kelly* was repainted in Home Fleet Grey on 3 September. The Italian reluctance to enter the war made it possible to bring the 'I' class back to Britain in November without immediately replacing them. On the 4th, *Kelly* was exercising with *Acheron* and a anti-submarine motor boat off Portland when torpedo tracks were reported. Both destroyers obtained contacts and dropped charges and Mountbatten, *Kelly*'s captain, optimistically claimed a U-boat destroyed. There was no U-boat and this was a prime example of early war wishful thinking. *Kelly* was joined by the second member of the flotilla, *Kingston*, before sailing for Cherbourg on 12 September to pick up the Duke and Duchess of Windsor and bring them to Plymouth.

Kingston's commissioning had been uneventful but on 2 September, White's, her builders, had written to the Admiralty asking to be indemnified for any loss or injury to her employees as a result of enemy action. After consultations with the official solicitor this was agreed and White's were notified. *Kingston* was accepted on the 15th and sailed to Portland to begin working-up trials. *Kelly* was next involved in the rescue of survivors from the aircraft carrier *Courageous* which was hit by two torpedoes on 17 September. *Kelly* raced at full speed through a half gale in response to *Courageous*'s SOS and found that an American liner had picked up about four officers and thirty-four men which were transferred aboard her. For the rest of the month *Kelly* and *Kingston* continued working up at Devonport.

FIRST COLLISION

The 7th Destroyer Flotilla had been split, with part working out of Plymouth and the rest patrolling out of Immingham, screening the 2nd Cruiser Squadron between there and Rosyth. Patrols consisted of one or two destroyers sailing on a fixed course (usually to a point or light vessel) each day or night. Screening the cruisers, on the other hand, involved high-speed operations requiring precision and skill. Frequently taking place in bad weather and at night, considerable ability and experience were needed, experience the Royal Navy did not possess in the early stages of the war and collisions were inevitable. The first of these involved *Javelin* and *Jersey*. Both were escorting the 2nd Cruiser Squadron at night on 23 September when *Jersey* ran into the stern of *Javelin*. *Jersey* was travelling at some 30kts at the time and damaged her stem, holing her port bow near the waterline. She had to reduce speed and was out of action until 9 October. *Javelin* was repaired at Newcastle and was out of action until 22 October.

NEW PLANS AND ORGANISATION

Early in October 1939 the Director of Plans conducted an evaluation of the current situation with regard to destroyers and anti-aircraft ships. Four specific functions for destroyers were identified.

(a) Anti-ship action.
(b) Anti-submarine action.
(c) Offensive mining.
(d) Anti-air action.

The 'Js', 'Ks' and 'Tribals' were considered the most suitable to perform function (a) as they possessed powerful gun armament and high performance. They were also considered suitable for function (d), their main armament being considered very useful for long-range and barrage AA fire. Great store was also set by their close-range armament. Function (b) was to be filled by old destroyers and function (c) by the two convertible 'E' class and four 'I' class.

Priority targets for the enemy were thought to be the Norwegian convoys, the East Coast traffic and convoys through the Straits of Dover, in that order. The 'Js' of the 7th Flotilla were to concentrate on the East Coast, relieving the 29th Destroyer Division ('V & W' class) whilst the 'Ks' were to relieve the 'B' class ships of the 19th Flotilla at Dover as they entered service and worked-up. The 'Bs' were then to transfer to the Western Approaches. However, the 'Js' would be initially based at Rosyth to cover the Norwegian convoys before transferring to Immingham to protect East Coast shipping. The 'Ks' would join the Home Fleet as they completed their working-up periods rather than stay at Dover. Lack of availability in both classes would later also cause problems for the planners.

OPERATION 'CATHERINE'

When Churchill returned to the Admiralty as First Lord in September 1939 he brought with him an aggressive spirit and a desire to take the war to the enemy as much as possible. One of the first suggestions he produced was a scheme to force the Baltic Sea and station a fleet there in early 1940. This idea was not as rash as might have seemed at first glance and certainly deserved further consideration. The planned fleet for Operation 'Catherine' included three battleships, three 8in cruisers, six 6in cruisers, two AA cruisers, three modern destroyer flotillas, one minesweeping flotilla of old 'S' class destroyers and various repair ships and other auxiliary vessels. The destroyer flotillas were to comprise of one 'Tribal' flotilla and the 'J' and 'K' class ships.

Operations in the Baltic entailed various modifications to these ships chiefly to combat cold and ice. As a result the 'Js' and 'Ks' were to receive the following:

Another view of *Jackal*, which unusually shows her starboard bow quarter rather than the expected port view. Her colour scheme is overall AP507B with the upper part of her foremast painted white.

(IMPERIAL WAR MUSEUM: FL9785)

(a) lagging of mess deck spaces; this was not the case when they were built;

(b) additional electric radiators;

(c) heating and lagging to fresh water supplies, sanitary and fire main services and galley oil fuel services;

(d) de-icing jets on the gun mountings, depth charge release gear, searchlights and torpedo tubes;

(e) heating to pom-poms and pom-pom tanks;

(f) heating to the 0.5 inch machine guns; and

(g) heating and lagging to other exposed equipment.

The shell plating forward was also to be reinforced by means of wood sheathing and additional intermediate frames in the fuel tanks, magazines and shell rooms. This was much needed anyway as later troubles with *Kingston* and *Kashmir* were to demonstrate. The final addition was a kite balloon which would be tethered to a mast located on the aft deckhouse. This device was an effective tool against low-level air attack and initially *Kandahar* and then *Kimberley* were allocated as trial ships before *Jaguar* was actually designated as the trial ship for tests. Ships fitted with kite balloons were to carry a tripod mainmast with gaff on the foreside of the aft superstructure. However, *Jaguar* did not receive this mast.

Operation 'Catherine' envisaged ships being resupplied from Norwegian ports via rail which was not really feasible given the likelihood of air attack. The whole plan foundered on the problem of air defence, despite three squadrons of Spitfires being added to the forces allocated. But the potential difficulties continued to multiply. For example the plan made use of Swedish anchorages which would have been vulnerable to U-boat attack. In January 1940, after much discussion, the plan was postponed indefinitely as no longer feasible because of improved air defences and mine barriers. The 'Js' and 'Ks' did receive their extra strengthening and heating, so the plan was not a total loss as these features were needed.

EARLY ACTION

At the beginning of October there were two of the 'J' class under repair. Two 'Ks' were operating out of Plymouth, shortly to be joined by a third (*Kandahar* on the 10th). The rest of the 'Js' were split between Plymouth (*Janus, Juno* and *Jackal*) and Rosyth (*Jervis* and *Jupiter*). *Jaguar* was on her way to Rosyth and would shortly be docked to fit new propellers. After this she would join the Rosyth group. About 8 October the Plymouth destroyers received orders to join their compatriots at Rosyth. *Juno* was undergoing repairs so only *Jackal* and *Janus* sailed. *Jervis* and *Jupiter* initially had been screening the 2nd Cruiser Squadron (*Southampton* and *Glasgow*) as part of the hunt for *Gneisenau* and *Köln* which were reported to be at sea. However, by this time they were hunting a submarine, leaving only *Jaguar* to cover the cruisers. *Jackal* and *Janus* were ordered to join the hunt after refuelling but news was received of a German breakout and they were diverted to join the cruisers. *Jervis* and *Jupiter* found themselves unable to join the cruisers and so steered for Rosyth.

The fuel situation was becoming critical for the destroyers, as they had been steaming at high speed in rough weather, and *Jaguar* had to be detached to Rosyth to refuel. It was then that the ships were attacked by aircraft for the first time. *Jaguar* was caught alone in two separate attacks and several bombs were dropped. No damage was caused and *Jaguar* claimed one aircraft forced down by anti-aircraft fire. The cruisers were also attacked on several occasions and it was decided that the sweep should be terminated. The air attacks on *Jervis* and *Jupiter* on 9 October were of a more serious nature, because the oil suction to *Jupiter*'s boilers failed and she was forced to heave to. The problem was rapidly repaired but at 3.10pm three aircraft attacked *Jervis* but scored no hits. Twenty minutes later *Jupiter*'s engines broke down. Another group of three aircraft appeared and dropped a series of bombs. Yet another aircraft made an attack but once again this was ineffective and *Jervis* was finally able take *Jupiter* in tow. The attacks revealed the inadequacies of the 4.7in as a high-angle weapon, being only able to fire at the aircraft after they had made their bombing runs and were escaping. The 'Js' were also affected by equipment failures caused in part by flooding. *Jackal* suffered a turbo-generator failure and *Janus* had her pump to all guns fail and was unable to train her mounts fast enough by hand to counter the dive-bombing attacks on *Southampton*.

Jervis towed *Jupiter* towards Scapa but was rapidly running out of fuel herself. The 2nd Cruiser Squadron, with *Janus, Jackal* and *Jaguar*, had safely arrived at Rosyth. Meanwhile, *Jersey* had arrived at Rosyth after completing her col-lision repairs and fuelled from the oiler *War Nizam*. She and *Jaguar* were ordered out of Rosyth to assist *Jervis* and *Jupiter* but due to bad weather were unable to depart. Fuel was becoming critical for *Jervis* and she was ordered to put into Kirkwall if she was unable to make Scapa. In the event, help was not needed and *Jervis* and *Jupiter* arrived at Scapa on the 10th. *Jupiter*'s problems were quickly rectified and the two ships were later joined by *Glasgow, Southampton, Jackal* and *Janus*.

After two days at Scapa the force sailed to provide cover for a convoy though *Janus* and *Jackal* returned to Scapa on the 15th. This patrol was quite productive as *Jervis* intercepted the oiler *Gustaf E Reuter* and put a prize crew on board and *Janus* intercepted the SS *Bonde* and sent her to Kirkwall. Apart from these incidents the destroyers indulged in their usual depth-charging of any asdic contact remotely resembling a submarine before returning to Rosyth. It is unlikely that any of these attacks involved submarines as a lot of contacts were produced by schools of fish, wrecks and pockets of water at different densities all of which could cause submarine-like echoes, especially to the inexperienced asdic operators of the period. Another incentive to depth-charge anything that 'pinged' was the automatic award of the Distinguished Service Order (DSO) to any captain who achieved a confirmed U-Boat kill.[2] However, it should be noted that the habit of depth-charging anything and everything did at least have the effect of restricting the activities of any submarines which might be in the vicinity.

KELLY, KINGSTON, KANDAHAR AND JUNO

Plans for the *Kelly*s had anticipated them staying at Plymouth but urgent Home Fleet requirements changed this and the 5th Flotilla was ordered to Scapa as and when the ships worked-up. *Kelly* and *Kingston* had spent the first half of October escorting coastal convoys and searching for suspected submarines. First *Kingston* then *Kelly* left Plymouth and sailed up the west coast to join the Home Fleet at Scapa. In time the whole flotilla would make that journey. *Kingston* joined the Home Fleet on 19 October with *Kelly* arriving two days later. After a short period at Scapa the two ships put to sea to screen (with the 'Tribal' class destroyer *Bedouin*) the battlecruiser *Hood* between 25 and 28 October. *Kelly* then sailed for Sullom Voe in the Orkneys and *Kingston* returned to Scapa. *Kandahar* continued to work-up at Plymouth, she would not join the Home Fleet until 3 November. At the end of the month *Kelly* was detailed to search for the *City of Flint*, a merchant ship which had been captured by the 'pocket battleship' *Deutschland* and used

---

[2] The first of the 'J' and 'K' class captains to achieve this coveted award would be Lieutenant Commander Phillip Somerville of *Kingston* (see below).

to hold British seamen from her other captures. She was making her way to Germany via Norwegian waters and *Kelly* was one of several ships detailed to intercept her. This search proved to be fruitless though the ship was later interned by the Norwegians. *Kelly* entered Norwegian waters and was promptly ordered out by the small Norwegian destroyer *Drauge*. She returned to Sullom Voe on 31 October.

Juno completed her repairs on 15 October and set off for Rosyth to join the rest of her flotilla the day after. During her voyage she rescued the crew of a shot-down Do24 flying boat. On the strength of her captain, Commander Wilson's report of the incident, measures were put in hand to equip British destroyers with D/F equipment. *Juno* arrived at Rosyth on 17 October and spent the rest of the month escorting coastal convoys between Harwich and Rosyth and patrolling out of Immingham. A new 'K', *Kashmir*, also commissioned at the end of October and started her working up at Portland.

BACK TO THE HUMBER AND THE SECOND COLLISION
The 'Js' of the 7th Flotilla continued to work out of Scapa and Rosyth. *Jervis, Jersey, Janus, Jackal, Juno* and *Jupiter* had all returned to the Humber by the end of October and were mainly operating patrols out of Immingham and escorting

Juno shortly after commissioning, on her trials. Clearly visible in this view are the panels which made up the hull plating. Also visible is the framework for the Mountbatten roof which was also carried by *Janus* and *Jersey* and the covers for the anti-aircraft armament. Note the galley chimney is now installed inside the funnel – *Juno* was the only member of the 'J' class to be completed with the internal installation.
(COURTESY OF GLASGOW CITY ARCHIVES)

convoys. *Jaguar* was testing her new propellers – which would eventually be installed on all twenty-four Kellys. *Javelin* had completed her repairs and sailed on 21 October. At 1.35am on 22 October her Officer of the Watch mistook a starboard light belonging to SS *Moidart*, a 1262-ton coastal steamer, off her starboard bow for a stern light. *Javelin* turned hard-a-starboard and ordered full ahead both but to no avail. The collision completely ripped open her side from her stern to Station 71. *Jupiter* and *Afridi* arrived and the former took *Javelin* in tow. This was transferred to the Tug *NER No 3* (North Eastern Railway) which towed *Javelin* to the Old Fish Quay at Hartlepool. On the 23rd she was towed to Smiths Dock Middlesborough for repairs that would take two months.[3]

---

[3] Her captain at the time, A F Pugsley, only mentions this second collision in his book *Destroyer Captain* and omits the collision with *Jersey*.

NOVEMBER

Admiral Forbes, C-in-C Home Fleet, summed up the conditions in his command as follows. 'The weather experienced in northern waters from October onwards can only be described as foul; one gale has followed another with monotonous frequency.'[4] It is important to bear this in mind as troubles with the 'Ks' (and to a lesser extent the 'Js') began to appear about this time. These were as a result of a small design flaw which had serious consequences[5] and which is discussed in the chapter on design. The 7th Flotilla had two important duties to perform. They provided ships for the Outer Dowsing patrol, which involved two destroyers of the 7th sailing leaving their base about 2.00pm and returning at around 9.30am the next day. On patrol the destroyers would keep an anti-submarine watch on both sides of the Outer Dowsing shoal. The other duty was escorting coastal convoys. This latter duty did not entail the escort of a convoy from beginning to end but rather a pair of 'Js' and possibly an anti-aircraft cruiser would reinforce a convoy for a day at the most risky stage of its voyage. The destroyers would take station on the seaward side of the convoy and keep watch for threats such as aircraft or surface craft. On a single sailing a pair of destroyers could act as cover for several convoys such as on 11 November when *Juno* and *Jupiter* provided cover for Convoys FS34, FN34 and FN35. On the same day *Jaguar* and *Jersey* were on the Outer Dowsing patrol. *Janus* had just returned to Immingham from convoy escort duty, *Jervis* was at Immingham and *Jackal* was in dry dock at Hull. Throughout November, both patrols and escort duty was uneventful with no enemy being encountered and, more importantly, no collisions.

Kandahar sailed to join the Home Fleet on 5 November. Returning to Scapa on the 6th she joined *Kelly* there, which had lost her motor boat and sustained some damage due to steaming at excessive speed in a North Sea gale. She had also lost a man overboard on the 3rd. *Kingston* had no trouble until the 8th when she developed a leak in her reserve feed tank. This problem would affect all the Kellys at one stage or another but ensured a trip to Leith Dry Dock for *Kingston* on this occasion. *Kelly* (after repairs) and *Kandahar* sailed to hunt for a submarine reported in Yell Sound, not far from Sullom Voe. *Kashmir* left Portland for Scapa on 10 November. She was ordered to escort the base ship *Dunluce Castle* to Scapa but missed this signal and proceeded independently to Scapa, arriving on the 12th, and officially joined the Home Fleet. The arrival of *Kashmir* brought operational strength of the 5th Flotilla up to one division or half a flotilla. Back at Portland *Khartoum* had

arrived on 8 November from her builders at Wallsend-on-Tyne and was starting her working-up period.

Working-up periods had been cut due to the war and so *Kashmir* found herself despatched from Scapa on the 15th to locate the tanker *Arne Kjode* which had been torpedoed and broken in two. However, the tanker had already been found and sunk by gunfire from the Armed Merchant Cruiser *Chitral*. *Kashmir* was then ordered to rendezvous with the Home Fleet but was unable to do so as she was damaged[6] and returned to Scapa on the 18th. *Kandahar* joined her from Scapa to escort her in. *Kelly* was also at Scapa but was due to sail to the Tyne to repair storm damage and clean her boilers. *Kingston* had just finished her repairs at Leith and sailed for Rosyth for the final touches.

On 21 November *Janus* and *Juno* were detailed to take part in Operation BT2, a minelaying sortie for which the destroyers would provide the escort. 'J' class destroyers were only used occasionally on these operations as they were much more valuable for convoy escort. However, BT2 had to be cancelled because of bad weather. On 23 November

---

[4] ADM 199/393 Home Fleet War Diaries 1939-1940.
[5] D K Brown, conversation with the author September 2000.

[6] I have been unable to find out how.

Juno, Jaguar, Janus and *Jersey* sailed for Operation GT1, an early example of inter-service co-operation which involved a rendezvous with an aircraft for a search. This was successfully accomplished but like so many early patrols found nothing. On her return *Juno* collided with an oiler and had to be docked at Immingham for a week to have the damage repaired. *Jervis* went to Grimsby for a boiler clean and refit emerging on 8 December.

The Royal Navy's operations in late 1939 included the Northern Patrol, part of the blockade of Germany, which was initially carried out by armed merchant cruisers. These were passenger liners requisitioned at the start of the war and fitted with guns and basic fire control. They were fine for intercepting merchant vessels but were at a serious disadvantage when faced by anything resembling a warship. One such ship, the *Rawalpindi*, was patrolling off Iceland on 23 November when she encountered the German battlecruisers *Scharnhorst* and *Gneisenau*. Totally outgunned, she nevertheless engaged them with predictable results, but managed to get off an enemy report, attributing her attack to the *Deutschland*. The Home Fleet sailed immediately and the 18th Cruiser Squadron took up interception positions.

Photographs taken during the early war are rare and this view of *Kandahar* is especially interesting because of her unusual and early camouflage . The 5th Flotilla did not carry funnel bands but Kandahar does show the divisional leader's bar. No information exists on this scheme or how long it was carried for but she was still in a variant of this scheme in June 1940.

(NATIONAL MARITIME MUSEUM, LONDON: 6720)

Kingston and *Bedouin* which had been due to escort Convoy ON3 to Norway immediately joined the search and ON3's sailing was postponed. *Kandahar* and *Kashmir* which had put to sea with *Tartar* were ordered to locate and shadow the German ships whilst *Southampton, Edinburgh, Aurora, Afridi, Gurkha* and *Kingston* initially took up a patrol position in the Fair Island Channel to intercept *Deutschland* should she attempt to head that way though this was changed the next day. All destroyers were ordered to concentrate on *Aurora* except *Kingston* which was ordered to join the end of a patrol line consisting of *Southampton, Edinburgh, Glasgow, Sheffield* and *Newcastle*.[7] However, the

---

[7] *Newcastle* had in fact fleetingly sighted *Gneisenau* late on 23 September but had lost her in a rain squall.

German ships would return home unmolested. *Kingston* returned to Scapa on the 27th to refuel and immediately put to sea again where she joined *Kashmir*.

THE SINKING OF *U-35*
As part of the operations in support of the *Gneisenau* and *Scharnhorst* sortie, Admiral Doenitz had set up a line of four U-boats, *U-31*, *U-35*, *U-47* and *U-48*, near the Shetland Islands to intercept British warships. *U-47* had fired a torpedo at *Norfolk* on the 28th without success. The *U-35* was cruising on the surface when she was seen by the destroyer *Icarus* which turned to attack. The U-boat's lookouts sighted the *Icarus* quite late but she managed to dive and tried to evade the destroyer. *Icarus*, which was having trouble with her asdic, summoned assistance which arrived in the form of *Kashmir* and *Kingston*. *Icarus* remained in the area and when they arrived the two Kellys commenced a search which eventually led to *Kingston* obtaining an asdic contact at 11.02am. *Kingston* made the first attack at 11.23am, dropping three charges from her rails but did not fire her throwers because of the proximity of *Kashmir*. *Kashmir* then ran in to attack but her asdic malfunctioned and she had to abort.

Kingston then made a second attack and this time the throwers failed to function due to wet firing charges caused by the bad weather. However, the middle charge of the three from the rails hit the *U-35*, jamming her diving planes and rupturing fuel and ballast tanks. The U-boat took on a bow-up attitude and all attempts to right her failed. Believing her doomed, her commanding officer surfaced, intending to fight a gun action with the destroyers. This was discouraged by *Kashmir* who fired a shot across the bows of the submarine. The crew then scuttled their boat and surrendered to the British destroyers who rescued them all.

After *Kashmir* had picked up thirty-one officers and men, *Kingston* took on the other eleven survivors. There were no casualties among the U-boat's crew. The Director of Submarine Defence thought this an 'extremely accurate' attack and that Lieutenant Commander Somerville's DSO was well earned.[8] *Kashmir* and *Kingston* sailed for the Clyde to land their prisoners and to repair damage caused by the bad weather.

KELLY'S FIRST MINE AND OTHER INCIDENTS
Khartoum left Plymouth on 29 November and sailed for Belfast. The next day she sailed for Scapa and joined the Home Fleet. *Kelvin* had completed her acceptance trials on 27 November and sailed for Portsmouth to begin working-

up. On arrival at Portsmouth on 30 November she collided with the SS *St Helier* as she was berthing. This caused damage to her plates and frames on her starboard side. The next day she was examined by dockyard staff and had to be towed to the Tidal Basin for repairs. *Kelvin* would not begin working-up trials until 13 December.

After *Kashmir* and *Kingston* had deposited their prisoners from *U-35*, they joined their sister-ship *Khartoum* in providing an anti-submarine screen for the *Hood,* due to provide distant cover for the Norwegian convoys. As they sailed, *Kashmir* picked up a submarine contact at a range of 600 yards. She dropped two patterns of depth charges on what was thought to be a submarine but without any success. At sea they were joined by *Kandahar* which had been escorting Convoy HN3 from Norway. *Kandahar* and *Khartoum* were detached to refuel at Sullom Voe in the Shetland Isles on 4 December and *Kingston* and *Kashmir* on the 5th. The whole force then covered Convoys ON4 and HN4 before returning to the Clyde on the 11th. Two days later the four destroyers put to sea with *Somali, Bedouin, Mashona, Eskimo, Ilex, Imperial* and *Fearless* to provide cover for the first Canadian troop convoy, TC1. Returning on the 17th with the convoy which had been delayed by bad weather, *Kingston* and *Kashmir* sailed to the Clyde for repairs whilst *Khartoum* sailed as part of the escort for *Barham* and *Repulse*. *Kandahar* remained in harbour.

It was during her escort duties for the *Repulse* that *Khartoum* made her first attack on a submarine. Three and a half miles from Holy Island Light, *Isis* obtained a contact and dropped a depth charge. Later a torpedo track was seen which passed up the starboard side of *Khartoum*, very fine on her starboard quarter. *Khartoum* turned and ran down the track of the torpedo obtaining contact shortly after and attacked. Contact was lost but regained shortly afterwards and three more attacks made. *Khartoum* continued the search for another two and a half hours before rejoining *Repulse*. She was then ordered to search between Pladda and Sanda Islands and picked up several German signals on her radios. The next day, she again made an attack on a contact but could only fire three charges because the firing charges on her throwers had not been replaced. The contact was lost after this attack and could not be re-located despite a search by *Khartoum* and elements from the 6th Destroyer Flotilla ('Tribals'). *Khartoum*'s performance was heavily criticised in the after-action evaluation. Certain elements of depth charge drill were very poor, particularly those relating to the throwers, and needed correction. Furthermore, the signals she had picked up had in fact come from a German police station which ought to have been recognised immediately rather than allowing the search to

[8] Report contained in PRO ADM 199/28.

go on based on these.[9]

Kelly had been undergoing repairs for storm damage and strengthening for Operation 'Catherine'. She finally emerged from Hawthorn Leslie's yard on the Tyne on 13 December and was required to escort the depot ship *Woolwich* to Scapa. However, the next day *Kelly* and *Mohawk* were ordered to go to the assistance of two tankers in trouble. Reaching the open sea, *Kelly* sighted the *Atholl Templar* at about 4.00pm. She was on fire and sinking so *Kelly* prepared to go alongside and take off survivors. At 4.12pm a curious bumping was felt followed by a large explosion. *Kelly* had hit a mine which for some reason did not function properly and exploded just behind the ship rather than on contact. Even so the damage was quite extensive. She was partially flooded and all steering was lost. *Kelly* was able to steam only with great difficulty and had to be towed back to Hawthorn Leslie's for further repairs.

Kelvin in the meantime had completed her repairs and begun her trials at Portsmouth. On the 17th, whilst conducting torpedo trials, *Kelvin* picked up survivors from the Polish schooner *Maud Mary* which had been sunk by a U-boat. These were taken to Portsmouth. Trials completed, she conducted anti-submarine sweeps off the Isle of Wight before sailing to Portsmouth to embark her medical officer and Lord Mountbatten. Whilst *Kelly* was in dry dock, *Kelvin* was to be the flotilla leader. The last two ships of the class also commissioned about this time. *Kipling* on the 20th at Eldenslie Dock, Scotstoun and *Kimberley* on the 21st at Woolston. Both sailed for Portsmouth to begin working-up trials, *Kipling* picking up the survivors of MV *Edenwood* – which had collided with the Armed Merchant Cruiser *Derbyshire* – on the way. Further north, *Kingston* and *Kashmir* sailed with the *Hood* to provide cover for Convoy ON6 before forming part of the escort for the second Canadian troop convoy, TC2. *Khartoum* escorted *Repulse* to Liverpool on 29 December. *Kandahar* had not yet completed her repairs and remained on the Clyde for the rest of December.

THE TORPEDOING OF *JERSEY*

The Outer Dowsing patrols were usually fruitless with no enemy sighted at all. *Juno* and *Jersey* left Immingham on 6 December for this routine patrol and were due to return the next day. At the same time a German destroyer force consisting of *Hans Lody*, *Bernd von Arnim* and *Erich Giese* put to sea on a minelaying mission off Cromer. *Bernd von Arnim* experienced trouble with her boilers and was ordered to return to base leaving the other two ships to continue the operation. The German destroyers sighted two darkened

ships just after midnight which proved to be *Juno* and *Jersey* on patrol but they did not notice the German ships even though visibility was 9 miles. This was fortunate for the German ships as *Erich Giese* still had a full load of mines on board. The Germans commenced laying mines at 1.12am using the Haisborough Lightship as a guide and despite two premature detonations succeeded in laying them successfully. They then retired and as they were doing so detected two darkened ships at about 8700 yards. These were *Juno* and *Jersey* who were still on patrol. The German ships altered course to run parallel and having closed to 5800 yards fired torpedoes, *Hans Lody* firing three at *Juno* and *Erich Giese* firing four at *Jersey*. *Hans Lody* missed with her torpedoes but *Erich Giese* did not. The first the British destroyers knew of the presence of the German ships was when a noise was heard in *Jersey* at 2.30am which turned out to be one of *Erich Giese*'s torpedoes. *Jersey* put her wheel hard to port but to no avail as the torpedo hit her abreast of her aft torpedo tubes on the port side. A flame 100ft high followed the impact and when this had subsided there was a ferocious oil fire burning aft. Luckily the turn to port blew the fire away from the ship but even so the engines came to a stop five minutes later. A further stroke of luck was the escaping steam from ruptured steam pipes which helped put out the fire. Flooding was extensive and the port engine was out of action due to a badly cracked turbine casing. As a result it was decided not to flood the aft magazine because of a possible loss of buoyancy and hands were piped to fire stations. *Juno* immediately turned to assist *Jersey*, laying a smokescreen to hide her. However, she was still unaware of the presence of the German ships which now made their only mistake of the evening. Rather than finish *Juno* and *Jersey* off, both turned for home and arrived later on the 7th. *Juno* took up the tow at 5.00am but at 8.00am *Jersey*'s steering failed when the tiller flat had to be abandoned as a result of flooding. As she neared Immingham the tow was passed to the tug *Biddy* which also pumped out the tiller flat. *Jersey* had suffered nine casualties and was lucky to survive. She was under temporary repair for a month in Humber Graving Dock before transferring to Amos Smith and Co for more permanent repairs.

On emerging from dry dock, *Jervis* immediately returned to the 7th Flotilla activities of patrolling and escorting FS and FN series convoys up and down the coast. *Jupiter* arrived at Hull for a boiler clean and refit on the 21st followed by *Jervis* again on the 26th. Earlier the 7th Flotilla had been transferred to the Nore Command, and were based at Sheerness. However, they were frequently being borrowed by the Home Fleet and the Rosyth command for other duties. Rosyth in particular used them to provide escorts for the Norwegian convoys.

---

[9] See ADM 199/126 19 Dec 1939, Admiral Forbes (C-in-C Home Fleet) was highly critical of this failure.

6
1940: The Norwegian Campaign

Kingston and *Khartoum* arrived at Plymouth on the last day of 1939 after escorting the battleship *Revenge* from the Clyde to Devonport. After a short stay they sailed again on the 3rd. *Kingston* would join *Rodney*, *Repulse* and seven other destroyers for an offensive sweep departing on the 5th whilst *Khartoum* would sail with her sisters *Kashmir* and *Kandahar* to escort Convoy ON7 on an uneventful passage. *Javelin* had completed her repairs and sailed for Immingham to join her sister-ships. The 7th Flotilla had been due to sail for Rosyth on 4 January but was instructed to remain at Immingham. *Janus* departed to refit at Hull on 5 January whilst the rest of the flotilla continued their escort and patrol duties. *Jackal* stood by and evacuated the crew of SS *Keynes* which had been damaged by a bomb and then escorted *Juno* as she towed *Keynes* back to port. *Kelvin* completed her working-up trials on 8 January and sailed for Greenock, on the way making two attacks on a supposed submarine detected by the sloop *Scarborough* but was ordered to break off by C-in-C Western Approaches. Oil which had come to the surface was analysed and found to be furnace fuel oil, suggesting the contact had been a wreck on the bottom, not a U-boat.

ANOTHER COLLISION

Kimberley sailed two days after *Kelvin*, initially for exercises with *Kipling* then to Greenock and the Home Fleet, arriving on 12 January. Both *Kimberley* and *Kelvin* remained at Greenock for the next few days before joining a force consisting of *Manchester*, *Newcastle*, *Maori*, *Inglefield*, *Icarus*, *Tartar* and their sisters, *Khartoum*, *Kandahar* and *Kashmir* in assisting the *Aurora* hunt for the German blockade runner *Trautenfels* on the 15th. The next day at 1.50 am, *Kelvin* and *Kimberley* collided.[1] *Kimberley* received damage to her No 3 gun platform, the starboard TSDS davit and her side abreast the stewards mess and tiller flat, creating a small hole 6ft above the waterline but was not seriously damaged as she was able to carry out an anti-submarine patrol with *Inglefield* before sailing to Scapa for repairs. The damage to *Kelvin*'s damage was more significant, her lower mess deck and cable locker being flooded, and she needed the assistance of *Bedouin* to make it to the Clyde. However, both ships were repaired in short order and back on operations, *Kimberley* engaging in a U-boat hunt by the 19th with other ships before going into dock for permanent repairs.

---

[1] See ships' logs for *Kimberley* and *Kelvin*, also Home Fleet Destroyer Command War Diary.

Kipling, the last of the Kellys to commission, arrived at Scotstoun on the 17th. She put to sea for exercises but had to return to port for repairs to her turbines, one of which fractured. It was found that the turbines made excessive noise anyway and these had to be re-cut at Fairfield Yard. Whilst she was in dock a fire broke out in the officers' galley but this was discovered and extinguished before any real damage was done. These repairs, though, kept *Kipling* out of action for the rest of the month. Meanwhile, due to increased submarine activity, *Jackal*, *Javelin* and *Jaguar* were borrowed by the Rosyth command for two weeks. Whilst this was going on, *Jervis*, *Juno* and *Jupiter* sailed to Rosyth to provide cover for Convoy HN9B. *Kingston*, which was suffering from cracked hull plates remained on the Clyde for the rest of the month. This problem, which was caused by slamming effects in the rough weather the lightly-constructed destroyers operated in, would affect other members of the class in the coming months. At this time *Kandahar* also entered dock for repairs.

Kashmir and *Khartoum* continued to escort the Norwegian convoys, Convoy HN8 proving particularly interesting for the former (*Kimberley* was also part of the escort). Due to extreme bad weather, she was forced to heave to with a blocked oil fuel pipe on the 19th. After this was fixed she rejoined the convoy but was detached to pick up the survivors of the SS *Nautic* on the 20th which had radioed an SOS. When she rejoined the convoy the next day she was again detached, this time for an unsuccessful anti-submarine search with *Khartoum*. On arrival at Methill Roads (the assembly point for all Norwegian convoys) the two destroyers sailed for Rosyth, *Kashmir* to join Convoy ON9 and *Khartoum* for repairs to weather damage. The convoy was uneventful and on arrival in Norway, *Kashmir*, *Inglefield*, *Isis* and *Escort* joined the cruisers *Edinburgh* and *Glasgow* for an anti-submarine sweep before escorting Convoy HN9A to Scotland, arriving on 30 January.

At the beginning of February, the 'Js' were assigned as a striking force for the TM/MT convoys. These convoys sailed between Methill Roads and the Tyne. Merchant ships would sail to the Tyne in an FN convoy and then head for Methill in a TM convoy. Conversely, ships from Norway and other destinations would congregate at Methill before being escorted to the Tyne to join an FS convoy heading southwards. Normally, the escort for these convoys consisted of a 'V & W' class destroyer as anti-submarine escort, a sloop for anti-aircraft duty and a 'J' class destroyer as a striking force. They also included one or two trawlers as well. The FN/FS and TM/MT convoys operated on a fairly frequent cycle and

A magnificent shot of the 5th Flotilla in line abreast probably taken in late 1940 when they were serving on the Humber station. The picture was taken from *Kelvin* and the others that are identifiable are *Kashmir*, *Jaguar* and *Javelin*. Colour scheme is overall AP507B and *Kashmir* carries an extension to the roof of her rear deckhouse. This was intended to carry an Oerlikon but was abandoned when No 3 mount was altered to train directly through the rear. (IMPERIAL WAR MUSEUM: A1070)

generally comprised between twenty and twenty-six ships. Unfortunately, the beginning of February was not a good period for the availability of the 7th Flotilla – *Janus* damaged herself (and *Jupiter*) as she came alongside on the 7th and only *Javelin* and *Jaguar* were available for service. At this time both the 'Js' and 'Ks' also needed regular degaussing as they were not fitted with internal degaussing coils and this affected their operational availability as well. But by mid-February degaussing gear began to be fitted to all Kellys, *Jackal* and *Jervis* being first, followed by *Jupiter*. The degaussing coil was fitted round the edge of the weather deck where it met the side except for *Kipling* whose coil would initially run round her hull, just below the weather deck.

The 'Ks' were engaged in various escort duties. *Kashmir* and *Khartoum* escorted the Armament Stores Issuing Ship *Sardis* to Aberdeen and then took the *Cyprian Prince* up to Scapa. On the return journey on 2 February, *Khartoum* came across a raft from the Swedish merchant vessel *Fram* which had sunk in Aberdour Bay, rescuing the survivors and taking them to the Clyde. *Kandahar* was due to join *Isis* in escorting *Cyprian Prince* but had so many men sick that she had to remain at Rosyth. The third Canadian troop convoy was due at the Clyde on 7 February but had been delayed by bad weather. A significant fleet, consisting of the battleships *Malaya* and *Valiant*, and twelve destroyers including *Kelvin* and *Kingston* - was despatched to locate it. *Kelvin*, *Kingston* and *Hunter* successfully located the second part of the convoy and *Kelvin* escorted the liner *Empress of Japan* up the Clyde late on the 7th. Then it was back to the Norwegian convoys for the 'Ks' before they were allocated to Operation 'WR' in mid-February.

OPERATION 'WR'

On 11 February the tanker *Imperial Transport* was torpedoed by *U-50* and lost her bows. She was able to steam very slowly and was making her way towards Scapa when *Kingston*, *Forester*, *Mohawk* and the sloop *Gleaner* arrived on the 14th. *Kingston* was ordered to stand by her until help could arrive. Due to bad weather the tanker had to heave to and although *Kingston* was unable to take the ship in tow, she did take off the survivors of the crew once tugs had arrived. *Kingston* sailed to join NP57 after disembarking the crew at Scapa.

Operation 'WR' was a sweep by the cruisers and destroyers of the Home Fleet against possible blockade-runners. *Kashmir* sailed to join the cruiser *Manchester* on the 17th. *Kimberley*, in company with *Manchester*, was to detach and refuel when *Kashmir* arrived, in line with new Admiralty orders on destroyer refuelling. On the 18th *Kashmir* sighted the Danish freighter SS *Bergenhus*, which she boarded and

sent to Kirkwall, the inspection point for all such suspect merchant vessels. Later *Kashmir* had to heave to in abysmal weather and secure her motor boat and whaler. On the 19th it was her turn to refuel and *Kashmir* sailed for Scapa being replaced by a fully-fuelled *Kimberley*. The next two days were uneventful apart from a full gale blowing but on the 21st *Manchester* sighted a suspicious ship leaving the Spanish port of Vigo. She was intercepted by *Manchester* and *Kimberley* but the weather was too bad to attempt a boarding. However, a few pom-pom rounds from *Manchester* dissuaded the crew from scuttling and the next day *Kimberley* was able to put an boarding party on board the ship which turned out to be the German freighter *Wahehe*. *Manchester* then ordered *Kimberley* to escort *Wahehe* back to Kirkwall and also ordered *Khartoum* to join her. *Khartoum* detached about 6.00pm to refuel and was replaced by *Kingston* which was then replaced at 1.00am on the 23rd by the trawler *Wastwater*. *Kimberley* and her prize arrived at Kirkwall at 9.15 am on the same day. *Kingston* and *Khartoum* then sailed to join *Ghurkha* in hunting a submarine which had been seen off the Faeroe Islands. *Kingston* returned to the Clyde after the search but *Khartoum* joined *Sikh* in escorting the west-bound portion of Convoy HN15 before leaving for the Clyde for urgent repairs to her gun mountings.

THE 'JS' IN THE LATTER HALF OF FEBRUARY, *KIPLING* AND THE RETURN OF *KELLY*

As they completed their repairs the 'Js' continued their patrol and convoy escort duties. On 27 February, the tanker *British Governor* was holed by a bomb but was able to proceed at 10kts and *Janus* was ordered to escort her back to port. Later *Jackal* managed to collide with the Swedish steamer SS *Storfoss* off Longstones and once again *Janus* stood by, escorting her to the Tyne where she would be under repair for two months.

After spending time at Scapa and escorting individual ships, *Kipling* began a series of anti-submarine hunts and escort duties on 14 February, with an abortive, day-long search for a suspected U-boat reported by *Gurkha*. The next day *Kipling* sailed to escort the tanker *Greatfield* but she had already been sunk. On the 16th she sailed in response to an SOS from the Danish freighter *Sleipner*, which had been sunk by a surfaced U-boat, rescuing thirteen survivors who she took to the Tyne. She then joined *Encounter* and *Brazen* to escort two oilers but the destroyers were diverted (with *Diana*) to hunt the *U-23* which had just sunk the destroyer *Daring* off Duncansby Head in Scotland, but they were unsuccessful. By this time *Kipling* needed a refit and sailed to the Tyne on 20 February, as *Kelly* was nearing the end of her repairs there. During her long lay-off her old crew had been dispersed and she recommissioned with a considerable number of hostilities-only seamen, several of whom had never been to sea before. Her full-power trials were successfully held on the 28th and the next day *Kelly* sailed to Scapa to join the Home Fleet. On 2 March she sailed as part of the escort for *Hood* and *Valiant*, attacking an asdic contact the next day but she lost it after one attack and rejoined the screen, arriving back at Scapa on the 6th. She and *Kandahar* were then allocated to cover Convoy ON18 but *Kandahar* was unable to sail as she was unfit for sea in heavy weather, her defects being similar to those experienced by *Kingston* earlier.[2] *Kimberley* was then allocated to replace *Kandahar* but was grabbed by the Home Fleet instead as part of their screen, so finally *Kelly* alone sailed to reinforce the convoy, taking over from *Cossack* as senior officer. She joined the convoy on the 8th and the next day was attacked by Heinkel bombers but suffering no damage. Also at sea at that time was the inbound Convoy HN17 which due to bad weather was out of position. ON18 and HN17 met during the night and *Kelly* collided with *Gurkha* which was escorting HN17.[3] *Ghurkha* suffered little damage, and the collision was blamed on *Kelly*'s watch keeping officer who should have seen *Ghurkha*. However, after the collision the Admiralty routed convoys even further apart during the hours of darkness. *Kelly* returned to Scapa for temporary repairs to the 30ft gash in her hull before sailing to Blackwall for repairs, arriving on 16 March.

Kandahar had also sailed for repairs arriving at Hull on the 11th. She would be out of action until 30 April, with *Kelly* returning to service on the 26th. March was quite a dreadful month for 'K' class availability. On the 1st *Kelvin* arrived at Liverpool for repairs to her petrol tank compartment which would take until the 27th, and *Kingston* and *Khartoum* sailed to Falmouth for major repairs taking from 10 March to 10 and 12 May respectively. Only *Kashmir* and *Kimberley* were available for service and of these two, *Kashmir* was out of action at Govan between the 6th and 13th March. Admiral Forbes, Commander-in-Chief Home Fleet commented in the Home Fleet War Diary for 10 March that; 'It is unwise to count on any of the 5th Destroyer Flotilla being available in the near future as five are casualties due to longitudinal construction. Hope light construction due to striving for extra half knot not being perpetuated in new construction.'[4]

Availability of the 'Js' was better, with *Juno* under repair from 9 to 18 March and also having degaussing cables fitted, but the other five (*Jackal* and *Jersey* being still under repair) were able to continue escorting coastal convoys without problems. However, from 18 March the 'Js' began to move to Scapa to cover the Norwegian convoys. The first to go was *Jupiter* and she was followed by *Javelin*, *Janus* and *Jervis* who sailed from the Humber. *Juno* sailed straight to Scapa from the Humber where she had completed her repairs. Unfortunately, on 19 March *Jervis* collided with a Swedish merchant ship, SS *Tor*, ripping open her side from the stem to nearly adjacent to her No 2 gun mount. Two men were killed and fifteen reported missing. *Javelin* and *Janus* stood by *Jervis* until she managed to reach Newcastle, *Janus* assuming the role of flotilla leader.

KIMBERLEY AND KASHMIR

On 7 March, *Kimberley* sailed with the Home Fleet for Scapa which was to be reactivated as the Fleet's main base. She was detached to go on ahead of the fleet with the First Sea Lord and the Prime Minister. *Faulknor* provided an escort but the journey was uneventful. The next day *Kimberley* sailed to join Convoy HN18, arriving back at Scapa on the 13th. On the 15th *Kashmir* returned from repair and the next day both ships sailed to escort Convoy ON20. For the rest of the month, these convoys would come under frequent air attack, but the attackers were usually driven off by the escorts. ON20 ran into bad weather and ships straggled and finally had to heave to. Then *Kashmir*'s gyro compass failed and the attempted repairs were not wholly successful. The bad weather continued with the return convoy, HN20, and this time *Kashmir*'s degaussing coil failed as a result of penetration of the insulation by seawater. Both *Kashmir* and *Javelin* fired on enemy aircraft, but neither side suffered any damage. During one of these engagements *Kashmir* discovered that she lacked a small lamp which illuminated her fuse-setting machine, so she was unable to engage aircraft with her main armament at their favoured time of attack, dusk, as the crew were unable to read the fuse settings.

More serious was the attack on Convoy ON21 by HE111s. Bombs hit one ship of the convoy but failed to cause any damage. The escort, which consisted of *Jupiter*, *Janus*, *Javelin* and *Eclipse* also came under attack on 20 March with *Janus* in particular being singled out for attention. Bombs fell 50 yards away from her but one Heinkel was hit and was seen retiring trailing smoke. The next day *Jupiter* suffered a recurrence of her boiler troubles and had to return to Scapa, being relieved by *Juno*.

Kelvin completed her repairs on 27 March and was immediately ordered up to Scapa but was unable to leave

[2] These defects were likely to be the splitting of her hull plates as the reserve feed tank problem had already been dealt with during *Kandahar*'s earlier refit.
[3] After the mine incident in the Tyne, Lord Mountbatten had drafted an emergency message to be sent if his ship was hit. The message read 'Have been hit by mine or torpedo. Am uncertain which'. This message was sent after the collision provoking the response from *Ghurkha*, 'That was not mine but me'.
[4] PRO ADM 199/361 Home Fleet War Diaries 1940.

Liverpool due to fog, finally arriving on the 30th. At the beginning of April, *Kashmir* and *Kelvin* were based at Rosyth. *Kashmir* damaged herself on 2 April going alongside an oiler to refuel but she remained operational. *Kimberley*, based at Scapa, was escorting Norwegian convoys but on the 7th she and *Jupiter* were reallocated to the Home Fleet screen with news of the invasion of Norway. *Kashmir* and *Kelvin* worked as part of the 2nd Cruiser Squadron and on 4 April *Kelvin* and the Polish destroyer *Burza* attacked a contact without result. The squadron next put to sea on the 7th and two days later, *Kashmir* and *Kelvin* collided. *Kashmir* was flooded aft, her side opened up to her aft torpedo tubes and her steering gear put out of action whilst *Kelvin* was damaged forward. *Cossack* and *Zulu* were detached to escort the two ships to Lerwick, with *Kashmir* having to be towed by *Cossack*, so that only *Kimberley* of the 5th Flotilla was actually available for service until the 13th when Kipling completed her refit and sailed for Scapa. The 7th Flotilla was in a much better state, with *Javelin*, *Janus*, *Juno* and *Jupiter* all operational. Until the German invasion of Norway they were mainly engaged in escorting the fleet.

THE NORWEGIAN CAMPAIGN

Both Britain and Germany had drawn up plans for an invasion of Norway, the Germans in the event being quicker off the mark. The fleet sailed on 7 April to prevent a German breakout into the North Atlantic and so was at sea when the invasion started. *Kimberley* was part of the close screen for the battleships but on the 8th was detached as part of the escort for the *Repulse*. She was then despatched to assist *Glowworm* but was recalled when it was realised that that ship already had been sunk. Back as part of *Repulse*'s screen the force joined up with *Renown* after her successful action with *Scharnhorst* and *Gneisenau* before being detached with the other destroyers to cover the withdrawal of the 2nd Destroyer Flotilla from Narvik. *Janus*, *Juno* and *Javelin* were part of the fleet screen which was joined on the 10th by *Jupiter*.

In the meantime, *Kimberley* was ordered to stand by the cruiser *Penelope* which had run aground. She took on 173 ratings and 16 prisoners of war from the captured German ship *Alster* before being ordered to investigate a report of German transports at Bodo. This proved to be a wild goose chase and *Kimberley* returned to stand by *Penelope*. However, on the 13th she was allocated to the screen of the battleship *Warspite* for the Second Battle of Narvik.

Kimberley left *Penelope* and sailed with *Cossack* to join *Warspite* in Operation DW, an attack on the German destroyers trapped in Narvik harbour. *Warspite* sat in the centre of a broad screen of destroyers. Ahead of her she had *Icarus* with bow sweeps deployed and to her left and right

were *Hero* and *Foxhound* trailing their TSDS. *Cossack*, *Kimberley* and *Forester* were off her port beam with *Bedouin*, *Eskimo* and *Punjabi* on the starboard beam. *Kimberley* sighted the German ships at 12.32pm but was not in range until 1.08pm when she opened fire. She then continued to fire without interruption until 2.30pm. Problems were encountered with several of the guns failing to run out fully after the 100th salvo but this was cleared by the shock effect of the other gun firing. The hydraulic pumps stopped twice as a result of the starters failing due to blast effects and an Admiralty Fleet Order would later be issued to correct the defect. All other damage was caused by the shock of the guns firing, the gun shield of No 1 mount splitting and several items falling off the gun shields. The most serious damage was the Direction Finding office which was completely wrecked and the D/F equipment rendered useless. Rate of fire met design specifications, the loading interval of five seconds being easily maintained.

About 1.18pm *Kimberley* was straddled and until 2.20pm salvoes continued to land near her. Her evasive manoeuvres were somewhat restricted by having to maintain station with *Warspite* which was only making 14kts. Several torpedoes were seen including two which passed down *Kimberley*'s side but none of these necessitated any evasive manoeuvres. *Cossack* then ordered *Kimberley* to follow her into Narvik harbour which was difficult as *Kimberley* had to pass *Warspite*. Once she had managed this, *Kimberley* joined *Cossack* in opening fire on an enemy destroyer moored in the harbour. This ship returned fire, hitting *Cossack* and causing her to run aground. *Kimberley* was not damaged in the engagement but could not get past *Cossack* into the harbour. As orders were received to concentrate on Rombaks Fjord, *Kimberley* abandoned attempts to tow *Cossack* and joined *Hero* which was firing at enemy destroyers further up the Fjord. One, *Hans Lüdemann* (Z18) was abandoned and both *Kimberley* and *Bedouin* lowered boats to investigate. However, *Kimberley* was ordered back to join *Warspite* and tow *Cossack* off but this could not be done before nightfall and so she decided to wait until the next morning. Her only casualty had been a stoker who had been stunned by a shell fragment and dropped a 4.7in cartridge on his foot. However, she did have about fifty holes in her side varying from about 1 to 4ins in diameter.

Cossack floated off at dawn without assistance but *Kimberley* was ordered to remain in Narvik harbour and show the flag whilst the rest of the force withdrew. This was uneventful for most of the morning, barring odd exchanges of fire with patrolling German aircraft, one of which attempted to bomb *Kimberley*. At 3.00pm she received orders to ensure that no German merchant ships attempted to discharge their cargoes. These seemed to be deserted but a large flying boat was found to be moored in the harbour which had not been there the day before. *Kimberley*'s captain decided to sink it but, because he want to avoid damage to the port facilities sent his cutter in to do the job, but when the cutter was about 30 yards from the flying boat, positions on the shore opened up, killing one officer and four ratings and wounding six others. *Kimberley* returned fire but had difficulty locating targets in the houses. Despite this resistance, the flying boat was successfully cut from its moorings and sunk. *Kimberley* finally received instructions to depart at 10.00pm and rejoined *Penelope* in Skjel Fjord, transferring her wounded to the cruiser. She then sailed to rendezvous with the Home Fleet and spent 16 April as part of the close screen. On the 17th she was detached to join the battlecruiser squadron and sailed with them to escort the damaged cruiser *Suffolk* back to Scapa, arriving on the 18th.

Kipling *and the raid on Stavanger*

After her refit on the Tyne, *Kipling* arrived at Scapa on the 15th. The very next day she sailed with the heavy cruiser *Suffolk* and the destroyers *Janus*, *Juno* and *Hereward* for Operation 'Duck', a bombardment of Sola Airfield just outside Stavanger in support of Operation 'Primrose'. They arrived off Stavanger on the 17th and *Suffolk* commenced her bombardment at 5.00am at a range of about 10 miles, but with little effect. The force was then ordered to sweep northwards to hunt for enemy destroyers rather than retire immediately. The ships came under continuous air attack and *Suffolk* was seriously damaged by a large bomb which hit her near X turret. *Kipling* was also attacked and at 11.30am was near missed by two bombs which caused serious damage to her shaft tunnels, the port and starboard HP turbines and the aft torpedo tubes. The force struggled back under constant air attack, though there were no more hits. The Home Fleet detached the battlecruiser squadron to cover them and all ships arrived safely at Scapa on the 18th. *Kipling* sailed for Portsmouth and then Southampton for repairs whilst *Kimberley* enjoyed a short break before joining *Ark Royal*'s screen for the rest of the month.

The 'Js' *during the Norwegian campaign*

Jackal finished her repairs on 17 April, the same day that *Juno*, *Janus* and *Kipling* were escorting *Suffolk*, and sailed to Scapa on the 18th. By this time destroyers were in such short supply that once a ship finished her repairs she invariably returned to service immediately. On the 23rd she was escorting the *Empire Ability* to Cape Wrath where she was relieved and returned to Scapa. *Juno* went Greenock for minor repairs before taking part in Operation 'DX', a series

of air operations by *Ark Royal* and *Glorious* in support of the Norwegian campaign, as part of the destroyer screen for the carriers. By the 25th the destroyers were running short of fuel and was ordered to Sullom Voe to refuel, returning on the 27th. Meanwhile, *Javelin* and *Jackal* sailed to escort a convoy of two troop ships and a supply ship to Aandelsnes from Aberdeen. The supply ship *Cedarbank* was sunk by *U-26* as the convoy approached Romsdals Fjord but due to the need to stay with the troopships, neither *Jackal* or *Jaguar* made any attempt to hunt the submarine. Both destroyers came under air attack, *Jackal* being bombed by He115s and He111s.

Javelin was due to escort the collier *St Magnus* back to Scapa on the 22nd but had to wait whilst the collier refuelled at Aelsund, moving to a small fjord to moor under some cliffs for protection from air attack. But she was still attacked by four Ju88s which bombed and strafed her. *Javelin* replied with all the guns she could bring to bear and was rewarded with the sight of one of the bombers departing trailing smoke. After a series of attacks lasting two and a half hours, *Javelin* emerged unscathed and was able join up with the *St Magnus*, arriving at Kirkwall on the 23rd.

Jackal and *Javelin* next sailed together on 27 April and were joined for a full-calibre shoot by *Janus* which then returned to harbour with *Javelin*, *Jackal* sailing to rendezvous with the cruiser *Arethusa* and escort her and Convoys TSM2 and FS3 to Scapa. After she arrived at Scapa, *Jackal* left with *Javelin* on the 28th to escort the cruiser *Glasgow* to Molde where she was due to pick up the Norwegian royal family, government and the bullion of the Bank of Norway. Whilst *Glasgow* entered Molde and took on her cargo and passengers, *Javelin* and *Jackal* patrolled outside coming under ineffective air attack during the night. The whole squadron then sailed for Tromso where the royal family and government disembarked. The ships then sailed for the Clyde where *Glasgow* transferred the gold into the care of the Bank of Scotland.

Janus then sailed to deliver of the new Royal Navy ciphers to *Bittern* and *Carlisle* at Namsos. Arriving on the 30th, she was in time to rescue survivors from the sinking *Bittern*,[5] and scuttle her with a torpedo. She was then detailed to transport supplies and reinforcements for the army from Namsos to Mosjoen. On 1 May she embarked 130 troops and a pair of Bofors guns together with a quantity of ammunition, stopping to refuel at Skjel Fjord, and unloaded her cargo at Mosjoen the next day. *Jupiter* had arrived on the Tyne on the 26th and would shortly be docked for a two-month refit with repairs similar to *Kingston* and *Khartoum*.

---

[5] *Bittern* had had her stern blown off by a bomb from a Ju87 causing a fire which spread throughout the ship.

The withdrawal from Norway

It soon became clear that the army would have to withdraw from Norway. *Kelly* had completed her repairs on 25 April and was available for some of the early withdrawals whilst *Kandahar* would be available after she had received degaussing equipment on 5 May but would only play a very small part in the evacuation. *Kelly* arrived at Scapa on the 29th after a short work-up period and immediately sailed as part of the escort for an evacuation convoy. In the meantime *Kimberley* was on her way back to Scapa escorting the freighter *Gunvormaersk* with *Wolverine* and *Brazen* having been released from *Ark Royal*'s screen. Arriving at Namsos it had been planned to evacuate all the troops on the night of 1 May but due to logistical difficulties this was not possible. Mountbatten volunteered to lead a division of four destroyers into the harbour and take off as many troops as he could. This was approved and *Kelly*, *Maori*, *Grenade* and *Griffin* charged up the fjord at 26kts with *Kelly* just avoiding running onto rocks. The success of this operation was dependent on the cover of fog but not only did the fog clear but what remained was lower than the tips of the masts of Mountbatten's force. This meant that German bombers were still able to find his ships, *Maori* suffering twenty-three casualties from splinter damage. The harbour proved to be totally devoid of any fog cover at all and with German bombers overhead the attempt was abandoned and it was decided to try again during the night.

On the night of the 2nd the cruiser *York*, *Kelly*, three other destroyers and three transports sailed into Namsos and successfully evacuated the whole of the force there, *Kelly* herself taking 270 French troops. The ships then headed out to sea to escape the inevitable air attacks but *Afridi* and *Bison* (which had remained outside the harbour) were both sunk. The journey back was uneventful and *Kelly* reached Scapa on the evening of the 4th. The next day she sailed for the Clyde escorting several troopships which were heading there to unload. She then sailed to Rosyth to join the Nore Command along with *Kimberley* and *Kandahar*.

Jaguar completed her repairs on 1 May and escorted the ASIS *Cromarty Firth* to Scapa. On arrival she was allocated to *Ark Royal*'s screen when she sailed for Narvik on the 4th. *Janus* had unloaded her troops and was ordered to escort three important Norwegian pulp ships from Norway to Scapa. She was then sent to join the Nore Command. On the 30th *Juno*, which had had to return to Scapa with a leaking condenser tank, sailed with *Nubian* to locate and escort the troopships *Ulster Prince* and *Royal Scotsman* from Mosjoen, returning to Rosyth on the 13th and heading south to Harwich in company with *Jaguar*.

Javelin and *Jackal*'s last few days in the Norwegian campaign were a bit more eventful. Assigned to escort Convoy NS2 to Vest Fjord with two French destroyers, they set sail at 2.30am on 7 May. Almost immediately, two ships of the convoy ran aground, but *Javelin* and *Jackal* continued with the remaining two ships while the others returned to harbour with the French ships. The convoy arrived without

Kimberley on the evening of 8 or 9 May 1940 at speed photographed from *Kelly*. She would shortly turn back for harbour to refuel. The white effect on the funnel is a salt deposit formed when spray hit the hot sides of the funnel. Of interest is the fact that she carries her D/F equipment on the front of her rear deckhouse, not on her foremast.

further mishap on the 8th and the destroyers were ordered back to Scapa. This order was countermanded and they were diverted to Mo in Norway. On arrival a short bombardment of Hemnes was carried out and *Jackal* embarked 100 troops for transport to Bodo. There the ships easily evaded high level air attacks and *Jackal* unloaded her troops. They remained in Norwegian waters for the next couple of days until assigned to cover the arrival of a transport. They then headed for home, being attacked by He111s on the way but beating off the attacks without too much trouble. They arrived at Scapa on the 13th and sailed on an anti U-boat patrol before sailing for Rosyth and then Harwich to join the Nore Command.

THE E-BOAT EPISODE

Part of the duties for the Kellys under the Nore Command were to intercept enemy destroyers and minelayers, and *Kelly* sailed from Rosyth on one of these missions with *Kimberley* on 8 May.[6] They were then to rendezvous with and escort the cruiser *Birmingham*. Both ships were low on fuel (*Kelly* had 185 tons remaining and *Kimberley* 120 tons) and hoped to refuel from the cruiser when they met her. *Kelly* and *Kimberley* formed one force and *Kandahar* and *Hostile* another and were to patrol until 4.00am on the 10th looking for German minelayers, concentrating on the *Birmingham* after that. By 7.20pm on the 9th *Kimberley* was seriously low on fuel and was detached to Sheerness, as was *Hostile*. A signal was received that the enemy minelaying forces were retiring and the destroyers were ordered to concentrate on *Birmingham* and return to Sheerness. As they headed towards *Birmingham*, Captain Mountbatten in the *Kelly* received a report from an escorting aircraft of a submarine and diverted to hunt for it. This was quite contrary to orders and left the *Birmingham* without an anti-submarine escort.

Eventually Mountbatten was persuaded to terminate the search and head for the *Birmingham*. On the way they were joined by *Bulldog*, which was also heading back to base and had lost her flotilla. At 10.44pm a blurred white object was seen off the port beam which was identified as an E-boat. This identification was too late, as the E-boat had already launched a torpedo which passed under the bridge of *Kelly* and exploded underneath her. The force of the explosion blew the bottom of her boiler rooms out, blowing No 1 boiler over to starboard and flooding No 2 boiler room immediately. About 50ft of the ship's side and bottom disappeared and *Kelly* took on an immediate list and lost all power. *Bulldog* was ordered to attack with depth charges but this was quickly countermanded as it was realised that

the attacker had been an E-boat. She then took *Kelly* under tow, but a large white E-boat suddenly appeared out of the dark and tried to ram *Kelly*, bouncing off her side and then hitting *Bulldog* before sinking. Some sources indicate that the E-boat's steering had failed and she hit *Kelly* by accident. *Kandahar*, which had left the area until the situation was clear, returned to give assistance. She took off *Kelly*'s wounded and non-essential personnel and stayed with her flotilla leader until *Birmingham* appeared. Admiral Layton aboard *Birmingham* was astonished by *Kelly*'s appearance and initially suggested that she be scuttled but allowed himself to be persuaded that she could be saved. *Birmingham* could not stay more than two hours and so departed leaving *Kelly* with an escort of *Fury*, *Bulldog*, *Gallant* and *Kandahar*. Later on the 10th the cruisers *Manchester* and *Sheffield* arrived to give further support and protection against air attack.

Kandahar departed during the night to refuel but on the 11th the wind and seas had increased, and *Kelly* was in danger of foundering. Mountbatten's damage control measures up until then had been excellent, disposing of all available top weight but more was needed. In a sudden brainwave, Mountbatten realised that by getting rid of the crew he could possibly make enough difference to save the ship. Eighteen volunteers were all that remained but it has been calculated that if the crew had not been evacuated *Kelly* would have sunk[7] *Kandahar* returned on the 12th with the tug *Watermeyer* which took over the tow from *Bulldog*. Later, a second tug joined. *Kelly* was under continuous air attack throughout her tow but was not hit. She finally arrived at Palmers Yard, Hebburn-on-Tyne at 6.30pm on the 13th having suffered twenty-seven killed and twenty-one wounded. *Kelly* had been in service for all of eleven days since her last repair.

REORGANISATION AND REINFORCEMENTS

Kimberley did not sail to assist *Kelly* after she was torpedoed but remained at Sheerness waiting to take a British naval representative to Holland. On 12 May he embarked and *Kimberley* sailed for Flushing, arriving at 10.45am. Also at Flushing was the Head of the British Military Mission to the Netherlands, Major-General Heywood who needed to get to Ymuiden. *Kimberley*'s captain agreed to take him by sea. However, before she could depart that evening the ship received a signal from the British Vice-Consul that nine British refugees needed evacuating and so waited for them. The Vice-Consul was not of much assistance but the refugees were loaded and *Kimberley* sailed for Ymuiden, rather to the disappointment of the refugees.

---

[6] This was only the second time *Kelly* and *Kimberley* would operate in company.

[7] D K Brown, correspondence with the author.

Kelly after she was torpedoed by an E-boat. The recovery of the damaged destroyer was a magnificent feat of seamanship but she should never have been torpedoed in the first place. She has her twin Lewis guns mounted on her searchlight platform.

(IMPERIAL WAR MUSEUM: FL14304)

Kimberley arrived off Ymuiden at 10.00am on the 13th, but was unable to enter the harbour as a merchant ship had hit a mine. A launch was sent to investigate and while *Kimberley* was waiting a German bomber appeared, dropping four bombs, one of which fell 40 yards away from the wildly manoeuvring destroyer. On the return of the launch Major-General Heywood and his staff embarked in it and once it was recovered *Kimberley* sailed for Sheerness. On the way back she came across a Greek freighter which had been bombed and whose compass was out of order. She was lent a boat's compass to help her reach port. *Kimberley* arrived at Sheerness on the 14th and received orders to sail for Plymouth with *Mohawk* to join reinforcements for the Mediterranean.

The initial transfer of the 5th Flotilla to the Nore Command had been a temporary measure, but with the invasion of the Low Countries this was made permanent. Three flotillas were transferred to the Nore Command, being based at Harwich. The 1st, 5th and 7th replaced the 2nd, 4th and 8th Flotillas which were transferred to Scapa for duties with the Home Fleet. These arrangements had very little time to take effect, as the increasing indications coming from Italy that she would soon enter the war meant the Mediterranean Fleet

would need significant reinforcement. This was organised extremely quickly and nine destroyers from the 'A' to 'I' class, a division of 'Ks' (four ships), a division of 'Tribals' an AA cruiser with radar and three sloops from the Rosyth Command were allocated by the Admiralty. All ships were to assemble at Plymouth for departure on 16 and 17 May. Two of the 'Tribals' were still under repair and because destroyers were needed immediately Captain Mack (7th Flotilla) was ordered to take two from *Janus*, *Juno* and *Jaguar* and sail for the Mediterranean himself. He chose *Juno* and *Janus*. From the initial request for reinforcements to the first sailing only six days elapsed and as the ships assembled at Plymouth they re-provisioned and took on ammunition.

The first group to set off were the two sloops which sailed at 4.30pm on the 16th followed later by *Egret*. At 8.00pm on the 16th Group 2, *Kingston*, *Khartoum*, *Kandahar*, *Nubian*, *Hostile* and *Hasty*, sailed. The last and largest group sailed on the 17th at 3.00pm, consisting of the AA cruiser *Carlisle, Kimberley, Mohawk, Havock, Hereward, Hero, Ilex, Janus* (carrying Captain Mack), *Juno* and *Imperial*. *Hyperion* sailed later. The passage to Alexandria was uneventful with all ships arriving by 24 May.

Two divisions of destroyers had been due to be assigned to the East Indies command to operate out of Aden at the mouth of the Red Sea, but this was reduced to one with the cruiser *Carlisle* and three sloops. The Kellys and the two 'Tribals' had been allocated to a new flotilla, the 14th, and it was the four 'Ks' of the 28th Division which were sent to the Red Sea, arriving at Aden on 28 May, eventually forming an independent command under Commander Robson of *Kandahar*. *Janus* and *Juno* stayed in Alexandria as part of the 27th Division with the two 'Tribals'. Captain Mack took *Nubian* instead of *Janus* as his flotilla leader. This left ten Kellys back in home waters, with six ships of the 7th Flotilla without a leader, though *Jackal, Javelin* and *Jaguar* were temporarily working with the 1st Flotilla. Effective from 1 June they would all become part of the 5th Flotilla under Captain Mountbatten based at the Humber as part of the Nore Command. At the time only *Kelvin, Javelin* and *Jackal* were operational and so the flotilla was augmented by ships from other classes. Mountbatten was to command the ships from the County Hotel at Immingham, going to sea when necessary in whichever ship he chose until *Kelly* was repaired. *Jervis* would never actually be part of the 5th Flotilla but sail for the Mediterranean as soon as she worked up after her repairs.

OPERATION 'QUIXOTE'

Operation Quixote concerned the location and cutting of the submarine telephone cables between Britain and Europe. In all, three pairs of cables were to be cut, each by a separate group of one destroyer and two trawlers supported by the sloop *Puffin*, which would mark the safe limit of a newly laid minefield, and Blenheims from No 16 Group RAF. The three destroyers allocated to the operation were *Jackal, Javelin* and *Jaguar*. The cables ran in pairs about 5 miles apart and 20 miles between the pairs.

The plan was for each destroyer to mark a datum point with an extra heavy dan buoy at a previously-established position. The trawlers would then work towards it until they had located the cable. During this time the destroyer would patrol the area to protect the trawlers. Once a cable was located it would be hauled to the surface, cut and sealed before being dropped back over the side. The trawler would then be escorted back to Yarmouth by the destroyer which would return for the second trawler. Once the operation was complete, the destroyers would rendezvous in Yarmouth

Roads and return to Harwich.

On 18 May *Jackal* and *Javelin* left Harwich and rendezvoused with the trawlers at 10.30pm. *Jaguar* sailed later and arrived in her area with the trawlers at 3.45am on the 19th. *Javelin* picked up the crew from a crashed Whitley bomber and laid her buoys. She then discovered that she had to relay them 3 miles further south. An abandoned tug appeared in *Jackal*'s area which turned out to be the Dutch tug *Hector*. A prize crew was put on board and the tug eventually arrived at Great Yarmouth on the 21st. *Jaguar*'s group were the only ones to complete their cutting operations on the 19th and after escorting her trawlers back she joined *Javelin*, whose group did not complete their cutting operations until the next day when the two trawlers were then escorted back to Yarmouth by *Jaguar* and *Javelin*. *Jackal*'s group also had to work through to the 20th but were successful and then the three destroyers returned to Harwich and their patrol duties.

THE RETURN OF *KELVIN* AND THE DUNKIRK EVACUATION

When she collided with *Kashmir*, *Kelvin* had come off the better and so was available for service by late May. Completing her refit on 24 May, she was ordered to Scapa Flow, escorting the supply ships *Arbroath* and *Ngkoa* on the way. *Kelvin* arrived at Scapa on the 28th and was to spend the first half of June with the Home Fleet.

Only two of the Kellys would be involved in the Dunkirk evacuation and then only for a short time in late May. *Jackal* would remain at Harwich throughout this period whilst *Javelin* and *Jaguar* would sail to the beaches direct from Harwich. On the 27th *Jaguar* hit a buoy which caused a slight dent in one of her propellers but did not affect her capabilities in any way. On the 28th she sailed with *Javelin, Codrington* and *Grenade* to patrol between the *North Goodwin Light Vessel* and Kwinte Bank. At 6.00am the destroyers came across wreckage and boats from the SS *Aboukir*, torpedoed by an E-boat, and *Jaguar* picked up seven survivors who were later transferred to *Grenade*, which took the survivors back to port. *Codrington, Javelin* and *Jaguar* then sailed for Dunkirk to take part in the evacuation there. *Jaguar* and *Javelin* were ordered to Braye beach to pick up troops. Both ships lowered their cutters and motor boats but they were immediately swamped. Commander Pugsley in *Javelin* then ordered *Jaguar* to Dunkirk and after bailing out the swamped boats she was were able to take on board 700 men from the beach. With *Codrington* which had also taken on 700 men from the East Mole she sailed for Dover. *Jaguar* embarked another 700 men at Dunkirk and then sailed for Dover with *Impulsive*.

Janus and *Juno* at Alexandria newly arrived in the Mediterranean and painted in overall Mediterranean grey. They carry the 14th Flotilla identification bands of one red over one black band. *Janus* has had her galley funnel internalised. The nearest destroyer in the background is *Hero*.   (AUSTRALIAN WAR MEMORIAL: 133594).

On the 29th both ships sailed separately. *Javelin* sailed with *Intrepid*, *Ivanhoe*, *Icarus* and *Vanquisher* at 1.45am. At 4.25 am they sighted *Grafton* which had been bombed and was sinking and *Ivanhoe* was detached to assist her. *Javelin* arrived at the harbour breakwater at 8.20am and had embarked troops and sailed an hour later. On her return to Dover, she was ordered to Havant but this was counter-manded and she returned to Dover, returning to the Nore Command on the 30th.

Jaguar refuelled and took on more ammunition before sailing from Dover with *Grenade* and *Gallant*. When they had reached Snouw Bank, the force was attacked by dive bombers and *Gallant* was damaged, but one bomber was damaged by pom-pom fire and finished off by a fighter. *Jaguar* arrived at Dunkirk at 12.50pm and moored along-side *Grenade*. She then loaded approximately 1000 troops before sailing at about 3.30pm. To leave the harbour ships had to sail through a narrow channel which restricted their speed and manoeuvrability. Bombers concentrated their attacks at this point and *Jaguar* was attacked fourteen times. Towards the end of the attacks one aircraft dropped four bombs which fell about 10 yards abreast of the searchlight platform. The explosions caused serious splinter damage, causing *Jaguar* to list to port and her engines and steering to fail. She came to a stop near a wreck and there was a very real risk that she would drift on to it. Because she had about

70 tons of extra weight on board (the troops) all the tor-pedoes and twenty-three depth charges and pistols were jettisoned. Luckily for *Jaguar*, *Express* was nearby and she passed a line over and took her under tow at 4kts. *Jaguar* was also able to transfer the majority of her troops to *Express* and *Rika* but could not start her engines. At 7.00pm the tow broke and *Express* came alongside to take off *Jaguar's* wounded and at 7.40pm prepared to depart rather than risk two destroyers being sunk but requested a tug from Dover. However, 10 minutes later *Jaguar* finally managed to repair her engines and was able to steam at 20kts, reaching Dover by 11.50pm. She had lost three men killed and seventeen wounded. Her troop cargo had suffered one officer and nine other ranks killed (one suicide) and forty-seven wounded. Her captain commented that *Express's* help had been vital and that some form of kite balloon defence as had been fitted in the trials for Operation 'Catherine' would have been very useful. *Jaguar* remained at Dover until 31 May and then sailed for Harwich. She would be under repair until 16 June.

7

The Kellys in Home Waters to April 1941

FROM 1 JUNE 1940 all 'Js' and 'Ks' in home waters joined Captain Mountbatten's 5th Flotilla, the 7th Flotilla ceasing to exist for the time being, although of the ten Kellys in home waters only three, *Kelvin*, *Jackal* and *Javelin*, were actually operational. *Javelin* entered dock at Sheerness to refit on 5 June and, as a result, was unavailable until the 23rd, but *Kelvin* was highly active with the Home Fleet. On 5 June she sailed with *Renown*, *Repulse*, *Newcastle*, *Sussex*, *Zulu*, *Maori*, *Forester* and *Foxhound* to cover the withdrawal of Group 2 of the Norwegian evacuation force, but the force was diverted to search for reported German forces off Iceland. These reports were, however, false. *Renown*, *Zulu* and *Kelvin* returned to Scapa on the 9th and sailed again at 12.50am with *Inglefield*, *Amazon*, *Electra* and *Escort* to continue covering the withdrawal from Norway, *Kelvin* and *Escort* being detached on the 13th to escort the *Ark Royal* back to Scapa.

On the 16th the armed merchant cruiser *Andania* was torpedoed and sunk by the German submarine *U-A* and *Kelvin* put to sea to rescue the survivors. However, these had already been picked up by an Icelandic trawler and she returned to Scapa. The next day she was transferred to the Nore Command and sailed to Immingham to join the rest of the 5th Flotilla. *Kashmir* and *Jupiter* had both finished their refits and arrived at Immingham the same day. With *Jackal* already available and *Jaguar* available on the 22nd this pushed the strength of the flotilla up to five ships of which two, *Jaguar* and *Jackal*, were immediately borrowed by the 18th Cruiser Squadron to escort it from Rosyth to the Humber (arriving on 2 July).

The 5th Flotilla then settled down into a pattern of patrols, convoy escort duties and exercises. Captain Mountbatten embarked on each of his destroyers on a rotating basis, generally at weekly intervals, from 14 August. At this time he was also responsible for all destroyers on the Nore Command including the 20th (Minelaying) Destroyer Flotilla which with the minelayer *Teviot Bank* was engaged in laying the North Sea mine barrage. The 5th Flotilla's only participation in one of these operations was on 28 June when *Javelin* and *Jupiter* left their patrol line and escorted *Teviot Bank*, *Express*, *Intrepid* and *Icarus* on Operation 'BS19'. Initially, the ships of the 5th had been responsible for Patrol 'P' from the Inner Gabbard to Smiths Knoll but in July would take over Patrol 'U', the line of which ran from

Jupiter and *Jackal* on convoy escort duty with *Kelvin* (camera ship). *Jupiter*'s colour scheme is a simplified version of her earlier elaborate camouflage, chiefly around the bridge. *Jackal* is fitted with a Type 286 whilst *Jupiter* still carries the D/F aerial.

(IMPERIAL WAR MUSEUM: A688)

Flamborough Head to Sherringham Float. At night they would be reinforced by one of the cruisers of the 2nd Cruiser Squadron and a further destroyer until the beginning of August, when Patrol 'U' was suspended between 5 August and 12 September. These patrols were totally uneventful with no enemy ships being sighted at all and the only incident worthy of note was on 2 August when *Jackal* had to abandon her patrol as a result of damage to her port propeller blades. The coastal convoys were a bit more exciting and *Jaguar* was bombed on 22 July by a Dornier Do215 whilst escorting one, but no damage was done. *Kelvin* was also bombed with Convoy FS38 on 1 August, once again without damage.

COLLISIONS AND OTHER DAMAGE

The Home Fleet continued to borrow the ships of the 5th Flotilla. On the 12 August, due to serious losses in the Northern Approaches, *Javelin, Jaguar, Jupiter* and *Kelvin* were all temporarily attached, being relieved in rotation. This would also involve *Kipling* when she completed her repairs on 21 July but she did not actually sail until 4 August as further defects needed repairing. On that day she sailed to test her new degaussing equipment but was unable to carry out steam trials as the port was closed because of fog. Her degaussing gear needed repairs which were finished on the 5th but she was not able to carry out the steam trials until 8th August. These were not successful, the turbine casing leaking, and *Kipling* had to enter the Humber basin for repairs. This drew comment from the C-in-C Nore that the situation was unsat-

isfactory as the continuing problems with *Kipling* coupled with the damage to *Kashmir* and *Jackal* meant that *Javelin* and *Jaguar* had to forego their boiler cleaning and were in consequence not up to full efficiency. The trials were rescheduled for the 13th and were successful after which *Kipling* was immediately borrowed by the Home Fleet, arriving at Scapa on 15 August and remaining there until the end of September when she returned to Immingham just in time for the transfer of the 5th Flotilla to the Western Approaches Command. As she arrived in the Humber she collided with another ship but fortunately this caused only slight damage and she was able to continue in service.

Kashmir managed to stay out of trouble until 31 July when she collided with the minesweeping trawler *Kurd*, remaining out of action until 21 August when she too would be borrowed by the Home Fleet to work with *Kipling*, sailing direct from her Home Fleet station at Rosyth with *Jupiter* and *Jackal* for Plymouth on 1 October. *Jaguar*, as mentioned above, was borrowed by the Home Fleet for several duties, one of which was providing anti-submarine escort for Atlantic convoys, and on 12 August she and *Cattistock* sailed to rendezvous with Convoy HXA61. The weather was extremely poor and they came across the corvette *Primrose* standing by MV *Albula* which was in danger of foundering after a collision. After unsuccessful attempts to take the *Albula* in tow, during which the two ships collided with minor damage to the destroyer, *Jaguar* took off her crew and she later sank. No blame was attached to *Jaguar* for this collision as she had been attempting a difficult operation in

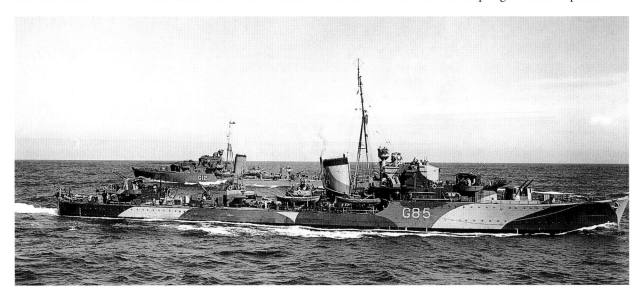

Jupiter with *Kashmir* behind, probably on 24 August 1940 just before *Kashmir* sailed for Scapa Flow. *Jupiter* is acting as flotilla leader (note the black band) and still has her galley exhaust wrapped around her funnel. *Kashmir* sports a false bow wave which is just visible above

Jupiter's No 3 Mount. Also of interest is the way that *Jupiter*'s camouflage is carried over the Carley floats.

(IMPERIAL WAR MUSEUM: A238)

extremely bad weather. She returned to Scapa where her damage was repaired by the depot ship *Woolwich*.

THE MINING OF THE 20TH DESTROYER FLOTILLA

On 31 August the 20th Destroyer Flotilla departed the Humber on another of their minelaying missions, CBX.5. *Jupiter*, *Jackal* and *Kelvin* of the 5th Flotilla and *Vortigern* were at sea for exercises upon completion of which, *Jupiter*, *Kelvin* and *Vortigern* sailed to support the minelayers on receipt of reports from aircraft indicating that the 20th Flotilla was under observation. The 20th itself was ordered to intercept German ships which had been reported by air reconnaissance and, while doing so, *Express* struck a mine. Both *Esk* and *Ivanhoe* then struck mines whilst attempting to go to her assistance and *Esk* was sunk. *Intrepid* and *Icarus* avoided the minefield and radioed for help. Mountbatten, who was approaching at 23kts (*Vortigern*'s maximum speed), decided to wait till daylight. In the meantime he directed his flotilla to mark Gap D in the British minefields to enable *Icarus* and *Intrepid* to exit the mined areas.

At 7.00am on 1 September, *Jupiter* and *Kelvin* sailed to locate the two damaged destroyers whilst *Vortigern* remained behind to mark Gap D. *Kelvin* found *Express* and took her under tow but fouled her propeller with the tow line which then broke. *Jupiter* was unable to find *Ivanhoe* and returned to tow *Express*, later handing over to the tugs *St Cyrus*, *Wheeldon* and *Irishman*. *Kelvin* and *MTB30* were then ordered to locate *Ivanhoe* but received contradictory information as to her location. It was finally the destroyer *Garth* which found *Ivanhoe* being bombed by a German

A superb photograph of *Kelvin* at Scapa Flow in September 1940. Her 4in gun is protected by splinter mats as is her searchlight platform. There is evidence of re-painting along her waterline, near the bow and it is possible that at some time she carried a false bow wave but no photographs have been found to back this up. Her colour scheme is overall AP507B. (IMPERIAL WAR MUSEUM: A1524)

floatplane. After the aircraft had been driven off with AA fire, *Kelvin* and *MTB30* were summoned. The proximity of an enemy minefield, meant that it was too dangerous to attempt to take *Ivanhoe* in tow and *Kelvin* sank her with a torpedo, rejoining the rest of the flotilla at 6.10pm but she was shortly detached to return to port at full speed and land *Ivanhoe*'s wounded. As she departed she was attacked by a Ju88 which sheered away when it saw the rest of the flotilla approaching. The whole force, escorting the damaged *Express*, arrived back on the Humber on 2 September.

Meanwhile, *Jaguar* and *Javelin*, which were operating out of Rosyth with the Home Fleet, sailed with *Punjabi* and *Tartar* to escort in the cruiser *Fiji* which had been torpedoed by *U-32* whilst on her way to take part in Operation 'Menace', an attempt to capture Dakar, arriving back at the Clyde on 1 September.

THE 'N' CLASS

The 'N' class ships of the 1939 Programme, which would all be foreign-manned, were still under construction. The first to be allocated were the Australian ships, following a letter written by Admiral Cunningham, C-in-C Mediterranean Fleet, on 17 April 1940. At the time he had a flotilla of old Australian destroyers under his command and wrote to the Admiralty;

> There is one point for your consideration. The officers and men of the Australian destroyers out here are magnificent material and are quite wasted in these old ships. Tovey has suggested that they might be transferred lock, stock and barrel to 5 new ships and used at home. They certainly are the most lively and undefeated fellows I have ever had to do with.[1]

This suggestion fell on fertile ground and on 14 May an approach was made to the Australian Navy in Melbourne offering the loan of five new destroyers. This was quickly accepted and the choice of destroyer type rested between the new 'L' class and the 'N' class. Five of the 'Ns' were chosen which would have meant an increase of 400 ratings over the compliments of the existing five destroyers.[2] However, the Australians offered to go on manning the old ships and provide totally new crews for the new ships. This was accepted but meant a change in the allocation. The first of these crews would not be ready in time for the commissioning of *Nerissa* and rather than delay this, another ship was allocated. Conversely, *Noble* would be commissioning too late and so she too was replaced by a different vessel and a revised allocation of *Napier*, *Nizam*, *Nestor*, *Norman* and *Norseman* was settled on.

The RAN had already accepted financial liability for the crewing of the destroyers[3] and as a result the ships were to fly the Australian ensign despite being under Admiralty control. With the allocation of *Napier* (the flotilla leader) Captain Steven Arliss RN was loaned to the RAN to act as flotilla commander on 14 September. The 7th Flotilla was resurrected, though now it was a mainly Australian outfit, and a Confidential Admiralty Fleet Order was issued on 31 July[4] instructing that all five Australian ships were to be referred to as 'His Majesty's Australian Ship' (HMAS). Skilled ratings were borrowed from the Royal Navy for technical duties until suitable Australians could be trained. This caused some friction as the RN ratings were paid at considerably lower rates than the Australians but it proved impossible to persuade the pay section to change things.

Of the small Polish navy, three destroyers, *Burza*,

Javelin in the Channel in late 1940 with *Jersey* behind her. *Javelin* has been fitted with a Type 286 and painted unusually in AP507C. She would be camouflaged shortly after this photograph was taken in November 1940.

(IMPERIAL WAR MUSEUM: A2035)

---

[1] PRO ADM1/11141.
[2] *Stuart* (leader), *Voyager*, *Vampire*, *Vendetta* and *Waterhen*.
[3] Australian Navy Board, Letter of 8 June 1940 in PRO ADM1/11141.
[4] CAFO 1530/40.

Blyskawica and *Grom*, managed to escape to the United Kingdom and continue the fight against the Germans. During the Narvik campaign, *Grom* had been sunk by air attack and Churchill promised the Poles a new ship to replace her. Initially, destroyers of the 'G' class were considered as possible replacements (particularly *Grafton*, *Greyhound*, *Griffin*, *Grenade* or *Gallant*) and the Poles in fact were quite happy to have *Gallant* as *Garland* of the same class had already been transferred and they would be able to form a homogenous unit. There would be a delay of about a month whilst the ship was withdrawn and refitted to re-emerge as the new *Grom*.[5] *Burza* was in need of a refit and so it was decided to offer the Poles three more 'Gs' and refit *Burza* as a training ship. But *Gallant* was mined in the

[5] See M010663 in PRO ADM 116/4098.

Piorun on commissioning in November 1940. She has been fitted with a 4in gun as part of her commissioning equipment but does not have Oerlikon platforms by her searchlight platform. Unusually she also has the framework for the Mountbatten roof. (IMPERIAL WAR MUSEUM: FL10070)

Mediterranean and declared a constructive total loss, creating the problem of what to offer the Poles in her place and finally on 14 July Admiral Pound (the First Sea Lord) offered them the ex-French destroyer *Ouragan* and the Auxiliary Patrol Boats *Pomerol* and *Medoc* (former coasters) together with the submarine chasers *CH11* and *CH15*. The Poles were none too pleased at this, pointing out that *Ouragan* needed re-arming due to a lack of French ammunition and that the Prime Minister had promised them a new destroyer. Casting around, the Admiralty realised that *Nerissa* would be available in mid-October 1940 and promptly

offered her instead.[6] The Poles were delighted and accepted immediately. However, there was still the matter of where she would serve. There was no intention of *Nerissa* operating with other Polish ships but rather as part of the 7th Flotilla. The Poles were not happy at this and did not want to serve in a flotilla manned by Australians. Eventually a compromise was reached whereby if *Nerissa* did go overseas it would be for only short periods and the Poles agreed to accept the administrative inconvenience this would cause.

The final matter to be resolved concerned the ship's name. She was commissioned as *Nerissa* on 24 October 1940 as an independent command with a Polish crew and commanding officer. However, her name was too feminine for the Polish Navy's taste so on 21 October they requested permission to rename her as they had been promised a replacement *Grom*. They did not have any suitable names beginning with N and wanted to avoid giving the new ship the same name as *Grom*, so they suggested that she be renamed *Piorun* (meaning clap of thunder) which was very similar to *Grom* and which had been planned as a name for a pre-war destroyer. The Admiralty agreed to this and so on 13 November *Nerissa* was renamed *Piorun*. Whilst she would serve with Force H and take part in the Italian campaign she only sailed with the Australian 'Ns' at the very beginning of her career.

At a Controllers New Construction meeting on 12 November 1940 the question of allocating two new vessels to the Dutch Navy came up. Two Dutch ships, the cruiser *Jacob Van Heemskirk* and the destroyer *Isaac Sweers*, had escaped from Holland before the invasion and were being completed in the United Kingdom. The Dutch government was anxious for these ships to serve with the Royal Navy on completion but they had originally been intended for the Dutch East Indies Fleet. To placate the colonial authorities, they wanted to purchase two or three new destroyers to serve out there. The Admiralty were happy for two destroyers to be sold to the Dutch, and the meeting discussed which ships to allocate, concluding that *Norman* and *Norseman*

---

[6] *Ouragan* would serve with the Polish Navy between 18 July 1940 and 30 April 1941 after which she was returned to Free French service.

One of series of posters produced to elicit funds for the new *Van Galen*.

(MARINEMUSEUM/DUTCH NAVAL MUSEUM)

would be the most appropriate. However, Australian crews for these ships were already on their way and so it was decided to sell the Dutch the two unallocated members of the 'N' class, *Noble* and *Nonpareil*, due to be completed in November 1941 and January 1942 respectively. There was opposition to the sale as it would reduce the 'N' class by two ships but an arrangement was worked out whereby the ships would be under the operational control of the Royal Navy serving under the C-in-C Eastern Fleet. This was accepted by the Dutch naval command on 20 November. There was no problem with renaming them as the Dutch would own both ships unlike the Australian and Poles whose vessels were only loaned. *Noble* became *Van Galen* after the Dutch destroyer sunk during the defence of Rotterdam by German aircraft and *Nonpareil* was named after *Tjerk Hiddes* which was scuttled before completion by the Dutch. Both ships would commission in 1942.

THE 5TH FLOTILLA AT PLYMOUTH

The 5th Flotilla had been transferred to the Western Approaches Command as a destroyer striking force. Initial orders issued on 30 September were for there destroyers of the 5th to reinforce the Western Approaches Command forming the Channel Striking Force – *Jackal*, *Jupiter* and *Kashmir* being the three chosen. *Jersey* was due to join them when she completed her repairs. What actually happened was that all the ships of the Flotilla in fact went, *Javelin*, *Kelvin* and *Jaguar* on the 30th, *Kashmir*, *Jupiter* and *Jackal* on 1 October and *Kipling* – which had returned from Home Fleet service on 30 September sailed on 2 October with Captain Mountbatten on board. *Jersey* had completed her repairs by 23 September and joined the rest of the flotilla on the 28th. However, she still needed time to work-up and so remained at Immingham. On 10 October she arrived at Sheerness and the next day as she left port she hit a mine which exploded close under her port bow, causing severe damage, but she was fortunate. The motor yacht *Aisha* which sailed with her also hit a mine and sank a as a result. Both mines had earlier failed to explode when a whole

convoy of thirty ships passed over them. *Jersey* would be out of action for the rest of the month.

The 5th Flotilla was quickly in action, *Kelvin* sailing with the Polish destroyer *Blyskawica* on 2 October for a patrol between Eddystone and Wolf Rock. On her return on the 3rd she immediately sailed with *Wanderer* to sweep off Lands End and the Scilly Isles in support of MASBs *42*, *43* and *51*. The whole flotilla put to sea on the 7th to hunt for a U-boat following an aircraft report. A raft belonging to the *SS Diana* was found near the position of the report but there was no sign of the U-boat.

On 10 October the battleship *Revenge* sailed from Plymouth escorted by *Javelin*, *Jupiter*, *Jackal*, *Jaguar*, *Kashmir* and *Kipling* to bombard Cherbourg (Operation 'Medium'). With her were a separate force consisting of *Newcastle*, *Emerald*, *Wanderer*, *Broke*, *Garland* and *Burza*. Mountbatten, following his practice of rotating through the ships of his flotilla, had embarked in *Jackal*. The ships arrived off

Jersey and *Javelin* on exercises with an MTB. *Jersey* has not been fitted with radar yet and possibly never was. She is in overall AP507B.

(IMPERIAL WAR MUSEUM: A2036)

Cherbourg undetected to coincide with an RAF raid. *Newcastle* and *Emerald* then fired starshell to illuminate the target and stationed themselves west of the bombardment force to screen them from any German destroyers which might attempt to intervene from Brest. *Revenge* and the 5th Flotilla opened fire at 3.32am on harbour installations, oil depots and shipping in the harbour. Eighteen minutes later the bombardment was over, the German shore defences having not responded immediately thinking that it was an air attack. When they finally opened fire, finding the range at about 4.00 am, they forced the attackers to zig-zag and lay a smoke screen. None of the British ships were hit and the 5th Flotilla and *Revenge* returned to Portsmouth whilst the cruiser force went to Plymouth, the destroyers having fired 801 rounds. On the way back the 5th was diverted to intercept a convoy but were further diverted to hunt the two small German warships which had sunk two trawlers *L'Istac* and *Warwick Deeping*. Contact was made but the enemy ships escaped in the darkness.

On 17 October the German destroyers at Brest sailed for an offensive sweep, which could have had quite serious consequences for the British as there were three lightly escorted convoys in the area, HG45, SL50 and OG44 all of which were diverted. The German force, consisting of *Hans Lody*, *Erich Steinbrink*, *Friedrich Ihn* and *Karl Galster* (a fifth, the *Theodore Riedel*, had had to return to port with engine trouble), were spotted by a Blenheim aircraft at around 8.30am, and the cruisers *Newcastle* and *Emerald* together with the 5th Flotilla were ordered to intercept, *Jackal*, *Jupiter*, *Kashmir*, *Kelvin* and *Kipling* sailing with Mountbatten still in *Jackal*. A course was set to intercept the German ships which were sighted at around 4.00pm and shortly after *Newcastle* opened fire at extreme range, followed by *Emerald*.

The range gradually decreased as the German ships were making only 29kts whilst the British force was at 33kts and the 5th Flotilla was then able to open fire. Due to engine trouble *Jupiter* fell behind and was ordered to investigate two sailing ships travelling independently. The rest of the force continued, coming under increasing air attack – both sides had plenty of air support and the Germans were bombed by Blenheims on the way back. But lacking fighter cover the British force decided to break off the chase and return to harbour. The German air attacks petered out and the British force returned to harbour unharmed. On the 20th *Jaguar*, *Kashmir* and *Blyskawica* sailed to investigate a suspicious vessel but returned after an abortive search and the rest of the month was uneventful apart from the arrival of *Jersey* from Sheerness on the 29th, escorted by *Kelvin*.

On 2 November *Jersey* sailed with *Newcastle*, *Nigeria*, *Jackal*, *Jaguar*, *Jupiter* and *Kashmir* to intercept a German destroyer force. However, this operation was cancelled when the German ships were reported to have reached Brest. Routine patrols continued throughout this period, with two or three ships of the flotilla sailing on each occasion. Frequently during this period the flotilla used Dartmouth as a base as Plymouth was closed due to mining, sometimes creating logistical problems as on the 15th when the arrival of *Kelvin* and *Jersey* completely filled the harbour up. *Jaguar* and *Kelvin* were detached on 15 November to escort the cruisers *Manchester* and *Southampton* to Gibraltar and both were retained by Force H. *Kelvin* would be replaced by *Jersey* for a short period but *Jaguar* would remain with Force H until she joined the Mediterranean Fleet (see next chapter). On the 23rd the whole flotilla sailed to patrol between Lizard Point and the Scillies to intercept a German convoy. They returned on the 24th having missed it and sailed again almost immediately to try to intercept three German destroyers. Once again they were unsuccessful. Captain Mountbatten embarked in *Kashmir* but was shortly to transfer to *Javelin* which had been fitted with a brand-new Type 286 radar set.

THE TORPEDOING OF *JAVELIN*

Mountbatten's policy of using ships of his flotilla in rotation whilst the *Kelly* was repaired did not meet with universal approval, Commander King of *Kashmir* and Commander Pugsley of *Javelin* both expressing doubts,[7] but it would continue until *Kelly* was repaired. On 28 November *Javelin*, *Jupiter*, *Kashmir*, *Jackal* and *Jersey* left Plymouth for patrol duties between Lands End and Start Point. *Kipling* was also due to sail but managed to get a mooring line wrapped round her propeller and was delayed. Rather than patrol along a line Mountbatten decided to remain in the western area of his patrol and put the flotilla through various evolutions based on different lines of bearing. This formation required ships to steam in an oblique line which was based on a compass measurement. For example, a line of bearing of 240° would mean that all ships would be in an oblique line with the foremost ahead of the rest on that particular bearing. The advantage of this formation was that it allowed ships to gain ½-1kt in speed as they were not impeded by each other's wakes and to be able to get more guns into action more quickly.

A German force consisting of the destroyers *Karl Galster*, *Richard Beitzen* and *Hans Lody* had sailed from Brest to hunt British shipping. They managed to sink some small vessels but their gun flashes were spotted by *Kashmir*. The German ships were in an unenviable position, three against a flotilla of five powerful 'J' and 'K' class ships. The German

---

[7] For King's comments see Philip Ziegler, *Mountbatten*, p139 in particular. Pugsley's comments are included in his book *Destroyer Man*.

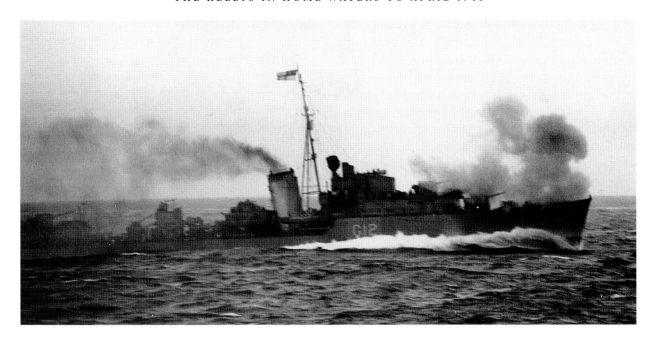

Kashmir firing at German destroyers during the engagement of
17 October 1940. The German ships escaped without damage but
caused no damage themselves. Once again one can see the heavy salt
encrustation on the destroyer's funnel and also *Kashmir*'s battle ensign.

(IMPERIAL WAR MUSEUM: A1383)

destroyers were sighted about 5.40am on the 29th and the
British opened fire 3 minutes later. The Germans responded
though their salvoes fell over (this was the case for the
British as well). At this time the 5th Flotilla was in oblique
formation heading towards the German destroyers at a right
angle, but then Mountbatten ordered a turn to port to run
alongside the German ships. This would have been justi-
fied if the ships had been in line-ahead but was question-
able in the current circumstances. As they turned the British
ships lost the targets on their directors and steamed right
into the paths of torpedoes launched by the German ships.
Most missed but two torpedoes hit *Javelin* in the bow and
stern. The first hit almost blew the stern off up to Station
64 and ignited the oil tanks. The stern dropped off 2 minutes after the explosion but luckily the aft magazine did not
explode. The second hit blew off the whole bow forward
Station 30 and caused rapid flooding up to Station 35, flooding No 2 Magazine at a rate of 6in per hour. The German
ships turned away, pursued by the rest of the flotilla, but
escaped undamaged. The four ships then returned to stand
by *Javelin* which had been reduced from a length of 356½ft
to 155ft. At midday the tug *Caroline Moller* arrived and by
passing a line round *Javelin*'s torpedo mount was able to
tow her back to Plymouth at 2kts, arriving on the 30th.
Mountbatten made great play of how the crews of the Kellys
thought their ships were invincible and could survive any-

Two photos which show the aftermath of *Javelin*'s torpedoing. Very
little of her was left and her survival is a testament to the strength of
her design. Visible in the original is her Type 286.

(IMPERIAL WAR MUSEUM: A1810 AND A1815)

thing, but the Admiralty considered that he had blundered and blundered badly. The criticism of the action hinged on the turn to port. It was felt that the ships should have continued straight at the enemy ships. Whilst Ziegler[8] has pointed out that this would have put the flotilla behind the enemy he has not come up with any convincing explanation as to why this was necessarily a bad thing. It is possible that the German ships would still have escaped but also unlikely that *Javelin* would have been torpedoed. Furthermore, the turn to port did not confer any advantage, the enemy still being able to escape after the turn. In fact, Mountbatten's turn handed victory to the German destroyers. Confronted by a superior force, they not only got away without damage themselves but were also able to seriously damage one of their opponents. Unlike the encounter with *Juno* and *Jersey* where the German ships should have stayed to finish off their foes, they were wise to withdraw in this case. They were still outnumbered and could not be assured of any further success. *Javelin* would be under repair until January 1942 when she returned, completely rebuilt. The German destroyers had also proved to be faster than the Kellys and it was suggested that the 6th Flotilla of 'Tribals'

---

[8] Philip Ziegler, *Mountbatten*.
[9] This speed advantage turned out to be illusory and would not have enabled the British ships to catch up with the German destroyers which were significantly faster.

replace them as the Channel Striking Force, but the advantage was only 1-1½kts[9] and the ships of the 6th were less experienced. Furthermore, they had a larger, more visible silhouette and the Home Fleet wanted to keep the 6th Flotilla as escorts for the battlecruiser squadron.

OTHER OPERATIONS

On 3 December, *Icarus* sailed to lay mines off the Ile de Bus light. She was escorted to Torbay by *Kashmir*, *Kipling* and *Punjabi* who then patrolled off the Lizard and awaited her return. This operation passed off without trouble and on the 4th the same three ships with the addition of *Jupiter* sailed to hunt a small submarine which had been reported heading for L'Orient, but were unsuccessful.

The cruiser *Manchester*'s return to the UK after Operation 'Collar' was covered by the 5th Flotilla. *Jersey* sailed for Gibraltar on 5 December returning with *Manchester* and *Kelvin* and being met by *Kashmir* and *Jupiter* who then escorted her into Plymouth on 11 December. *Jackal* sailed to the Humber for a refit on 8 December, returning at the end of the month. With *Jackal* and *Javelin* out of action it was necessary to strengthen the flotilla and 'Tribals' from the 6th Flotilla were temporarily attached. The ships changed in rotation, the first being *Mashona* and *Punjabi*. *Kelvin* was also recalled from Gibraltar as previously mentioned. *Jersey*

Jersey in the Channel shortly before the 5th Flotilla departed for the Mediterranean. She is already painted in overall AP507C but does not yet have her Oerlikons installed on their platforms. All ships of the 5th received two Oerlikons just before sailing. *Jersey* seems to have been the only ship of the flotilla not to have received a Type 286.

(IMPERIAL WAR MUSEUM: A2754)

A fine view of *Kelly* before departure to the Mediterranean. She has her Oerlikons already fitted. Also visible are the ready-use shell holders along the extended aft deckhouse. (IMPERIAL WAR MUSEUM: A4081)

and the French *Le Triomphant* conducted a U-boat search off North Cornwall on 12 December, once again without finding anything and on the 14 *Jersey* and *Jupiter* sailed to rescue survivors of the small French destroyer *Branlebas* which had foundered in a storm off Land's End.

The cruiser *Kent*, which had been torpedoed by Italian aircraft in the Mediterranean, was returning to the United Kingdom. After successfully passing the Straits of Gibraltar she was ordered to rendezvous with *Kelvin* and *Kipling* on 24 December, the two destroyers forming an anti-submarine screen and escorting the damaged cruiser back to Devonport where they arrived on the 25th. As they tied up others of the flotilla were just departing: a troop convoy (WS5A) had been attacked by the German heavy cruiser *Admiral Hipper* and though she had been driven off by the escort, reinforcements were ordered to sail. These consisted of *Kenya*, *Punjabi*, *Kashmir* and *Jersey*, but in the end they were not needed and the next mission for *Jersey* would be to escort the French submarine *Surcouf* with *Jupiter* on 28 December.

THE KELLYS AT SCAPA

Captain Mountbatten had travelled up to Newcastle from Plymouth to recommission *Kelly* after she completed her repairs on 3 December. But as she left the Tyne she man-

aged to ram the SS *Scorpion* and had to return for more repairs. Finally on 16 December she was able to leave the Tyne and commence her working-up trials. By now the first of the 'Ns' had entered service. *Piorun* was working-up on the Clyde, *Nizam* was almost ready and *Napier* had completed her trials and had been working out of Scapa since the 21st. During *Napier*'s trials, conducted with the *Kelly*, the galley funnel on the aft deckhouse was blown overboard but apart from this they were uneventful. On 4 January 1941 *Napier* and *Piorun* sailed to join two armed merchant cruisers escorting a convoy to Iceland, returning to Scapa on the 11th. *Kelly* had completed her trials and sailed for the Clyde on the 7th. On the way she met the SS *Temple Moat* which had been machine-gunned by a Focke Wulfe Condor and had a seriously wounded man on board. *Kelly* took off the seaman and sailed to Greenock where he was disembarked to a hospital. She then continued her voyage to Plymouth being met by *Kipling*, *Kashmir* and *Jersey*. *Kelvin* had gone to the Humber for a refit and was not due to return until 22 February but *Jackal* and *Jupiter* were at

Plymouth along with *Punjabi*, still on loan, giving the flotilla an operational strength of seven ships.

Kelly, true to form, managed to suffer storm damage and lost her motor boat and whaler on the 15th. She was repaired at Devonport and then with the rest of the flotilla she continued patrol duties in the Channel. There were no more encounters with German destroyers, most of which had returned to Germany for refit or been transferred to other duties. On 8 February *Kelly*, *Kipling* and *Kashmir* left Plymouth for Scapa to escort the Home Fleet as they hunted the German battlecruisers *Scharnhorst* and *Gneisenau* which were supposed to be at sea. The search was called off but *Kelly*, *Kashmir* and *Kipling* were ordered to hunt a U-boat which had been reported by *Nelson* near Skaale Fjord in the Orkneys. On the 11th they were joined by *Boreas* and *Jackal* which had sailed to Scapa the previous day. Having found nothing *Kelly* and *Kashmir* sailed for Londonderry but *Kipling* was left behind to tow *Boreas*, whose boilers had broken down, to Scapa, after which she sailed directly to Londonderry to join her two flotilla mates.

Jupiter and *Jersey* had sailed to Gibraltar to join Force H on 26 January for a short period and replace *Jaguar*. They returned on 3 March and two days later *Jupiter* went into dock for a refit which was to last until 23 May. Meanwhile *Kelvin* had finished her refit and on 24 February arrived at Scapa to carry out degaussing trials, after which she sailed

to join the rest of the flotilla at Plymouth. *Jackal* remained at Plymouth and on 29 January sailed to reinforce Convoy SC19 which was under attack by U-boats. On 2 February she was forced to sink the fore part of the tanker *W B Walker* which had broken in half after being torpedoed by *U-93*.

MINELAYING AND THE GERMAN CAPITAL SHIPS
The 5th Flotilla's next minelaying operation was on 29-30 December 1940 when *Kashmir*, *Jersey* and *Jupiter* escorted the minelayer *Adventure* on Operation 'GQ'. Most of these operations in early 1941 were intended to keep the German battlecruisers *Scharnhorst* and *Gneisenau* and the heavy cruiser *Admiral Hipper* penned up in Brest. These were mostly the provenance of ships of the 20th Flotilla which had been reconstituted with *Intrepid*, *Impulsive* and *Icarus* as its members. A couple of operations also involved the brand new minelayer *Abdiel* (Operations 'GV' and 'GY') escorted by *Kipling* and *Kashmir* on 24 March and *Kelly*, *Kashmir*, *Kelvin* and *Jackal* on 28 March. The most elaborate operation was Operation 'GX' on 27 March which consisted of the 20th Flotilla escorted by *Kelly*, *Kashmir*, *Jackal* and *Kelvin* and was timed to coincide with a diversionary air raid by six Blenheim bombers from 19 Squadron. Unfortunately the results of the operation were not observable due to low cloud.

When not escorting minelayers the 5th Flotilla conducted Channel patrols. These patrols could be risky: on 8 March,

Another view of *Kelly* on her trials and showing her final configuration minus her Oerlikons. Her Type 286 is clearly visible. Mountbatten was a keen exponent of radar and used all his influence to get as many ships of his flotilla as he could fitted with radar. Visible on the front of the bridge is the new type of D/F aerial. Note also the elongated rear deckhouse for flotilla staff which precluded leaders carrying TSDS equipment.

(IMPERIAL WAR MUSEUM: A2787 AND A2909)

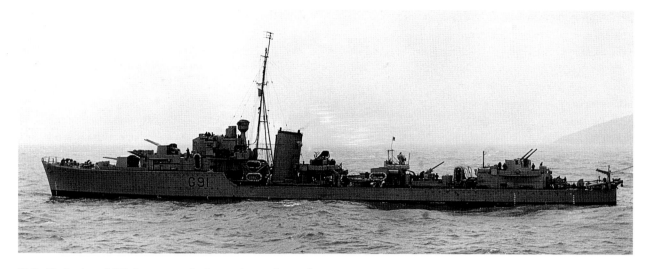

Kelly, Kashmir and *Kelvin* came under intermittent air attack whilst in the Channel, but the nearest bombs fell 200 yards astern of *Kashmir* and *Kelvin* managed to hit one of the aircraft with AA fire. German coastal convoys were also frequently sighted by patrolling aircraft. This generally resulted in the 5th Flotilla putting to sea to intercept the convoy but in all their time at Plymouth the flotilla were unable to catch any of them. One operation on 22 February had to be abandoned due to appalling weather, in which the destroyers were only able to make 10kts which made them quite useless. In early April the German capital ships could not be found which caused panic at the Admiralty and so on 5 and 6 April *Kelly, Kashmir, Kelvin* and *Jackal* sailed to intercept the *Scharnhorst* and *Gneisenau* if they left Brest. They were joined by *Jersey* for the patrols on the 7th and 9th by which time their orders had quite sensibly changed to shadowing the ships rather than attacking them, but no contact was made.

KIPLING AND CONVOY 'SAPPER'

In April *Kipling* was escorting shipping in the waters around the Bristol Channel and on the 16th was re-forming a convoy for Bristol. Several ships were straggling badly and *Kipling* was rounding them up when aircraft were heard but not seen. At 2.00am one of the lead ships of the convoy, *Bolette*, caught fire and sank stern first, *Kipling* lowering a boat to search for survivors. Another aircraft was seen but was driven off by gunfire and when the trawler *Pearl* arrived to join the escort she was ordered to continued hunt for survivors and *Kipling* rejoined the convoy. As she did so she came upon a boatload of survivors from the *Anglesea Rose* which had been sunk by a near miss. *Kipling* was continuously opening fire on aircraft using RDF and sound bearings. The stragglers were left to fend for themselves as was *Amiens*, another ship hit by a bomb. A Dornier flying boat was sighted towards morning and damaged by AA fire after

this the convoy was left in peace. *Kipling*'s captain, Commander St Clair Ford, believed that barrage balloons would have been an excellent deterrent to such low-level attacks and recommended that all merchant ships carry them.

THE TRANSFER OF THE 5TH FLOTILLA TO THE MEDITERRANEAN

After the fall of Greece the 5th Flotilla was allocated to reinforce the Mediterranean Fleet as a temporary replacement for the 14th Flotilla as the Malta Striking Force against the Tripoli convoys. At the time the operational strength of the flotilla was six ships, *Kelly, Kipling, Kelvin, Kashmir, Jackal* and *Jersey. Kashmir* was already at Gibraltar when the other five ships left Plymouth on 21 April. To replace the 5th as Channel Striking Force, the 4th Flotilla of 'Tribals' was allocated from the Home Fleet. Arriving at Gibraltar on the 24th, the flotilla refuelled and then feinted eastwards before sailing through the Straits to Malta, together with the minelayer *Abdiel* and the cruiser *Dido,* where they arrived on the 28th.

THE 'NS' IN HOME WATERS

Napier next left Scapa on 15 January where she embarked the Prime Minister, Lady Churchill, Harry Hopkins and Lord and Lady Halifax. Lord Halifax was due to head out to the USA on the battleship *King George V* and Winston Churchill was seeing him off. After a night on board the battleship he and Lady Churchill returned to Thurso on the 16th. *Nizam* had commissioned on 8 January and spent the next two weeks on working-up exercises in the Clyde. She

RIGHT: *Kashmir* photographed from *Kelvin* with *Kelly* behind. Like all ships of the flotilla she has been painted in overall AP507C for Mediterranean service. She is also equipped with a Type 286 but her Carley float complement does not seem to have been enhanced. This series of photographs was taken in March 1941.

(IMPERIAL WAR MUSEUM: A2917)

BELOW: *Jaguar* photographed from *Kelvin* before service with Force H. Note that she still has her external galley funnel. Also of interest is the aircraft recognition chart behind *Kelvin*'s 4in gun.

(IMPERIAL WAR MUSEUM: A880)

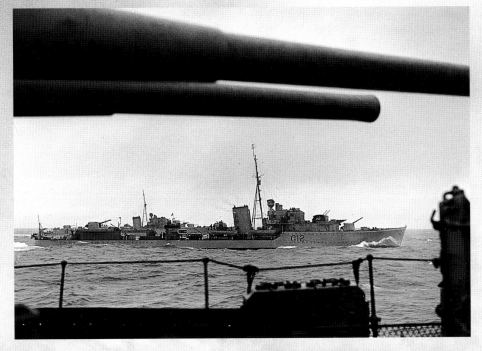

sailed to join *Napier* at Scapa on the 23rd but damaged her propeller on the wreck of the *Royal Oak*, delaying her working-up trials until the 29th. *Napier* had sailed the previous day to escort a tanker and then continued to Skaale Fjord to await the return of *King George V* from America, rendezvousing with the battleship and her escort on 3 February and staying with them for the next two days before being detached to Greenock, suffering minor damage in heavy weather. *Nizam* had arrived at Greenock and on the 9th she and *Napier* sailed to escort a large troop convoy of thirty-six ships, arriving back at Scapa on the 16th. *Nestor*, the fourth member of the class, commissioned on 3 February and worked-up at Greenock, arriving at Scapa on 1 March.

Napier next departed Scapa for Rosyth on 19 February to escort the battleship *Queen Elizabeth* and the cruiser *Dido* to Scapa. She and *Nizam* continued exercises before both sailing to the Clyde where they both underwent repairs for damage received during the past two months before departing for Gibraltar on 21 March. They would escort a troop convoy taking a roundabout route to evade German raiders and arrive on the 29th. After exercising with *Ark Royal* on the 30th, the two ships left Gibraltar for the Mediterranean Fleet taking the long route round the Cape of Africa, the first Kelly to do so. The move to the Mediterranean was the natural conclusion of the re-institution of the 7th Flotilla. It had always been intended that the Australian ships should serve in the Mediterranean and this had been confirmed on 9 December 1940. At the same time *Piorun* transferred to the Western Approaches Command, ceasing to be a member of the 7th Flotilla.

Nestor's first duty at Scapa was to escort *Hood* into the base on 2 March, almost colliding with the battlecruiser in the fog but returning to Scapa safely. She next sailed on the 26th to rendezvous with *Rodney* before escorting a convoy to Iceland. Returning to Scapa she continued working-up exercises and on 8 April sailed with *Prince of Wales* to avoid an air raid. Whilst the battleship returned to Scapa, *Nestor* sailed to the Clyde for a refit between 10 and 28 April and the installation of a new Type 285 radar set, returning to Scapa on 1 May.

8

The Mediterranean Theatre, 1940-41

TABLE 10:

Composition of forces for Operation MD2, 16 June 1940

Destroyer	Flotilla	Force
Nubian	14th	M
Mohawk	14th	M
Janus	14th	M
Juno	14th	M
Hyperion	2nd	H
Havock	2nd	H
Hereward	2nd	H
Hasty	2nd	H
Stuart	10th	S
Vampire	10th	S
Dainty	10th	S
Voyager	10th	S

AFTER THEIR ARRIVAL in the Mediterranean *Juno* and *Janus* remained in harbour at Alexandria from 24 May to 10 June, until Italy declared war commencing at one minute past midnight on 11 June. *Warspite*, *Malaya*, *Eagle*, *Nubian* (D14), *Janus*, *Juno*, *Hasty* (then part of the 14th Destroyer Flotilla) and the Australian 19th Division of *Stuart*, *Dainty*, *Vendetta* and *Vampire* sailed at 1.00am for an offensive sweep returning to harbour on the 14th. It was at this time that comprehensive instructions were issued for destroyers: one division was to be permanently on patrol, one division at 2½ hours' notice with the rest of the force on four hours' notice for 24kts and eight hours' for full speed. All ships were to ensure that their close-range AA weapons were manned at all times.

The next operation was Operation MD2, an anti submarine sweep north-west of the mouth of the Rosetta. Three destroyer forces, M, H and S, left Alexandria at 2.00pm on 16 June.

The 14th Flotilla were soon diverted to intercept a force of enemy ships sighted off the Syrian coast, sweeping along the coast before diverting to the Scarpanto Straits without sighting anything and returning to Alexandria on 19 June. *Jervis* had completed her repairs on 9 June and after a short working-up period sailed for the Mediterranean on the 27th. To ensure that she was not 'borrowed' by the local commander, the Flag Officer commanding the North Atlantic Station was ordered to sail her from Gibraltar to Malta at the earliest opportunity.[1] The rest of the 14th Flotilla were due to sail on a fleet operation on 22 June but, given the Fall of France, this was postponed.

Juno escorting a convoy in the Mediterranean. She is little changed from commissioning and has none of the improvements that characterised the ships of the 5th Flotilla. The photograph shows her between May and September 1940. (MARITIME PHOTO LIBRARY: 2023)

The outbreak of war had brought the convoy system to the Mediterranean and the first sailed on 27 June from the Dardenelles and Greek ports for Port Said and one transporting supplies from Alexandria to Malta. *Ramillies, Royal Sovereign* and *Eagle* sailed to provide cover for the Malta convoy (Operation 'MA3') escorted by the 3rd Destroyer Division and *Hasty, Janus* and *Juno*, but this had to be postponed after the 7th Cruiser Squadron had expended a large proportion of their ammunition in sinking the Italian destroyer *Espero*. The ships already at sea were diverted to provide cover for the Aegean convoy, AS1, and on 29 June the destroyers were detached to hunt submarines but without result. The convoy was heavily bombed, but suffered no losses and the War Diary noted that:

> 4. As a result of the continued bombing of the Aegean Convoy, Commander-in-Chief has represented to the Admiralty that he has no ships with sufficient AA armament suitable for convoy escort work and that he is forced to use 'Tribals' and 'J' class destroyers for this duty, thus wasting ammunition and wearing out their guns. He therefore requests the provision of escort vessels in the Eastern Mediterranean.[2]

The convoy arrived safely at Port Said on 2 July and the covering force sailed on to Alexandria. *Jervis*, which had arrived at Malta the same day, was bombed the next day whilst waiting for Operation 'MA5'. This was the sailing of two convoys, a slow and a fast one from Malta to Alexandria, carrying non-combatants and supplies for the fleet from Malta. MA5 finally got underway on 7 July. *Juno* and *Janus* were part of the screen for the battleships *Royal Sovereign* and *Malaya* in Force C. The Italian Fleet was also at sea, covering one of their own convoys but received orders not to engage the British fleet. However, on 9 July the British fleet, which was looking for the Italians, found them. The British were split into three forces, the 7th Cruiser Squadron ahead, followed by *Warspite* and then *Royal Sovereign* and *Malaya* 8 miles behind them. The battle of Punta Stilo has been recounted elsewhere so I will just concentrate on the role of the 'Js' in it. They were escorting *Malaya* with *Dainty* and *Decoy*, but the battleship was too slow to get in range of the Italian fleet. When the Italian ships retired behind a smokescreen, the destroyers were released from their screen in pursuit. Almost immediately they all split up, managing to join their respective flotillas which surprised Captain Mack, who later recommended that it be normal practice for destroyers of the same flotilla to screen together. *Juno*'s performance in this respect was considered particularly excellent. She was 4 months out of dock and 800 hours out of overhaul, yet was still able to maintain full power and keep up with the rest of the ships. Hits were claimed on one Italian destroyer and the British ships did come under fire from the Italian cruisers but without being damaged. They did not pursue into the smokescreen and with the Italian destroyers retiring returned to the *Warspite*, joining her at 6.45pm. With all the day's high-speed steaming, the destroyers needed to refuel and on the 10th *Stuart, Dainty, Defender, Hyperion, Hostile, Hasty, Ilex* and *Juno* were detached to Malta. Once they had refuelled, *Hero, Hereward, Decoy, Vampire* and *Voyager* arrived, followed by *Royal Sovereign, Nubian, Mohawk* and *Janus*. The convoys sailed at the same time with *Jervis* as part of the escort to the fast convoy MF1. *Warspite* had sailed ahead with an escort of *Nubian, Mohawk, Juno* and *Vampire* and on the way back was attacked five times by Italian bombers. The rest of the fleet was also bombed but MF1 escaped unmolested arriving at Alexandria on 13 July. The 1st Battle Squadron including *Janus* as part of the screen arrived on the same day but sailed almost immediately to provide cover for the slow convoy MS1, which reached Alexandria on the 15th.

Captain Mack transferred to *Jervis* which became the 14th Flotilla's leader and sailed with the squadron as part of the fleet screen on 19th July to support the Australian cruiser *Sydney* after her successful action with *Bartolomeo Colleoni* and if possible intercept the other Italian cruiser involved, which had however escaped so the fleet returned to Alexandria the next day, with *Jervis* being detached to search for one *Warspite*'s spotter planes which had had to ditch. It was around this time that the destroyer readiness instructions were also modified so that one sub-division (two ships) were to be on permanent notice for one hours'

Jervis newly painted as leader of the 14th Flotilla. She is not fitted with a 4in gun in this photograph though some sources say that she did have one for her passage from the United Kingdom. (COURTESY OF JOHN ROBERTS)

---

[1] Destroyers straying into a different operational command were frequently retained by that command for as long as possible. This would later happen to *Jaguar*. This instruction was a hands-off order.
[2] ADM 199/386 Mediterranean War Diary 1 July 1940.

steaming. On 27 July, the fleet sailed again to cover the southward passage of Convoy AS2. *Jervis* and *Juno* sailed as part of the screen and on putting to sea were heavily attacked by Italian bombers with *Jervis* being bombed by four aircraft. The convoy was sighted on 28 July and the fleet assumed an escort formation. The next day *Warspite* sailed ahead and was met by *Janus* and *Hostile* and escorted into Alexandria. The convoy and the rest of the fleet arrived on the 30th.

On 31 July, the 14th Flotilla was at sea again as part of Operation MA9 which had two purposes; to provide a diversion for Operation 'Hurry'[3] by Force H and to exercise contraband control in the Gulf of Athens. *Juno* sailed with Force A for the Gulf of Naples and *Jervis* sailed with Force B for gunnery exercises followed by a sweep to the west of Gavdo Island. Force B returned to Alexandria on 1 August whilst Force A continued their operations until the next day. On 3 August *Jervis* sailed with *Juno* and *Janus* for a shoot at a battle practice target before sailing the next day with *Liverpool*, *Gloucester* and *Hostile* to cover shipping movements in the Aegean and maintain pressure on the Italians. This operation included the escort of a very important convoy of Danube barges from Athens to Alexandria with *Jervis* and *Hostile* forming the close escort. The convoy was sighted on 7 August by a Sunderland which then directed *Jervis* and *Hostile* to it. Six Italian aircraft were seen bombing the town of Hieraptra and *Jervis* turned towards them and opened fire. They had already found two of the barges, *King George* and *Lord Byron* and located the other two *Princess Elizabeth* and *Scotland* in Hieraptra harbour. All were undamaged and after forming up the convoy set off at 4.10pm for Alexandria. At 5.30pm two groups of Italian aircraft attacked unsuccessfully, one aircraft being damaged by *Jervis*'s pom-pom fire. *Lord Byron* broke down on the 8th and after repairs was only able to make 4kts. *Liverpool* and *Gloucester* provided distant cover and carried out dazzle experiments at the same time. The next day the convoy had 'a rather startling encounter with *Eagle*'s screen'.[4] The convoy arrived at Alexandria on 10 August at the same time as a local convoy from Port Said. This had also been bombed but the escort of *Hasty* and *Janus* had fought off the attackers successfully with *Janus* damaging one of her assailants. Captain Mack then led as many destroyers from the 2nd, 10th and 14th Flotillas as he could find out for high-speed target practice.

FURTHER OPERATIONS

The high tempo of operations continued. On 15 August, *Juno*,

Ilex, *Hero* and *Hyperion* sailed from Alexandria to carry out an anti-submarine patrol followed by a TSDS sweep off Sollum Bay during the night before rendezvousing with the fleet for Operation 'MB2', the bombardment of Bardia. During this operation *Juno* managed to lose her starboard paravane.

On joining the fleet, the destroyers were split between the two fleet forces, with *Juno* and *Hero* joining Force B as part of the screen. From the destroyers' point of view this was another uneventful screening operation and the ships arrived back at Alexandria on 17 August. Operation 'MD7' was next, another offensive sweep by cruisers whilst destroyers escorted shipping in the Aegean. Force B, consisting of *Orion*, *Liverpool*, *Jervis* and *Janus*, sailed on 21 August and were immediately located by Italian aircraft. *Juno* and *Ilex* sailed on 22 August to join *Loch Melfort* in an anti-submarine hunt but as the contact was in the vicinity of a minefield it was considered to be a mine and they returned to harbour. Meanwhile, *Janus* and *Jervis* continued their convoy escort duties but on 23 August *Janus* was ordered to leave the convoy and proceed with all despatch to Alexandria to prepare for Operation 'HATS'. *Jervis* was to continue with the convoy until it reached Alexandria.

Juno left Alexandria with the 10th Flotilla to provide cover for Operation 'MB1', the bombardment of Bardia Harbour by the gunboat *Ladybird*, by bombarding the Italian seaplane base at Bomba and Jez-el-Marakab. The force passed *Jervis* and *Janus* on the way in and at 7.45pm detached *Waterhen* to escort *Ladybird*. *Juno* and *Ilex* found that they could not make their echo-sounding recordings agree but a marked path of electric lights was sighted shortly before 1.00am. As these could only be the seaplane base the ships assumed bombardment positions and opened fire at 1.19am ceasing 4 minutes later after each ship had fired twenty-four HE shells. The ships raced out of the area at 25kts, being rejoined by *Waterhen* as they retired. The return to Alexandria on the 24th and a rendezvous with *Sydney* was uneventful.

Operation 'HATS' was a complex affair, in which a supply convoy sailed for Malta at the same time as reinforcements for the Mediterranean Fleet and twelve Hurricanes for Malta were arriving from Gibraltar, coupled with a bombardment. *Janus* sailed to Malta and then to Gibraltar with *Nubian*, *Mohawk* and *Hero* to provide an escort for the incoming forces. The convoy for Malta sailed on 29 August escorted by *Jervis*, *Juno*, *Diamond* and *Dainty* and the next day the fleet left Malta in support. At 12.45pm the convoy was 6 miles from Elephansi Island when several aircraft were sighted. These concentrated on the SS *Cornwall*, hitting her with three bombs. Ten minutes after this attack the planes reappeared but were driven off by *Juno*'s gunfire. *Cornwall*'s steering had been disabled and both her AA guns were out

[3] The flying-off of Hurricanes for Malta from *Argus*.
[4] Report of Proceedings Captain Philip Mack.

of action. A little later the fire resulting from the attack reached No 5 hold causing her magazine to explode, but the fire was brought under control and *Cornwall* was able to proceed at 9½kts. Even so, it was decided to send the rest of the convoy ahead with *Dainty* and *Diamond* whilst *Jervis* and *Juno* escorted the damaged ship. *Calcutta* and *Coventry* were also detached from the reinforcement fleet to provide extra AA cover. They all arrived in Malta on 2 September, one day behind the rest of the convoy.

Janus had sailed with the reinforcement force on 29 August and rendezvoused with the fleet south of Sicily, arriving at Malta on 2 September to refuel and unload several sacks of mail for the garrison before returning. *Jervis* and *Juno* left shortly after with four other destroyers to provide the escort for Operation 'MB3', a dawn air attack on Maritza and Kalatho airfields in the Dodecanese. The rest of the fleet then set course for Alexandria with the bombardment force following them once the attacks had been completed, all ships arriving on 5 September. Five days later *Juno* and *Janus* sailed to Port Said to escort Convoy AN3 to Athens. Setting off on the 11th, the convoy could only manage 6kts, delaying its rendezvous with the AA cruiser *Calcutta* by a day until the 13th. They were attacked by aircraft on the 13th and 15th with *Juno* driving off a torpedo attack on the former date but with no casualties or damage to any of the ships. On the 15th she dropped ten depth charges on an asdic contact which was probably not a submarine. The escort left the convoy as it entered Piraeus and then sailed through the Kaso Strait for a sweep of the Dardenelles and the Gulf of Salonika returning to Alexandria on 16 September.

Juno and *Janus* sailed the next day to join *Ladybird* at Mersah Matruh. The Italian army had finally begun its offensive in the Western Desert and as a result Royal Navy ships were required to bombard the forces advancing along the coast. After obtaining the latest information, they sailed to cover *Ladybird* and to bombard the Sollum area. Both destroyers bombarded enemy concentrations in the Barrini area and then sailed for Buq Buq shooting at anything that looked interesting on the way. This duty was interrupted as they both ordered to go to the assistance of the heavy cruiser *Kent* which had been torpedoed by Italian SM79 bombers during a bombardment of Bardia with *Jervis*. *Jervis* had the cruiser in tow when *Juno* and *Janus* arrived to help, and they reached Alexandria on 19 September.

On the 21st they were back on bombardment duty, *Jervis*, *Janus*, *Juno* and *Mohawk* arriving at Mersah Matruh for instructions before sailing to bombard Barani, attacking the aerodrome and motor transport concentrations in a very successful shoot before returning to Alexandria. *Juno* joined *Hyperion*, *Hereward* and *Mohawk* for another bombardment on 24 September. This one must have hit something significant as the fires it caused were still visible from the ships two hours after they retired. On her return, *Juno* got a few days rest as she and her flotilla mates were allocated to the next big convoy to Malta, Operation 'MB5' carrying troops and RAF personnel for Malta. As part of the operation Convoy AN4 also sailed with its own covering force which would join the fleet once they had finished their escort duty. The whole force sailed late on 28 September and then split up into their various units. *Jervis* was detached to investigate a submarine contact early on the 29th but found nothing. She, with *Janus* and *Juno,* was part of the screen for the main fleet (Force A) as they headed for Malta and settled down to endure the inevitable air attacks. The Italian fleet was at sea but made no attempt to intervene and the convoy successfully arrived at Malta. The fleet then turned for home and arrived on 2 October with *Havock* sinking an Italian submarine shortly after she rejoined the fleet from AN4.

Having augmented the garrison of Malta, the British now needed to re-supply the island and so the fleet sailed on 8 October for Operation 'MB6' covering Convoy MF3. *Jervis, Juno* and *Janus* were part of the fleet screen. *Jervis, Juno* and *Ilex* searched ahead of the formation on the 10th, following up the report of a submarine but nothing was located and the passage to Malta was uneventful. On the way back things were a bit more lively with several air attacks. *Ajax, Jervis* and *Janus* were detached from the fleet to cover Convoys AS4 and MF4 from the Gulf of Athens and *Nubian, Juno* and the 10th Flotilla were sent ahead to Alexandria to refuel. The convoys were bombed on the 14th but the high-level attacks were so ineffective that no evasive action was necessary. However, on the same day *Liverpool* was torpedoed by Italian SM79 aircraft and her bows blown off. The destroyers in Alexandria were ordered to join *Liverpool* as soon as possible and on the 15th *Mohawk* was detached to take over AS4 from *Jervis. Liverpool* and her escorting destroyers arrived safely at Alexandria on 16 October but she needed extensive repairs.

Convoy operations continued and if possible were combined with other activities. For example, 'MAQ2' was combined with an attack on Maltezana Airfield by Swordfish from *Eagle.* Departing from Alexandria on 25 October and splitting into several forces, each section of the fleet pursued a different objective. *Janus* stayed with the main fleet whilst *Juno* and *Jervis* sailed with *Orion* and *Sydney* for a patrol of the Kaso Strait and Duro Channel, stopping and examining several ships for contraband, *Jervis* even boarding one Greek steamer before allowing it to proceed. At nightfall the force split up and *Jervis* and *Sydney* patrolled Cape St Mikolo in Khios, Cape Sigri in Mityhens and Cape Kara Burun. *Orion* and *Juno* patrolled between Estratios Island, Limnos Island and the Muselim Channel, stopping two ships. The two groups rejoined the next morning and spent the rest of the day stopping more ships before locating and escorting the convoy. Another force joined them with the AA cruiser *Calcutta* but she does not seem to have been needed as no air attacks were recorded. The attack on Maltezana was also successful with eight Swordfish involved achieving surprise.

The various units all arrived back in Alexandria on 28 October to the news that Italy had declared war on Greece that day and as a result, the Greek ports were now open to the Royal Navy. Of particular interest was the island of Crete. Its strategic position in the centre of the eastern Mediterranean made it an ideal refuelling base and on 29 October the fleet sailed to establish facilities in Suda Bay. The first ships to take advantage of this were *Juno* and *Defender* returning from a sweep north-westwards with the fleet on 31 October. On 6 November the Royal Navy initiated its most complex and ambitious operation yet, Operation 'MB8'. This involved all operational ships and initially started out with the fleet escorting Convoy MW3 to Malta with three ships to be detached for Suda Bay. *Warspite, Illustrious, Malaya* and *Valiant* screened by the 2nd Destroyer Flotilla sailed to carry out the famous air attack on the Italian fleet at Taranto (Operation 'Judgement') whilst a separate force led by *Orion* carried out a raid on shipping in the Straits of Otranto. At the same time Force H was carrying out Operation 'Coat' from Gibraltar which involved escorting reinforcements for the fleet to Malta. These reinforcements, consisting of the battleship *Barham,* the cruisers *Berwick* and *Glasgow* and the destroyers *Greyhound, Gallant* and *Griffin* first called at Malta to unload troops for the island and then joined the fleet for 'Judgement'. The 14th Destroyer Flotilla sailed with the battleship *Ramillies* which after re-fuelling at Malta was to escort Convoy ME3 of four empty ships back to Alexandria. As a final element, cover was provided for Convoy AN6 in the early stages of the operation. One Swordfish from *Illustrious* crashed on 9 November, its crew being rescued by *Juno.* Two of the ships from the flotilla, *Mohawk* and *Nubian,* did join the raid into the Straits of Otranto which successfully sank an Italian convoy but *Jervis, Janus* and *Juno* carried out escort duties throughout the return to Alexandria on 13 November.

THE GREEK CONVOYS AND OPERATION 'COLLAR'

Convoy AN7 was a change from the normal supply operation as for the first time the ships involved transported troops for Greece. As a result it had a large escort, including the 1st Battle Squadron and the 3rd Cruiser Squadron. *Jervis* led the destroyer escort with the new members of the 14th Flotilla, the operation being codenamed 'Barbarity'. It was also the first time the fleet used Suda Bay as a staging post. The convoy reached its destination without challenge and the fleet returned to Alexandria on 19 November. The next operation would not be so fortunate. This was Operation 'MB9', another of those complex operations so liked by the Mediterranean Fleet. As usual there were several convoys to cover, ME4 and MW4 to and from Malta, Operation 'Collar', the transportation of RAF personnel to Egypt in *Manchester* and *Southampton* and the movement of *Ramillies* and *Berwick* out of the Mediterranean via Malta. There was also a raid on Port Laki by aircraft from *Illustrious*. In this operation, *Jervis*, *Juno* and *Janus* were part of Force A, the main battle fleet, and left Alexandria on 25 November. *Illustrious*, covered by *Gloucester*, *Glasgow*, *Janus*, *Juno*, *Nubian* and *Mohawk* detached from the fleet on the 26th. This first stage of the operation, the attack on Port Laki, went well but caused little damage.

Reunited, the fleet sailed through the Kithera Channel to cover Convoy ME4 which was nearing Alexandria, all ships of the convoy reaching port unharmed. They then sailed on to rendezvous with the 'Collar' convoy. Convoy MW4 had arrived safely in at Malta covered by the slower ships of the fleet which then sailed to cover the 'Collar' convoy. The convoy had run into the Italian fleet and had an interesting time which will be covered in a later section on *Jaguar*'s service with Force H. After meeting the 'Collar' ships, the fleet escorted them to Alexandria without incident.

It had been anticipated that further 'Js' would be sent to the Mediterranean and in fact *Javelin* was expected shortly. However, her torpedoing effectively ended that hope for over a year and the rest of the class were retained at Plymouth to combat German destroyers. Bombardments in support of the army continued with fleet units being enlisted at times. On 10 December, *Barham*, *Valiant* and *Coventry* covered by various destroyers including *Juno* sailed to bombard Sollum. *Jervis*, *Nubian*, *Janus* and *Hereward* also sailed and bombarded the Sollum area before returning to Alexandria on the 11th. On the way *Janus* was detached to Mersah Matruh to refuel the gunboats of the inshore squadron, an unusual task for a destroyer. She then embarked 200 prisoners of war for the trip back to Alexandria. *Juno* arrived back with even more, carrying 450.

Whilst involved in these duties, the cruiser *Coventry* was torpedoed by the Italian submarine *Neghelli* on 13 December. *Jervis*, *Janus* and *Hereward* were ordered to escort her back to Alexandria arriving on the 14th. The destroyers then were required to put to sea in support of Operations 'MC2' and 'MC3'. Operation 'MC2' was a resupply operation to Malta consisting of four convoys (MW5A and B and ME5A and B) coupled with a small raid in the Dodecanese and the passing of the battleship *Malaya* to Force H at Gibraltar. Operation 'MC3' was another raid on the Straits of Otranto and the bombardment of the port of Valona (now Vlore) in Albania, the main supply port for the Italian army. Cover was also provided for Convoy AN10. The fleet sailed on 16 December with *Jervis*, *Juno* and *Janus* attached to Force A.[5] At Suda Bay the destroyers refuelled and Force A

sailed separately with the 14th Flotilla escorting *Illustrious* and *Valiant* on a quick raid on Rhodes. They rejoined *Warspite* and on the 18th the 7th Cruiser Squadron with *Jervis*, *Juno* and *Mohawk* were detached for the sweep of the Straits but found nothing. The rest of the force prepared for the bombardment which was delayed by the weather but was successful, causing serious damage to the airfield. Rejoined by the 7th Cruiser Squadron the fleet then sailed for Malta arriving on the 20th and *Warspite* entered Grand Harbour escorted by *Jervis*, *Juno* and *Janus*.

After a short stay the three 'Js' – now designated Force D – left Malta on the 21st to carry out a sweep ahead of the incoming Convoy MG1 and *Malaya* to clear the area of E-boats or U-boats. On 22 December the *Hyperion* struck a mine and *Jervis*, *Juno* and *Janus* were ordered to stand by.[6] They found that *Ilex* had already taken her in tow but this had parted. As it was impossible to tow the badly-damaged *Hyperion* more than 10kts, Captain Mack decided to sink her, *Janus* firing one torpedo which broke her in half. *Jervis*, *Janus* and *Juno* then sailed to rejoin Force A, rendezvousing at 11.30am whilst *Ilex* took *Hyperion*'s survivors to Malta.

Force A returned to Alexandria on 24 December. The last operation of 1940 was an uneventful anti-submarine sweep as far as Tobruk on 29-30 December. Destroyers would conduct many sweeps like this but due to poor asdic conditions would rarely locate submarines.

JANUARY 1941

Early on 2 January 1941 *Juno*, *Greyhound*, *Griffin* and *Ilex* sailed as escort to *Illustrious* which was to embark aircraft for Operation 'MC5', a major bombardment operation in support of the army assault on Bardia. The main fleet sailed in the afternoon with *Janus* as part of the escort. As they approached Bardia on the 3rd the fleet reduced speed to 8kts and *Janus*, *Juno*, *Greyhound*, *Griffin* and *Ilex* ranged ahead and deployed their TSDS gear.[7] The fleet then accelerated and commenced the bombardment at 8.10am with the destroyers engaging targets of opportunity. Twenty minutes later the fleet reversed course with the TSDS screen turning to starboard in succession and commenced another run. After this devastating show of firepower the fleet set course for

---

[5] Force A consisted of, *Warspite*, *Illustrious*, *Valiant*, *Gloucester*, *York*, *Jervis*, *Janus*, *Juno*, *Mohawk*, *Greyhound*, *Dainty*, *Hyperion*, *Ilex*, *Hero*, *Hasty* and *Hereward*.
[6] Several sources state that *Hyperion* was torpedoed by the Italian submarine *Serpente* but she seems to have fired her torpedoes at a different ship earlier and was not near *Hyperion* when the explosion happened. See in particular, Lenton and Colledge, *Warships of World War II*, Whitley, *Destroyers of World War II* and Brown, *Warship Losses of World War Two*. Cunningham in *A Sailors Odyssey* states that she was mined as do Greene and Massignani, *The Naval War in the Mediterranean 1940-1943*.
[7] TSDS paravanes could not be deployed at speeds over 8kts but could be used at speeds of up to 25kts.

Alexandria arriving on 4 January. Bardia fell the next day.

The next operation commenced on 6 January and was another massive fleet affair designated Operation 'MC4' and 'MC6'.[8] Six convoys were to be escorted (MW5½, ME5½, ME6, 'Excess', AN12 and AS10). It started with *Gloucester*, *Southampton*, *Ilex* and *Janus* (Force B) sailing at 1.00pm with troops for Malta. A day later Force A sailed with *Jervis*. They arrived at Suda Bay on the 8th and were joined by Forces C and D which had been escorting convoys in the Aegean. At the same time Force H left Gibraltar with the 'Excess' convoy. Force B had arrived at Malta on the 8th and *Janus* was docked for repairs to her asdic dome. The rest of the force refuelled and sailed to meet the 'Excess' convoy. *Janus* joined the fleet on the 10th which had arrived at Malta with MW5½. As that convoy entered the harbour, Convoy MW6 left for Alexandria and Convoy ME5½ sailed to join the 'Excess' convoy. It was on the 10th that the fleet suffered its first losses. The destroyer *Gallant* hit a mine and had to be towed to Malta where she would remain for the rest of the war. *Illustrious* was attacked and badly damaged by aircraft from *X Fliegerkorps*, a German anti-shipping unit which had recently arrived in the Mediterranean to shore up the crumbling Italian efforts.

Jaguar, which had stayed with the 'Excess' convoy and then joined the fleet screen, was ordered to escort *Illustrious* as she attempted to reach Malta with *Hasty*. After a great struggle she was finally brought into harbour. The next day *Southampton* was hit by at least two bombs and brought to a standstill. *Orion*, *Perth Jervis* and *Janus* were detached to stand by her but it was clear that she could not be saved and so was scuttled. The two destroyers then rejoined the fleet and sailed for Alexandria. *Juno* and *Nubian*, which were part of the screen, reported being short on fuel and were detached

Juno at Alexandria in January 1941. This is likely to be her first camouflage scheme which was simplified later by the painting out of the false bow wave. Note that even at this stage her No 3 mount is still trained forward. The bows of a 'Tribal' are visible in front of her and *Jaguar* is moored to the left. (MUSÉE NATIONAL DE LA MARINE: 6632)

to cover the 'Excess' convoy which arrived safely at Piraeus. The losses suffered by Cunningham forced him to suspend the shipping strikes he had planned but amazingly not one of the merchant vessels had been hit. The freighter *Essex* was later hit by a bomb in Malta harbour but did not sink. On 14 January *Orion* sailed with *Bonaventure* and *Jaguar* to reduce the concentration of ships in the harbour. Half-an-hour after leaving port *Jaguar* reported damage to No 8 fuel tank which would prevent her from using 120 tons of oil unless she flooded the damaged tank to compensate. Permission to do this was granted but it resulted in the destroyer leaving a highly visible track all the way back to Alexandria. They were met by the 1st Battle Squadron (*Barham*, *Eagle*, *Ajax*, *Stuart*, *Dainty*, *Juno*, *Griffin* and *Hasty*) at Suda Bay and escorted to Alexandria arriving on the 16th. After escorting the Piraeus portion of 'Excess', *Juno*, *Hasty* and *Ilex* arrived at Suda Bay on 13 January to join *Barham* for the air strike element of Operation 'MC6'. This was cancelled due to bad weather but *Juno* had been allocated to Operation 'Blunt', a raid on Kaso Island by commandos. The ships intended for this operation had included *Ilex*, *Hereward*, *Mohawk* and the cruiser *York*. The four destroyers were ordered back to Alexandria in preparation for Operation 'MBD2', the extraction of *Illustrious* from Malta. *Jervis* was due to cover Operation 'IS1', a bombardment of enemy positions near Mersa-el-Sahal by the inshore squadron but this was also cancelled due to the weather and the ships which had sailed on 18 January were recalled. *Janus* sailed to escort Convoy AS12 on the 18th and stood by the torpedoed *Clan Cumming*, ensuring that she arrived in Piraeus safely.

---

[8] Several sources refer to this operation as 'Operation Excess' or the 'Excess Convoy'. These titles only refer to the military transport aspect of what was a complex naval operation.

In contrast to earlier operations, 'MBD2' was a much simpler affair. A small group of destroyers would dash into Malta and pick up *Illustrious* then sail back to Alexandria, rendezvousing with a cruiser squadron on the way back. The whole operation would be covered by a battle squadron. Should *Illustrious* not be ready, the destroyers would escort several Military Supply vessels out of Malta. *Illustrious* was ready and the destroyers *Jervis*, *Janus*, *Juno* and *Greyhound* made their high-speed dash on 20 January, refuelling at Suda Bay on the 21st and arriving at Malta the next day. They left the island with *Illustrious* on the 23rd and arrived at safely Alexandria on the 25th, only the cruiser squadron coming under air attack. At the same time Cunningham signalled Force H that he intended to hold onto *Jaguar* temporarily. Operation 'MBD2' would have been the ideal opportunity to return her to Force H but she was in need of repairs for several defects and Malta was a dangerous place for a ship to be. The Mediterranean Fleet was short of destroyers and no doubt he felt the opportunity was too good to miss. *Jaguar* would remain in the Mediterranean until sunk and was allocated to the 14th Flotilla with the rest of the 'Js'. Her first duty was escorting the netlayer *Protector* to Suda Bay with *Dainty*. She was detached to patrol Kithera on 26 January before escorting *Protector* part of the way to Tobruk. On the same day Cunningham sent a further signal to the Admiralty regretting retaining *Jaguar* but giving the excuse that destroyers attempting to transit the narrows west of Sicily needed bow protection against mines.[9] *Jaguar* and *Dainty* then joined up with *Calcutta* and swept the Kaso Strait ahead of Convoy AN14 on the night of 30/31 January.

FEBRUARY AND MARCH

The aircraft carrier *Formidable* was due to join the Mediterranean Fleet within the month and would be met at Aden by two of the fleet destroyers and escorted up the Red Sea. These were to have been *Greyhound* and *Griffin* but *Greyhound* had collided with *Warspite* on 31 January and was unavailable. *Juno* was allocated as a replacement and so when the fleet sailed for Operation 'MC7' on 1 February she peeled off from the screen for Port Said. After waiting two days with *Griffin* for the Suez Canal to clear, the two ships sailed for Aden, meeting *Formidable* on 5 February. For the next two weeks *Juno* and *Griffin* escorted *Formidable* as she carried out air operations in the Red Sea, finally sailing for Suez on 20 February. However, on arrival at the canal the ships had to wait for it to be cleared of mines and

were only able to sail for Port Said on 9 March.

Back in the Mediterranean, Operation 'MC7' went ahead as planned despite being delayed slightly by the repairs to *Warspite*'s bulges after the collision with *Greyhound*. This was intended to provide a diversion for two Force H operations ('Pickett' and 'Result'), cover two convoys and bring the destroyer *Decoy* to join the Mediterranean Fleet. The destroyer *Defender* would also sail for Malta for a refit. *Juno* was in the Red Sea but *Jervis* and *Janus* remained with the fleet as part of the screen. On 2 February, *Perth*, *Ajax* and *Jaguar* joined the fleet from the Aegean on completion of their screening operation. *Wryneck* then left the fleet screen to join the inshore squadron, her place being taken by *Jaguar*. This operation passed off without incident though Operation 'Result' had to be abandoned due to bad weather and 'Pickett'[10] failed. All ships had returned to Alexandria by 4 February.

It was decided to take advantage of the size of the 'J' class and use them for offensive duties in the Aegean in conjunction with the cruiser *York* and 815 Squadron FAA. *Jervis*, *Janus*, *Jaguar* and *Mohawk* arrived at Suda Bay on 7 February. They had four main roles which were, in descending order of importance:

(a) to patrol Kithera Strait at intervals;
(b) night sweeps into the Dodecanese and round Rhodes:
(c) to cover convoys in the Aegean; and
(d) to act as an anti-submarine striking force.

From 8 to 11 February the destroyers of the 14th Flotilla patrolled the various straits and channels around Rhodes and Kithera, but without result. After a few days the sweeps resumed on the 15th but were cut short when *Jervis*, *Mohawk* and *Jaguar* were ordered to return to Alexandria on the 17th to take part in Operation 'MC8'. *Janus* returned to Suda Bay with *York* and *Bonaventure* but was also ordered to Alexandria. 'MC8' was another Malta re-supply operation transporting two battalions of infantry and urgently-needed supplies to the island. *Jaguar* was allocated to screen *Eagle* which sailed separately to carry out exercises and joined *Jervis* and *Janus* with the fleet as it left Alexandria at 4.30pm, the operation being completed successfully, although bad weather prevented a planned air attack on Rhodes and the fleet returned to Alexandria on 23 February.

Jaguar was then detailed to take part in Operation 'Abstention', the attempted capture of the island of Castelorizzo, which failed due to unexpectedly strong Italian resistance. *Decoy*, *Hasty* and *Hero* sailed on 27 Febru-

---

[9] This is an interesting excuse given that less than three months later the whole of the 5th Flotilla would sail through those waters and they of course also lacked bow protection.

[10] This was an attempt by Swordfish to torpedo the dam at Lake Tirso in Sardinia.

ary to take off the troops whilst *Jaguar* and *Bonaventure* provided the escort. After a failed attempt to torpedo a ship in the harbour, *Jaguar* was then attacked by the Italian destroyer *Francesco Crispi* which fired two torpedoes at her. These narrowly missed and *Jaguar* opened fire on the Italian ship scoring two hits. Unfortunately the searchlight jammed on which delayed the firing of starshell and allowed the enemy ship to escape. *Jaguar* could not regain contact and then sailed southwards to rejoin the rest of the British force. In the meantime, *Ajax* and *Nubian* had arrived to take charge of the withdrawal and *Jaguar* was ordered to join them. Together with *Hasty* and *Nubian*, *Jaguar* carried out a sweep between Castelorizzo and Rhodes to intercept any Italian reinforcements for the island. Nothing was found and the destroyers returned to Alexandria arriving at 6.00pm on 1 March.

March began with the 'Lustre' convoys to Greece transporting the army from the Western Desert. These convoys, sailing every 3 days, were covered by a battleship or cruiser force. *Jervis* joined the first of these operations with *Jaguar* and *Janus* on 6 March. After refuelling and carrying out gunnery exercises they sailed to support the cruisers on 8

March. At about the same time, *Formidable* was finally able to transit the Suez Canal and arrived at Alexandria on 10 March. *Juno* and *Griffin* then escorted *Illustrious* to Port Said for her voyage to America for repairs before returning to Alexandria on the 11th. *Jaguar* was assigned to convoy duty starting with Convoy GA2 from Piraeus to Alexandria on 9 March. In the meantime *Jervis* and *Janus* continued to provide cover for Force A (the battleship force) off Crete before finally returning to Alexandria on 18 March. This was to allow time to prepare for the next Malta resupply operation, 'MC9'. *Jervis*, *Juno*, *Janus* and *Jaguar* all sailed as part of Force A on 20 March with the battlefleet covering Force B and the convoy. On the 21st an enemy reconnaissance aircraft was shot down by fighters from *Formidable* but the convoy reached Malta safely. The fleet turned back on 22 March and arrived at Alexandria on the 24th. *Jaguar* and *Juno* sailed the next day with *Defender* to escort Convoy AG8 to Piraeus. They joined the AA cruiser *Carlisle* but she suffered engine defects and had to detach to Suda Bay escorted by *Jaguar*, which then sailed for Piraeus but sighted a torpedo track which passed astern of her. No hydrophone or asdic contact had been made but as her dome was dam-

Janus later in 1941 coming alongside *Valiant*. She is wearing a simplified version of her earlier scheme created by painting out the white lines. Of interest is the obvious wear and tear around the bows and the fact that her configuration has not changed significantly since she arrived in the Mediterranean. (NATIONAL MARITIME MUSEUM, LONDON: D1091)

aged this was unsurprising. *Jaguar* conducted a brief search but as she was unsure whether the torpedo had been fired by an E-boat or a submarine she did not linger and did not want to be late into Piraeus. *Juno* had had an uneventful convoy and was waiting for *Jaguar* when she arrived at 6.20am on the 28th. After *Jaguar* refuelled both ships went to 2 hours notice until midnight when they came to immediate notice. Designated Force D, they sailed for a patrol of Kithera Channel in the aftermath of the Battle of Matapan but were ordered to join the fleet as it returned to Alexandria. During the patrol *Juno* picked up the crew of Albacore 5A from *Formidable* which had been forced to ditch.

THE BATTLE OF MATAPAN

The Battle of Matapan was the result of German pressure upon the Italian Navy to attack British convoys to Greece with their surface fleet. Several books cover this action in detail so this account will concentrate on the role played by *Jervis* and *Janus* rather than an overview of the battle. *Jervis* and *Janus* sailed from Alexandria on 27 March as part of the fleet screen in response to a sighting report from a Sunderland flying boat. During the initial engagements the two destroyers stayed with the fleet but on receipt of the news that the Italian battleship *Vittorio Veneto* had been torpedoed *Jervis* together with *Janus*, *Nubian*, *Mohawk*, *Hereward*, *Hasty*, *Ilex* and *Hotspur* were detached to hunt her and make a night attack. Captain Mack in *Jervis* planned to pass up the starboard side of the battleship out of visual range and then turn to attack from ahead. But first he had to find the battleship and the estimate he had of her position was wrong, being based on a speed of 13kts rather than her actual speed of 19kts.

As the destroyer force steamed towards the Italian ships a signal from *Ajax* was intercepted which reported three ships on her radar. Mack plotted these and as they corresponded very closely to his own position assumed that they were his ships whereas they were in fact Admiral Cattaneo's cruiser squadron going to the assistance of the torpedoed *Pola*. Mack held his course, assuming that he was overhauling the *Vittorio Veneto* which was further ahead than anticipated. About this time and to avoid confusion in any forthcoming night action, Cunningham signalled that all ships not engaging the enemy were to retire north-eastwards. Mack assumed that this included his force and turned northeast at the same time signalling the Commander-in-Chief to confirm that he was correct. However, he was instructed to complete his attack first and so turned back to the west to locate the battleship which by this time was out of range and steaming in a different direction. At 12.30am Mack intercepted a signal that *Havock* was in touch with a stopped

Italian battleship (actually the cruiser *Pola*) and turned back to engage. Seeing gun flashes and starshell, the eight destroyers steered towards them and arrived at the scene of action at 2.00am. Mack signalled that only *Jervis* was to fire torpedoes to avoid the danger of hitting the other ships. The rear destroyers were ordered to pick up survivors whilst *Jervis* fired a salvo of five torpedoes at the stopped *Zara*. The cruiser blew up in spectacular fashion and sank very rapidly and the destroyers started to pick up her survivors. The rescue work ceased suddenly when a red and white signal was seen to the east. This was *Pola* which had been torpedoed by the Fleet Air Arm but had survived the night action unscathed. *Jervis* went alongside and took off the crew who still remained[11] and then fired a torpedo at the cruiser. This hit but only caused the ship to settle slowly and so another was fired by *Nubian* which had the desired effect.

The 14th and 2nd Flotillas then rejoined the fleet at 4.10am on the 30th and later they were joined by *Juno* and *Jaguar* from the Aegean. Matapan had been a significant victory for the Royal Navy and a disaster for the Italians. Three heavy cruisers had been sunk and *Vittorio Veneto* herself would be out of action for three months.

THE MALTA STRIKE FORCE AND THE CONVOY INTERCEPTION OF 16 APRIL

With the collapse of the Italian empire in Africa there was thought to be a danger that their naval forces would attack through the Suez Canal and on 3 April *Jaguar* and *Janus* were despatched from Alexandria to Port Said to counter any threat but nothing happened and the destroyers returned the same day. On the 4th, however, *Janus* sailed back to Port Said to cover part of Convoy AN25. The Alexandria part sailed on 5 April covered by *Jervis* and *Coventry* and was met the same day by *Janus* and the Port Said section, the whole convoy then heading for Piraeus. The convoy was uneventful but *Janus* and *Jervis* would be relieved by *Hero* and *Defender*.

Due partly to the success of the Italians in passing convoys to Libya, the pressure on the British forces there was quite severe. The arrival of the Afrika Korps under Rommel had created serious problems and it was felt that something needed to be done to interdict the convoys. The answer was to form a striking force operating out of Malta consisting of *Jervis*, *Janus*, *Nubian* and *Mohawk*. The latter two were escorting Convoy AG11 when they were ordered to Suda Bay to join their flotilla mates. After refuelling the four destroyers

[11] Several accounts (*eg* Pack and Connell) mention that the crew were drunk but have recently been contradicted by other sources. However, Mack's own Report of Proceedings written shortly after the battle states that 'many of them [the crew] were half drunk and the ship's upper deck was an indescribable mess of clothing, bottles, packets of cigarettes, etc'.

set off on 10 April covered by the cruisers *Ajax* and *Perth*.

On 11 April, as *Jervis* and her cohorts arrived at Malta, the other two 'Js' joined Operation 'MBD3', an offensive sweep by cruisers and destroyers along the Cyrenaican coast. The operation lasted for several days but nothing was seen and *Juno* and *Jaguar* returned to Alexandria with *Hasty* and *Perth* on the 14th just as *Kimberley* left for her first Mediterranean duty. The oiler *Pericles* had been damaged by an explosive motor boat attack on Suda Bay which had immobilised the *York*, and had broken in half. *Kimberley* was sent to help but by the time she arrived *Grimsby* had taken off the crew and all that was left for *Kimberley* to do was to sink the two halves. She was able to sink one but the other drifted into a minefield and sank of its own accord after hitting a mine. The Malta destroyers were initially unsuccessful, two sweeps on 11 and 12 April being aborted when the convoys they were supposed to intercept turned back.

Their first success came on 15 April, when following an aircraft report, the force led by Captain Mack in *Jervis* put to sea to intercept an Italian convoy consisting of four German ships (*Iserlhon*, *Aegina*, *Arta* and *Adana*) carrying troops and supplies and one Italian ship (*Sabaudia*) loaded with ammunition, escorted by three Italian destroyers, *Luca Tarigo*, *Lampo* and *Baleno*. Captain Mack arrived off Kerkenah Bay at about midnight and proceeded on the assumption that the convoy was actually slower than its estimated speed and sailed to the farthest interception point and then worked back. *Nubian* detected the convoy on her radar at around 1.58am and sighted it 2 minutes later. The British destroyers were in a perfect position to attack, the ships of the convoy being silhouetted against the moon whilst the they was hidden, approaching from behind the convoy in its blind spot.

Jervis was the first to open fire but her salvoes were initially over as she was the only ship not equipped with radar. *Janus* opened fire next on the destroyer *Baleno* using her Type 286 set for gunnery ranging.[12] These initial salvoes were devastating and destroyed the ship's bridge rendering her totally unmanageable. The crew managed to beach her but *Baleno* was a total loss. *Nubian* and *Mohawk* fired at any target visible but concentrated mainly on the merchant ships. The destroyer *Tarigo*, in charge of the convoy, turned back and attacked the British ships, passing through the line as she did so, but was instantly engaged by *Nubian* and *Jervis* and rapidly reduced to a sinking condition. Whilst this was going on *Janus* fired at a merchant ship and then

put a torpedo into the ammunition carrier *Sabaudia* which blew up in a spectacular explosion, showering debris onto *Jervis*. A 3000-ton freighter[13] attempted to ram *Jervis* but missed and was sunk by her guns. The other Italian destroyer, *Lampo*, had also suffered heavily and was shelled by *Janus*, *Nubian* and *Mohawk* together. She managed to fire her torpedoes at *Janus* but missed and had to beach herself. *Lampo* would later be salvaged by the Italians and finally sunk in April 1943 by air attack.

Tarigo, despite being severely damaged, managed to fire one then another torpedo. The first hit *Mohawk* on her starboard side and the second hit the port side as she was turning, disabling her. She beached on a sandbank and after taking off the crew the rest of the British force sank her with gunfire. The British did later bomb the wreck to destroy the radar set which the Italians had attempted to raise but found too heavy. Of the freighters, one managed to beach but was blown up by a party from the submarine *Upholder* which meant that, apart from *Lampo*, the convoy had been entirely destroyed. The loss of *Mohawk* was regrettable but the Admiralty felt that this was an acceptable price to pay for such a victory. The three surviving destroyers returned to Malta on 16 April.

Further Malta re-supply operations, 'MD2' and 'MD3', now commenced, which also included a bombardment of Tripoli. The transport *Breconshire* sailed with the fleet from Alexandria on 18 April. Also with the screen were *Juno* and *Jaguar* and *Kingston* and *Kimberley* on their first Mediterranean Fleet mission. Following what was now normal practice the battlefleet sailed through the Kaso Strait and then stopped off at Suda Bay the next day to allow the destroyers to refuel. Also on the 19th but after dark Convoy ME7 sailed from Malta escorted by *Jervis*, *Janus*, *Nubian* and *Diamond*. When the convoy was sighted by the fleet on the 20th, *Jervis* and *Janus* detached from it and joined the fleet screen for the bombardment of Tripoli. The fleet was now formed in two groups with *Formidable* and four destroyers as one and *Warspite*, *Barham* and *Valiant* the other, with the cruisers and the six Kellys as screen. The bombardment started with an attack by RAF and FAA aircraft followed by the battleships which opened fire using the submarine *Truant* as a datum point. Damage was thought to be greater than it was but even so was fairly significant. As the fleet retired they were joined by *Kandahar* at noon on 22 April. *Jervis* and *Janus* had already returned to Malta with *Juno* and *Jaguar* to continue as a striking force.

The fleet arrived back at Alexandria on 23 April and the next day Convoy AG14 consisting of six 12kt ships sailed,

---

[12] Some accounts state that the ship fired at by *Janus* was *Lampo* but she was able to play an active part in the battle whilst *Baleno* was rapidly disabled as a result of hits taken early in the battle. As *Nubian* and *Mohawk* concentrated mainly on the transports with their initial salvoes I have taken it that *Janus* attacked *Baleno*.

[13] This was probably the *Iserlhon* but due to the confused nature of the melee it is impossible to be sure.

Kimberley at Crete during the evacuation from Greece. The similarity to the scheme carried by Kandahar is obvious with the panel near the bow being the major difference. Kingston carried exactly the same scheme. Her funnel bands are red.

(IMPERIAL WAR MUSEUM: MH3888)

escorted by *Carlisle*, *Kandahar* and *Kingston*. Convoy AG15 which had an escort of *Auckland*, *Kimberley* and *Vampire* sailed a day later. The Malta strike force had sailed to intercept a convoy of three ships escorted by four destroyers. To make things more interesting this convoy also had a cruiser covering force. Near Lampedusa, *Jaguar* intercepted an aircraft signal which reported a vessel which a little later was sighted by *Juno*. This was a single-funnelled auxiliary, the *Egeo*, which was crippled by gunfire, *Jaguar* accidentally firing starshell. *Juno* was ordered to finish her with a torpedo which she did, hitting her amidships and the force raced off to locate the convoy. Unfortunately, the convoy had seen *Jaguar*'s starshell and reversed course and so the destroyers returned to Malta. The four ships were due to be replaced by the 5th Destroyer Flotilla which had been loaned to the Mediterranean Fleet. Captain Mountbatten would be bringing the *Kelly*, *Kipling*, *Kelvin*, *Kashmir*, *Jersey* and *Jackal* to Malta shortly and the Admiralty suggested on 25 April that Mack's ships stay in Malta to operate with them against the Tripoli convoys. This was rejected by Cunningham who wanted as many light forces as he could muster in Greek waters. Also due to arrive at Alexandria soon were the first two members of the reconstituted 7th Flotilla under Captain Arliss. The ships, *Napier* and *Nizam*[14] had taken the long route round the Cape and carried LL gear for the fleet.

OPERATION 'DEMON'

The war in Greece was not going well for the Allies. The initial defeat of the Italians had caused the Germans to invade and in a highly-efficient campaign they drove the Greeks and British back. With Greek surrender imminent, the Navy put into action its plans to evacuate the British army. Most of the evacuation was carried out by military transport ships but destroyers and cruisers also played a part. The 'Ks' of the 28th Division (*Kingston*, *Kandahar* and *Kimberley*) played a significant role, starting on 26 April. *Kingston* and *Kimberley* arrived at the port of Raftis to embark troops along with *Carlisle* and *Havock*. *Kingston* is recorded as taking on 850 troops. They were then joined by *Glengyle* and the whole force sailed for Suda Bay where they disembarked their passengers. They were back at Raphtis on the 27th, this time with *Kandahar* and *Hero* but were only able to find 332 men to evacuate.

They were more successful on the 28th, *Kimberley* taking on board 700 troops with *Kingston* taking 640. This left them seriously overloaded and any violent manoeuvring would have been very risky. This load would be the last from Greece for the destroyers (except *Kimberley*) as on 29 April they were ordered to join *Carlisle* to escort Convoy GA15 to Alexan-

---

[14] In *Eagles War*, Peter C Smith notes their arrival in Mombassa on 26 April but misidentifies them as *Kingston* and *Kandahar* who were by then escorting Aegean convoys.

dria. The convoy set off from Suda Bay at 11.00am escorted by *Carlisle*, *Kandahar*, *Kingston*, *Kimberley*, *Decoy*, *Defender*, *Hyacinth* and *Auckland*. It was uneventful until about 11.00pm when *Kingston* sighted two unknown ships to starboard. She challenged them and opened fire which was returned. Flashes were seen which were thought to be the launching of torpedoes which were heard to explode at the end of their runs. *Kingston* then pursued the ships, identified as E-boats, but they escaped due to their superior speed. Later *Kandahar* spotted further E-boats and turned to drive them off. The senior officer of the escort in *Carlisle* thought that these attacks were intended to draw off the escorts and cautioned captains not to be lured away from their charges.

The 28th also saw the completion of Operation 'Salient', the successful sailing of *Dido*, *Abdiel* and the 5th Flotilla from Gibraltar and Malta. *Dido* and *Abdiel* did not remain long but sailed the same day with *Breconshire*, escorted by *Jervis*, *Juno*, *Jaguar* and *Imperial*. *Janus* remained at Malta as she needed repairs. The 1st Battle Squadron had also left Alexandria to escort GA15 in and *Juno* and *Jaguar* were ordered to join it whilst *Jervis* continued on to Alexandria. The convoy was a natural target for submarines and one was detected on 30 April by *Jaguar* and *Juno*. On *Juno's* fourth attack the charge from the port thrower exploded prematurely on the surface killing five seamen and injuring eleven. The ready-use locker for No 3 mount was holed and one charge set on fire and the ships side was holed in two places. What had happened was that a copper disc which prevented the charge detonator exploding as it hit sea was missing from the charge pistol. As a result of this accident *Juno* was detached for Alexandria to land her casu-

alties.[15] After repairs she sailed again on 2 May to cover the battlefleet with *Kandahar*, *Jaguar*, *Imperial* and *Hasty* and relieve the 19th Division. *Napier* and *Nizam* arrived at Port Said and Suez respectively, *Nizam* having been delayed by TSDS duties for Convoy US10A in the Red Sea.

After their arrival at Malta, *Gloucester*, *Kelly*, *Kashmir*, *Kipling*, *Kelvin*, *Jackal* and *Jersey* sailed to intercept a Tripoli-bound convoy on 1 May but were too late as it had already made port. Another convoy was reported north of it but heavy seas made this one impossible to intercept in time and the ships returned to harbour on the 2nd. *Kelly*, *Jackal* and *Kelvin* had successfully entered harbour when the fourth ship in line *Jersey* struck a mine. It seems that she sank very quickly with the loss of two officers and thirty-four men.[16] Unfortunately she completely blocked the entrance to the Grand Harbour leaving *Gloucester*, *Kipling* and *Kashmir* stuck outside. These three ships were ordered to Gibraltar but could only steam at 25kts due to *Kipling's* shortage of fuel. They were repeatedly attacked by aircraft and *Gloucester* was hit by a bomb which failed to explode.

On arrival at Gibraltar all three ships were prepared for Operation 'MD4' which involved the passing of two convoys (MW7A and MW7B) to Malta and the 'Tiger' Convoy all the way from Gibraltar to Alexandria, carrying tanks for the desert army and including reinforcements for the fleet. It was a bold move conceived by Churchill to shorten the time supplies took to reach Egypt. The Mediterranean Fleet

---

[15] The submarine was able to make good its escape.
[16] Other sources give two officers and thirty-three other ranks killed and one officer and forty-six ratings wounded. The war diary for the period gives the figures I have stated in the main text.

Jaguar photographed whilst serving with Force H, probably in late 1940. She has received some updates, such as the 4in gun and enhanced splinter protection, but not others, the Oerlikon platforms being the most obvious, and the galley funnel is still in evidence.

(IMPERIAL WAR MUSEUM: A696)

A heavily retouched photograph of *Jaguar* taken by one of the French convoy intercepted on 1 January 1941. The pennant number appears to have changed colour but has been pencilled over making this difficult to assess. The message of the torpedo mount is fairly emphatic.

(MUSÉE NATIONAL DE LA MARINE: 18116)

departed from Alexandria with the two Malta-bound convoys on 6 May. Included with it were no less than eight Kellys (*Jervis, Janus, Juno, Jaguar, Kandahar, Kingston, Kimberley, Napier* and *Nizam*) under Captain Mack in *Jervis*. The escorting destroyers would refuel from *Breconshire* over two days but due to the weather they had an uneventful passage to Malta with both convoys arriving intact on 9 May. By then the wreck of *Jersey* had been cleared away from the entrance to the Grand Harbour, but there was still the problem of unexploded mines and no minesweepers at Malta. The fleet brought with them the sweep-equipped corvette *Gloxina* which successfully swept the entrance allowing the convoys in and the 5th Destroyer Flotilla out to join the fleet which added *Kelly, Kelvin* and *Jackal* to the Kellys in the screen.

The 'Tiger' Convoy had left Gibraltar on 5 May covered by Force H with *Gloucester, Kipling* and *Kashmir*. It was located by enemy aircraft which attacked quite vigorously but only managed to damage one merchant ship. More seriously, the *Empire Song* struck two mines and blew up but she was to be the only loss from the convoy. The fleet met the convoy about 50 miles south of Malta on 9 May, adding *Kipling* and *Kashmir* to the screen, incidentally making the greatest concentration of Kellys ever assembled, fourteen ships in all. This state of affairs did not last long and the reunited 5th Flotilla were detached to bombard Benghazi. Captain Mountbatten had planned for the 9th Division (*Kelly, Kelvin* and *Jackal*) to stand on a position 3 miles north-west of the lighthouse on the north-west mole and bombard the ships anchored near that mole. The 10th Division (*Kashmir* and *Kipling*) were to remain in support. However, due to faulty navigation and too high an approach speed the vital turn was missed and the bombardment was not as effective as it could have been. In all 866 rounds of SAP and 84 of starshell were fired for one ship damaged. The 5th Flotilla then withdrew, pursued by enemy aircraft.

Kelvin was missed by one bomb which fell 30 yards abreast of her after superstructure and *Jackal* by one bomb which failed to explode. Cunningham was disappointed with the results of the operation and thought that if they had withdrawn to the south as ordered they would have caught a supply convoy which arrived at Benghazi the next day. The 5th Flotilla arrived back at Malta on the 12th but this was the end of their role as the Malta strike force as on 21 May they would be ordered to the Eastern Mediterranean to join the fleet and participate in the battle of Crete.

On 13 May *Orion, Ajax, Kingston, Kandahar, Juno* and *Nubian* sailed for Operation 'MD8', the bombardment of El Fateyah aerodrome. They were attacked by twelve Ju88s at about 4.30pm without success. The bombardment itself was a failure. The cruisers and destroyers could not fix their position and were unable to make contact with the spotting aircraft. As a blind bombardment was considered inadvisable none of the ships actually opened fire. The destroyers were detached to bombard Derna harbour but on arrival found it empty and so did not open fire either. They had been supported by part of the fleet which included *Jervis* and *Jaguar* who also saw no action. On 15 May Force C was formed which consisted of *Kandahar, Kingston, Juno* and *Nubian* with the cruisers *Coventry* and *Dido*.[17] Force C sailed from Alexandria for a sweep towards the Kaso Straits but sighted nothing and was recalled to Alexandria on 17 May. It refuelled and sailed again on 19 May, being joined by *Naiad* and *Perth* ready for the battle of Crete.

---

[17] *Dido* did not join until 16 May and was the flagship of the Rear-Admiral Destroyers, Rear-Admiral Glennie.

THE *KELLYS* AND FORCE H

Force H was the Gibraltar-based force covering the Western Mediterranean to Malta. They always had a significant destroyer force, consisting mostly of 'F' class ships of the 8th Destroyer Flotilla. As discussed in the previous chapter, *Kelvin* and *Jaguar* had been assigned to escort *Manchester* and *Southampton* to Gibraltar and been retained by Force H. Their first operation was Operation 'Collar', the passing of *Manchester*, *Southampton*, *Despatch* and *Coventry* to the Mediterranean Fleet with a convoy for Malta. The fleet set sail on 27 November with *Kelvin* and *Jaguar* providing the escort for *Renown*, *Ark Royal* and *Sheffield*. They were sighted by Italian aircraft and an enemy fleet sailed to intercept. As aircraft reports were received of this force on the British side, *Renown* ordered *Despatch* to take charge of the convoy and *Manchester* and *Southampton* to join him. The destroyers were ordered to concentrate on *Renown* except for *Forester* and *Jaguar* which were ordered to screen *Ark Royal*. As *Jaguar* hauled out of the screen, *Kelvin* saw this and joined her. *Faulknor* (Captain D8) noticed what happened and, because of the familiarity of *Kelvin* and *Jaguar* in working together, ordered *Forester* to rejoin him. Throughout the action the two destroyers worked together covering *Ark Royal* but could only fire anti-aircraft barrages at retiring aircraft, being restricted by the elevation of their main armament.

The Italian fleet did not succeed in getting to grips with the convoy and retired after an inconclusive engagement. *Manchester* did not remain long in the Mediterranean, but was escorted back to Plymouth by *Kelvin* and *Jersey* arriving on 11 December. *Jaguar* had remained in Gibraltar for repairs and this perhaps is the reason that Force H were able to retain her. Prior to this *Kelvin* had attacked a submarine whilst escorting *Royal Sovereign* in the Atlantic Ocean on 2 December. *Royal Sovereign* had actually seen the submarine but initially *Kelvin* had had difficulties in locating it. However, after dropping individual charges she obtained a contact and was able to hit it with a full pattern of six charges. This brought oil and bubbles up to the surface and the contact was lost. A poor contact was later obtained and a single charge dropped on it but after a further search nothing could be found and *Kelvin* rejoined the *Royal Sovereign*. It was thought that she had attacked an Italian submarine but failed to destroy it. *Jersey*'s stay at Gibraltar was short, she departed with *Kelvin* as soon as *Manchester* was ready.

On completion of her repairs, *Jaguar* rejoined Force H on 31 December for Operation 'Ration', an attempt to stop Vichy French supply ships from running the blockade then in force. The force involved in this operation was *Duncan*, *Foxhound*, *Firedrake*, *Hero* and *Jaguar* supported by *Bonaventure*. On 1 January 1941 a convoy was intercepted

and the ships ordered to prepare for boarding. This was resisted by one vessel, the *Chantilly*, and *Jaguar* fired a burst from her 0.5in machine guns into the water, several bullets of which ricocheted, killing two French seamen and wounding four. There was no more trouble after that and the French ships were escorted to Gibraltar. *Jaguar*'s last operation with Force H was Operation 'Excess' on 7 January. This convoy escort operation sailed in two groups, Group 1 which comprised Force H including *Jaguar* and Group 2 which comprised the convoy. On 8 January *Malaya*, *Jaguar* and *Firedrake* were detached from Group 1 to augment the convoy escort and on the 9th the screen was further augmented by *Southampton*, *Gloucester* and *Ilex*. The convoy came under air attack at 2.05pm and *Jaguar* opened fire on a formation of ten aircraft. Initially she was able to fire with her 4.7in guns but a little later could only fire with her 4in as they passed out of the elevation of the main armament. After driving this attack off *Malaya*, *Firedrake* and *Duncan* turned back for Gibraltar and *Jaguar* assumed the port wing position for the passage through the narrows.

The next day saw an attack on the convoy by two Italian torpedo boats, *Circe* and *Vega*, which fired several torpedoes but failed to hit. They were initially engaged by *Bonaventure* and *Jaguar* stayed with the convoy until she saw *Southampton* haul out of the screen at which point she increased to 32kts and followed. She then opened fire on *Vega* as soon as *Bonaventure* cleared the range, closing to six cables and obtaining several hits before rejoining *Bonaventure*. All this time she continued to pummel *Vega* obtaining hits which started fires fore and aft. *Jaguar* came under fire probably from *Circe* which she did not see but at the time the shell splashes were thought to be from the shore batteries at Panterella. On seeing that *Southampton* was heading back towards the convoy *Jaguar* fell into formation with her.[18] As she departed *Hereward* torpedoed *Vega* which blew up but neither destroyer joined the convoy screen, going instead to the fleet screen where *Jaguar* screened the damaged *Illustrious* with *Juno*. *Jaguar* fired at any aircraft which came into range and was quite effective in driving them off. *Jaguar* and *Hasty* escorted the carrier into Malta at 9.45pm and *Jaguar* secured alongside the oiler *Plumleaf* to refuel. She would not return to Force H but as described earlier would join the Mediterranean Fleet. The 'Excess' convoy is frequently considered a German victory because of the bombing of *Illustrious* and the loss of other warships but in fact it was considered a failure by the Germans. Not one of the merchant ships in this very complex operation was actually sunk, though the *Essex* would be damaged later whilst unloading at Malta.

---

[18] Most sources do miss *Jaguar*'s part in the sinking of the *Vega* but her report of proceedings is quite specific. She fired eighty-eight 4.7in SAP, six 4in HE and forty-one pom-pom rounds during the engagement.

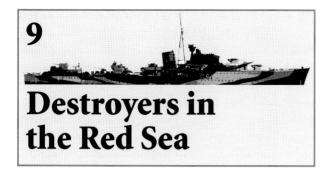

9

Destroyers in the Red Sea

THE RED SEA, coming under the East Indies Station, was a strategically vital waterway, being the exit for the Suez Canal and the only alternative entrance to the Mediterranean if the Straits of Gibraltar were closed. With the prospect of war with Italy it became imperative to strengthen the Red Sea Command. The Royal Navy had a base at Aden and from there conducted inspection and contraband patrols, the most important being the Perim Patrol. This was centred on the island of Perim located in the middle of the mouth of the Red Sea and involved a box patrol of 5 days in the Straits of Bab-el-Mandeb. Italian forces in the area consisted of a squadron of seven destroyers, two torpedo boats and eight submarines based at Massawa in Italian Somaliland, posing a considerable threat to traffic in the Red Sea.

On 18 May 1940 the Admiralty informed the East Indies Command that they would be receiving reinforcements consisting of the cruiser *Carlisle*, the sloops *Auckland*, *Flamingo* and *Grimsby* and two destroyer divisions. This was later amended to just one destroyer division, the 28th,

consisting of *Kandahar* (divisional leader), *Kingston*, *Kimberley* and *Khartoum*. Other cruisers would also be available as they passed through the Red Sea. The 28th Division left Alexandria on 24 May arriving at Aden four days later. On the 31st they were allocated to the Perim patrol initially in pairs though this would later change.

At first the patrols were uneventful but on 9 June the duties of the 28th Division were expanded to include protection of shipping against attacks by the Italian forces at Massawa, the first of which were launched by submarines. The large submarine *Galileo Galilei* sank the Norwegian tanker *James Stove* on 18 June off Aden. She was sighted and bombed by an aircraft but incurred no damage. *Kandahar* and the sloop *Shoreham* were detached to hunt for her and, as a result of excellent judgement by *Kandahar*'s captain, found the submarine on the surface the next day. The Italian submarine dived but was forced to the surface by *Shoreham* and the trawler *Moonstone* which had joined the attack. The crew intended to fight it out on the surface but *Moonstone* opened up such an effective fire that all the officers on the bridge were killed and the submarine was forced to surrender. *Kandahar* then put a prize crew on *Galilei* and attempted to take her in tow but the line parted. However, two of her officers, Lieutenant Fox and Lieutenant Commander Havergal, cleared the helm and got her engines started. The tow was re-established and *Galilei* entered the harbour under the White Ensign.[1] After collecting her prize crew, *Kandahar* left Aden to rejoin *Shoreham*, *Kingston* and

---

[1] The *Galilei* was re-commissioned into the Royal Navy as *X2* finally being scrapped in 1946.

I have only been able to find two photographs of the 28th Division in the Red Sea and these come from the early months. This one shows the submarine *Galileo Galilei* under tow by *Kandahar* after being captured by the trawler *Moonstone*. *Kandahar* seems to have one funnel band but it is difficult to ascertain many other details. Her pennant

number has been censored and she appears to be in a dark hull/light upper works variation of her 1939 scheme. This could have been applied as early as February 1940 but see the chapter on camouflage.

Khartoum which had attacked and damaged the submarine *Luigi Toricelli* on the 21st.

Knowing that there were likely to be more Italian submarines, the Royal Navy determined on an aggressive policy to locate and destroy as many as possible. At 4.00 am on 23 June the three ships of the 28th Division (*Kimberley* was at Bombay) and *Shoreham* formed a line of bearing of 225° to hunt the *Toricelli*. *Kingston*, on the port wing, spotted an object 3 miles away which turned out to be the submarine which dived on being sighted. An anti-submarine search commenced and *Shoreham* dropped a charge on the contact before Commander Robson in *Kandahar* ordered the search line to be reformed. As this was being done *Kingston* spotted the submarine again and turned to attack, giving six short blasts of her siren to alert the other ships of the force. This time the submarine made no attempt to dive but headed for the coast of French Somaliland at full speed. *Kingston*'s forward 4.7in guns opened fire at 5.36am and from that point the submarine was doomed. *Kandahar* and *Khartoum* also opened fire but ceased shortly after when it was clear that the submarine was being abandoned by her crew. The *Toricelli* finally sank at 6.24am with the only damage to the British ships being caused to *Kingston* when one of her pom-pom shells struck the aerial lead to the Sound Reproduction Room, wounding eight men.

THE LOSS OF *KHARTOUM*

After the *Toricelli* operation the force split up, with *Khartoum* sailing to take up the Perim patrol. But at 11.50 am a torpedo in the wing tube of the aft quintuple mount suddenly exploded. The warhead was blown through the rear deckhouse, passing through the officers' galley and cutting the leads to the gravity-fed oil tank on No 3 gun deck, immediately starting a fire. The warhead continued on its way through the support and the power unit of No 3 gun and disabled the valves to No 3 magazine before exiting the deckhouse and coming to rest against the starboard TSDS winch. The fire took hold very rapidly throughout the after lobby, filling it with dense smoke. Unfortunately, fire fighting attempts were ineffective, and the aft shell room could not be flooded as the valves were inoperable and the hoses rigged could not provide enough force to bring the fire under control. As a result her captain, Commander Dowler, shaped course for Perim Harbour (which was a little over 7 miles away) and ordered all the torpedoes in the fore mounting to be fired and all ready-use ammunition to be tossed overboard as well to reduce top weight.

As she passed the harbour's entrance *Khartoum*'s steam failed but by a supreme effort was re-started and she was able to struggle past the buoy and drop her anchors between Princes Shoal and Murrays Point. Nos 1 and 2 magazines were flooded and the ship abandoned with the crew swimming towards the approaching launches of the previously-notified Perim police. As the crew escaped from their ship, the fire finally reached No 3 magazine which exploded shortly after 12.45pm and was followed by an even greater explosion when the augmented depth charges and remaining torpedo warheads also went up. It was at then that *Khartoum*'s crew incurred their only fatality when debris from the explosions struck and killed a seaman swimming away from the ship. These explosions sank the ship and later examinations concluded that salvage was impossible.

The loss of such a modern destroyer caused great concern and as soon as possible the Admiralty instituted an inquiry into the circumstances of her loss. Damage from the engagement with *Toricelli* was quickly ruled out as the nearest shell had landed well past the ship and she had not been hit by any splinters, as was sabotage, since despite having

This is the only photograph of *Khartoum* that I have been able to locate. It shows her after she was sunk in Perim Harbour. The boat nearby is attempting to recover her confidential books.

(AUTHOR'S COLLECTION)

prisoners from the submarine onboard, there had been no opportunity for them to cause the explosion. Attention rapidly focused on the torpedoes themselves, particularly the compressed air vessels. *Khartoum*'s torpedoes had been landed at Devonport on 10 March because her torpedo officer was worried about pitting on the air vessels which he thought excessive. After examination they were reported to be well within tolerances and re-embarked on 11 May. Examination of *Kandahar* and *Kimberley*'s torpedoes also showed similar pitting which was deeper than it initially appeared. However, this was not considered likely to be the problem and examination of the warhead showed that the vessel had split near its top end suggesting a flaw in the casing as the cause of the explosion. As a precaution the pressure in the air vessels was reduced from 3100 to 2900lbs per square inch. What was noted with satisfaction was the fact that the warhead had not exploded unlike American or French ones in similar circumstances.[2] No blame was attached to any members of the crew who were considered to have performed excellently. There was also some concern about the disposal of the confidential books and the Perim Police were asked to keep an eye open for any that might turn up.

THE CONTINUING ANTI-SUBMARINE CAMPAIGN
Despite the loss of *Khartoum* the anti-submarine campaign continued. On 24 June, *Kimberley* and *Falmouth* intercepted the submarine *Galvani*. *Falmouth* found the *Galvani* on the surface and rammed her, and then launched an accurate depth charge attack which forced her back to the surface where she surrendered. *Kimberley* lowered her boats and picked up the survivors. Two days later, *Kingston* was returning from an abortive search for an Italian liner when a sharp eyed lookout spotted a submarine (*Perla*) on the surface. *Kingston* attempted to close the range without being seen but opened fire at 5500 yards when the submarine started to dive. No hits were scored but good asdic contact had been obtained and three patterns of charges dropped, which *Kingston*'s captain considered sufficient to have destroyed the submarine and he cancelled a signal ordering *Kandahar* and *Flamingo* to join him and withdrew at high speed. Later this error came in for some criticism. Rear-Admiral Murray, C-in-C of the Red Sea area, wrote

> I consider that you could have afforded to wait for a couple of hours if the submarine were to be forced to the surface – observing that it was dark – and that there probably would not have been time for her to make a full report including position.

2/ The fuel consumed in withdrawing at 30 knots was hardly warranted either.

3/ Nevertheless, the opportunity fortune gave you was well taken and your lookouts are to be congratulated.

4/ Note and return for transmission to Commander in Chief East Indies Station.

Kingston and *Kandahar* sailed on the 27th with the cruiser *Leander* to locate and finish off the *Perla* which was found beached and abandoned. She was hit seven times by shellfire and near-missed by a 100lb anti-submarine bomb dropped by *Leander*'s Walrus. Despite this, about a month later the wreck was salvaged by the Italians and towed to Massawa for repair.[3] The *Perla* engagement practically ended the Italian submarine threat in the Red Sea. Half the Italian submarine force had been put out of action in under six days and in their later escort of convoys in the Red Sea the 28th Division never lost a ship to submarines.

ESCORTING CONVOYS
In keeping with other theatres of action a convoy system was initiated in the Red Sea. This was in addition to the US (Fremantle to Alexandria) and WS troop convoys which passed through on their way to and from the Mediterranean. The main convoys in the Red Sea were the BN and BS convoys between Suez and Bombay. Whilst the BN series consisted of mainly merchant vessels carrying cargo, the BS series was a lot more varied and consisted of the following categories of ships:

1. Returning troop transports.
2. Vessels loaded in the Eastern Mediterranean bound for the UK.
3. Vessels discharged in the Eastern Mediterranean and proceeding under instructions from the Ministry of Shipping to load for the UK in India.
4. Vessels returning to Australia on the Australia-Middle East run.
5. Vessels returning to India or South Africa to load coal for the Middle East.
6. Vessels proceeding to various overseas ports for supplies for Greece.
7. Tankers proceeding to the Persian Gulf or Dutch East Indies.

The main role of the Kellys was to provide an anti-shipping and anti-submarine escort for the BN convoys between

---

[2] Exploding air vessels were a problem that would crop up throughout the war with *Newfoundland*, *Partridge* and *Tjerk Hiddes* being affected as well as some torpedoes intended for *Quality*.

[3] *Perla* would eventually be captured by the British off Beirut and commissioned into the Royal Navy before being transferred to Greece.

Aden and the Red Sea before returning to Aden with the corresponding BS convoys. They were also to provide a minesweeping capability by deploying their TSDS gear as the convoys moved through shallow and restricted waters. The convoys themselves were not constant and numbers varied quite considerably as various portions attached and detached along the route. The first BN convoy sailed on 30 June and was joined by the Red Sea escort on 5 and 6 July. As it was the first, the escort was very strong and consisted of Force Q (*Leander, Shoreham, Hindustan, Carlisle, Kandahar, Kingston, Flamingo, Hobart, Ceres* and *Auckland*) and Force S, the close escort (*Grimsby* and *Clive*). Force Q sailed with the convoy to a point roughly parallel to Jiddah in Saudi Arabia before dispersing. *Kingston* and *Leander* departed on the 15th and joined the southbound Convoy BS1 on the 17th. This set the pattern for convoy duty on the following BS and BN convoys and it was considerably helped by the existence of a base at Port Sudan which was used for re-fuelling and resting.

Throughout July the destroyers carried out what were uneventful but important escort duties. There were never more than two of the division escorting a convoy at any one time and frequently only one. Force Q was still in existence but was much reduced from the high point of BN1. The other destroyer would be on the Perim patrol before swapping roles with her compatriot. Enemy action was restricted to the occasional ineffectual air attack, but the Italian invasion of British Somaliland would cause a temporary change in this routine.

THE EVACUATION OF BERBERA

British Somaliland lay on the opposite side of the Gulf of Aden to the port of Aden giving a strategic hold on both sides of the gulf and the entrance to the Red Sea. Surrounded by Italian territory since the invasion of Abyssinia, capture of it would give the Italians an important strategic advantage. The Italian offensive began in July and was slow but relentless, the British forces being heavily outnumbered. It rapidly became apparent that the British would have to evacuate or face total defeat and so arrangements were made to withdraw them from the port of Berbera.

Kimberley had been helping to delay the advance with *Auckland*, carrying out a bombardment on the 14th and patrolling off the coast the next day. Meanwhile, a comprehensive force of eleven ships was allocated for the evacuation which would also include Abyssinian refugees and their families. *Kandahar* and *Kimberley* arrived separately on 16 August. *Kimberley* took up the role of anti-submarine guard ship with *Shoreham*, whilst *Kandahar* assisted with the evacuation, loaning her motor boat for the pur-

pose. On the 17th *Kimberley* embarked the Governor and his staff and *Kandahar* took over the anti-submarine patrol. On the 18th *Kandahar* requested permission to bombard the advancing Italian forces. This was approved but she was warned to be careful as elements of the rearguard, the Camel Corps, were also expected in the area. She sailed up the coast and shelled a column of Italian tanks which were brought to a halt. Later she provided cover for a couple of RAF lorries heading along the Berbera road. The evacuation itself continued smoothly, the transports loading and sailing across the Gulf to the port of Aden. The Italian squadron did not attempt to interfere and even aggressive patrolling by *Kimberley* towards Port Sudan provoked no response. However, submarines were still a danger for ships sailing independently and the Greek freighter *Atlas* was sunk on 6 September. *Kingston* was detached to pick up her survivors and take them to Aden, then carrying out a sweep towards the Island of Kamaran but failing to locate the submarine.

MORE CONVOYS AND THE BATTLE OF HARMIL ISLAND

Troop convoys were beginning to arrive in the Red Sea as reinforcements for the Western Desert passed through on the way to Suez. The first important troop convoy to take this route was WS2A (Capetown to Suez) and *Kingston* and *Kandahar* were detailed as part of the escort to the fast group of the convoy. The two destroyers were stationed ahead of the three transports with TSDS streamed in shallow waters and as an anti-submarine escort in deeper waters. Joining early on 12 September the two destroyers kept station ahead of the convoy until *Kingston* was detached to investigate a suspicious ship. This proved to be the Greek freighter *Ann Stathatos* which was advised to wait for and join Convoy BS4¾. *Kandahar* departed for Port Sudan at 8pm but *Kingston* stayed with the convoy until 10.30pm before following her with *Coventry*. She then joined BS4¾ on 15 September as it made its way down the Red Sea towards the Gulf of Aden. *Kimberley* was also part of the escort. The destroyers do not seem to have been involved in the escort of Convoys BN5 or BS5 but *Kingston* was part of the escort for BN6. Prior to this, on 3 October she had carried a representative of the French government to Aden from Djibouti for a conference with the Governor of Aden.[4]

About this time Italian aircraft became more active, attacking ships on patrol and convoys. *Kimberley* was bombed on 4 October whilst on the Perim patrol but it was difficult to say whether she or the island was the target as the nearest bomb fell over 7000 yards away from her. Convoy BN6 was bombed on 5, 6 and 7 October with no

---

[4] This is when the Italian forces supposedly controlled the whole of that area of coastline.

damage to any of the ships. Yet again, this attack exposed the unsuitability of the Kellys' main armament for anti-aircraft fire as *Kingston*'s 4.7in guns could not elevate enough to fire on the enemy aircraft. The Italian destroyer force then made what was its first sortie to attack Convoy BN7 on 21 October. *Kimberley* was zigzagging a mile astern of the convoy when at 2.22am *Auckland* signalled that she was engaging an enemy destroyer. *Kimberley* altered course and increased speed to 30kts. The Italian destroyers returned shortly after and were driven off again as *Kimberley* accelerated past *Leander* on an interception course intending to make contact before the enemy could reach Massawa.

At 3.54am she sighted two ships crossing from starboard and turning away. To avoid her own smoke being spotted, *Kimberley* reduced speed first to 27kts, then to 12kts. She then altered course to cruise around until daybreak, due at 6.12am. However, at 5.40am she sighted a object and steered towards it, increasing speed to 30kts as she did so. This was identified as an enemy ship and at 5.55am *Kimberley* opened fire with her forward turrets at a range of 12,400 yards, the enemy ship replying 2 minutes later as *Kimberley* altered course to open her A arcs. About the same time the shore battery on Harmil Island also opened fire on *Kimberley* but its shooting was poor. By 6.11am the range had reduced to 10,300 yards and *Kimberley* was hitting her opponent regularly. Ten minutes later the destroyer was stopped with smoke coming from her bridge and *Kimberley* fired a torpedo which missed. It was only then that she was able to identify her opponent as the *Franceso Nullo* from the letters 'NL' visible on the bows in red. She fired another torpedo at 4000 yards which hit and the Italian ship blew up.

Kimberley then tempted fate and opened fire on the shore batteries. A shell from one of the guns struck the port side of her engine room but failed to penetrate. However, splinters from the damaged plating cut the steam pipes for the port engine in addition to several other pipes and conduits forcing the evacuation of the engine room. All steam was shut off using the emergency valves on the upper deck and the main boiler room valves, unfortunately bringing the ship to a complete stop. All the while the engagement with the shore guns continued, though only No 3 mount could bear, but *Kimberley*'s shooting was good and it was thought that two out of the three guns in the battery were hit and put out of action. The starboard engine was restarted and *Kimberley* left at 15kts. She would later need to be taken in tow first by *Leander* and then by *Kingston*, as she had insufficient feed water for her starboard engine. During the engagement *Kimberley* had fired 596 SAP shells and 97 HE for numerous hits. *Nullo*'s gunnery had not been good and the only hit on *Kimberley* had been by the shore batteries

which had wounded three men. *Kimberley* would be under repair at Port Sudan until 31 October. Admiral Murray considered that, excluding *Kimberley*, the escort had performed poorly and by showing more aggression could have achieved an even more complete victory.

By now the three destroyers were in need of refits but facilities at Aden were insufficient, the nearest suitable base being Bombay. *Kandahar* was the first to go, departing on 7 November. *Kingston* continued to escort convoys and *Kimberley* carried out patrol duties. This pattern continued until December when *Kimberley* began to escort convoys as well, starting with BN10 on the 3rd. Escorting Convoy BS9¾ on 4 December *Kingston* was informed of a mutiny at the Abu Ali Lighthouse and landed an armed party to deal with the problem, rejoining the convoy at 3.00pm.

Kandahar returned from her refit on 7 December and with *Kingston* and *Carlisle* sailed to escort the troop convoy US7 (Fremantle to Alexandria). The destroyers were escorting convoys along the entire length of the Red Sea, *Kingston* taking three faster ships from one convoy all the way to Suez with the aim of avoiding later congestion. *Kingston* had one more convoy to escort, BS11, on 25 December before leaving for her refit at Bombay on 3 January 1941. On the way she investigated clandestine dhow traffic to Somaliland. *Kandahar* and *Kimberley* were kept busy in January escorting the extensive convoy traffic that was flowing between the Indian Ocean and the Suez Canal. They provided cover for SW, US, BS, BN, BNF and BSF convoys. The only incident of note occurred on 4 January when *Kandahar* depth charged a contact which was later classified as non-submarine.

Kingston returned from her refit on 27 January, once again investigating dhow traffic to Somaliland and diverting via Mukalla to do so. Two days later, *Kimberley* in turn sailed for Bombay for her refit which would last until 14 March. *Kingston* resumed convoy escort duty on 1 February when she joined Convoy BN14 to Suez. The rest of February saw her escorting convoys up and down the Red Sea with a short spell on the Perim patrol from 15 to 17 February.

Having such valuable destroyers tied up in the Red Sea was considered a waste of resources and as early as 19 December consideration had been given to their replacement. Four 'Hunt' class destroyers had been mooted as potential reliefs though it was acknowledged that this could not be before March 1941 as they would need modifying for tropical service. Once the 'Ks' were released they could then relieve *Mohawk* and *Nubian* from the Mediterranean Fleet which could then return to the Home Fleet. However, when the three 'Ks' did rejoin the Mediterranean Fleet *Mohawk* and *Nubian* stayed with it and in fact others of the 'Tribal' class would be sent to the Mediterranean from the Home Fleet.

OPERATIONS 'CANVAS' AND 'APPEARANCE'

After the victories in Egypt and Libya, the collapse of the Italian empire was only a matter of time. The first target was Italian Somaliland (Operation 'Canvas') and an invasion force assembled at Mombassa in Kenya. *Kandahar* sailed from Aden on 9 February to provide an anti-submarine escort for the covering cruiser squadron, Force T, which was intended to destroy or demoralise the seaward defences of Kismayu before the occupation of the town. *Kandahar*, however, was diverted on the 11th to place an armed guard on the intercepted Italian freighter *Ermina Mazella* and then proceed to Mombassa. After refuelling *Kandahar* sailed to cover the invasion force which landed near Kismayu on 12 February. The next day she abandoned her patrol and closed Kismayu Island to see if she could provoke any response. Three salvoes were fired but the Italian batteries located there were not drawn. On the 14th *Kandahar* provided an anti-submarine screen for the cruiser *Shropshire* as she bombarded the island but was then detached to resume her patrol.

Being the only destroyer available for the force created conflicting priorities. It had been intended that she should sail to Brava on 15 February to sink the freighter SS *Pennsylvania* and several loaded petrol lighters which were trapped in the harbour. However, there was also an important convoy due in at Kismayu which needed an escort. *Kandahar* did not have enough fuel to perform both tasks. The convoy was judged more important but before she could depart a periscope was sighted by a lookout on *Shropshire*. *Kandahar* and three aircraft were detached for what proved to be a futile hunt which further depleted the destroyer's fuel reserves. By the time she was detached to locate the convoy, she was in serious need of refuelling so when she found the convoy on the 16th, she ordered it to anchor for the night while she sailed to Mombassa to refuel. She returned on the 17th and under orders from *Ceres* escorted the steamer *Al Said* into Kismayu harbour before returning to the rest of the convoy the next day. After refuelling at Mombassa she sailed on the 20th to relieve *Emerald* as the escort for Convoy WS5BX while that ship refuelled at Mombassa. Arriving with the convoy at Mombassa on 22 February, *Kandahar*'s role in the invasion of Italian Somaliland was over and she sailed for Aden the same day.

Operation 'Appearance' (the reoccupation of Berbera) took place in March. *Kandahar* had detached from the escort of Convoy US9½ and hurried back to Aden to pick up the six troopships for the reoccupation. Sailing on 14 March this force was overhauled the next day by the main naval force consisting of *Glasgow*, *Caledon*, *Kingston* and *ML109* and they all reached the rendezvous at 11.30pm.

Here *Kandahar*'s special knowledge of the coastline gained when she covered the retreat in 1940 proved invaluable and the ships sighted Berbera lighthouse at 2.03am. The warships which were carrying Somali commandos went ahead to land their troops on the beaches either side of the town. The force then split up, *Kandahar* and *Kingston* sailed for the beach east of the town and *Glasgow* and *ML109* headed for the entrance to the western beach. *Glasgow* had considerable difficulty locating this gap, having to lower a boat to do so, whilst *Kandahar* and *Kingston* found theirs immediately. The orders to land were given and 5 minutes later *Kandahar* opened up on the shore defences which were silenced by 4.35am. The troops had occupied Berbera by 10.00am without suffering a single casualty.

Kandahar and *Glasgow* stayed off the beach for the next few days whilst *Kingston* hurried off on the 17th to join the escort of Convoy BN20. She was ordered to detach on the 18th and escort the troopship *Sagitta* to Berbera as that ship might have been needed to evacuate casualties, then rejoining the convoy before sailing for Port Sudan, arriving on 22 March. *Kimberley* on her return from refit sailed from Aden on 20 March for Suez to escort the damaged aircraft carrier *Illustrious* through the Red Sea. *Illustrious* joined Convoy SU2 on 24 March and *Kimberley* returned to Aden to refuel. *Kandahar* returned to Aden on 22 March and two days later sailed with the Armed Boarding Vessel *Chakdina* on a political department mission, an old fashioned piece of gunboat diplomacy in fact. The Fahdi Sultan had been giving trouble and chastisement was needed. This took the form of landing 150 government guards at Shukra and blowing up the Sultan's palace up. He himself escaped but later surrendered and promised to behave himself. *Kandahar* and *Chakdina* then returned to Aden.

As the British advanced further into the Italian empire it was becoming clear that its collapse was near. The German blockade runner *Bertram Rickers* attempted to escape from Massawa on 29 March where she had been moored. British Intelligence was forewarned and *Kandahar* was despatched to intercept which she did on 31 March. Rather than surrender *Bertram Rickers* scuttled herself on sighting *Kandahar*.

THE ELIMINATION OF THE ITALIAN SQUADRON

There remained the Italian surface squadron which was still considered a potential threat. Convoys were still escorted by cruisers and a 'K' up to Port Sudan and on 29 March steps were taken to guard against an Italian breakout. *Kimberley* and the cruiser *Caledon* were based on the Red Sea side of the Suez canal and *Kingston* and *Capetown* operated out of Port Sudan. It had been intended that the aircraft carrier *Eagle* be brought through the canal to assist but this was not possible as the canal was blocked. However, her aircraft were still able to play a significant role in the operations that followed. All that remained of the Italian naval forces were the destroyers and a few auxiliary vessels and MTBs.[5]

As part of the occupation of Abyssinia and Eritrea, the British planned the establishment of an advance base at Mersa Kuba (Operation 'Atmosphere'). Practically all the ships based at Port Sudan were involved. *Kingston* sailed first with *Parramatta* on 1 April to be joined later in the day by *Capetown*. Their role was to carry out minesweeping in advance of the arrival of the troopships. *Capetown* provided cover whilst *Parramatta* carried out a double oropesa sweep and *Kingston* laid dan buoys every 100 yards inside the eastern limit of the sweep, marking the various swept channels. This continued until 2 April when news was received that Italian destroyers had been sighted fleeing northwards. *Capetown* and *Kingston* were ordered to cover Convoy BN22 which was passing against possible attacks from the direction of Harmil Island and joined it at 10.10pm. At 4.40am on the 3rd both ships left the convoy but rejoined it when reports were received that enemy destroyers were concentrated off Port Sudan. At 11.00am *Kingston* was detached to sink a damaged enemy destroyer reported to be at Position 21° 02'N, 38° 42'E. However, on reaching this position she could find no trace of the destroyer and decided to patrol up towards Jeddah.

The Italian destroyers from Massawa were the *Leone*, *Tigre* and *Pantera* which had sortied on 1 April with the aim of attacking shipping at Suez. Unfortunately, the *Leone* had struck an uncharted rock and had had to be scuttled by her compatriots who returned to port. With the fall of Massawa imminent, another Italian destroyer force departed on 2 April. This consisted of the *Daniele Manin*, *Cesare Battisti*, *Nazario Sauro*, *Tigre* and *Pantera*, intending to attack British shipping off Port Sudan. *Cesare Battisti* suffered an engine breakdown and had to drop out of the force. She was scuttled on the 3rd off the Arabian coast. The other ships continued but had been spotted by British aircraft and came under constant air attack which included the Swordfish from the *Eagle*, which bombed and sank the *Nazario Sauro*. A second Swordfish took off from Port Sudan and sank the *Daniele Manin*, leaving just the *Tigre* and *Pantera*. These proceeded northwards and were abandoned off the Saudi Arabian coast by their crews. Vickers Wellesley bombers from No 223 Squadron then appeared and commenced bombing runs after the ships had been abandoned.

Kingston appeared on the scene about 4.00pm and opened fire on one of the destroyers which seemed intact. Fire was ceased shortly afterwards when there was no response and *Kingston* approached to within 2 miles. *Tigre* was down by the stern and sinking, still being bombed by the Wellesleys. *Pantera* was on fire after being hit by *Kingston*'s shells but was still afloat. Because of the uncertainty of the location of the other destroyers *Kingston* decided to sink both ships. Her original orders had been to salvage both of them but it was judged not worth the effort. *Tigre* was sinking anyway so *Kingston* put a torpedo into *Pantera* which severely damaged her bows and then withdrew to Jeddah for the night. At dawn on the 4th *Kingston* returned but both destroyers had sunk. The masts and funnel of one ship and the forefoot of the other were visible and *Kingston* was able to recover an ensign from one of the ships which was later presented to *Eagle*. She then returned to Port Sudan arriving at 5.25pm.

Some dispute exists as to what eventually finished these destroyers off, with Italian records claiming that they were scuttled. Whilst this would be the logical action after abandoning the ships, the very fact that they both stayed afloat for so long after the crews had abandoned them does cast doubt on this. Furthermore, Italian records also claimed that *Kimberley*'s victim *Francesco Nullo* was scuttled which is not borne out by the evidence. The historian Peter C Smith[6] attributes their demise to *Kingston* only but it is clear from her action report that she only fired on the *Pantera*. Certainly *Kingston* sunk the *Pantera* but had no part in the demise of the *Tigre*, which seems to have been sunk by near misses from the Wellesley bombers which opened up her hull and caused her to sink slowly. Whatever the cause the Italian destroyer force had ceased to exist.

However, the Italian naval threat had not ceased and *Kingston* relieved *Caledon* as the escort for Convoy BS22 on 5 April. She was relieved herself by *Kimberley* on 6 April but both destroyers were then detached to stand by *Capetown* which had been torpedoed by the Italian MTB *MAS 213*. This was the last and only flourish of the Italian navy in the Red Sea, the MAS boats (*204*, *206*, *210*, *213* and *216*) all being scuttled off Massawa on 8 April along with the surviving torpedo boat. With the elimination of the Italian naval threat, there was no need to base a destroyer force in the Red Sea and so *Kandahar*, *Kimberley* and *Kingston* were re-allocated to the Mediterranean Fleet. *Kimberley* was the first to go, passing through the Suez canal into the eastern Mediterranean on 12 April. *Kandahar* arrived at Alexandria on the 13th April direct from the Perim patrol and Port Sudan. *Kingston* was the last to depart, arriving at Alexandria on 17 April. All three ships would once again form the 28th Division of the 14th Destroyer Flotilla.

[5] The submarines had left in January 1941 for Bordeaux.

[6] Peter C Smith, *Eagle's War*.

10

The Battle of Crete, 1941

AFTER THE FALL OF GREECE it was obvious that Crete would be the Germans' next target. As a naval base and fortress it left a lot to be desired and preparations to defend it were both slow to start and inadequate. Significantly, air support for the Royal Navy was virtually non-existent. The initial German attack would be with airborne troops, but the invasion would still require reinforcements and heavy equipment that could only come by sea. To prevent this, Admiral Cunningham had organised several patrol lines and on 15 May there were four main forces at sea. The only Kellys involved at this time were *Kandahar*, *Kingston* and *Juno* which were patrolling off Heraklion with Force C (*Dido*, *Coventry* and *Nubian*) under Rear-Admiral Glennie to intercept any planned invasion force and to cover any attempt to land at Sitia as well. *Janus* was also at sea, returning to Alexandria after searching for some missing MTBs and having been part of the escort of Convoy ANF30 to Suda Bay. Force C were recalled for refuelling at Alexandria on 18 May and at 8.00pm the same day Force A1, consisting of the battleship *Valiant*, the light cruiser *Ajax* and the destroyers *Napier*, *Kimberley*, *Isis*, *Janus*, *Griffin*, *Hereward*, *Decoy* and *Hero*, sailed to patrol westwards of Crete to relieve Force A in preventing any intervention by the Italian fleet. Force C refuelled and, joined by *Naiad* and *Perth*, sailed for the Kaso Straits on 19 May.

On 20 May the invasion of Crete began and this led to the activation of another squadron, Force E, consisting of *Jervis*, *Nizam* and *Ilex* which sailed to bombard the airfield on Scarpento Island, withdrawing before dawn. Afterwards, they were supposed to link up with Force C but ended up patrolling Kaso Strait before returning to Alexandria on 23 May. There had also been some shuffling between the squadrons and *Isis*, *Kimberley*, *Imperial* and *Janus* had joined Force D from Force A1. Force C, now under Admiral King, reached the Kaso Strait on the night of 20 May when they intercepted a force of Italian MASBs. Their earlier instructions to sweep round Stampalia had been cancelled and they had been diverted to patrol north of Crete with Force D. *Juno* sighted three of the MASBs and tried to ram them before opening fire on four others. Two of these were probably the

same boats she sighted earlier. Faced with an active and aggressive opponent and with *Naiad* and *Kandahar* coming up rapidly to join the action the Italian boats departed rapidly. One of them had been damaged by *Juno*'s pom-pom.

With the coming of daylight both Forces C and D came under constant air attack. At 12.49pm *Juno* was attacked by a formation of five SM79s.[1] They approached from ahead at an angle of 50° and released five bombs. *Juno* increased her speed to 28kts and turned hard to port to avoid the attack, but it was too late. Two bombs near-missed her whilst three hit simultaneously abaft her bridge. One exploded in the boiler room, one in the engine-room and the third in the aft magazine, with devastating effects. *Juno*'s side was blown outwards and she immediately heeled to starboard. The order was given to stop the engines but 20 seconds later the heel had increased to 70° and the order to abandon ship was given. Within 60 seconds of the ship being hit by the first bomb she had broken in two and the stern section had sunk. The bow section (from the pom-pom forward) was already vertical and sinking rapidly and was gone in 2 minutes. *Nubian*, *Kingston* and *Kandahar* were able to rescue six officers and ninety-one ratings from her crew.

Early on 21 March a fleet of about twenty-five commandeered caïques set sail from Milos with urgently-needed reinforcements and ammunition for the German forces on Crete. For the last stage of their journey they were escorted by the Italian torpedo boat *Lupo*. This flotilla had been detected and Forces B, C and D were ordered to intercept. It was Force D (then *Orion*, *Ajax*, *Kimberley*, *Janus*, *Hasty* and *Hereward*) which found the flotilla at about 11.30pm. *Janus*, which had lost touch with the rest of her force, was the first to encounter the enemy when she sighted *Lupo* whom she initially mistook for *Kimberley*. The Italian fired torpedoes which missed and *Janus* opened fire and turned her searchlights on. Her next target was a large schooner which she set on fire, followed by a caïque which she tried to ram twice before opening fire and blowing it up with the second round from A gun. *Janus*'s final victim was another caïque she located with her Type 286 radar and successfully rammed. The other ships of the force were also successful, the cruisers locating the enemy ships by searchlight and the destroyers finishing them off. At least nineteen caïques and

Kingston at Crete shortly before the invasion. Just visible is the camouflage on her gun barrels and the faded camouflage on the roofs of her shields. (IMPERIAL WAR MUSEUM: MH3880)

---

[1] Accounts differ as to whether they were Italian or German aircraft. *Juno*'s reports indicate that she was attacked by SM79s but the Germans also claimed to have sunk her. As the SM79 is a fairly unmistakable trimotor aircraft this was unlikely to be a misidentification and the German claims are probably false.

Jackal rescuing an airman from a ditched aircraft. Once again her funnel is heavily encrusted. The photograph also shows the flaps of her 0.5in platforms lowered, a detail not often seen. Whilst this photograph was taken before the arrival of the 5th Flotilla in the Mediterranean the only difference in *Jackal*'s configuration was the two Oerlikons she later carried. (IMPERIAL WAR MUSEUM: A3574)

three small steamers were sunk, though *Lupo* and three other vessels from the convoy did survive. Most of the troops were saved, the final casualty total being 13 officers and 311 other ranks.

A second invasion convoy had also sailed on the same day bound for Heraklion escorted by the torpedo boat *Sagittario*. Force C, which still included *Kingston* and *Kandahar*, was also in the area and had been under air attack since daylight. About 9.30am *Perth* and *Naiad* sank a small merchant vessel and, as they were rejoining, more ships were sighted. This was part of the convoy and *Kingston*, steaming ahead of the cruisers, reported even more ships. About the same time *Sagittario* sighted Force C and immediately reversed the course of the convoy and then steered to cover it. As she did so she came under fire from *Kingston* and received some damage. However, her efforts were not in vain as Admiral King, worried about the air attacks he was facing, ordered his squadron to withdraw. The convoy escaped but the attempt to reinforce the forces in Crete by sea was abandoned. Admiral King came under considerable criticism for his withdrawal, Cunningham believing that he could have safeguarded his ships from air attack by closing with the convoy and would have been able to cause significant damage. Force C continued to be attacked by aircraft as it withdrew but by 3.00pm they were able to join the battleship force, A1, and receive a greater measure of protection. About this time *Kingston* and *Kandahar* were detached to rescue the survivors of *Greyhound* which had been sunk by dive-bombers after being detached to sink a large caïque. *Kingston* and *Kandahar* arrived and under

heavy air attack rescued as many men as they could. Admiral King, who had assumed command of the fleet when he joined it,[2] ordered the cruisers *Fiji* and *Gloucester* to go to the assistance of the destroyers. Both were low on anti-aircraft ammunition and this would prove fatal.

The first to be sunk was *Gloucester*, hit first by two bombs and later by two more. She turned over and sank but *Fiji* was ordered to continue on her mission, leaving boats for *Gloucester*'s survivors. She made contact with the two destroyers but as they were withdrawing was herself hit by a bomb which disabled her. Thirty minutes later she was hit by three more bombs and rolled over and sank. *Kandahar* and *Kingston* did not linger in the area but returned after dark to pick survivors up. They were able to rescue 523 men but both ships were now dangerously low on fuel and ammunition which restricted their speed of return to the fleet. Both destroyers were able to refuel from the battleships but ammunition remained a problem.

Captain Mountbatten of the 5th Destroyer Flotilla wanted to be involved in the battle of Crete and asked permission to bring his ships into action. This was an attrac-

---

[2] He was senior to the Force A1 commander Rear-Admiral Rawlings.

tive proposition as the Mediterranean Fleet needed all the destroyers it could get and all of Mountbatten's destroyers were equipped with Oerlikons and radar. Consequently, the 5th Flotilla departed Malta on 21 May. The flotilla joined the fleet off Crete at 4.00pm and almost immediately were split into two groups, *Kelly*, *Kashmir* and *Kipling* being sent to rescue survivors of *Fiji* and *Kelvin* and *Jackal* to rescue those of the *Gloucester*.

Too late to help, the flotilla was ordered to re-group and sweep Kissamo and Canea Bays. *Kelvin* and *Jackal* were ordered to investigate some unexplained lights in Canea Bay which proved to be innocuous shore lights and as a result returned independently to the rest of the flotilla. *Kipling* developed steering defects which caused her to fall back to make repairs, leaving *Kelly* and *Kashmir* to carry on alone. As they entered Canea Bay, *Kelly* and *Kashmir* encountered a troop-carrying caïque which they engaged and destroyed. They then carried out a short bombardment of Maleme airfield in support of New Zealand troops fighting there and withdrew. As they did so they spotted another caïque which blew up spectacularly when fired on. By morning *Kelly* and *Kashmir* were withdrawing from Maleme and *Kipling* was about 6 miles away from them having repaired her steering and hurrying to rejoin the fleet.

They were located by twenty-four Ju87s from I/G St G 2 led by Captain Hitschold and attacked 13 miles south of Gavdo. *Kashmir* was the first to be hit by aircraft from the third wave of attacks. One bomb struck amidships on the upper deck, just before her funnel. This broke the ship's back and she sank in 2 minutes. *Kelly* continued to evade the enemy but as she turned under full helm, a bomb struck her on No 3 mount just abaft the engine-room and blew the port side open. *Kelly* was heeling as she sped round at 30kts and continued to do so without righting herself. She listed to port and capsized, sinking after about 30 minutes. The bombers continued to attack, machine-gunning the survivors in the water but with *Kipling* nearby this ordeal did not last long. During the time she was rescuing survivors she came under forty separate air attacks. As she manoeuvred to avoid the attacks and at the same time rescue the survivors from both ships, *Kipling* hit the wreck of *Kelly* suffering significant damage and flooding several compartments. Her stern was badly damaged. As if this was not enough, her hull was holed and ripped in several places causing her to list 6° and be down at the bow by about 6ft. *Kipling* manoeuvred carefully to pick up survivors but in one unfortunate incident the fast motor boat was lowered to help with the rescue work during a lull but as the falls were being released a bomber appeared and *Kipling*'s captain, St Clair Ford, gave the order for full ahead. Mount-

batten shouted for the falls to be cut but only the foremost ones were released in time and as a result the boat was towed under stern first and both *Kelly* and *Kipling*'s first lieutenants were drowned. After picking up 279 officers and men *Kipling* left the area at her maximum speed which, due to damage, was only 22kts.

Kipling had lost a significant amount of oil and was running out of fuel by the time she neared Alexandria on 24 May. The netlayer *Protector* came to meet her and transferred 15 tons of oil, enough for *Kipling* to reach port. The whole fleet turned out to cheer the destroyer into her berth but she would be out of action for four weeks. After these losses the 5th Flotilla was disbanded and the surviving three ships divided up between the 7th and 14th Flotillas, with *Jackal* and *Kipling* going to the former and *Kelvin* to the latter. Later the 5th Flotilla would be reformed with 'Hunt' class escort destroyers. The 5th Flotilla had lost 50 per cent of its strength in the month it had been in the Mediterranean though none of the losses could be blamed on Mountbatten, unlike several of the earlier mishaps.

On 22 May *Jaguar* and *Defender* loaded up with 50 tons of urgently-needed ammunition for the troops on Crete and left Alexandria. Their initial aim was to rendezvous with Force A1 for part of the passage to gain extra air protection and so they sailed westwards to meet it. At about 6.30am on the 23rd they sighted *Kelvin* and *Jackal* in the distance obviously heading in the same direction and engaging a bomber. Several minutes later they were attacked and increased speed to 30kts but *Defender* found this speed difficult to maintain and they were slowly overhauled by *Kelvin* and *Jackal*. By the time *Kelvin* and *Jackal* had drawn near, *Defender* was better able to keep up and all four destroyers continued together making contact with Force A1 at 11.15am. *Jaguar* and *Defender* were detached in the afternoon and on the way in they were both attacked several times. *Jaguar* was attacked twice and *Defender* eleven times but despite several near-misses were not hit. The two ships arrived at Crete and unloaded their ammunition and then took on board 250 naval officers and ratings not needed for the defence and set off for Alexandria. They were attacked on the way back but once again suffered no damage and arrived back in harbour late on the 24th.

Force A1 also arrived back in Alexandria on the same day but reports were received that the Italians were planning a landing on Sitia Bay located at the eastern end of Crete and *Ajax*, *Dido*, *Kimberley* and *Hotspur* departed to intercept this. If no invasion forces were sighted the force was to bombard Maleme airfield. No invasion force was sighted but the obvious folly of attempting to bombard the airfield with no air cover for the withdrawal ensured that the operation was can-

Crews of the 14th Flotilla cheer *Kipling* into Alexandria Harbour with the survivors of *Kelly* and *Kashmir* on 24 May 1941. Behind her can be seen the netlayer *Protector* which had sailed to transfer oil to enable her to enter harbour under her own power. She is also slightly down by the bows, a result of her collision with the wreck of the *Kelly*. She is fitted with two Oerlikons and a Type 286.   (IMPERIAL WAR MUSEUM: A4348)

celled and the ships returned through the Kaso Strait. As the squadron withdrew *Kimberley* and *Hotspur* were relieved by *Napier*, *Kelvin* and *Jackal* and headed off to Alexandria. Also on the 24th *Nizam* joined *Isis* and *Hero* in an attempt to land a special force ('Layforce') on Crete. Unfortunately the weather deteriorated and by the time the force had reached Crete a landing was too hazardous. In fact the weather was so bad that *Nizam* lost two 27ft whalers and the whole force returned to Alexandria frustrated. The next day (25 May) *Nizam* and *Hero* tried again, this time joined by *Abdiel*. This time the operation was successful and the three ships then took off 930 surplus personnel. It was also the last troop reinforcement for the Crete garrison.

At the same time an ill-conceived operation was getting under way – Operation 'MAQ3' – a raid on Scarpanto airfield. The aircraft carrier *Formidable* sailed with what was basically Force A with an escort which included *Jervis*, *Janus* and *Kandahar* on 25 May. The air raid went ahead the next day and caused some damage and the force was joined by *Ajax* and her destroyers at 7.00am, but *Formidable* was badly damaged by counter-attacking German aircraft and put out of action. It had been proposed to detach *Kandahar*, *Nubian* and *Janus* to raid Melos harbour but, in the circumstances, this was cancelled. *Jervis* and *Nubian* came under attack from high-level bombers and *Nubian* had her stern blown off. Surprisingly she was still able to steam so *Jervis* stood by until relieved by *Jackal* who escorted the damaged ship back to Alexandria. *Janus* was detached with *Hasty* to go to the assistance of *Defender* which had been caught on her own and was being attacked by aircraft. She survived the attack and was escorted back to Alexandria. The rest of Force A (*Queen Elizabeth*, *Barham*, *Jervis*, *Kelvin*, *Kandahar*, *Napier* and *Hasty*) remained at sea to cover *Abdiel*, *Hero* and *Nizam* on their reinforcement mission. During this period *Barham* was hit by a bomb on X turret and Admiral Cunningham recalled the force to harbour.

By 27 May it had been decided that Crete was no longer tenable and that the garrison would have to be evacuated. This created difficulties as the only good anchorage, Suda Bay, was already held by German forces and all that were left were small fishing ports. However, before the evacuation started *Napier*, *Nizam*, *Kelvin* and *Kandahar* (Force C) left Alexandria on 28 May carrying small arms ammunition and provisions for the troops on Crete. Like most of the operations to Crete this one was subject to continuous air attack. The destroyers landed their supplies without a hitch and left Sphakia at 3.00am the next day carrying 700 troops. On the way back, *Nizam* was near-missed by a bomb which landed 15ft off her port quarter, causing only minor damage.

On 30 May the force returned again to take off more troops but *Kandahar* developed a mechanical defect and was detached to Port Said joining *Janus* and *Flamingo* in escorting *Barham* there. *Kandahar* returned to Alexandria on 1 June where her defects were repaired the next day. *Napier*, *Nizam* and *Kelvin* continued their mission but at 3.30pm were attacked by Ju88s. Most bombs missed but one fell close to *Kelvin*, and exploded underneath her hull and. Significantly more serious than the near miss to *Nizam*, the explosion was directly beneath watertight bulkhead No 77 and its force lifted the propellor bearings out of alignment. This resulted in the shafts running eccentrically creating considerable wear and reducing her maximum speed to just 20kts. She also suffered significant hull damage. *Kelvin* returned to Alexandria but it was found that she could not be repaired there. She would escort the gunboat *Aphis* to Port Said on 8 June before sailing for permanent repairs at Bombay.

Napier and *Nizam* continued with the mission and arrived at Sphakia just after midnight on 31 May. Accounts differ as to how many men the destroyers took on board but the

Nizam returning from Crete on 3 June 1941 during the evacuations. She is in a dark hull/light upperworks scheme, also carried by *Napier* and *Nestor* and is fitted with a Type 286. Interestingly she is not yet fitted with Oerlikons though she does carry a 4in gun. (IMPERIAL WAR MUSEUM: E3361)

figure was in the region of 1500.[3] Having loaded up they then departed at 2.30am for the journey back to Alexandria. The destroyers had, for once, RAF fighter cover but this proved insufficient and at 9.15am an attack was made which caused serious damage to *Napier*. Two bombs just missed her port side, one of which landed within 10ft. Four other small bombs also landed close by at the same time but it was the larger bomb which caused the most damage. The feet of the pumps to No 2 boiler were shattered by the explosion and as they broke connections to the boiler also parted spraying fuel oil all over the compartment. The crew's reaction was prompt and efficient and No 2 boiler was immediately shut down so that the loose fuel could be mopped up. Damage was also caused to the HP turbines, both the fixed and sliding feet being broken. The port turbine was slightly forced out of alignment, the casing cracked around the entire circumference and it had to be shored-up as a precaution. Whilst all this was happening *Napier* came to a dead stop but once the boiler room was cleared out she was able to proceed. Speed was increased gradually until 20kts could be maintained. No more damage was suffered and the two ships arrived back at Alexandria at 7.00pm.

Stuart and *Jaguar* had been assigned, with the cruiser *Coventry*, to cover the troop transport *Glenroy* as she sailed to land reinforcements at Tymbaki beach on Crete. The force sailed on the 25th but, after *Glenroy* was hit by a bomb, withdrew to Alexandria. At the same time, Forces B and D sailed to carry out the evacuation, Force B consisting of *Orion, Ajax, Dido, Imperial, Hotspur, Hereward, Decoy, Kimberley* and *Jackal* whilst Force D was made up of *Perth, Glengyle, Calcutta, Coventry, Jervis, Janus* and *Hasty*. A day later *Stuart, Jaguar* and *Defender* sailed to reinforce Force D. All forces were bound for Sphakia and Force B in particular would be in for a rough ride. *Jaguar* would be shaken by near misses but none of the Kellys involved would actually incur any damage. The same could not be said of *Kingston* which, on 30 May, was attacked whilst on anti-submarine patrol. Four near-misses sprung her joints and led to flooding in several of her oil and water tanks putting her out of action until 14 June. The final evacuation run sailed on 31 May and consisted of *Phoebe, Abdiel, Kimberley, Hotspur* and *Jackal*, all the ships that were available. These ships were able to load 3710 troops between them and thanks to RAF fighter cover had an uneventful passage, arriving back in Alexandria on 1 June.

THE SYRIAN CAMPAIGN

The German victory on Crete was the catalyst for the Iraqi

leader Raschid Ali to declare his support for the Axis and request material support. Both Germany and Italy sent aid via Vichy-controlled Syria and despite the collapse of the Iraqi insurgency on 31 May, the British decided that they needed to rid themselves of the threat that Syria posed. Relations between Britain and Vichy had never been particularly good and up until then a kind of hostile and uneasy truce had existed. The invasion of Syria began in June but stretched the already thin resources of the army and navy even further. The naval forces opposing the British consisted of the contre-torpilleurs *Guepard* and *Valmy* and three submarines based at Beirut. The British naval forces were divided into two forces, Force A consisting of *Ilex, Isis, Hotspur, Hero, Coventry* and *Glengyle*, and Force B including *Phoebe, Ajax, Kandahar, Kimberley, Jackal* and *Janus*. The campaign opened with an attempt by *Glengyle* to land commandos to seize the Damur bridge but this was frustrated by bad weather. The next day (8 June) *Kimberley* closed the shore to bombard French positions near the Kahn bridge in support of troops attacking Tyre. On 9 June she and *Kandahar* were ordered to hunt for a submarine which had attacked *Phoebe*, but the search proved abortive. *Janus, Jackal* and *Hotspur* were then ordered to carry out another

Kimberley as she comes alongside *Valiant* to refuel during the Crete operations. Interestingly her camouflage still appears pristine suggesting that it had been recently repainted. No 3 mount is still trained forward. Also of interest is what appears to be a camouflage panel under the overhang behind No 1 mount. This is actually shadow and illustrates how deceptive black and white photographs can be in interpreting camouflage schemes. (NATIONAL MARITIME MUSEUM, LONDON: D1100)

---

[3] Captain Arliss's action report gives a figure of 1403 officers and men but at Alexandria an army count gave 1510 officers and men.

sweep to support the army. *Kandahar* and *Kimberley* rejoined the cruisers.

At 1.35pm local time *Janus* was in the lead with *Jackal* about eight cables behind and *Hotspur* a mile further back when two French warships were sighted.[4] These were *Guepard* and *Valmy* which had left Beirut to bombard British positions. They opened fire on *Janus* at a range of 17,000 yards, taking her by surprise as British destroyer practice was normally to close the range before firing. *Janus* responded at 15,000 yards and summoned *Jackal* and *Hotspur*. She did not attempt to close or withdraw but let the French ships dictate the course of the engagement. When the range had closed to 10,000 yards *Janus* was hit five times in quick succession. The first shell hit at Station 76 and exploded causing a 4ft diameter hole in the lower deck and a tear in bulkhead 77. The second penetrated the 20in projector platform and continued through the bridge deck and exploded outside the captain's sea cabin killing everyone on the bridge apart from the captain. The third was the most serious as it disabled No 1 boiler room and carried away the saturated steam pipe. The fourth shell hit the port fan intake but failed to explode and the fifth and final hit was once again on No 1 boiler room penetrating the hull in five places. Both boilers were put out of action and with steam escaping in No 1 boiler room, No 2 boiler could not be restarted as the diesel generators and oil fuel hand pump were located in the former. *Janus* was still able to continue firing in local control but with steering and way lost Mounts 1 and 2 gradually ceased to bear and only Mount 3 was able to respond. Smoke floats were dropped and these seemed quite effective as French fire deteriorated after the hits. However, *Janus* was in a serious situation and what saved her was the arrival of *Jackal* which immediately turned to port to open her A arcs and, increasing speed to 30kts, closed the French. At 2.00pm she fired three torpedoes but none hit. Twelve minutes later the French ships altered course and retired under cover of a smokescreen. *Jackal* increased to full speed and pursued them, zigzagging to avoid their fire. *Hotspur* also arrived and gave chase but she was 1½ miles behind *Jackal*. *Isis,* which had been summoned from her bombardment duties, was a further mile back at the time. At 2.15pm the French altered course and opened fire. *Jackal* turned to run parallel to their course and returned fire. After a short while *Guepard* and *Valmy* returned to their original course and retired making more smoke being pursued by *Jackal* once again. This happened again at 2.40pm but the range was gradually increasing due to the superior speed of the contre-torpilleurs. Finally, about 10½ miles from Beirut, *Isis* called

Jackal back and the French ships reached port safely. During the engagement, *Jackal* had been hit once by a shell which had penetrated the upper deck and started a small fire in the tiller flat, but it had been quickly dealt with and caused minimal damage. One rating had been wounded in the shoulder by a fragment from the shell and *Jackal* had fired 611 rounds of 4.7in during the engagement.

Janus was taken under tow by *Kimberley* which had been ordered to assist. Shortly after the tow commenced a fire broke out in No 1 boiler room probably due to oil in the furnace and all ventilation was immediately closed off. Steam from No 2 boiler which had been restarted was piped to extinguish the fire but this meant that No 2 boiler was too short of water to raise steam. Initially the approach was successful and the fire was left to die down but it then flared up again and by 8.30pm was glowing red hot and could be seen through the splinter holes in bulkhead 42. *Janus* was now listing slightly to port and as a precaution, the mess deck was evacuated and No 2 magazine and shell room flooded. About this time a tug came alongside and, using its fire-fighting equipment, was able to drive the fire back from bulkhead 42. *Janus* finally reached Haifa and secured alongside the cargo jetty where a fire-fighting float with foam equipment was brought alongside. About an hour later she was moved to the oil jetty where there was unlimited foam available but the fire was not finally extinguished until 5.00am the next morning.

The post-mortem on the action was not favourable towards *Janus*, the DTSD considered that she should have waited for the rest of the destroyers to come up and support her before engaging. The Admiralty concurred with this view, as *Janus*'s captain had allowed himself to get caught in two minds, whether to attack or fall back. The French gunnery was also noted. Whilst three of the hits did have an element of luck attached, it had been generally very good, particularly one ship and they had demonstrated an ability in long-range gunnery far surpassing the Royal Navy destroyers. All in all this action was considered a well-earned French victory. *Jackal* was considered to have performed extremely well and it was only due to her presence that *Janus* was not sunk. It was also noticed that despite not being fitted with cross-levelling gear her shooting had been better than that of *Janus* and she had been able to straddle the French ships frequently. *Janus* would be towed to Port Said by *Protector*, patched-up and thereafter sent to Simonstown for more permanent repairs, arriving on 19 July. She would be out of action until March 1942.

Following this action new instructions were issued to Admiral King in charge of the naval forces at Haifa. He was ordered:-

---

[4] This account is based on the reports of the captains of *Jackal* and *Janus*.

1. To prevent any repetition of the French bombardment of our troops;
2. To hunt French submarines if at sea;
3. To destroy French surface craft that might again put to sea; and
4. To support the left flank of the army.[5]

Once she had towed *Janus* to Haifa, *Kimberley* returned to the battle zone on 10 June where she conducted a very effective dawn bombardment of French forces with *Kandahar*. *Kandahar* would also bombard on the 11th and 12th before joining *Jaguar* to escort *Ajax* back to Alexandria on the 13th. On the same day *Jervis* arrived at Haifa with *Hasty* and initially started on bombardment duties. *Jaguar* had joined *Kimberley* and *Kandahar* in their bombardment and had blown up an ammunition dump and destroyed two guns before sailing up and down the coast with *Isis*, dispersing Vichy troops who were moving to intercept the invasion forces. The bombardment performance of all the Kellys throughout the Syrian campaign would be very effective. Ranging up and down the coast *Kimberley* encountered *Guepard* and *Valmy* on the 16th just off Beirut. This time the tactics used were different. *Kimberley* increased to full speed and closed the French ships rapidly, claiming hits as she did so. This aggressive approach had more effect and the French ships withdrew to Beirut. As she neared the port, *Kimberley* came under attack from torpedo planes and bombers and was ordered to rejoin her squadron. French air attacks were initially quite effective. *Jackal* came under attack from a dive bomber on the 15th and a bomb struck her where her side plating and upper deck joined, just behind station 84. The bomb bounced off and exploded in the sea, the only damage being an 18in hole in her deck. She was able to continue in service unaffected and on 21 June intercepted the French hospital ship *Canada*. She escorted the ship back to Haifa but was relieved and proceeded back to Alexandria on the 22nd.

Further reinforcements arrived from Alexandria on 17 June in the form of *Naiad*, the repaired *Kingston, Jaguar* and *Nizam. Phoebe, Jackal, Jaguar, Kingston* and *Nizam* immediately sailed to search for the contre torpilleur *Chevalier Paul* which was due into Beirut with ammunition and supplies for the French squadron. However, she had been torpedoed and sunk by a British aircraft and so they carried out a sweep between Tripoli and Beirut instead. In pursuance of their new orders, the British squadrons initiated a pattern of nightly sweeps and daylight bombardments. A strong force consisting of one or two cruisers and several destroyers would patrol every night whilst the rest of the forces

involved would carry out bombardments during the day. Every so often the ships would swap roles and ships taking part in the sweeps frequently remained on station to carry out bombardments duties the following day. The next encounter with the French destroyers occurred on 23 June when they ran into *Naiad, Leander, Jaguar, Kingston* and *Nizam* who were engaged in one of the nightly sweeps. *Naiad* sighted first one then another destroyer and turned to intercept. The French ships opened fire and retired under smoke to the cover of the shore batteries. The British ships also opened fire and claimed hits though the only confirmed hit from this engagement was a 6in shell from *Leander* which failed to explode. *Kandahar* rejoined the operation on 27 June having escorted *Warspite* to Port Said and in a change from usual practices took *Griffin* and *Havock* out for a TSDS sweep. However, no mines were found. *Jaguar* had returned to the fleet on 25 June and sailed the next day with *Kandahar, Kimberley* and the rest of the fleet for exercises.

On 29 June *Nizam* and *Jervis* returned to Alexandria and three days later *Jackal* rejoined the operation. She was acting as the flotilla leader for the 7th Flotilla as *Napier* was still under repair after her damage at Crete. The next day, 3 July, *Phoebe, Nizam* and *Kimberley* rejoined the operation as reinforcements were sent out. *Kandahar* then returned to Alexandria with *Decoy*. By now the success of the campaign was just a matter of time. The French warships were bottled up in Beirut and the Royal Navy controlled the seas completely. The 15th Cruiser Squadron was recalled and replaced by the 7th Cruiser Squadron on 14 July, two days after the Vichy administration asked for an armistice, bringing *Kimberley* back to Alexandria. *Jackal, Nizam* and *Kingston* stayed off the Syrian coast a bit longer. The French forces had performed surprisingly well before being overwhelmed. Once access to Beirut was secured Convoy LE25 sailed to establish port administration and defences. The first part of the convoy sailed from Alexandria on 16 July escorted by *Jaguar* with *Kandahar* sailing to Port Said to take over the second group. *Kandahar* met her two ships and escorted them to Beirut on the 17th. The destroyer shortage eased slightly when *Kipling* completed her repairs and rejoined the fleet on 16 July. She had had to wait several days for the Suez Canal to be cleared of mines before being able to sail to Alexandria. In the meantime *Jervis* sailed to replace *Jackal* and prepare for Operation 'Guillotine'.

'GUILLOTINE', 'SUBSTANCE' AND THE TOBRUK RUNS

Jackal, Nizam, Hasty and *Kingston* stayed off the Syrian coast for a few days after the armistice was signed to forestall any German or Italian interference. The first three ships returned to Alexandria on 17 July whilst *Kingston* lingered

---

[5] See PRO ADM 199/415 Mediterranean Fleet War Diary 1941.

slightly longer before returning to Haifa for Operation 'Guillotine', the reinforcement of the Cyprus garrison. This operation was carried out with considerably less interference from the enemy than the Crete adventure. Throughout the rest of July, a steady stream of ships shuttled backwards and forwards between Haifa and Famagusta. *Neptune*, *Abdiel* and *Kimberley* joined the operation direct from Operation 'ME3'. *Kandahar* and *Jaguar* first escorted *Formidable* to Port Said on 24 July before joining the troop runs. The only hiccup occurred two days later when the *Latona* collided with *Jaguar* but the damage was not serious. *Jackal*, *Nizam*, *Kipling* and *Kimberley* sailed on Operation 'ME3' on 22 July with Captain Arliss still using *Jackal* as his flotilla leader. They were met on the 23rd by *Leander*, *Jervis*, *Jaguar*, *Kandahar* and *Kingston* which had sailed from Haifa. The operation was uneventful and the fleet returned to Alexandria on 24 July.

With the first phase of 'Guillotine' successfully completed the Kellys began to return to Alexandria and for the first half of August were mainly involved in exercises, anti-submarine or anti-shipping patrols. On 1 August, *Jervis* left Alexandria with *Kingston*, *Nizam* and *Jackal* under her command to hunt a submarine that had been seen several times off Bardia but without success. The next phase of 'Guillotine' was due to start and so *Neptune* and *Abdiel* sailed with *Jackal* and *Kipling* from Alexandria to initiate it before going on to relieve the Haifa force. Also at this time, the Kellys began to be used on the more dangerous supply runs to Tobruk. The first ships to attempt this trip were *Nizam* and *Jaguar* which sailed on 4 August. Destroyers made a high speed dash to Tobruk timed to arrive well after dark. The amount of time

in harbour was limited to about half-an-hour before the ships left. Entering the harbour itself was a hazardous operation as various sunken wrecks had to be avoided and no lights could be used. On this occasion they did not come under air attack but this would not be the case in future. In fact it was on their very next run, on 6 August, that they were attacked by three SM79s which dropped torpedoes, which all missed though one passed down *Nizam*'s side. Both ships increased speed to 31kts after the incident.

Kandahar and *Kimberley* were to leave Alexandria to set up a striking force operating out of the port of Mersah Matruh. This was cancelled twice and though the ships did eventually arrive at Mersah Matruh on 12 August it was to salvage stores from a sunken lighter and then take them to Tobruk. the two destroyers were then drafted onto the Tobruk runs and were attacked on every run, but the only damage was to *Kandahar*'s upper works from splinters. On 21 August, *Kandahar* was also attacked by torpedo bombers but evaded them. On 15 August it was decided that pairs of destroyers should sail for Tobruk every day rather than every two days as before. Thus, as *Kandahar* and *Kimberley* returned, *Jaguar* and *Hasty* sailed until 18 August when they were replaced by *Jackal* and *Kingston*.

In late August the destroyers of the Mediterranean fleet were engaged in the following operations: Tobruk supply runs, Operation 'Guillotine' to Cyprus, patrols off Haifa, shipping strikes and exercises. They also had to contend with one-off operations as well. For example on 14 August, *Coventry*, *Nizam* and *Kingston* escorted the MT ship *Glenroy* to Port Said. They were then joined by *Jackal* and *Kipling* to escort her sister-ship *Glengyle* and the battleship *Barham* to Alexandria.

Kimberley at Alexandria during the early Tobruk resupply operations. It is likely that this colour scheme was applied shortly after the Syrian operation in which the destroyer distinguished herself. Colours are AP507C and AP507A. Her funnel is heavily weathered and she still retains her two quintuple mounts. Note that she has lost the D/F aerial of a year ago. (MUSÉE NATIONAL DE LA MARINE: 181163)

If this was not enough, the Australian government decided it wanted its troops serving with the garrison at Tobruk withdrawn. This placed an extra burden on the Navy which also still had to continue to supply the garrison. The troops chosen to replace the Australian 18th Infantry Brigade were the Polish Carpathian Brigade and the operation was to be conducted on the nights of the new moon, starting on 19 August, codenamed 'Treacle'. The first run was carried out by *Jervis*, *Kimberley* and *Hasty* and inevitably they were attacked by aircraft. These three ships continued on this duty, joined by *Abdiel*, and were occasionally given cruiser protection until 23 August. As the Tobruk trips were two-day affairs, *Latona* and three other Kellys were allocated to run alternately with *Abdiel*. Initially the three ships chosen were *Kipling*, *Nizam* and *Kingston* and they first sailed on 20 August. However, returning from their first run the force was attacked by a Ju88, which dropped two bombs, one of which fell 5 yards abreast of *Nizam*'s funnel and exploded underneath her. The other bomb landed 15 yards from No 2 mounting. *Nizam* shuddered violently and the

oil pumps were torn from their feet. Oil sprayed everywhere and both boilers were shut down to reduce the risk of fire. The shock of the explosions also damaged the starboard turbine and reduced the oil pressure to 10lbs. As *Nizam* came to a halt *Kingston* and *Kipling* started circling her to protect her from further air attack. Another aircraft attacked *Kipling* but was successfully driven off whilst repairs and damage assessments were made. No 1 boiler was out of action but No 2 was still useable despite being damaged. The wireless and gyro compass were also disabled and the magnetic compass was found to be unreliable. *Kingston* attached a line but this broke and preparations were made to tow by *Kipling*. However, it was discovered that *Nizam* could steam at 15kts and so she was escorted back to Alexandria where all ships arrived safely.

Nizam's place was immediately taken by *Griffin* and *Latona* and the destroyers continued with Operation 'Treacle' until it was suspended on 28 August to wait the next new moon. *Napier* returned from repairs at Port Said on 22 August and immediately sailed with *Jackal* to intercept

Kandahar during the same period as *Kimberley* with much the same configuration. Her camouflage is an overpaint of the earlier hull pattern she carried but being extended onto her superstructure. Colours are also AP507C and AP507A. She has abandoned the divisional leader's bar though she remained the leader of the 28th Division during this period.

(MARITIME PHOTO LIBRARY: 2024)

After completion of her refit which prevented her from joining the 5th Flotilla *Jupiter* finally arrived in the Mediterranean in September 1941 and this photograph is taken shortly afterwards on 2 October showing her newly painted in her Mediterranean scheme (profile 10). Her stay was brief and she left in November to join the Eastern Fleet.

(MUSÉE NATIONAL DE LA MARINE: 181168)

enemy shipping in the Ras-el-Melh area but like so many sweeps this was unsuccessful and they returned to Alexandria on 24 August. Immediately after the completion of the operation, *Kingston* and *Hasty* sailed to operate out of Haifa, though *Kingston* was replaced by *Griffin* on 6 September. *Kandahar* suffered the attentions of bombers in Alexandria harbour when she was near-missed off her starboard bow, suffering splinter damage from the forecastle deck to the water line and from the stern to bulkhead, and superficial damage to the crew spaces. The Tobruk re-supply operations started again on 8 September when *Kipling, Jaguar* and *Decoy* left Alexandria. As she was entering Tobruk, *Kipling* was attacked twice and one bomb fell 5 yards abreast of her funnel, breaking the feet of two oil pumps and shattering the brickwork in the galley. She was also attacked three times when leaving, again receiving only minor damage.

The rest of the fleet began to carry out normal movements, various units sailing for exercises. The battleship *Queen Elizabeth* put to sea with *Latona, Abdiel, Nizam* and *Jackal* on the 10th. The next day *Jackal* and *Hotspur* sailed as an escort for *Naiad* which was acting as a fighter direction ship. No enemy aircraft were seen but *Jackal* rescued a party of two army officers, three soldiers and nine Greeks who had escaped from Greece in a caïque. *Kingston* joined *Havock, Hero, Hasty, Hotspur* and *Vendetta* for an anti-submarine sweep along the Alexandria-Port Said-Haifa shipping routes following increased U-boat activity. Nothing was found and she and *Havock* then returned to the Tobruk runs on 11 September with *Napier*. Despite the sweep not locating any U-boats in the difficult conditions of the Mediterranean, *Kipling, Jackal, Hasty* and *Havock* were again despatched to hunt a submarine after an Allied freighter, SS *Murefte*, was sunk, but without success. *Kipling* and *Hasty* returned to Alexandria on the afternoon of 13 September. Following a refit, *Jervis, Jaguar, Kimberley* and *Kingston* sailed for exercises on 14 September. *Kingston* and *Kimberley* were detached for an unsuccessful sweep returning the next day. *Kimberley*, however, was towing another caïque she had come across which was carrying soldiers and civilians escaping from Crete. *Jervis* and *Jaguar* joined *Abdiel* and *Hasty* on a stores run to Tobruk.

With the coming of the moonless period on 17 September the next phase of the troop replacement programme (Operation 'Supercharge') commenced. The first run consisted of *Abdiel, Jervis, Jaguar* and *Hasty* on the 17th followed by *Latona, Napier* and *Nizam* the next day. *Nizam* did not seem to have much luck on these runs. As she was berthing in Tobruk near the wreck of *Serenitas* she had been hit by a strong crosswind. This caused significant damage to her forecastle deck and despite being able to return to

Alexandria she was out of action for 14 days.[6] *Kingston* replaced *Nizam*, and *Kimberley* replaced *Jaguar*. *Jackal* and *Hero* sailed for an abortive anti-submarine sweep on 20 September and then escorted *Glengyle* to replace *Glenroy* at the combined services training centre at Port Said. *Jackal* took part in the final run of Operation 'Supercharge' on 26 and 27 September.

Another Kelly, *Jupiter*, joined the 14th Destroyer Flotilla. After completion of her refit and duty with Force H, she had sailed round the Cape and arrived at Suez on 23 September. Before she could join the flotilla she needed docking for repairs to serious leaks in her oil fuel tanks. But she did not remain in port for long, for on 26 September she joined the rest of the fleet in a diversionary operation in support of the 'Halberd' convoy, intended to give the impression that the convoy was heading for Alexandria. Also with her were *Jervis, Kingston* and *Kipling*. *Napier* was due to join but was delayed by the need to refuel and joined the fleet at 2.30pm that afternoon. The diversion did not have the desired effect as the fleet was not sighted by the enemy at all and it returned to Alexandria the next day. *Napier* and *Jackal* joined the Suez Canal escort force for two weeks from 29 September. This proved to be quiet and if anything a welcome rest from the rigours of the eastern Mediterranean. Meanwhile the anti-submarine sweeps continued. As soon as a ship was sunk or a report of a submarine received destroyers would sail to try and locate the vessel. *Kandahar* and *Jaguar* investigated one on 2 October and *Kipling, Jupiter, Griffin* and *Hotspur* sailed on the 4th, but both were uneventful.

A further abortive operation took place on 10 October. An erroneous report had been received that Italian warships were at sea in the Tobruk area and the fleet sailed to intercept. *Jervis*[7] led *Jaguar, Jupiter, Kandahar, Griffin, Hasty, Hotspur, Decoy, Avon Vale* and *Eridge* out to escort *Barham, Valiant* and *Ajax* to intercept. The next day *Jervis* conducted a three-hour hunt for a submarine as the fleet was returning but this also yielded no results. *Kandahar* was detached to sweep an area where a submarine had been seen with *Jupiter, Griffin, Decoy* and *Avon Vale* under her command but returned to Alexandria on 11 October after another unsuccessful hunt. The fleet was at sea on 12 October, once again to intercept Italian warships but also to cover the start of Operation 'Cultivate', the third and final phase of the relief of the Australian troops from Tobruk. Once again *Jervis, Jaguar, Jupiter* and *Kandahar* were involved and this

---

[6] In a reply to an enquiry from Admiral Cunningham about the damage her captain is reputed to have said, 'I am sorry Sir, I can't report that it was mice'. See L J Lind and M A Payne, *N Class*, p59.

[7] Captain Mack of *Jervis* was the senior destroyer captain in the Mediterranean. He was also senior to many of the captains of larger warships.

time the three 'Js' were detached with *Ajax*, *Hobart* and *Galatea* to intercept an enemy cruiser and destroyer force, but the weather was particularly abysmal and nothing was sighted. 'Cultivate' itself was to involve a run to Tobruk every night by a force consisting of one fast minelayer and three destroyers. By the time the fleet returned, *Napier* and *Jackal* had returned from Suez and *Jackal* was immediately allocated to the Tobruk runs.

'Cultivate' was different from 'Treacle' and 'Supercharge' as destroyers were not allocated to one group on a semi-permanent basis. For example, *Nizam* was part of the *Latona* group with *Jackal* and *Havock* on 17 October but she had also operated as part of the *Abdiel* group earlier. Other Kellys involved throughout the runs were *Kipling*, *Kandahar*, *Jaguar* and *Kingston*. *Jupiter* does not seem to have been involved this time, and neither was *Jervis*. They escorted *Glenroy* to Port Said on 18 October but apart from that enjoyed a few days in port. *Kandahar* had sailed for Tobruk on the same day and on the 19th sighted a submarine on the surface. Hoping to surprise it she closed to 1000 yards, opened her A arc and commenced director firing. The shooting was not good and the submarine dived without being hit. *Kandahar* then prepared to fire a pattern of charges but could not locate the target which she most likely overshot as a result of her captain being blinded by flash

from the guns. A further hindrance was the congestion on her decks as she had a full load of troops which would have made reloading the depth-charge trap and throwers very difficult. In the end, she broke off the attack and returned to Alexandria.

As part of the operations supporting the army, *Ajax*, *Hobart* and *Galatea* sailed, escorted by *Griffin* and *Jaguar*, to bombard a gun position near Tobruk. Their shooting was not particularly effective, and neither was that of *Jervis*, *Jupiter* and *Kandahar* as well when they were despatched on 21 October to bombard the Bardia port facilities. On 22 October in keeping with the increased activity, *Griffin* linked up with *Jervis* and carried out an anti-submarine sweep in front of the merchant ship *Toneline* and the trawler *Kos 19* which had departed Tobruk. *Jupiter* and *Kandahar* were detached to hunt a submarine reported by a Sunderland but *Jupiter* was low on fuel and had to return to Alexandria. *Decoy* was detached to replace her. Bombardment operations continued, *Ajax*, *Neptune* and *Hobart* leaving Alexandria on 23 October with *Napier*, *Nizam*, *Jupiter*, *Hasty*, *Eridge* and *Avon Vale* for the Sollum area. There were two separate bombardments with *Napier*, *Nizam*, *Jupiter* and *Hasty* bombarding the Sollum village area and then returning separately to Alexandria. On 25 October they were at it again, this time with the addition of *Jervis*, *Jaguar*

Napier and *Nizam* hunting a U-boat with air support on 25 December 1941. Both ships carry the bands of the 7th Flotilla and are painted in the scheme that was applied to all ships of the flotilla until the advent of the Admiralty Standard Types in late 1944. No U-boat was found on this occasion. (IMPERIAL WAR MUSEUM: A8051)

Kimberley in late 1941 with a slight variation on her earlier camouflage scheme. Her funnel has now been camouflaged but she has received the full armament update as well. The 4in has been installed and the Oerlikons by the searchlight platform though her quarterdeck Oerlikon still has to be added. Also of interest is the fact that the pennant number has been censored. (IMPERIAL WAR MUSEUM: FL2552)

Jervis in late 1941, with an unusual variation on her previous camouflage with a black panel added to the stern. She still retains her twin sets of tubes and 0.5in machine guns but has had four Oerlikons fitted, two on her aft deckhouse and two adjacent to the searchlight platform. She also now carries a Type 286 on her foremast.

(MUSÉE NATIONAL DE LA MARINE: 6750)

and *Kimberley*. However, the destroyer bombardment was cancelled with the sinking of *Latona* by German aircraft during a supply run to Tobruk. The destroyer *Hero* was also damaged and needed escorting back to Alexandria and *Jervis*, *Jaguar* and *Kimberley* were detached from the bombardment force to do this. *Hero* was successfully escorted back to Alexandria but this was the end of action for the destroyers in the month. Orders for the next major operation, Operation 'Glencoe', were issued on 31 October and this would involve almost all the Kellys.

OPERATION 'GLENCOE' AND FORCE K

Operation 'Glencoe' was the relief of the Cyprus garrison by the 50th Division which were transferred from Haifa to Famagusta. Three groups of ships were involved, sailed at 2-hour intervals. Group A consisted of *Abdiel*, *Jaguar* and

Hasty, Group B *Jervis*, *Kandahar*, *Kimberley* and *Kingston* and Group C *Napier*, *Nizam*, *Kipling* and *Jackal*. Each destroyer carried 250 troops, with *Abdiel* carrying 300 troops and about 70 tons of stores. Each force would arrive at Famagusta and take roughly 2½ hours to unload and load up with departing troops before returning to Haifa. The operation commenced on 2 November and continued without interruption until the 8th. *Kipling* broke down with condenser problems on 3 November and her troops had to be transferred to *Jackal* which then towed her part of the way to Alexandria. She was met by *Decoy* which took up the tow for the rest of the journey whilst *Jackal* returned to the operation, *Jupiter* sailing from Alexandria to take *Kipling*'s place. By 5 November, the intervals between the groups had been widened to four hours but the operation was proceeding smoothly. On 7 November, *Kingston* had to remain at Haifa also with condenser problems and her

On 1 December 1941, *Jackal* was hit on the stern by an aerial torpedo which damaged her severely. Here she is seen under tow with the damage clearly visible. She wears the camouflage and markings of the 7th Flotilla with black pennant numbers. She would get back to port successfully. (IMPERIAL WAR MUSEUM: AD NO. 6880)

troops were distributed between the other ships of Group B. The operation was completed on 8 November without a single casualty. The officer commanding the force, Rear-Admiral Glennie, had referred to the ships as 'my grey painted removal vans' and so on their return to Alexandria on 9 November all the destroyers flew a green and red flag with the words 'Carter Paterson Ltd' (a well-known removal firm) emblazoned on them, while *Abdiel* flew a black flag with Pickfords Limited, a rival firm, on her upper yardarm.[8]

Kipling in the meantime had been repaired and had sailed with *Hotspur* to hunt a submarine. The two destroyers then joined a third, *Encounter*, for a practice bombardment at Aboukir before returning to Alexandria, also on the 9th. The pace of destroyer operations continued unabated, *Kandahar*, *Kingston*, *Kimberley* and *Jupiter* sailing on 10 November to screen *Barham* and *Galatea* on exercises. The next day, the 7th Destroyer Flotilla were at sea and *Napier* and *Nizam* joined *Valiant*, *Hobart*, *Kandahar* and *Hotspur* for a sweep south of Crete. During this period, the Tobruk supply operations continued and *Nizam* took part in Operation 'Approach' with *Abdiel*, *Hero* and *Hotspur* which included transporting twelve urgently-needed 25pdr guns for the garrison. On 13 November *Kipling* had transported the Polish prime minister, General Sikorski, to the fortress to visit his troops.

Jupiter had been in the Mediterranean less than two months when she was ordered to join the Far Eastern fleet. Relations with Japan had been deteriorating and plans had been made to reinforce the fleet. The battleship *Prince of Wales* and the battlecruiser *Repulse* were sent out from Britain and modern destroyers were needed to escort them. This included borrowing ships from the Mediterranean fleet. *Jupiter* was chosen because she had had an unenvi-

able series of problems with her engines. She left Alexandria on 15 November escorted by *Napier* and *Nizam*. By 19 November she had arrived at Aden and the next day sailed for Colombo with *Encounter*, another Mediterranean Fleet destroyer. The two ships arrived on 26 November and left two days later for the naval base at Trincomalee but had to return when *Encounter* developed engine problems. On 29 November *Jupiter*, *Encounter*, *Express* and *Electra* escorted *Prince of Wales* to rendezvous with *Repulse* and then sailed for Singapore, arriving on 6 December. *Jupiter* operated out of Singapore till the end of the month when she sailed for Batavia to join the ABDA[9] fleet.

Back in the Mediterranean, normal destroyer operations continued. After leaving *Jupiter*, *Napier* had joined *Kandahar*, *Hasty* and *Eridge* in what proved to be a fruitless submarine sweep. The Mediterranean fleet embarked on Operation 'ME4', another diversionary operation, this time to draw aircraft from the Western Desert where the relief of Tobruk, Operation 'Crusader', was getting underway by simulating the passage of a convoy. *Napier*, *Nizam*, *Kipling*, *Jackal*, *Jervis*, *Kimberley* and *Kingston* all took part. The fleet sailed on 18 November and the next day *Kipling* and *Jackal* were detached to bombard the Helfaya area before returning to Alexandria. The next diversionary operation got underway on 21 November and consisted of Operations 'ME7' and 'Landmark'. They were intended to support a dummy convoy from Malta and simulate an attack on

---

[8] GG Connell, *Mediterranean Maelstrom*, p135.

[9] American, British, Dutch, Australian.

Tripoli. Once again *Jervis, Kandahar, Kimberley, Kingston, Napier, Nizam, Kipling* and *Jackal* were all involved. The 15th Cruiser Squadron was detached after dark to make diversionary wireless signals whilst the rest of the fleet returned to Alexandria. 'Crusader' was successful and the garrison was able to break out of Tobruk and link up with the relieving forces. The MT ship *Glenroy* was despatched with a harbour clearance party and lighters for the port but was torpedoed on 23 November. *Napier, Nizam, Kipling, Jackal* and *Hasty* sailed to join her escort but she was too badly damaged and had to be beached near Mersa Matruh.

As the destroyers returned to Alexandria, two enemy convoys were reported at sea and Force B, *Ajax, Neptune, Euryalus, Galatea, Kandahar, Kingston, Kimberley* and *Hotspur*, sailed to operate south of the battlefleet which was at sea to support them. *Jervis* sailed with the fleet but *Napier*'s group had to return to Alexandria to refuel before joining the fleet. On 25 November Force B was at sea searching for the convoys outside Ju87 range, the *Napier* group had also joined the screen and the fleet was patrolling between Crete and Cyrenaica. At 4.17pm *Jervis*'s asdic picked up a contact. This was reported to the officer on watch and the duty staff officer who decided that it was not a submarine and should be disregarded. Unfortunately it was a submarine –

U-331 – which put three torpedoes into the *Barham* at 4.30pm. The battleship heeled over and blew up with heavy loss of life. *U-331* broke trim and surfaced 150 yards off *Valiant*'s starboard bow. The battleship tried to ram but not being that manoeuvrable was not able to before the latter dived and escaped. Immediately, *Jervis* and *Jackal* were ordered to hunt the submarine which would, however, make good its escape. *Nizam* and *Hotspur* were ordered to rescue survivors of which there were 450. The rest of the fleet continued westwards and returned to Alexandria on 26 November. The destroyers arrived later. The subsequent Court of Inquiry considered the mistake by *Jervis*'s officers to be significant. Also seen as important was the fact that *Jervis* had not conducted an asdic exercise for ten months.

Force B, meanwhile, had returned to Alexandria but sailed again on 27 November to reinforce Force K which was having some success intercepting enemy convoys which were at a peak. They were ordered to intercept an Italian torpedo-boat sighted leaving Navarin but could not locate it and headed for Malta on the 28th. They arrived on the 29th and sailed the day after with Force K to intercept a convoy sighted in the Ionian Sea. The Italians were running several small convoys and these were recalled when it was learned that the British were at sea. British aircraft sank or

An excellent photograph taken from the Dutch destroyer *Isaac Sweers* on 2 December 1941. *Kingston* is shown passing the Dutch ship in what was possibly her last camouflage scheme and at least her third of 1941. She is not yet fitted with radar but now carries a 4in gun and two Oerlikons. Colours are AP507A and AP507C.

(IMPERIAL WAR MUSEUM: A8054).

damaged several of the ships, one of which was the tanker *Irido Mantovani* which was torpedoed. The Italians detached the destroyer *Alvise da Mosto* to escort her but Force K found the two ships. Both were quickly sunk and Force K returned to Malta where Force B had already arrived on 1 December.

Back in the eastern Mediterranean, *Jervis*, *Jaguar*, *Jackal* and *Kipling* sailed from Alexandria on 30 November to patrol 30 miles north of Derna. As backup they had *Naiad*, *Euryalus*, *Hero* and *Hasty* and the aim was to intercept three Italian destroyers which had been reported in the area. The patrol was uneventful but due to lack of fuel could not be continued the next night and the ships returned to Alexandria on 1 December, conducting an anti-submarine sweep on the way. At 1.00pm five aircraft was seen, three of which commenced a torpedo attack on *Jackal*. The aircraft intelligently divided their attacks and one torpedo hit *Jackal* in the stern at station 92 just below the waterline on the port side putting her steering gear out of action and jamming her rudder 24° to port. The torpedo also damaged her plating and lower deck. As a result the TSDS was out of action but no damage had been caused to *Jackal*'s main machinery. This was a blessing and it enabled her to return to Alexandria at a speed of 14½kts even though the journey took her 22 hours and left her with only 23 tons of fuel in her tanks when she finally arrived on 2 December.

In a tragic incident that occurred after the torpedoing, *Jervis*'s No 2 gun mount still had a shell in the barrel. The gun captain asked permission to clear the barrel by firing off the shell to *Jervis*'s disengaged side. Unfortunately, *Jackal* was 2000 yards away, unseen by the lookouts and the shell burst near the unlucky destroyer, killing her captain, Lieutenant Commander J W Hine, and an able seaman who were on the bridge. Another seaman was mortally wounded.

Jackal would be out of action until May 1942. The day she arrived at Alexandria, *Napier* led *Griffin*, *Hotspur* and *Decoy* out to patrol along the Cyrenaican coast. The force returned on 4 December having sighted nothing and *Jervis* sailed with *Hero* and *Havock* to patrol off Derna. They had to return to Alexandria on 5 December to refuel as they had indulged in a high-speed chase of a hospital ship which was thought to be suspicious. They sailed again the same day and finally returned to Alexandria on 6 December.

THE FIRST BATTLE OF SIRTE AND THE LOSS OF *KANDAHAR*

At Malta, it had become necessary to send the *Breconshire* back to Alexandria and she departed on 5 December escorted by *Kingston* and *Kimberley*. The convoy was met by *Carlisle*, *Griffin* and *Hotspur* and the whole force arrived safely on 8 December. Operation 'ME9' was next, an attempt to intercept enemy units operating in the Ionian sea covering convoys to Libya. *Jervis*, *Kingston*, *Kimberley*, *Napier* and *Nizam* all joined in but unfortunately the operation did not work out as planned when the cruiser *Galatea* was torpedoed and sunk by *U-557*. The destroyers rescued 144 survivors but the subsequent anti-submarine hunt was unsuccessful. On 15 December *Breconshire* sailed, fully loaded with fuel and disguised as a battleship, massively escorted by three cruisers and eight destroyers once again including *Jervis*, *Kimberley*, *Kingston*, *Napier* and *Nizam*. This escort also contributed to the illusion that a fleet was at sea and resulted in the Italian fleet sailing to cover one of their own convoys. The end result of this would be what is known as the First Battle of Sirte. *Carlisle*, *Kingston* and *Hasty* were detached from the escort on 16 December to set up a radio diversion before returning to Alexandria separately. In appalling weather, which was so bad that

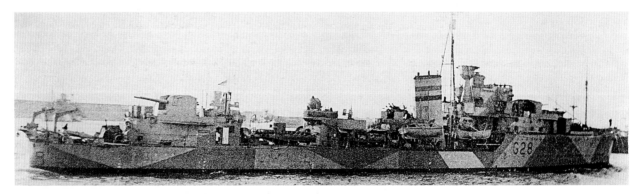

Kandahar at Alexandria on 2 November 1941. This photograph is interesting as it shows her final configuration before her loss a little over six weeks later and possibly her final camouflage scheme as well. Whilst Oerlikons have been added the 4in has not and would not be.

There also appears to be a light machine gun mounted on her quarterdeck, a rare view of one of these weapons which were frequently added for extra firepower (though how much they provided is debatable). (MUSÉE NATIONAL DE LA MARINE: 181164)

Breconshire had to turn south to make repairs, the ships struggled westwards. Force K sailed to meet the convoy, joining it on 17 December. The Italian force finally came into view on 18 December, consisting of the battleships *Littorio*, *Giulio Cesare* and *Andrea Doria*, the cruisers *Gorizia* and *Trento* and ten destroyers. However, despite locating the British the Italian admiral felt that by the time he could reach the enemy, it would be too late in the day to engage them. *Breconshire* again turned south with *Decoy* and *Havock* as escorts whilst the British force commander Admiral Vian led his cruisers and destroyers into a blocking position. His intention was not to engage unless *Breconshire* was seriously threatened.

A smokescreen was laid but when Captain Mack led the 14th Flotilla out for a torpedo attack they were recalled, as Vian had also received specific instructions from Cunningham in Alexandria not to attempt a night action. At the same time as it was being shelled by the Italian fleet, Vian's force was under attack from aircraft but succeeded in his aim to draw the Italian fleet away from *Breconshire* and fortunately incurred very little damage in carrying this out. The 7th Flotilla came under fire and *Kipling* received slight damage but after dark the Italians turned away and withdrew. Vian then returned to Alexandria, arriving on 19 December but as they passed through the boom three Italian human torpedoes[10] were also able to penetrate. These had been launched from the submarine *Sciré* and positioned themselves under the battleships *Queen Elizabeth* and *Valiant* and the stern of the oiler *Sagona*. *Jervis* was moored near the oiler and when the SLC exploded it damaged her bows, blowing in the plates of the communications mess deck, the paint store and the carbide compartment. The explosion ignited the carbide which then set off the spirits in the paint store but the fire was quickly bought under control. *Jervis* would be under repair for a month but the damage to the battleships was much more serious and they would require extensive repairs.

As this blow befell the Mediterranean fleet, Force K also suffered a disaster on what was a very good day for the Axis. They had escorted *Breconshire* into Malta and refuelled before sailing to try and intercept the Italian convoy. To avoid Italian mines, interception forces were to stay outside a line of 100 fathoms depth but this was flexible and they could approach to up to 90 fathoms as this depth was considered safe. Force K was in line ahead with *Neptune* leading followed by *Aurora*, *Penelope*, *Kandahar*, *Havock*, *Lance* and *Lively*. Speed was 30kts and course 195°. About 23 miles north of Tripoli Force K sailed into an excep-

tionally deeply-laid minefield. *Neptune* was the first to hit a mine followed rapidly by *Aurora* and *Penelope*. *Aurora* managed to turn and followed by *Penelope* was able to steam out of the minefield. However, *Neptune*'s engines had been disabled by the mine and she drifted into another two. Captain Agnew in *Aurora* ordered Commander Robson in *Kandahar* to detail one destroyer from his division to go alongside *Neptune*. This Robson refused to allocate to anyone else but himself and as the other ships of the force waited outside the minefield *Kandahar* entered the minefield. When she was about seven cables from *Neptune*, *Kandahar* touched off a mine under her stern. Shortly after, *Neptune* struck her fourth mine and turned over and sank. There would be only one survivor. *Lively* attempted to go to the assistance of *Kandahar* but was ordered away by Robson who also suggested that the rest of Force K return to Malta. Very reluctantly they did.

The explosion blew had blown *Kandahar*'s stern off up to bulkhead 68 which was perforated but bulkhead 61 held and the ship remained afloat. Both boilers and the auxiliary machinery remained in working order but the *Kandahar* was not steerable as the propellers and rudder had been blown away. Her fire control was out of action but Nos 1 and 2 mounts were workable by hand. Her 0.5in machine guns and Oerlikons were also operational but the pompom was out of action. The crew were also able to get the radio equipment working but not the lights which were out of action due to the flooding of the aft electrical switchboard. As much top weight as possible was jettisoned but only three of the ten torpedoes could be fired. For most of the 19th *Kandahar* drifted unnoticed and eventually she drifted clear of the minefield but started to list as the sea rose. About 4.20am on the 20th *Jaguar*, which had been despatched from Malta, arrived guided in by an ASV Wellington. *Jaguar* attempted to go alongside bow-to-bow but could not hold this position in the bad weather as *Kandahar* was yawing badly by now and would have caused serious damage if he had remained. Her captain therefore held off and *Kandahar*'s crew swam across to *Jaguar*. Seven officers and 150 ratings were saved but one officer and fifty-four ratings were missing. There remained the question of what to do with *Kandahar*. *Jaguar* faced the problem of towing the wrecked ship back to Malta in the remaining hours of darkness. For this she needed to be able to maintain a speed in excess of 10kts which in the sea conditions and with *Kandahar*'s state was not possible. Reluctantly the decision was taken to scuttle her and *Jaguar* fired one torpedo at 5.45am on 20 December. *Kandahar* sank shortly afterwards and *Jaguar* returned to Malta. The Board of Enquiry that met to consider the debacle concluded that

---

[10] Known as *Siluro a Lenta Corsa* or SLC. Translated this literally means 'Slow Speed Torpedo'.

no one was to blame and endorsed all the decisions that had been taken. The cause of the losses was the extremely skilfully-laid minefield which could not have been anticipated. This minefield had an effect far beyond sinking two ships. It had neutered Force K and reduced Malta's effectiveness as a base for anti-convoy operations which allowed regular supplies once again to reach the Afrika Korps.

KIPLING AND THE SINKING OF U-75
German submarines which had been arriving in the Mediterranean were having considerable success. To combat this threat destroyer sweeps off Alexandria were instituted and *Kimberley*, *Nizam*, *Griffin* and *Sikh* sailed on such a sweep on 22 December. They were unable to locate any submarines and *Kimberley* and *Nizam* joined in another sweep with *Napier* and *Kingston* the next day, relieving the 2nd Flotilla. These sweeps would be stopped on 25 December as a waste of time. With the relief of Tobruk, small coastal convoys were now regularly running between Alexandria and Tobruk and the other ports. In a repeat of the practice with the UK coastal convoys, these were allocated destroyer striking forces, and *Kipling* and *Legion* sailed on 23 December to provide cover for Convoy AT6. This convoy had set sail in pretty rough weather and was struggling. On 24 December *Kimberley* had to sail to escort the freighter *Vavara* from the convoy back to Alexandria with a flooded engine room. The rest of the convoy was only able to make 3½-4½kts. This continued until the 26th when an explosion was seen in the stern of the Polish ship *Warzawa*. Assuming that this was from a submarine, *Kipling* and *Legion* began an anti-submarine hunt whilst *Avondale* stood by the stricken freighter and the corvette *Peony* took her under tow. Having located nothing the search was broken off at dusk and *Kipling* and *Legion* returned to cover *Warzawa*. The remainder of the convoy, the boom defence vessel *Burgonet* and the freighter SS *Alisa* continued independently to Tobruk. At 7.25pm a second torpedo finished off *Warzawa* and *Kipling* and *Legion* recommenced their hunt. Contact was obtained and *Kipling* made an attack followed by *Legion*. *Kipling* had to break off the attack to refuel at Tobruk and as she returned to the area she was attacked by four torpedo bombers but these were driven off with the help of *Legion*. The two destroyers then broke off their hunt and joined *Peony* and Convoy 'Barge'.

At 2.47am on 28 December, the SS *Volo* was torpedoed and sunk. Once again *Legion* and *Kipling* commenced a search and this time *Kipling* was rewarded with a contact. She initially attacked with just one charge which confirmed that the contact was indeed a submarine retiring at high speed. The submarine tried to evade *Kipling* by steering

towards and under her but at 3.55am *Kipling* obtained a firm contact and planted a six-charge pattern on it. Contact was lost and *Kipling* returned to the location where she had first made contact and was shortly rewarded with the sight of the submarine surfacing bows first, 1500 yards off her port quarter. The searchlight and 20in signal projector were immediately snapped on and *Kipling* opened fire with all guns and began to hit her. The submarine started circling but clouds of smoke were coming from her conning tower and the smell of chlorine gas was detectable even 800 yards away and she rapidly came to a stop and started to sink on an even keel. She was the *U-75* and had been sunk after a 2-hour hunt. *Kipling* and *Legion* rescued two officers and twenty-eight men before sailing to rescue three survivors from the *Volo* and then rejoined the convoy. *Kipling*'s pattern of charges had been very accurate, disabling the submarine's steering gear and aft hydroplane and damaging her hull quite seriously. Convoy 'Barge' arrived later on 28 December and *Kipling* and *Legion* sailed with Convoy AT10 on the 29th as the striking force with *Farndale* and the anti-submarine trawler *Southern Isle*. *Farndale* thought she saw a conning tower but *Kipling* could not make contact. *Legion* remained behind to search but was unsuccessful and returned to the convoy. Tobruk was reached with the convoy intact on 31 December and *Kipling* and *Legion* carried out a sweep to cover the departure of *Prince Badouin* and *Heythrop* with Convoy 'Merit' before joining the convoy for its journey to Alexandria.

With *Jervis* under repair most operations involving the Kellys came under Captain Arliss of the 7th Flotilla. *Jaguar* was based at Malta with Force K so he had at his disposal *Kimberley* and *Kingston* of the 14th and *Napier*, *Nizam* and *Kipling* of the 7th. On 26 December he sailed as part of Force B taking *Kingston* and *Nizam* with him to join the 7th Cruiser Squadron but the rendezvous was postponed due to bad weather until the 28th, when *Napier*, *Nizam* and *Kingston* sailed to take part in Operation 'MF1', the sailing of Convoy ME8 and reinforcements for the Mediterranean fleet to Alexandria. ME8 was the first convoy to be passed from Malta to Alexandria since the 'Tiger' convoy in May. It also brought the third Australian 'N' class destroyer, *Nestor*, into the Mediterranean to join her flotilla mates. On 31 December she sailed with *Ajax*, *Nizam*, *Gurkha*, *Kingston* and *Arrow* for a bombardment of Bardia.

PIORUN IN 1941[11]
The year began for *Piorun* with convoy escort duty when she and *Napier* escorted the Armed Merchant Cruisers

---

[11] Most of this section is based on an unpublished paper written by Marek Twardowski.

Cilicia and *Wolfe* to Djupvôgar in Iceland before sailing to Reykjavik to escort a convoy back to Scapa Flow. On arrival there, she damaged herself coming alongside an oiler to refuel and was repaired by the depot ship *Maidstone*. She was then loaned to the 10th Escort Group operating from Greenock but in fact did not join it until the end of the month. Before that she sailed with *Nelson*, *Rodney* and *Repulse* to intercept the *Scharnhorst* on 27 January. However, no sighting was made and *Piorun* had to detach from the fleet and return to Scapa with weather damage. Temporary repairs were made followed by more permanent repairs at Greenock. Finally, on 8 February, she joined the 10th Escort Group escorting a convoy bound for America. At this stage escorts did not cross the Atlantic and *Piorun* turned back on 12 February, arriving at Greenock on the 14th. Two more convoys were escorted in February before *Piorun* sailed for the Clyde to refit. Whilst in dock the Clyde shipyards were bombed and heavily damaged. Members of her crew helped extinguish a fire on the *Duke of York* but on 24 March it was back to convoy escort duty. This continued until 13 April when *Piorun* and *Legion* were diverted to pick up the survivors of the Armed Merchant Cruiser *Rajputana*, which had been torpedoed by *U-108*. The destroyers picked up 290 men and then joined a Canadian troop convoy to the UK. *Piorun* was with *Rodney* when the battleship rammed the unfortunate trawler *Topaze* on 20 April and sank her, and picked up four men out of the crew of twenty-five. She was back under repair from 3 to 20 May. Six days later she was part of the escort for the important WS8B troop convoy with the 4th Destroyer Flotilla.

On 20 May, the German battleship *Bismarck* had sailed on Operation 'Rheinübung', a cruise to raid British shipping. She had sunk the battlecruiser *Hood* on the 24th but had then been damaged by torpedo aircraft. The lack of destroyers for the Home Fleet battleships pursuing the *Bismarck* meant that some would have to be diverted from other operations. There was *Jupiter* but she was in the Irish sea and would not be available till well after the others. The 4th Destroyer Flotilla with *Piorun* were ordered to leave the convoy and proceed to join *King George V*. Captain Vian (D4) took *Sikh* and *Zulu* with him to join *King George V* whilst *Piorun* and *Maori* were ordered to join *Rodney*. *Jupiter* was also ordered to join up with the battleships as soon as possible. As they were steering to meet *King George V*, Vian picked up a report from a Catalina flying boat of a battleship and rather than steer towards the fleet, decided to head for this target. He ordered full speed but found that this was impossible in the sea conditions and had to reduce to 27kts. Even then it was difficult going, with the

small ships 'taking it green' and yawing wildly. By 10.00pm they had sighted the cruiser *Sheffield*, having already passed Force H and *Renown*, and Vian asked for the bearing of *Bismarck* and, once he received it, headed for the German battleship. At 10.50pm *Zulu* signalled that she had the *Bismarck* in sight.

Vian's destroyers were in line abreast, 2½ miles apart when *Bismarck* was sighted, firstly by *Piorun* though *Zulu*, as mentioned, made the sighting report. *Bismarck* sighted *Piorun* shortly afterwards and opened fire with both her main and secondary armament, but the Polish destroyer proceeded to trade fire with the battleship for the next half hour before hauling off out of range. Rather than go charging in, Vian decided to shadow *Bismarck* first and arranged *Sikh*, *Zulu*, *Maori* and *Piorun* in a box around the battleship whilst *Cossack* shadowed from astern. If an occasion for a torpedo attack offered itself Vian would take it but only if he could avoid losses to his own force. There then followed a confused action as *Bismarck* tried to drive the destroyers away and they manoeuvred to avoid the battleship's shells. All except *Piorun* tried torpedo attacks but without result. Conversely, *Bismarck*'s fire though unpleasantly close failed to score any hits. By 5.00am on 27 May *Piorun* was running low on fuel and she was ordered by Vian to return to Plymouth. Her captain continued to search to the north-west for the battleship for another hour before turning for home.

After her moment of glory *Piorun* then returned to convoy escort duty though it was once again the important WS convoys, this time Convoy WS8X from Greenock to Gibraltar. The convoy sailed on 30 May and also included the aircraft carrier *Victorious* and the cruisers *Norfolk* and *Neptune* in its escort. On 3 June *Piorun* and *Sherwood* were detached from the convoy to rendezvous with and escort the *Athlone Castle* to the UK. The latter proved very difficult to locate and it was not until 5 June that *Piorun* was able to find her charge and escort her to the UK. Throughout June she worked with a special escort group from Greenock and in July joined the Polish liner *Batory* in transporting Soviet gold to the United States. At the end of August she joined the 9th Escort Group and on 2 September rescued survivors from the *Fort Richepance* which had been torpedoed. *Piorun* left the escort group shortly afterwards as she and her consorts sailed to take part in Operation 'Halberd', a convoy to Malta from Gibraltar. At 6.15pm on 24 September, *Nelson* escorted by *Piorun*, *Garland* and *Isaac Sweers* feinted west out of Gibraltar before reversing course and sailing to join the convoy.

They met Convoy WS11X on 25 September and *Piorun* joined Group II of the escort which included the battleships *Prince of Wales* and *Rodney*. The convoy itself consisted of nine ships.[12] The two groups were divided into two forces, Force X consisting of cruisers and destroyers which would form the close escort to Malta and Force H which included the *Ark Royal*, battleships and all ships that were not part of the close escort. Initially the operation went smoothly but on 26 September they were attacked by Italian aircraft, one of which was able to torpedo *Nelson* despite a furious barrage. The convoy and escort steamed on and with the Italian fleet also at sea the battleships remained with the convoy. However, they did not intervene and *Nelson*, which was experiencing trouble, finally left the convoy on 28 September escorted by *Duncan*, *Garland* and *Piorun*, arriving back at Gibraltar on 30 September. The convoy itself was a success with only the *Imperial Star* being sunk. *Piorun* then returned to Britain where she was reassigned to convoy duty. This was more interesting as the escort groups now crossed the Atlantic with their convoys and in October *Garland* and *Piorun* were the first to do so. Normally they sailed to Halifax and moored at Argentia before returning.

[12] *Breconshire, Clan MacDonald, Clan Ferguson, Ajax, Imperial Star, City of Lincoln. Rowallan Castle, Dunedin Star* and *City of Calcutta*.

Nestor in July 1941 transferring correspondence prior to or during Operation 'Substance'. She is not fitted with Oerlikons but carries a Type 285 located on her rangefinder tower, the first Kelly to be so fitted. Also visible is her divisional leader's bar which she carried at least until November of that year.

(IMPERIAL WAR MUSEUM: A4680)

NESTOR BEFORE THE MEDITERRANEAN.

On 5 May *Nestor* joined the 6th Destroyer Flotilla for an operation in Arctic waters. This was an attempt to capture German weather trawlers. Three were supposed to be operating in the Arctic and the information they could provide would be invaluable. *Nestor* was lucky. On 7 May one of these vessels was spotted and ordered to heave to. Included in the haul of prisoners was a German naval intelligence officer and *Nestor* was immediately ordered back to Scapa Flow with her prisoner. She arrived on 9 May but on the 14th her senior officers were suddenly replaced.[13] With news that *Bismarck* was at sea, *Nestor* sailed with the rest of the Home Fleet at 10.15pm on 22 May. The weather was very rough and conditions on board all the destroyers became very wet and uncomfortable. *Nestor* remained in company

with the fleet until 25 May when the destroyers were detached to Iceland to refuel. She was therefore not present at the final destruction of the German battleship and was ordered to join *Prince of Wales* and escort her back before returning to sea to escort *King George V* and *Rodney* to Loch Ewe. She finally sailed for Scapa with *Jupiter* arriving on 30 May. *Nestor* spent June and part of early July operating with the Home Fleet out of Scapa. After the excitement of the chase these days were pretty quiet but things would change in July.

Nestor sailed for Greenock on 8 July and spent the next four days having modifications carried out.[14] On the 13th she sailed from Londonderry to escort a convoy and then later set off for Gibraltar to take part in Operation 'Substance', an attempt to run a six-ship[15] convoy to Malta. The

---

[13] L J Lind and M A Payne, *N Class*, quotes one of her ships officers who stated that the reason for this was that they were in no fit state to put to sea when ordered, after a wardroom party. A temporary captain was detailed from the Rear Admiral (Destroyers) staff until a replacement Australian captain was found. I have found no official account to back this up but it is true that *Nestor* had a temporary RN officer in charge. During the *Bismarck* chase her captain was Lieutenant Commander C B Alers-Hankey DSC, RN who was shortly afterwards replaced by Commander A S Rosenthal RAN and this lends some credence to the account as RAN destroyers were supposed to have RAN officers in charge.

[14] Lind and Payne claim that she had her 4in HA gun fitted during this period but this is unlikely. The instruction for the 4in had been issued in June/July the previous year and the 'Ns' were completed with it in place. The only reason a 4in gun would not have been fitted by the builders would be that there were none available at the time but once again this is unlikely. The only other possibility would be that she had a faulty gun replaced. Unfortunately I have been unable to find any photos earlier than September 1941 and so cannot confirm the assertion.

[15] *Leinster, Deucalion, Port Chalmers, Durham, Melbourne Star* and *Sydney Star*.

Leinster ran aground leaving Gibraltar in fog and had to be left behind. The rest of the convoy steamed on with *Nestor* screening *Nelson* on 20 July before being ordered to screen *Renown* instead. Opposition began to appear and on 22 July the Italian submarine *Diaspro* attempted to torpedo *Nestor* and *Renown* but missed both. *Nestor* had picked the torpedoes up on her hydrophones and then sighted the tracks. Her prompt warning enabled *Renown* to evade them as well. She then turned and ran down the tracks gaining a firm contact which she attacked with one five-charge pattern followed by two six-charge patterns. Contact was lost after the third attack and after an extensive search she was unable to regain it. *Nestor* rejoined the screen at 6.15am on 23 July just as the air attacks were getting into full swing. *Manchester* and *Fearless* were both hit by aerial torpedoes and *Nestor* missed by one. *Manchester* would survive but *Fearless* had to be scuttled. *Firedrake* was damaged by a near miss and had to return to Gibraltar.

During the night Italian MAS boats attacked. They were detected by *Cossack*'s radar but *MAS 532* and *MAS 533* successfully torpedoed the freighter *Sydney Star* and escaped. *Nestor* noticed *Sydney Star* dropping astern and went to investigate and after some trouble was able to ascertain that the freighter's Nos 1 and 2 holds had been flooded. *Nestor* took off the troops she was carrying, a process which took some 50 minutes and after completion of which she had 774 people on board.[16] *Sydney Star* did not seem to be sinking and so *Nestor*'s captain Commander Rosenthal concluded that her master, Captain Horn, was being unduly pessimistic about his chances. He then persuaded him that they could make Malta and promised that *Nestor* would stay with the damaged freighter. This had the desired effect and both ships set off for the island. They came under air attack and *Nestor* sent out an urgent request for help which resulted in the cruiser *Hermione* being sent back to provide extra support. The air attacks increased in ferocity and intensity but fortunately without any hits. However, *Sydney Star* did begin to swing and the pumps were no longer able to hold the influx of water but she was able to make Malta and the three ships were cheered into the harbour when they arrived at 2.00pm on the 24th. *Nestor*'s actions brought her high commendation from Admiral Somerville and later the Admiralty and her captain and several crew members received Distinguished Service Crosses for their efforts. *Nestor* did not stay long at Malta but departed the same evening with the rest of Force H escorting a convoy of seven empty merchant ships back to Gibraltar. One of these was lost but the force was met by *Ark Royal* which provided

much-needed air cover. Two of *Ark Royal*'s fighters were shot down but *Nestor* was able to rescue one crew. On 27 July the whole force arrived at Gibraltar.

Operation 'Substance' had only been a partial success as *Leinster* had not been able to sail with the convoy. She was due to carry vitally needed spare parts for the island's Beaufighters and 1700 troops and these had been left behind. These were loaded onto the cruisers *Arethusa* and *Hermione*, the fast minelayer *Manxman* and the destroyers *Sikh* and *Lightning* which then made a fast run to the island supported by Force H. This time *Nestor* remained in support with Force H which carried out a diversionary operation codenamed 'Style'. *Cossack* and *Maori* were detached to bombard Alghero in north-west Sardinia and the rest of Force H cruised between Minorca and Sardinia. The whole operation was a stunning success with all ships arriving safely though *Hermione* had damaged her bows ramming and sinking the Italian submarine *Tembien* on 2 August. The entire fleet returned to Gibraltar on 4 August.

Nestor next sailed to escort Convoy OG70 on 6 August. This proved to be quiet until 11 August when together with *Encounter* she sighted a U-boat on the surface, 3000 yards away. Shortly afterwards a torpedo passed along her side as she sped to attack. She then made two attacks but the U-boat seems to have successfully evaded these and disappeared. *Nestor* returned to Gibraltar on 12 August now firmly a part of Force H. She sailed with them on 14 August for gunnery exercises, acting as divisional leader. When the ships returned on 17th *Nestor* needed urgent repairs to A gun. Her next operation was Operation 'Mincemeat' which was aimed at destroying the Italian cork forests at Tempio in north-western Sardinia. It was also intended to divert enemy attention from the *Manxman* which was due to lay mines off Leghorn. Both operations were a success, *Ark Royal*'s aircraft causing extensive fires on 24 August. Later in the day it was reported that the Italian fleet was at sea and the force turned to meet them and prepared a air strike at dusk but the Italians did not venture further. Force H arrived at Gibraltar on 26 August.

Five days later *Nestor* started to venture further, escorting Freetown-bound convoys. At first she sailed as far as Ponta Delgarda but on 4 September she joined a troop convoy bound for the Middle East which would take her to join the Mediterranean Fleet but had to put into Bathurst in Gambia on the 5th to refuel. This was a result of *Repulse* using the oiler sailing with the convoy before the destroyer and emptying it. Her entry into the Mediterranean would be considerably delayed.

Nestor was leaving Bathurst on 11 September in shallow tidal waters when she picked up an excellent asdic contact.

---

[16] 231 crew, 56 army passengers and 487 from the *Sydney Star*.

She instantly attacked it but the shock of the depth charge explosions damaged her quite significantly. The shock had not affected the turbines but had fractured both sliding feet on the port HP turbine. This effectively reduced her speed to 18kts. The contact itself was likely to have been a school of fish. *Nestor* sailed to St Helena then Freetown where the damage was examined. It was beyond local resources to repair and so she returned to Gibraltar where she arrived on 25 September. After refuelling and taking on board three Fleet Air Arm officers *Nestor* sailed for Devonport arriving on 30 September.

Nestor was under repair from 1 October until 30 November. She then loaded provisions and sailed for a short period of trials. After a trip up to the Clyde she sailed with Convoy WS14 as senior officer of the escort. After detaching from the convoy on 12 December the destroyers were ordered to Gibraltar. On the 15th *Nestor*, *Gurkha*, *Foxhound* and *Croome* were carrying out an anti-submarine sweep 34 miles south of Cape St. Vincent when a U-boat was sighted 7 miles away on the horizon. N*estor* immediately turned towards it with *Foxhound* and *Gurkha* taking station on the beam. At 11,000 yards she opened fire with her foremost guns but scored no hits, and the U-boat dived. The ships reduced speed and commenced a sweep, picking the submarine up 4 minutes later. Immediately, *Nestor* made an attack with a five-charge pattern set for 100, 150 and 250ft. *Gurkha* could not obtain a contact but *Foxhound* did. This faded, however, and a little later an explosion was felt in *Foxhound*, comparable to a depth charge exploding deep under the ship. It was also felt by the other three ships. *Croome*, which had come up slightly later, obtained a doubtful contact and dropped two patterns of charges. These brought up oil, wreckage and human remains. The submarine, which turned out to be the *U-127*, had definitely been destroyed, probably by an internal explosion caused by *Nestor*'s attack, and she got the credit for the kill.

The destroyers returned to Gibraltar, arriving on 16 December. On the 22nd *Nestor*, *Gurkha*, *Zulu*, *Foxhound*, *Arrow* and *Dido* sailed for Malta. The Admiralty had decided to risk the passing of reinforcements for the fleet together with a convoy of empty ships through the Mediterranean. *Nestor* spent Christmas at Malta and sailed on the 26th with her consorts (Force C) and *Lance* and *Lively* (Force B). The convoy was made up of *Sydney Star*, *Ajax*, *City of Calcutta* and *Clan Ferguson*. An air raid delayed the departure of *Clan Ferguson*, *Ajax*, *Lance*, *Lively* and *Gurkha* and so the rest of the convoy slowed down to allow them to catch up. *Nestor* was in charge of the anti-submarine arrangements but the convoy also enjoyed air support on part of its journey. On 28 December they rendezvoused with Force D, *Carlisle*, *Napier*, *Maori*,

Nizam and *Kingston*, at which point *Lance* and *Lively* returned to Malta. *Nizam* detached to escort *Sydney Star* to Port Said whilst the rest of the convoy and its escort arrived at Alexandria at 10.15am on 29 December. During its passage it had come under heavy air attack but only *Maori* and *Clan Ferguson* had been damaged by splinters.

NORMAN IN THE ARCTIC

Norman, the fifth 'N' class destroyer, commissioned on 15 September 1941 and sailed to Scapa Flow to begin her working-up which was interrupted on 6 October when she was ordered to Seidis Fjord to pick up a British trade union mission for a visit to the Soviet Union. They had originally embarked on the destroyer *Antelope* at the end of September but she had suffered engine trouble and had to put into Iceland. *Norman* was the first destroyer that became available. She arrived at Seidis Fjord on 7 October having averaged 31kts on passage and collected the delegation. She refuelled and sailed at 8.00am the next day, this time averaging 18½kts on the passage to Archangel in arctic conditions. She arrived at Archangel and disembarked her passengers and then went alongside *Suffolk* before sailing for an anti-submarine patrol off the North Drivia Light Vessel on 15 October. Next day *Norman* was ordered back to Seidis Fjord and Scapa Flow but as she neared Bear Island was ordered back to Archangel. She arrived on 19 October but as she had no idea when the delegation would return she offered her services to the Soviet naval officer in charge there. These were accepted and it was requested that she carry out an anti-submarine patrol in the White Sea where German submarines had been active. *Norman* sailed on 21 October after a slight delay to clear her condenser inlets. She found nothing and returned to Archangel to refuel on 22 October and wait for the delegation, which returned on 26 October but did not embark until the 27th when *Norman* set sail for Seidis Fjord. She arrived there on the 31st and took on both fuel and provisions before sailing for Scrabster where she disembarked the delegates. Then it was back to Scapa arriving on 2 November.

Norman spent November escorting *Duke of York* and convoys. She arrived at the Clyde on 5 December and after repairs sailed for Southampton where she arrived on 9 December for a refit. During her time at the Clyde her sister-ship *Nestor* had arrived from Southampton on the 6th and for a brief time both destroyers were in port together. *Norman* entered dry dock at Southampton for a refit that would last until 4 January 1942. There were still three 'Ns' yet to enter service, *Nepal*, *Van Galen* and *Tjerk Hiddes* and they would all commission in 1942 which was to prove another tough year for the Kellys.

11

1942: The Second Battle of Sirte and the Java Sea

T HE 5TH DESTROYER FLOTILLA had been disbanded which left the 7th and 14th Flotillas in the Mediterranean and various ships of the 'N' class working-up or still building. At the start of the year, there were still nine Kellys operational with four under repair and three building. Of the ships under repair three would re-enter service early in 1942 although one, *Javelin*, would not join the Mediterranean fleet until halfway through the year.

JANUARY IN THE MEDITERRANEAN

The force from the moderately successful bombardment of Bardia returned to Alexandria on 1 January. The next day the Australian destroyers left for the Eastern Fleet at the request of the Australian government after the Japanese attacks on Pearl Harbor and Malaya. *Napier*, *Nizam* and *Nestor* departed for their first mission, escorting the aircraft carrier *Indomitable* which was carrying air reinforcements for Malaya, the remaining ships of the 7th Destroyer Flotilla, *Kipling* and *Jackal*, joining an enlarged 27th Division of the 14th Flotilla.[1] On 3 January *Kimberley* had sailed with *Hasty* as the escort for Convoy AT11 to Tobruk and Benghazi, arriving there without incident on 7 January, but bad weather delayed their return to Alexandria until the 11th.

On 12 January, while conducting a sweep off the approaches to Tobruk, *Kimberley* was hit by a single torpedo fired by *U-77*, on the starboard side, blowing the whole stern off with everything aft of bulkhead 73 bursting into

---

[1] The 28th Division consisted of *Maori*, *Sikh* and *Zulu*.

Jaguar leading *Lance*, *Lively* and *Glengyle* into Malta Harbour on 8 January 1942. *Jaguar* is now fitted with a Type 286 and Oerlikons but still retains her external galley funnel and was probably lost with it still in place, the only 'J' class not to be altered. (IMPERIAL WAR MUSEUM: A7368)

flames. The initial explosion was rapidly followed by a second one which was probably a depth charge primer going off. Immediately, the main engines were stopped and the manoeuvring valve closed. An attempt was made to flood the aft magazines but the valves had jammed. Fortunately the magazine was open to the sea and did not explode, otherwise *Kimberley* would have sunk. Several compartments were flooding rapidly through the stern glands and a fire was raging on deck. Top weight was jettisoned, including ready-use ammunition and depth charges. Only the starboard engine was still functioning, and both propellers and their shafts were badly damaged. Other damage was mainly due to the force of the explosion. The quarterdeck Oerlikon had vanished but No 3 mount could still be trained. The shell hoist to the gun could only be worked by hand and the guns themselves were damaged. The fire was put out by 3.40am on the 13th, and she was towed back to Alexandria on the 14th. Repairing *Kimberley* was beyond the capabilities of Alexandria or even Port Said and she would need to be sent to Bombay, a long, slow journey under tow all the way. On arrival at Bombay she would be repaired and then reduced to care and maintenance before being refitted in late 1943 and re-entering service in 1944.

Kipling and *Kingston* joined the 15th Cruiser Squadron[2] and other destroyers for Operation 'MF2'. This was an attempt to sail *Glengyle* and *Sikh* to Malta and got underway on 5 January. At the same time they were to meet and escort *Breconshire*, *Dido* and *Havock* to Alexandria. All went well and the

Caption: *Kelvin* on 15 February 1942 during Operation 'MF5' as she turns to screen what is possibly *Rowallan Castle* in the background. Her four Oerlikons are visible but her Type 286P aerials appear to have been censored. Her 4in gun is also clearly visible. (IMPERIAL WAR MUSEUM: A8262)

force was met by *Lance*, *Lively* and *Jaguar* on the 7th and the changeover effected. The rest of the force reversed course and returned to Alexandria, arriving safely on 8 January. *Kingston* then joined the newly returned *Kelvin* in escorting the oiler *Derwentdale* from Port Said to Alexandria.

Kelvin's first major operation was Operation 'MF3' providing cover for Convoys MW8A and MW8B to Malta. The opportunity was also to be taken to replace *Jaguar* with *Legion* as part of Force K. Once again they were joined by *Kipling* and the 15th Cruiser Squadron. Force B, as it was known, was due to sail at 11.59pm on 16 January, but as it departed *Kingston* and *Foxhound* collided in the dark. Both were rendered unseaworthy, *Kingston* being put out of action for three and a half weeks. The rest of the force left on the morning of 17 January and rendezvoused with the four ships of the convoy the next day. Later that day they met with Force K as scheduled and turned back for Alexandria with *Jaguar*, arriving on 20 January. *Kelvin* was detached to Tobruk to pick up the survivors from *Gurkha* which had been sunk by a U-boat and take them to Alexandria. She arrived at roughly the same time as the 15th Cruiser Squadron.

This was followed by Operation 'MF4' covering *Breconshire*'s latest fuel run to Malta. *Kingston* would also sail with the convoy for repairs in the dockyard there and *Lance* would join the Mediterranean Fleet. Two empty transports,

[2] For this operation *Naiad* and *Euryalus*.

Rowallan Castle and *Glengyle*, would also sail. The force for this operation was quite large[3] and Force K was also out in strength. The two convoys met and exchanged escorts on 26 January with *Kingston* continuing to Malta with *Breconshire* and Force K. January had been quite a successful month for the fleet, the Malta convoys all arriving intact but damage to destroyers continued to mount. *Jervis* also completed her repairs and was able to take her place leading the 14th Flotilla again.

INCREASING PRESSURE

Jervis's first operation after her repairs was to lead a force of seven destroyers including *Jaguar* and *Kelvin* from Alexandria on 4 February for an anti-submarine sweep westwards (Operation 'MDB4'), involving co-operation with ASV Swordfish and Wellingtons. *Jaguar* carried out an unsuccessful attack on a U-boat on 5 February and the ships returned to Alexandria the next day. *Kipling* and *Jaguar* also sailed to provide extra cover for the damaged 'Hunt' class destroyer *Farndale*, arriving safely with her at Alexandria on the 11th.

On 13 February Force B left Alexandria to escort two small convoys, MW9A and MW9B, to Malta. At the same time they would also pick up Convoy ME10 of empty ships from Malta to Alexandria (Operation 'MF5'). The eight

[3] Force B, *Naiad, Dido, Euryalus, Carlisle, Griffin, Kelvin, Kipling, Arrow, Jaguar, Hasty* and *Isaac Sweers*.

destroyers involved included *Jervis, Kipling, Kelvin* and *Jaguar*. The escort rendezvoused with Convoys MW9A and MW9B at 7.00 am on 14 February. Later that day they met with Force K and exchanged convoys but they had already been heavily attacked and lost two of the three transports. The one remaining, *Rowallan Castle*, was handed over to Force K but would be bombed and sunk the next day, so no loaded ships would reach Malta. Convoy ME10 was attacked but no ships were lost. *Breconshire* was taken directly to Alexandria but the other three ships were escorted to Port Said by *Jervis, Kelvin, Kipling, Jaguar* and *Fortune*. They arrived on 17 February, after which *Jaguar, Kelvin* and *Fortune* returned to Alexandria.

In a change to the regular programme of convoys and sweeps, in March *Kelvin* and *Jaguar* sailed with one company from the 11th Battalion Royal Marines to practice landings after dark on the coast of Cyprus as training for a series of planned raids on the Libyan or Cretan coasts. Exercises were carried out on the night of 6/7 March but did not go well. The sea was rough and several boats had capsized with one Royal Marine being drowned. Both ships arrived back at Alexandria late on 7 March.

Just as the British were been sailing convoys to Malta so the Italians were also running convoys to their bases on the Cyrenican coast in support of their troops and the Afrika Korps, and several had been able to get through despite British efforts to stop then. It was after one of these con-

Jervis during Operation 'Vigorous' on 13 to 16 June 1942. Whilst this photograph is out of sequence it is included here as it shows *Jervis* as she was during the Second Battle of Sirte. Note that she has now acquired a Type 286P and also her rear Oerlikons have been relocated on her bridge wings in place of the 0.5in machine guns. Funnel bands are red over black and the two unusual panels at the bow and stern are both black.   (IMPERIAL WAR MUSEUM: A10479)

voys that a false report was received of a torpedoed Italian cruiser. Force B, the 15th Cruiser with *Jervis*, *Kipling*, *Kelvin* and six other destroyers sailed from Alexandria on 10 March to intercept this vessel and at the same time to bring the repaired *Kingston* and the newly arrived cruiser *Cleopatra* away from Malta. The meeting with the two warships went off smoothly and it was soon discovered that there was no torpedoed cruiser so the force turned for home. As they were returning on 11 March the *Naiad* was torpedoed and sunk by *U-565*, *Jervis*, *Kipling* and *Lively* being detailed to rescue her survivors. The rest of Force B arrived at Alexandria on 12 March and the next day *Kelvin*, *Kingston* and *Kipling* sailed from Alexandria for Operation 'MF9' which consisted of anti-submarine sweeps off the Levant ports by day accompanied by three ASV Wellingtons and along shipping routes by night. Captain Mack had left the 14th Flotilla and his replacement Captain Poland had not yet taken command so when *Jervis* joined the force on 14 March it was actually Commander Allison of *Kelvin* who was in charge of the operation. The sweeps were without incident and the force was back in Alexandria on the 18th.

The vital moment of the Second Battle of Sirte on 22 March 1942 as the ships of the 14th Flotilla turn to make their torpedo attack. Already the seas were quite rough and waves can be seen breaking over the bows of *Kipling* as she races along at 30kts. She is still in the 7th Flotilla scheme. (IMPERIAL WAR MUSEUM: A8165)

THE SECOND BATTLE OF SIRTE AND THE LOSS OF *JAGUAR*

Operation 'MG1' was a desperate attempt to run another convoy (MW10) to Malta from Alexandria, the western route being temporarily closed. The four cargo ships were to have a massive escort of five cruisers and seventeen destroyers. Enemy surface forces were expected to intervene in addition to air attacks and so the commander of the force, Admiral Vian, organised it in seven divisions with *Jervis*, *Kipling*, *Kelvin* and *Kingston* being allocated to the 1st. Initially the operation went well and the convoy was in range of air cover from British land bases until 22 March, but then the air attacks began soon after, though all were beaten off. The expected Italian surface force was also at sea, consisting of the battleship *Littorio*, three cruisers and eight destroyers. The commander of the Italian fleet, Admiral Iachino, divided his force into two groups, the battleship and three destroyers and the cruisers. Despite being delayed by heavy seas which affected the destroyers in particular and restricted the fleet's speed to 22kns the Italian cruisers were in sight of the British force by 2.30pm. The British made smoke, there was a short exchange of fire and the Italians retired.

The convoy itself was under heavy air attack and the 7th Division escorting it was beginning to run low on ammunition, so Admiral Vian detached the 1st Division to assist them. But by 4.40pm the Italians were in a position to intercept the convoy again. Once again the British made smoke and their cruisers made occasional forays to ensure that the Italians did not work their way round the edge of the screen and get at the convoy. The Italian ships for their part showed a marked reluctance to venture into the screen. A chance gap in the smoke gave the Italian ships the opportunity they had been looking for but the 5th Division raced to intercept and engaged in a gunnery duel with *Littorio*. Vian, who had been covering the eastern flank of the convoy, raced back with his 4th, the 3rd and 2nd Divisions. Poland's 1st Division which had been covering the convoy also sped towards the 5th Division to render support. As they arrived they could see the *Littorio* 6 miles away and Poland decided on an immediate torpedo attack. The division was steaming north in line ahead in the order *Jervis, Kipling, Kelvin, Kingston* and *Legion* and turned together to the west to commence an attack in line abreast. Speed increased to 28kts and all ships opened fire on the battleship except *Legion*

which waited till the range dropped to 4 miles before engaging. The seas were by now very heavy and accurate firing was difficult but *Littorio* was hit by a 4.7in shell on her quarterdeck at this time. Unfortunately, *Kipling*'s fire gong short-circuited and sounded continuously, causing her gunners to go to rapid independent fire which made individual salvo spotting very difficult.

As they reached a point 2 to 3 miles from *Littorio*, Poland ordered the torpedo attack to commence. Turning to starboard in the same order as before each ship fired several torpedoes, *Jervis* firing four out of nine and *Kipling* all five. *Kelvin* had already fired two when she mistook a turn order for an order to fire and but fired another two. As she turned to fire *Kingston* was hit by a 15in shell but managed to get four out five torpedoes away. *Legion* turned to port instead and fired all eight of her torpedoes. The shell that hit *Kingston* had a quite devastating effect. Passing through the whaler at the starboard foremost davits it exploded under the port Oerlikon platform, blowing it off the ship and large splinters from the shell riddled the gear room, the engine room, searchlight platform and the 4in gun deck. *Kingston* came to a stop as a fire broke out in the port boiler room but this was rapidly extinguished. Power was rapidly restored and by 7.07pm she was able to steam at 16kts but with the weather deteriorating, *Kingston* and *Havock* were detached to join the convoy to Malta. None of the torpedoes hit and the *Littorio* had suffered only minor damage from the 4.7in hit, but the Italians withdrew without coming into contact with the convoy. Of the convoy two ships would not make harbour, both *Clan Campbell* and *Breconshire*

A fine photograph of *Kingston* in dock at Malta after incurring damage from a 15in shell. It was probably taken after her first bomb hit as she is down by the bows. The effects of the hit can be seen as her port Oerlikon platform has disappeared. It is unknown whether she wore this colour scheme during the battle but it is unlikely as her pennant number has been painted over. Her Type 286P is visible in what appears to be a damaged state at the top of her foremast.

(IMPERIAL WAR MUSEUM: A9636)

The end of *Kingston*. She lies on her side with her back broken. Given the circumstances in Malta at the time it was decided that she could not be repaired and she was declared a constructive total loss.

(COURTESY OF JOHN ROBERTS)

being bombed though it was possible to beach the latter and salvage most of her cargo. *Pampas* and *Talabot* were able to enter Malta but they were both hit by bombs before they could unload and *Talabot* had to be scuttled to avoid her cargo of ammunition exploding. Very little could be salvaged. *Kingston* arrived at Malta on 23 March and entered dry dock as did *Legion* which had been damaged by a near miss. The 14th and 22nd Flotillas returned to Alexandria with the cruisers and suffered damage in the heavy seas. *Jervis*, *Kelvin* and *Kipling* were initially thought to be out of action until 31 March but were able to sail on the 29th. The second battle of Sirte was a brilliant defence of a convoy. A superior force had been successfully held off by a much inferior force. No ship of the convoy had been damaged by the surface attackers. Inadvertently, however, the measures taken to evade the Italian ships helped render the overall operation a failure. Because they had turned away from the Italian fleet, the ships of the convoy were delayed in their approach to Malta and had to endure a far greater period under daylight air attack than would otherwise have happened. Even if the whole convoy had reached Malta they would probably have suffered the same fate as the two ships sunk in harbour.

Jaguar had not joined Operation MG1 as she needed docking. After two weeks she sailed with the anti-submarine trawler *Klo* and the Greek destroyer *Vasilissa Olga* to escort the Royal Fleet Auxiliary tanker *Slavol* to Tobruk on 25 March. The speed of the formation was 10kts and *Jaguar* took station ahead with *Vasilissa Olga* on the port bow and *Klo* on the starboard bow. All ships zigzagged independently to confuse submarines. *Vasilissa Olga* made an attack on a contact and then on what she thought was a periscope but obtaining no further contact rejoined the convoy. About this time *Jaguar* made it clear that if any of the escort was torpedoed the first responsibility of the others was *Slavol*. Early on 26 March the ships had reached Sidi Barrani when *Jaguar* was hit by a torpedo fired by *U-652* between the bridge and the funnel on her starboard side and broke in two. The fore part of the ship sank in 1 minute, the aft part at the 4in gun remaining afloat for 3 minutes after that before sinking. Despite her instructions to remain with *Slavol*, *Vasilissa Olga* went to the assistance of *Jaguar* and picked up fifty-three survivors. Whilst she did so another submarine, *U-205*, torpedoed and sank the *Slavol* whose survivors were picked up by *Klo*. Both submarines escaped unmolested and the two remaining escorts returned to Alexandria.

THE LOSS OF *KINGSTON*

With *Kingston* out of action at Malta, there were only three Kellys operational in the Mediterranean. *Kelvin* and *Kipling* took part in Operation 'Scaffold', another relief operation to Cyprus sailing from Famagusta on 29 March. *Kipling*, however, did not stay with the operation long but returned to Alexandria to join the escort for the damaged battleship *Valiant* to Port Said on 3 April. *Kelvin* had developed engine defects on 3 April and had to put in to Beirut for repairs but she was back in service on the 6th. Both ships concentrated on the Cyprus relief operation which ran smoothly without interference. *Kingston* meanwhile was moored in No 4 dock at Malta where repairs were hampered by the German air assault on the island. On 5 April she was hit by a bomb and suffered several near misses. On the 9th another direct hit pierced her forward but did not explode. *Kingston* flooded but this was controlled and she remained afloat. The most devastating attack came on 11 April when *Kingston* was hit by a third bomb, breaking the destroyer in two. In the same attack another bomb hit the tunnel where her crew were sheltering and killed her commanding officer and twenty-three others. After this attack she was declared a constructive total loss and she was sunk as a block ship in the entrance to the harbour at St Philip's Bay.

THE ATTACK ON KUPHONISI AND THE RETURN OF *JANUS*

Operation 'Lighter' was a landing on Kuphonisi Island to destroy the enemy radio station there. Two platoons of the 11th Battalion Royal Marines embarked on *Kelvin* and *Kipling* provided the escort. As she would have to land troops, *Kelvin*'s boat compliment was modified and consisted of three 27ft whalers located at the starboard whaler

davits, the port torpedo davit and a set of improvised wooden davits rigged on the port side of the forecastle. She also carried a dinghy on the port TSDS davit and a 32ft cutter on her port motor boat davits. Both ships sailed on from Alexandria on 15 April and approached the objective at 27kts. The conditions for the operation were ideal, a very dark night with little wind or sea and *Kelvin* entered Kuphonisi harbour at one minute to midnight, *Kipling* remaining outside on patrol. The boats were all lowered by 12.05am and at 12.45 am *Kelvin* joined *Kipling*. The wireless station was destroyed at the cost of three casualties and an hour *Kelvin* returned to pick up the boats which left the shore at between 2.06am and 2.25am. The only mishap was the loss of one of the cutters when the aft fall of the motor boat davit broke as *Kelvin* was leaving the harbour, and both ships returned to Alexandria on the 16th.

Janus completed her repairs, which included a new boiler, at Simonstown in March. She then spent a period for trials and working-up at Durban before finally setting off for the Mediterranean at the end of that month, reaching Alexandria on 19 April. The next day she sailed with *Vasilissa Olga* to escort the naval stores ship *Eocene* to Tobruk. Two Italian Ca135 torpedo bombers attacked and two torpedoes were dropped, both aimed at *Janus* but fortunately they seemed to run under the ship. The rest of the mission was uneventful and *Janus* returned to Alexandria on 3 May.

Escort duties and anti-submarine sweeps continued throughout April. *Jervis* and *Kelvin* shuttled between Famagusta and Haifa with the troopship *Princess Marguerite* in pursuit of Operation 'Adamstown', the continuing relief of the Cyprus garrison. This was completed safely on 28 April, despite the threat of mines, and the ships sailed for Alexandria arriving on the 29th April. On 4 May *Jackal* completed her repairs and rejoined the fleet. Her first mission after her return would be Operation 'MG2'.

OPERATION 'MG2'

With the neutralisation of the striking forces at Malta, supply convoys to the Afrika Korps were getting through on a regular basis, and attempts were made to attack them from Alexandria. Following a report of a convoy headed for Benghazi with only a single destroyer escort, Captain Poland in *Jervis* led *Jackal*, *Kipling* and *Lively* out of Alexandria on 10 May to intercept it. Poland had orders to return to Alexandria if sighted by aircraft and when this happened the next day he immediately turned the destroyers around and headed back for home at full speed. Air attacks started at around 4.00pm by aircraft of *II Fliegerkorps* which had recently transferred to Crete and excelled in anti-shipping attacks. Each attack consisted of eight to twelve Ju88s with an He111 acting as a shadower. Air cover was supposed to be provided for the British ships but the patrolling aircraft arrived too late and in insufficient numbers to be of any use.

The loss of *Kipling* on 11 May 1942. the first photograph (right) shows her sailing past survivors from *Lively*. Visible is her third Oerlikon located on the centre of her quarterdeck and her red pennant numbers. She is now in 14th Flotilla markings as opposed to the 7th markings she carried earlier (see profile 8). The second photograph shows the final attacks on the destroyer. She was sunk shortly after this was taken.

(IMPERIAL WAR MUSEUM: A9167 AND A9175)

Lively was hit at 4.45pm and sank shortly afterwards, bow first. *Kipling* picked up 117 survivors and the destroyers continued on their way. Sixty miles north of Mersah Matruh *Jackal* was hit by one bomb which passed through the upper deck above No 2 boiler room, through the boiler itself and out through the bottom, exploding underneath the keel amidships. The explosion lifted the destroyer up bodily and seemed to break her back. At the same time two bombs near-missed the destroyer. The explosion from the hit caused Nos 1 and 2 boiler rooms and the engine room to flood and all power was lost. *Jackal* immediately came to a standstill, listing but afloat. The bomb started a fire which could not be put out due to a lack of fire-fighting equipment. As much top weight as possible was jettisoned and *Jervis* came alongside to take her under tow, but the draft created by the tow fanned the flames of the fire and No 2 magazine had to be flooded as a precaution. This had the effect of eliminating the list but reduced her freeboard. At around 8.10pm the Germans attacked again, this time concentrating on *Kipling*. She was hit by one from a stick of four bombs with another near-missing her. The force of the explosion broke her back, the two halves being held together by the upper deck. *Kipling* was clearly doomed and about 10 minutes after the explosion sank vertically, stern first. *Jervis* rescued her survivors then continued her tow of *Jackal*.

Early on 12 May it was clear that *Jackal* was in serious trouble. The torpedo mess decks were in danger of catching fire and shortly after this the stem began to settle and the ship took on a 6° list to starboard. The tiller flat began to flood and had to be closed down preventing *Jackal* from steering and a little later the wardroom also began to flood and it was unlikely that she would reach Alexandria. *Jervis* took off her crew and at 4.45am sank her by torpedo. She returned to Alexandria later the same day carrying 650 survivors from the three ships. The shock of this defeat was quite profound. To have almost a whole destroyer force eliminated emphasised the need for much better air support and co-ordination and for the rest of May no Kellys put to sea.

JUPITER IN THE FAR EAST

Jupiter's duties in January mainly involved escorting ships and convoys between Batavia and Singapore. On 14 January she left Singapore and sailed for Batavia to pick up the American transport[4] *Mount Vernon* and escort her clear of Sundra Strait. On the morning of the 17th a signal was received that a Greek freighter had been torpedoed and sunk. *Jupiter* received permission to hunt the enemy submarine. As the freighter had been sunk 65 miles to the east *Jupiter*

commenced her search 30 miles away from the sinking anticipating that the submarine would have made for deep water. At 2.00pm she picked up an excellent asdic contact and dropped a five-charge pattern on it. Hydrophone readings confirmed that this was a submarine and an hour and a half later a six-charge pattern was dropped after which *Jupiter* opened the range to ensure the submarine did not escape. Five minutes after this attack the enemy submarine, the *I60*, surfaced 1000 yards off the starboard bow. *Jupiter* altered course to bring her short-range weapons to bear and the Oerlikons, 0.5in and pom-pom all opened fire causing several casualties among the submarine's crew. The Japanese replied with their main gun and hit A mount, disabling it and killing three of the crew and wounding nine. *Jupiter* hit the submarine with her main armament and continued to fire at a rate of seven to eight rounds a minute as she opened the range. She obtained a hit and fired all five of her torpedoes which missed. By now the submarine was listing to starboard and thick brown-yellow smoke was coming from her stern. She fired two torpedoes at *Jupiter* but missed. *Jupiter* hit her again several times and seeing that the guns were no longer manned closed in and as she passed close astern fired a depth charge from her starboard thrower. This fell five yards from the conning tower and had a spectacular effect, blowing a man off the tower and causing a sheet of flame to shoot out. The submarine sank slowly stern first and *Jupiter* rescued three survivors. *Jupiter*'s captain had considered ramming *I60* when she surfaced but mindful of Cunningham's instructions that destroyers were not to ram because of the damage they caused themselves, had refrained. *Jupiter* sailed to the Dutch naval base of Surabaya where the damage to A mount was assessed. According to Dutch sources[5] the seriously-damaged mount was removed for repairs and replaced by a single 4.7in mount. These do not say whether this was a Dutch or a British one but considering that the removal took place at the Surabaya naval base it was most likely to be the former. *Jupiter* would be in this configuration when lost in February.

As the Allied position in the Far East collapsed, *Jupiter* was more involved in evacuations. On 10 February she sailed with *Durban* and *Kedah* to evacuate 3000 RAF officers and men from Singapore to Batavia. After this was completed *Jupiter* and *Stronghold* were to cover ten merchant ships sailing independently to Batavia and Banka. The force was attacked by Japanese aircraft on 11 February initially flying too high for *Jupiter* to engage but when they attacked the destroyer herself she was able to fire at them. A second attack was driven off. The force arrived at Keppel Harbour

---

[4] The official British report classifies her as an AMC but she was actually a transport.

[5] In particular F C Van Oosten, *The Battle of the Java Sea*, Appendix 12.

on the 12th and as her contribution to the evacuation, *Jupiter* embarked 16 officers and 104 ratings before sailing to take up a position in the van of a convoy. As she left early on 13 February she saw five merchant vessels waiting for daylight before proceeding and began to pick up signals from ships being bombed. Around 11.30am the same day *Jupiter* found her convoy, two steamships which, after checking that there were no bombed ships in the Banka Strait, she returned to escort. Along the way they were joined by the minesweeping tug *Wo Kwang*. The rest of the day was uneventful but the next day would be different. First two Japanese aircraft attacked the convoy but were driven off by the destroyers. After requesting fighter protection for the two ships as one was carrying ammunition, *Jupiter* left her convoy and went to the assistance of SS *Surstad* which had radioed that she had been bombed. *Surstad* was found listing 25° but was able to make 12kts. Her captain wanted to wait until dark before proceeding but was told to get going by *Jupiter*, which then sailed off to look for the tanker *Elsa* but, before she could locate her, she came across the *Merula*. This ship was on fire but as the minesweeper HMAS *Toowoomba* was in attendance *Jupiter* did not linger but continued her search, taking *Toowoomba* with her. She found *Elsa* undamaged and ordered her to proceed to Batavia independently.

More bombed ships were encountered. The tanker *Manvantara* was completely on fire and unsalvageable and the *Ipoh* was in need of medical supplies. *Jupiter* sent *Toowoomba* to the *Ipoh*. An attempt was made to try and tow the hulk of *Merula* by the tanker *Herborg* but this was abandoned. *Surstad* had now corrected her list and was demanding immediate escort. On being told 'somewhat sulphurically' that she was not the only one and threatened with her master being reported she changed her tune and set off with *Jupiter* and the tanker *Erling Brovig* which had come up astern. *Jupiter* was also supposed to escort the *Bulan* but this ship could not be found. At dawn on 14 February *Bulan* appeared and joined *Jupiter*'s group. *Toowoomba* was in company with *Herborg* and *Elsa*. These ships were escorted to the examination vessel at Batavia. *Toowoomba* sailed to refuel and *Jupiter* re-joined *Durban*, *Stronghold* and *Kedah* and two days later sailed with them for Colombo arriving on 21 February. Her report of proceedings also earned the praise of the Commodore of the China Station.[6] On the 21st *Jupiter* was officially allocated to the 7th Destroyer Flotilla but in the event this did not take place.

THE BATTLE OF THE JAVA SEA

Jupiter did not stay long at Colombo but with *Exeter*, *Encounter* and *Electra* returned to the Java Sea, arriving at Surabaya on 25 February. All four ships were to be part of the ABDA Fleet under Rear-Admiral Doorman of the Dutch Navy which concentrated to repel the Japanese invasion of Eastern Java. The Japanese invasion convoys had left Camranh Bay on 18 February and Jolo on the 19th and both were large and well protected.[7] The ABDA Fleet sailed on the 26th to search for the enemy invasion fleets sailing north, then east and then west. Nothing was sighted and at dawn the next day the fleet was attacked by Japanese bombers. Most of these concentrated on *Jupiter* but she was not hit. After this attack Doorman decided to return to harbour but was directed to continue searching by the overall commander of Allied naval forces Admiral Helfrich. Doorman initially complied with this order but about 12.40pm turned his force for home ignoring Helfrich's instructions. As the force approached Surabaya definite information of the invasion fleet was received and they turned to intercept.

However, the Japanese were well served by their air reconnaissance and had plenty of warning of Doorman's approach. The destroyers and cruisers of the covering and escort forces sailed to meet the Allied ships and the transports of the eastern attack force, which were those in danger, were ordered to reverse course. Doorman's approach was faulty allowing the Japanese heavy cruisers guarding the invasion force to bring all their guns to bear whilst his ships could only fire their forward turrets. However, the Japanese gunnery was quite abysmal and no hits were scored. The Japanese light cruiser *Jintsu* opened fire on *Electra* and *Jupiter* guarding the van of the Allied cruisers but again without hitting. The Japanese also fired torpedoes to no effect but, guided by spotter planes, their gunnery improved and the Allied cruisers began to take hits. The *Exeter* was hit in her engine room and hauled out of the line, throwing the force into confusion. Realising what had happened Doorman ordered *Encounter*, *Electra* and *Jupiter* to prevent the Japanese from making a torpedo attack on the damaged cruiser. The three destroyers charged through the smoke screen, *Electra* considerably ahead of the other two. She ran into a Japanese flotilla, seriously damaged one and hit *Jintsu* but was herself sunk. *Jupiter* was engaged by two Japanese destroyers but drove both of them away with rapid and accurate fire. She and *Encounter* rapidly withdrew after achieving their aim. Doorman also withdrew his force without getting near the transports.

The Dutch admiral had not abandoned his aim of attack-

---

[6] '*Jupiter* appears to have acted with the usual skill and good judgement which the past month has led me to expect from him.' Commodore J A B Collins CB, RAN 23 February 1942.

[7] Camranh Bay convoy, fifty-six transports protected by three cruisers and six destroyers, Jolo convoy forty-one transports protected by one light cruiser and six destroyers. There was also a covering force of three cruisers and seven destroyers.

ing the invasion fleet but changed course to head for the coast of Java to be in a better position to intercept it. *Jupiter* was the fifth and last ship in line behind the four surviving cruisers. At about 10.15pm *Jupiter* was wracked by a massive explosion and signalled 'I am torpedoed', but she had in fact struck a mine from a field laid by the Dutch earlier in the day. The explosion blew a hole 20ft by 8ft in her starboard side, buckled her deck and she took on an immediate list and started to flood. Most of the boats could be got away and made for the nearby coast. Unfortunately the surf was too great and they were unable to land and had to return. At 12.55am on 28 February *Jupiter*'s list started to increase and at 1.30am she heeled over and sank. Most of

A poor photograph of *Piorun* which is included because of its rarity. Possibly taken sometime in late 1941 or even early 1942 it shows *Piorun* in a Western Approaches scheme of blue and white. There is a Polish emblem on her funnel indicating that she was serving with one of the Polish escort groups at the time. (COURTESY OF MAREK TWARDOWSKI)

her crew did make it to shore but were captured by the Japanese. The rest of the ABDA fleet would also be sunk.

KELLYS IN OTHER WATERS – HOME AND INDIAN OCEAN

The only Kelly to be based permanently in home waters was the Polish destroyer *Piorun*. Other ships usually served with

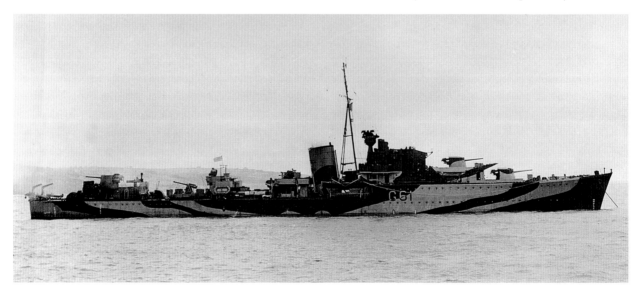

An incorrectly-dated photograph, this shows *Javelin* on completion of her re-building in early 1942. The camouflage scheme is probably symmetrical but no information exists to confirm this. Visible are her Type 286P and Type 285, the 286P being located at the top of the

mast. She carries four Oerlikons and one pom-pom as her close range anti-aircraft armament and a radar hut located between the legs of her foremast. (IMPERIAL WAR MUSEUM: FL10519)

the Home Fleet for a short period before moving on to their allotted stations elsewhere. Even *Piorun* was not permanently based there as she was heavily involved in transatlantic convoys and so spent significant amounts of time in Canada.

Piorun collided with the French destroyer *Mistral* on 12 January and was under repair until 6 February. On completion of the repairs she operated in the Irish Sea before joining her first convoy of the year, ON70 from Londonderry to Halifax, on 26 February. *Piorun* was quite active, depth-charging a couple of contacts on 10 and 11 March but without result. The convoy arrived at St Johns on 12 March and *Piorun* sailed to Argentia five days later to repair weather damage. On 21 March she sailed back across the Atlantic with convoy SC75 this time as senior officer of the escort. On 8 April she and the destroyer *Churchill* sailed on a more important convoy than usual, which was carrying a total of 20 tons of Soviet gold. The convoy was small consisting of the Polish liners *Batory* and *Letitia* which carried a total of 10 tons of gold, *Piorun* and *Churchill* each carrying 5 tons each. The weather was very rough and *Piorun*'s forward magazine was flooded but all ships made Halifax safely.

After a few days she sailed with Convoy SC81 and Escort Group B2 for the UK, arriving at Greenock on 10 May without incident. She underwent a short refit at Liverpool before setting off on another convoy. This would form the pattern for the next few months and *Piorun* would cross and re-cross the Atlantic with eight convoys up to 24 September when she would undergo another refit which would last from 28 September until 9 December. Her time on convoy

duty had been mostly uneventful apart from battling storms and trying to keep the convoys together. After this she would be allocated to the Home Fleet taking part in the Russian convoys, joining the 3rd Destroyer Flotilla.[8] *Piorun*'s first Russian convoy would be Convoy RA51 and she would sail with the fleet to provide distant cover on 31 December.

Early in January 1942[9] *Javelin* completed her repairs at Plymouth. She had been completely rebuilt with a new bow and stern and had received the latest anti-aircraft outfit and radars. After trials and exercises, she joined the cruiser *Cairo* on 6 February escorting a coastal convoy on her way to Scapa Flow, arriving on 8 February and spending the rest of the month either sitting at her buoy or engaging in exercises with other ships. Then on 25 March she sailed as part of the escort of Convoy WS17 to the Middle East. This was a heavily escorted troop convoy of thirty transports carrying 60,000 men. Part of the convoy was intended to take part in the forthcoming invasion of Madagascar.

A day out of Greenock the escort leader *Pakenham* picked up an asdic contact and ordered *Javelin* and *Inconstant* to investigate it. *Javelin* obtained an excellent contact and attacked with a pattern of six charges. She followed this up with a second attack two to three minutes later, picking up a 'whistle and rattle' effect on her hydrophones which was accompanied by a large disturbance on the surface. *Inconstant* was unable to make any contact and so attacked on calcium flares laid by *Javelin*. *Javelin* made a third and fourth

---

[8] *Milne, Meteor, Matchless, Musketeer, Iroquois* and the Polish *Orkan*
[9] This account is based on *Javelin*'s log for the period.

Van Galen on commissioning in February 1942 at Scapa Flow. Her configuration is almost identical to that of *Javelin* with the exception of a twin Mk V 0.5in machine gun tub located on her stern. Quite why this Coastal Forces weapon should be installed in a fleet destroyer is a mystery but several of the 'N' class received them. They were no more useful than the quad 0.5in guns before them. Note the small mainmast attached to the searchlight platform. (IMPERIAL WAR MUSEUM: FL9571)

attack and *Inconstant* made another one before re-joining the convoy. It was judged that they had attacked a U-boat although not sunk it. The convoy continued and *Javelin* refuelled at Ponta Delgarda on 29 March. When she returned to the convoy, *Javelin* joined the screen of the aircraft carrier *Illustrious* which remained with the convoy following a report of an unidentified warship nearby. Nothing more was seen and the aircraft carrier and escort arrived at Bathurst on 3 April. She then spent the next 6 days there before sailing on 10 April. On 18 April she rejoined the convoy and on the 19th escorted the battleship *Malaya* into Capetown.

She left Capetown on 29 April to join the Madagascar invasion force (Operation 'Ironclad'). *Javelin*'s role was mainly to screen the carriers *Illustrious* and *Indomitable* but she was detached on 7 May with the battleship *Ramillies* and other ships to bombard French positions which surrendered after 15 minutes. The next day, she took part in an anti-submarine hunt off Diégo Suarez[10] which led to *Active* sinking the French submarine *Monge*. *Javelin* remained at Madagascar until 19 May when she escorted *Illustrious* and *Indomitable* to Mombassa, departing on 29 May and arriving at Alexandria on 9 June with *Nestor*

---

[10] Now called Antsiranana.

and *Napier* having made a brief refuelling stop at Aden.

The first Dutch 'N', *Van Galen*, commissioned on 23 February and after working-up departed for the Eastern Fleet on 15 April, arriving at Mombassa on 31 May. On her arrival she was allocated to Force A along with the Dutch cruiser *Jacob van Heemskirk*. After a short period at Colombo, *Van Galen* sailed with Force A for fleet exercises which lasted from 12 to 17 June. She joined the fleet for their sweep to Port Victoria on 23 to 28 June and for a further round of exercises between 15 and 20 July. Another trip to Port Victoria followed and then at the end of the month she participated in Operation 'Stab' which was intended to be a diversionary operation for the American landings in the Solomon islands. This operation seems to have had little or no effect and was terminated on 3 August. *Van Galen* then returned to Colombo for a boiler clean.

The other Dutch destroyer, *Tjerk Hiddes,* commissioned on 6 May and was the last of the N class to enter service. After working-up at Greenock she joined the Home Fleet in June 1942 for further training. On 29 June she sailed as part of the escort for a westbound convoy before arriving at Liverpool and docking in Gladstone dock for conversion for tropical service. This mainly involved the removal of lagging, the adding of wind scoops to the scuttles, provision of

The 20th Destroyer Flotilla on manoeuvres on 25 June 1942. Visible in this photograph are *Tjerk Hiddes* followed by *Offa* and *Nepal*. *Tjerk Hiddes* and *Nepal* would shortly sail to join the 7th Flotilla in the Indian Ocean and *Nepal* is already carrying her flotilla markings. The other side of *Tjerk Hiddes*'s camouflage scheme is unknown.

(IMPERIAL WAR MUSEUM: A10300)

Nestor coming alongside *Formidable* in the Indian Ocean between 24 April and 10 May 1942. She has been repainted in the 7th Flotilla scheme and carries a Type 285 as well as her Type 286P. Unfortunately the original glass negative was broken and so the only one available was this censored version. The bow flare is very visible in this view.

(IMPERIAL WAR MUSEUM: A9060)

more refrigerators and canvas baths and adding of awnings. Once this was complete she left Liverpool on 17 January to the escort for join Convoy WS21. Arriving at Capetown on 13 August, she and *Nepal* joined Convoy WS21P on 19 August, detaching from the convoy five days later and sailing on to Kilindini. Between 25 August and 10 October *Tjerk Hiddes* patrolled the seas around her base at Kilindini. However on two occasions she did operate with her compatriot when the two ships screened an aircraft carrier between 28 to 30 August and on 3 and 4 September when they escorted an aircraft depot ship from Kilindini to Tanga.

On 6 September both destroyers sailed with Force M for Madagascar to take part in the final stages of the subjugation of the island. They took part in the Majunga[11] operation and then continued on to Diégo Suarez arriving on 15 September. The next day peace terms were presented to the Vichy governor general. On 17 September several ships including *Warspite*, *Jacob van Heemskirk*, *Van Galen* and *Tjerk Hiddes* sailed to participate in Operation 'Jane'. This was the seizure of the port of Tamarave[12] on the east coast of the island. A few salvoes from *Warspite* quelled initial resistance and by midday the port was in Allied hands. The ships returned to Diégo Suarez but as she was going along-

[11] Now Mahajanga.
[12] Now Toamasina.

side *Easdale* to refuel *Tjerk Hiddes* collided with her. The damage took a week to repair. *Van Galen* remained at Diégo Suarez for a couple of days before sailing for Operation 'Rose', the landing at Tulear,[13] on 23 September. Arriving on 29 September there was no resistance and *Van Galen* left for Kilindini the next day arriving on 3 October. *Tjerk Hiddes*, which had been delayed by her repairs. left Diégo Suarez on 3 October and arrived at Kilindini late on the 5th.

After the Madagascar operation the two destroyers were detached to reinforce the US Seventh Fleet in the Pacific, mainly undertaking escort duties out of the Australian port

of Fremantle. *Van Galen* and *Tjerk Hiddes* sailed with *Jacob van Heemskirk* on 10 October for Port Victoria, arriving at Fremantle on the 25 October. They would remain under Seventh Fleet control until January 1944. Their escort duties continued throughout November and December with *Van Galen* notably escorting the liner *Aquitania* several times and carrying out anti-submarine exercises. Late in December it was noticed that the ship was not responding to her rudder as she should and this would be investigated in the New Year.

December for *Tjerk Hiddes* was different. After leaving *Van Galen* she sailed to Port Darwin to operate as a supply and evacuation vessel for Allied forces fighting the Japanese

Kelvin (above) and *Javelin* (left) during Operation 'Vigorous' between 13 and 16 June 1942. The contrast between the two ships is quite interesting with *Kelvin* having her quintuple tubes restored and *Javelin* still equipped with a 4in gun. *Kelvin* does not carry a Type 285 and has had her TSDS equipment removed as well whilst *Javelin* has both. Just visible in the original photograph of *Javelin* is the red band above the standard black band. Her colour scheme was identical on both sides. *Kelvin*'s pennant number is red despite official instructions to the contrary.

(IMPERIAL WAR MUSEUM: A10855 AND A10856)

on Timor. En route, on 8 December near Cape Bougainville she was attacked by Japanese aircraft. These approached too high for the main armament to bear and beyond the range of the light armament, but the ships were able to avoid their bombs. One aircraft did try to attack from the rear and strayed into range, being driven off by intense fire. *Tjerk Hiddes* arrived at Port Darwin on 9 December and was allocated to Task Force 51. The next day she sailed for her first mission and on 11 December unloaded stores and supplies for the 4th Independent Company on Timor, taking off the sick and wounded, Portuguese evacuees and guerrillas. Unobserved by the enemy she returned to Port Darwin the same day. The next operation took place on the night of the 15th/16th, evacuating 240 Australian soldiers and about 30 nuns and priests. Her third and final run was on 18 December when 310 personnel and 4½ tons of rubber were loaded. The poor quality of fuel available and the marine growth on her hull was seriously affecting her performance and in her captain's opinion made it impossible for these operations to be completed in one day any more. Consequently, *Tjerk Hiddes* returned to Fremantle, arriving on 24 December. She sailed again on 31 December to escort the liner *Île de France* into port.

The Australian ships and the Eastern fleet

After leaving the Mediterranean fleet, *Napier*, *Nizam* and *Nestor* stopped at Aden on 7 January, leaving two days later to rendezvous with the aircraft carrier *Indomitable* which they escorted to Port Sudan to load fifty Hurricanes for transport to Malaya. *Indomitable* flew off her cargo on 27 January and the destroyers escorted her to Trincomalee. After arrival, the three destroyers remained in port whilst the Eastern Fleet built up its strength. *Napier* and *Nestor* conducted an anti-submarine sweep in Ceylonese waters on 14 February but found nothing. On 16 February they escorted *Indomitable* back to Port Sudan which took most of the rest of the month as she loaded another fifty Hurricanes, this time for Ceylon. Aden was reached on the 29th when they headed back to Trincomalee. On 3 March in a new departure for the Australian destroyers both refuelled at sea from the aircraft carrier. *Nizam* spent most of February in harbour, emerging on 24/25 February for an uneventful anti-submarine sweep.

Most of March was spent exercising and sitting in harbour but on 20 March *Napier* and *Nizam* sailed to escort the battleship *Resolution* to Addu Atoll. They arrived on 24 March and during the next two days most of the Eastern Fleet joined them. On the 30th they sailed to intercept the Japanese fleet but both forces missed each other by 90 miles. By now they were joined by the fourth Australian 'N',

Norman, which had arrived at Trincomalee on 12 March. She sailed to Addu Atoll to join the fleet and took part in her first anti-submarine sweep with *Napier* on 26 March. On 4 April all four 'Ns', *Napier*, *Nizam*, *Nestor* and *Norman* left Addu as escorts for *Indomitable*. This was to be their main duty.[14] After cruising with the fleet for several days they sailed for Bombay. *Nestor* and *Norman* remained there for six days and departed on the 19th for Colombo but *Napier* and *Nizam* were docked for refits. *Napier* would be in dock until 6 May and *Nizam* until 13 May. Both would have their anti-aircraft armament upgraded (see Appendix 3) and *Nizam* would also have her port shaft re-aligned.

Norman and *Nestor* returned to Colombo. The rest of April and most of May was spent escorting units of the Eastern Fleet mostly between the Seychelles and Colombo and engaging in fruitless anti-submarine sweeps. *Napier* and *Nizam* returned from their refits but *Nizam* had to be placed in quarantine when she arrived at Kilindini on 21 May having an outbreak of influenza on board, probably picked up in Bombay. About this time *Napier*'s commander, Captain Arliss, became Senior Officer (Destroyers) for the Eastern Fleet. This carried the rank of Commodore but Arliss kept *Napier* as his flagship for the time being. A change of scene was in the offing as the Mediterranean Fleet had borrowed several units from the Eastern fleet to take part in Operation 'Vigorous', another attempt to resupply Malta. On 25 May *Nizam* and *Norman* sailed with Group 1, *Birmingham*, *Pakenham* and *Fortune*. Two days later Group 2 consisting of *Newcastle*, *Paladin*, *Napier*, *Nestor*, *Inconstant*, *Hotspur* and *Griffin* followed them and all ships had arrived at Alexandria by 5 June. The 7th Flotilla would be based at Haifa and the four 'Ns' were all assembled there by 11 June.

The Mediterranean – Operation 'Vigorous'

Janus did not participate in 'Vigorous'. On 4 June whilst on an anti-submarine sweep an acoustic mine exploded in her wake. The shock damage to her machinery was quite severe and she had to return to Alexandria for repairs, initially taking three and a half weeks. 'Vigorous' and the corresponding operation from Gibraltar – 'Harpoon' – were attempts to resupply Malta. 'Harpoon' would be at best a partial success, 'Vigorous' a complete failure. As the Kellys were only involved in 'Vigorous' this account will confine itself to a detailed description of that operation alone. It began on 11 June when the dummy Convoy MW11C sailed with the hope of distracting the attention of the Italian fleet from the main event. When it reached a point roughly aligned with Tobruk it reversed course and steamed to join the main convoy, MW11 of eleven freighters, which had sailed in two portions, one

---

[14] The Pink Lists describe them as 'Attendants to Aircraft Carriers' throughout April.

from Haifa and the other from Port Said.

With the convoy were the ships of the 7th Flotilla and on the 13th *Jervis*, *Kelvin* and the rest of the 14th Flotilla sailed to relieve them. *Javelin* sailed later with the old target battleship *Centurion* used during this operation as an anti-aircraft platform and decoy. Air attacks continued on the 14th and 15th and a freighter was hit and sunk. E-boats damaged the cruiser *Birmingham* and torpedoed *Hasty* which had to be scuttled. Anti-aircraft ammunition was also becoming a problem with some ships having already used half their supply. Regrettably, the force commander Admiral Vian decided that the convoy would have to turn back.

At 6.06pm on 15 June *Nestor* was part of the convoy screen when she was straddled by two bombs from a high-level bomber. One landed 50ft from the starboard side, abreast the bridge and the other next to No 2 motor cutter. The shock extensively distorted the hull – on the starboard side the plating was dented and buckled but not holed. The port side was worse being holed and distorted abreast the motor cutter. No1 boiler room immediately flooded and all electrical power was lost as the diesel dynamos were in that compartment. Shortly after No 2 boiler room also flooded which meant a loss of steam power. Water was also entering the ship through sprung scuttles and a fire started in No 1 boiler room as a result of the bulkhead between the boiler room and Nos 3 and 4 oil tanks being damaged. The ship had settled by her head and was listing to port. Damage control measures were immediately initiated. The fire was brought under control and the contents of B magazine jettisoned to avoid flooding it and jeopardising the ship's stability. Other items of topweight were also jettisoned - torpedoes, depth charges (set to safe) and paravanes all went and ship's stores were placed on the starboard side of the upper deck to reduce the list. As a precaution the bulkheads at the far end of the engine room and aft end of the lower mess deck were shored up. *Javelin* came up and took *Nestor* under tow but despite on one occasion reaching a speed of 14½kts the tow broke twice due to *Nestor* yawing badly. Air attacks were continuing and it was 250 miles to Alexandria. The chances of getting *Nestor* to port before dawn the next day were nil and so it was decided to scuttle her. Consequently at 5.30am on 16 June *Javelin* took off her crew and then sank her with depth charges. Of *Nestor*'s crew four had been killed and one wounded. Her captain commented that if they had still had some power for steering *Nestor* might have been saved and strongly urged the separation of the diesel dynamos with one being located in the gear room. This was not practical but an extra dynamo was added in the gear room.[15]

---

[15] See AFO 5794/42, 26 November 1942.

The battered remains of the convoy returned to Alexandria on 16 June. Several warships had been damaged but apart from *Nestor* none of the Kellys were affected. The three 'Ns' of the 7th Flotilla left Alexandria on 22 June arriving at Port Said the same day. *Norman* and *Nizam* passed through the canal and sailed for Aden while *Napier* remained behind, finally sailing through the canal on 9 July. After arriving at Aden on 28 June *Nizam* and *Norman* sailed to assist *Newcastle* which had been damaged by E-boats and was sailing for Bombay. They finally returned to the Eastern Fleet on 2 July. *Napier* had remained behind to escort the damaged battleship *Queen Elizabeth* on her journey to the United States, sailing on 20 July.

BACK IN THE MEDITERRANEAN
Jervis, *Javelin* and *Kelvin* remained at Alexandria for most of the rest of June, until the threat to Alexandria from the advancing Afrika Korps forced the fleet to disperse to various other ports in the Mediterranean. On 28 June *Jervis* and *Javelin* helped escort the fleet repair ship *Resource* and destroyer depot ship *Woolwich* to Port Said. On the 29th *Janus* and *Kelvin* left for Port Sudan where they arrived on 4 July. *Janus* was still experiencing trouble and on 13 July sailed to Suez for repairs which would keep her out of action until 8 October. *Kelvin* would remain at Port Sudan until 28 July when she sailed for Port Said. Five days later she would join *Paladin* as escort for *Dido* on the way to Haifa. *Jervis* escorted the 15th Cruiser Squadron to Haifa on 1 July and then returned to her new home port of Port Said where she would operate as part of Force A with *Javelin*. On 19 July Force A put to sea for a bombardment of Mersah Matruh, destroying one petrol ship and damaging other. With the addition of *Belvoir* and *Hursley* they repeated the operation on 22 July but this time it was a failure. Low cloud covered the target and the bombardment was abandoned after only two salvoes.

Kelvin joined Force A on 5 August. The next day she and *Jervis* sailed with *Coventry* to Beirut. Operation 'MG3', the diversion for Operation 'Pedestal' commenced on 10 August. Three freighters escorted by thirteen warships including *Jervis* and *Kelvin* to simulate a convoy for Malta and draw the enemy air force away from the 'Pedestal' convoy, which would be a success but the diversion accomplished nothing. On 11 August the diversionary force split up and *Jervis*, *Pakenham* and *Paladin* escorted *Dido* to Port Said. The next phase of the diversion was a bombardment of Rhodes, Operation 'MG4'. *Javelin* and *Kelvin* joined two cruisers and two other destroyers for this, but results were poor mainly due to the presence of enemy E-boats and the use of searchlights by the defence which forced the bombardment to be carried out at a longer range than intended. On the way back *Kelvin* and *Javelin* were detached to Famagusta to refuel. Unfortunately there was not enough to fill both destroyers so they split what there was between them and sailed for Haifa arriving on 14 August. Once they had arrived they sailed for Port Said with the 15th Cruiser Squadron on 15 August. *Javelin* then sailed back to Haifa with *Euryalus*.

During this time the latest relief of the Cyprus garrison (Operation 'Robertsbridge') was underway with the transport *Princess Margeuritte* shuttling back and forth between Famagusta and Haifa. On 17 August she was torpedoed and sunk by *U-83*. *Kelvin* and *Hero* rushed to the scene and succeeded in picking up 1100 survivors. *U-83* did not escape unscathed as she was badly damaged by British aircraft. *Paladin* sailed to try and intercept the submarine and was joined by *Jervis* on 19 August but *U-83* escaped to Salamis. In the meantime *Kelvin* arrived at Port Said on the 18th to land her survivors. 'Robertsbridge' continued with *Princess Kathleen* and the convoy escort HMS *Antwerp* sailing from Haifa on 19 August escorted by *Javelin*, *Exmoor* and *Hurworth*. *Kelvin* sailed to Alexandria for repairs to her oil fuel tanks and on 25 August joined *Jervis* in escorting the submarine *Thrasher* on diving trials. Joined by *Javelin*, the destroyers searched fruitlessly for an enemy submarine throughout the day before returning to port. *Kelvin* was at sea again the next day this time to investigate the abandoned steamship *Empire Kumari*. The corvette *Gloxinia* took her in tow and she was escorted to Port Said by *Kelvin*, *Pakenham* and *Protea* but *Kelvin* left the escort on the 27th and sailed ahead to Port Said arriving on 29 August. *Jervis* and *Javelin*'s last duty in August was to carry out a night anti-submarine search with aircraft co-operation which once again was uneventful.

September began with the usual routine of exercises,

futile anti-submarine sweeps and rescue missions until the 13th when the cruiser *Dido* and the destroyers *Jervis*, *Javelin*, *Kelvin*, *Paladin* and *Pakenham* sailed from Port Said for Operation 'MG7', a bombardment of the Dabba area which was a diversionary operation for Operation 'Agreement', an ill-conceived raid on Tobruk.[16] The bombardment itself went off without a hitch and the ships returned to Port Said.

On 1 October *Kelvin* and *Jervis* were again involved in exercises with the cruisers. These may not have been satisfactory as the ships were out again on the 7th, this time *Javelin* and *Kelvin* being involved. *Jervis* was at Alexandria undergoing a boiler clean and so was lucky enough to miss the second set. After the exercises *Cleopatra* needed docking and so she was escorted to Alexandria on 7 October by *Kelvin* and *Javelin*. She was examined the next day but nothing seems to have been amiss so she was undocked the same day and returned to Port Said escorted by *Kelvin* and *Javelin* again. *Janus* returned to the fleet on 8 October but did not sail until the 10th. On the 19th she sailed with *Javelin* and the Greek destroyer *Spetsai* to hunt a U-boat which had been reported by aircraft, finding nothing after an all-night search and returning to Port Said the next day. On the same day *Kelvin* helped put out a fire on board the Greek freighter *Thirassa Nomicos* in Suez Bay.

November would see the first attempt since 'Vigorous' to pass a convoy through to Malta from the east. Convoy MW13 of four ships sailed for Operation 'Stoneage' on 17 November. *Jervis* and *Javelin* sailed as part of the escort which came under heavy air attack and the cruiser *Arethusa* was hit and damaged. She was taken under tow by *Petard* and made for Alexandria escorted by *Jervis* and *Javelin*. Once the tow was established *Jervis* and *Javelin* turned back to

---

[16] So ill-conceived that it would be a total failure and the Royal Navy would loose the cruiser *Coventry* and the destroyers *Sikh* and *Zulu*.

Nepal on commissioning in May 1942 wearing a two-colour scheme. Unusually whilst her pennant number has been censored her radar

equipment this colour scheme was also symmetrical.

Norman in the Indian Ocean during late 1942. Both sides of this interesting camouflage scheme are shown. This was a three-colour affair using AP507C, B5 and MS1and is similar to those carried by the 'Q' class destroyers. Of special interest are her reverse-shaded pennant numbers. Norman carries six Oerlikons and a Type 285 and Type 291.

(AUSTRALIAN WAR MEMORIAL: 301106 & 301099)

the convoy. The weather was abysmal which helped the convoy as it prevented air attacks and on 19 November Malta came into view. The destroyers turned for Alexandria but were thrown about quite badly in the rough seas, *Javelin* having to put into Tobruk. *Jervis* and *Kelvin* together with *Nubian* finally made Alexandria on 20 November. *Janus* sailed from Port Said on 19 November and joined the escort of *Arethusa*. However, she was due to return to Britain and on 23 November sailed for Suez. Two days later she passed through the canal on her voyage to Britain. She would finally arrive at Aultbea on 29 January 1943 and then go to the Tyne for a six-month refit.

MALTA AND FORCE K

With the successful offensive by the Eighth Army and the collapse of the German and Italian forces coupled with the Allied invasion of North Africa (Operation 'Torch') it became feasible to revive Force K again. On 25 November *Dido*, *Euryalus*, *Jervis*, *Javelin*, *Nubian* and *Kelvin* all departed Alexandria to form the new Force K. They made the passage in two days free from air attack. On 1 December Convoy MW14 arrived successfully and the build-up of Malta begun. The new striking force was quickly in action when *Jervis*,

Javelin, *Nubian* and *Kelvin* sailed to intercept an enemy convoy on 2 December. By the time they reached the reported position of the convoy the three merchant ships had all been sunk but their escort the torpedo boat *Lupo* was still in the area. Using radar the British ships had approached to under 2000 yards range when *Jervis* switched on her searchlight to illuminate the Italian ship and opened fire. The first salvo demolished her bridge and she was then pounded into a blazing wreck as each destroyer swept past her. She sank shortly after. The destroyers returned to Malta but only had time to refuel before they sailed again, this time with the whole of Force K to cover the 'Portcullis' convoy which was thought to be under threat from surface attack. They joined the convoy at daylight on 4 December and remained as close escort before returning to Malta on the 5th.

Part of Force K was granted a few days rest before sailing for Operation 'Quadrangle A' on the 10th to provide cover for Convoy MW15 which was thought to be under threat from Italian cruisers. They returned to Malta the same day when air reconnaissance established that the threat did not exist. *Javelin* did not take part in this operation as she was under repair in the harbour. She had sailed on 8 December with *Jervis* and *Nubian* for a sweep but the force had been sighted and all convoys at sea diverted. The ships arrived back at Malta on 9 December. On 13 December Force K split into two sections, *Cleopatra*, *Orion* and *Paladin* being one and *Euryalus*, *Jervis*, *Nubian* and *Kelvin* the other. However, the sweep was uneventful and all ships returned to Malta on 14 December. *Paladin* and *Kelvin* sailed the next day to assist *Petard* which had just captured the Italian submarine *Uarsciek* but she sank and the three destroyers returned to Malta empty-handed. Force K was working hard and *Kelvin* needed docking which she received after she returned to Malta, remaining in dock until 6 January 1943. *Jervis* and *Nubian* sailed again on 19 December and this time were rewarded with success. Near the coast of Ras Turgeuness they found a small freighter, the *Santarosa*, which was carrying supplies. In a clinical action *Jervis* first picked up the shadowing British aircraft on her Type 286 radar at 14 miles and then the freighter itself on her Type 285 at 10,500 yards. At 1.00am *Jervis* opened fire followed immediately by *Nubian*. Eleven minutes later the two destroyers ceased fire and turned for home leaving the freighter sinking. Back in service, *Javelin* sailed with *Nubian* on 26 December but returned the next day having sighted nothing. She then sailed with *Pakenham* to screen *Euryalus* which had sailed to cover Convoy MW19. *Euryalus* arrived back at Malta with *Javelin* and *Pakenham* at 11.00am on 31 December. This was the last mission of the year for Force K.

THE AUSTRALIANS IN MADAGASCAR

The Dutch role in the later Madagascar operations has been described earlier and this section concentrates on the role of the three Australian 'Ns'. After returning from the Mediterranean they rejoined Force A for its next operation. Initially the British seized Diégo Suarez hoping that the Vichy Governor-General would co-operate. However, it became clear that this was not going to happen and so it was decided to occupy the rest of the island. This operation was scheduled for early September which gave the fifth Australian ship, *Nepal*, plenty of time to arrive from Britain. She reached Diego Suarez on 4 September. *Napier* sailed later, on 6 September and rendezvoused with the transport *Empire Pride* the next day. She took on fifty commandos and sailed for Morandava to secure the wireless station and airfield. The landing took place on 10 September and was successful, only a few shots being fired and all objectives being seized rapidly.[17] The commandos returned to *Napier* on 12 September with six prisoners and *Napier* sailed for Diégo Suarez. *Nizam* had left Diégo Suarez on 7 September to take part in the assault on Majunga. This went ahead

on 10 September but there was very little resistance and the port was rapidly captured.

Nepal had sailed from Kilindini on 13 September to take part in the Tamtave operation described above. The other three 'Ns' were also present with their Dutch compatriots – the first time six 'Ns' of the 7th Flotilla had been assembled together. *Napier*, *Nizam* and *Norman* were then detailed to escort the *Illustrious* to Durban but on the 22nd *Napier* and *Norman* were detached to Majunga. *Nepal* sailed back to Kilindini arriving on the 21st. From Durban *Nizam* was to patrol and intercept Vichy merchant vessels and on 24 September she intercepted the *Maréchal Gallieni* south east of Laurenco Marques. The vessel was boarded and sent on to Durban as a prize. Five days later on 30 September she intercepted another freighter, *Amiral Pierre*, which scuttled herself rather than be taken. The scuttling was not successful but the ship could not be towed and was sunk by gunfire. *Nizam* arrived back in Durban on 1 October and sailed for Simonstown for a refit, arriving on 7 October. *Napier* and *Norman* were engaged in patrols and mopping-up operations around Madagascar. For *Napier* this would continue well into October until she sailed for Durban on the 18th. *Nepal* was operating out of Kilindini but returned to Madagascan waters on 14 October. She then sailed to Simonstown arriving on 21 October.

The reason for the concentration of 'Ns' in South African waters was an upsurge in U-boat activity. *Nizam* had her refit cancelled and on 8 October was at sea with *Foxhound*, rescuing survivors from the Greek freighter *Koumoundouros* which had been sunk by *U-68*. On 9 October she picked up more survivors, this time from the Dutch ship *Graateskerk*. At sea on 11 October, escorting the Polish vessel *Narwick*, *Nizam* sighted a submarine on the surface (*U-159*). She turned to attack and was joined by *Foxhound*. Asdic contact was made but before the attack could be carried out both destroyers were ordered to rejoin *Narwick*.[18] *Nizam* continued her patrol and escort duties until 20 October when she finally arrived for her refit. She would be in dock until 28 December.

Norman, *Napier* and *Nepal* patrolled mainly between Capetown, Durban and Simonstown spending several days at sea at a time. They did not locate any German submarines as even an addition of four destroyers was never going to cover all the possibilities but their tactics could have been better . *Napier* arrived at Durban on 14 December to begin her refit leaving just *Nepal* and *Norman* available. *Nepal* returned to Kilindini on 20 December and *Norman* to Diégo Suarez the same day.

---

[17] See Lind and Payne, *N class*

[18] Lind and Payne, *N class*, p118.

12
The Kellys in 1943

JANUARY 1943 saw more attacks from Malta by Force K against Italian convoys to North Africa. *Kelvin* completed her repairs on 7 January and joined *Nubian* in a sweep in which three schooners were found and sunk off Kuirat before the ships returned to Malta the next day. On 9 January, *Euryalus*, *Kelvin* and *Jervis* sailed to join Convoy MW19 which they successfully escorted into Malta on the 11th. The new practice of sending destroyers out in pairs was proving highly successful and *Nubian* and *Kelvin* left Malta at 4.30pm on 15 January. The early departure – usually forces would depart much later – was due to problems with *Kelvin* which could only manage 20-23kts maximum speed. Once they cleared Malta the routine was to follow a reconnaissance aircraft searching for enemy shipping. The aircraft dropped a flare every 10 minutes for illumination but *Kelvin*'s radar made the first contact. The first visual sighting was by *Nubian* of the torpedo boat *Perseo*. The Italians did not see the British ships and so it was a complete surprise when she was hit first by *Nubian* then *Kelvin*. Rapidly disabled she played no further part in the action and fled. *Perseo* had been escorting the freighter *Gabriele D'Annunzio* and she became the

destroyers' next target. *Kelvin* sighted her at 3.39am on the 16th and fired five torpedoes at least one of which hit and sank her. *Nubian* picked up the survivors whilst *Kelvin* patrolled nearby. Both destroyers were undamaged and they arrived back in Malta later that day.

On 16 January *Pakenham* and *Javelin* sailed to intercept a reported Italian freighter, the water stores carrier *Tanaro*. Despite opening fire on the two destroyers she was rapidly overwhelmed and sunk. Twenty-eight prisoners were taken and the two destroyers arrived back at Malta the next day.

The sweeps reached their peak on 19 January when *Javelin* and *Kelvin* sailed to patrol along the Tripolitanian coast. Course was altered towards a report of an enemy ship which was located by radar. *Javelin* opened fire and sunk the ship, a coaster, in 4 minutes. Two more ships were sighted which turned out to be armed trawlers and these were both sunk after a short fight lasting only 7 minutes. The destroyers turned eastwards but when *Javelin* sighted a floating mine they altered course northwards. As they turned onto their new course another ship was sighted which proved to be one of four in a small convoy consisting of a large schooner, a merchant ship, a torpedo boat and an unknown vessel. Both destroyers immediately attacked, *Kelvin* firing two torpedoes at the merchant vessel one of which hit and then went after the schooner, while *Javelin* sank the torpedo boat and finished off the merchant vessel. The fourth vessel escaped destruction as a report had been received that there were two more enemy vessels nearby.

These were thought to be minesweepers and one carried

A nice aerial photograph of *Nizam* escorting units of the Eastern Fleet in the Indian Ocean probably during the later Madagascar operations. She still carries her Type 286 and has not yet received a radar upgrade which would follow in 1943. As the later ships, *Norman* and *Nepal* commissioned they received radar outfits from the start. Note how the Oerlikons point vertically upwards, a common position for the guns when not in use and the TSDS davits are turned inwards to touch each other. This practice was unique to the ships of the 7th Flotilla.

(IMPERIAL WAR MUSEUM: A11659)

Napier at Port Victoria in the Seychelles in August 1942. This is during the period when she was operating as Commodore Arliss's flagship and she does not carry the leader's broad black band or 7th Flotilla markings but shows a commodore's pennant. She has received the updated anti-aircraft armament. Her Type 286 has been censored out.

(IMPERIAL WAR MUSEUM: A13562)

a large gun on her bows and both were sunk. At 4.00am yet another group was sighted which turned out to be a minesweeper and a corvette. The minesweeper was hit and sunk by the first salvo but the corvette fought back and was first hit by *Kelvin* and then disabled by *Javelin* before being sunk by depth charges. As they left the area they came across a motor schooner[1] which was also hit. By now the patrol limit had been reached and the two ships set course for Malta at a speed of 30kts. During the patrol, they had sunk eleven ships, *Kelvin* expending 300 rounds of 4.7in and *Javelin* 500 rounds. Both arrived safely at Malta on 20 January. Later the same day *Jervis* and *Nubian* left for a patrol between Kerkennah, Ras Turgueness and Zuara but, probably due to the action the previous night, found nothing. On 22 January, the whole of Force K sailed for a bombardment of Zuara. *Cleopatra* and *Euryalus* were screened by *Jervis* and *Kelvin* ahead of them with *Nubian* and *Javelin* on the starboard and port quarters respectively. The bombardment was successful, several explosions being seen, and 9 minutes later the force ceased fire and headed back to Malta.

CONVOY ESCORTS

Javelin and *Nubian* sailed later on 23 January for Benghazi where they embarked 600 RAF personnel for Malta, arriving back the next day. Tripoli had been captured on the 23rd and a convoy (XT1) sailed for the port with essential supplies and personnel to get it functioning again. This operation ('MH3') also included the Royal Fleet Auxiliary *Cherryleaf* for Malta and was met on 24 January by *Orion*,

Jervis, *Kelvin* and *Tetcott*. After covering the convoy for a day the force detached from the convoy and sailed with *Cherryleaf* for Malta arriving on the 26th. On 28 January, *Cleopatra*, *Jervis*, *Javelin* and *Kelvin* sailed to overtake Convoy ME16 for Alexandria, on their way to join and escort the latest large ship movement, Operation 'MH4'. the force remained with the convoy until after dark on 29 January when they accelerated to full speed and headed for Alexandria arriving on the 30th.

Operation 'MH4' consisted of two convoys, Convoy XT2 of six store ships for Tripoli and MW20 of six ships for Malta. MW20 was further divided into two parts, MW20A consisting of personnel and store ships and MW20B, a slow convoy made up of two tankers. *Jervis*, *Javelin* and *Kelvin* together with *Belvoir* were to escort MW20B. The whole operation got underway on 6 February and went smoothly, the convoys separating and reaching their respective destinations without trouble. MW20B and its escort arrived in Malta on 11 February. However, Captain Pugsley (D14)[2] considered that the convoy was routed too near the coast and recommended that in future such convoys be routed at least 6 miles out to allow room for emergency manoeuvres. During the voyage *Javelin*'s main steering gyro broke

---

[1] Unless survivors were rescued the names of the ships sunk were frequently unknown. Furthermore, misidentifications were common, for example *Kelvin* and *Javelin*'s corvette was very likely another minesweeper. Therefore, it is difficult to identify with any confidence just what was sunk at a particular time.

[2] Captain A F Pugsley had replaced Captain Poland in charge of the 14th Flotilla at the beginning of January.

down and she would remain at Malta until 16 February under repair. *Kelvin*, however, immediately sailed with *Paladin* and the Greek *Kondouriotis* to escort *Cherryleaf* to Tripoli. Two days later, *Jervis* sailed with Convoy ME17 but left it on 14 February to reinforce the escort of Convoy TX1, the first convoy from Tripoli back to Alexandria.

The voyage was uneventful until 17 February when *Paladin* picked up an asdic contact and attacked it with a five-charge pattern. *Paladin* had just concluded that she had attacked a false contact when a submarine, U-205, suddenly surfaced, too badly damaged by the depth charges to remain underwater. *Jervis*, which had been nearby, and *Paladin* opened up with all guns. At the same time a South African Air Force aircraft roared in and attacked the submarine with machine-gun fire and depth charges. The U-boat crew rapidly abandoned ship and forty-two survivors were picked by *Paladin* and *Jervis*. The submarine itself remained on the surface going round in circles at about 9kts and Captain Pugsley decided that an attempt should be made to salvage it. A party from *Paladin* boarded the submarine and removed files and other items. The corvette *Gloxinia* was summoned to attempt a tow of the submarine but unfortunately the submarine was settling and even though *Gloxinia* tried to reach shore and beach it, it sank 2 miles out. The convoy arrived safely at Alexandria the next day.

On her return to service, *Javelin* joined *Orion*, *Euryalus* and *Nubian* for exercises. After transporting Labour Corps personnel between Malta and Tripoli she sailed with *Nubian* on 27 February for an uneventful night sweep. The two destroyers returned to Malta the next day but sailed again after dark as escorts for *Orion*, bound for Alexandria. After an uneventful passage the three ships arrived on 2 March. *Jervis* was undergoing a boiler clean in the Alexandria Floating Dock from 27 February to 4 March and *Kelvin* had sailed to Port Said escorting Convoy XT4M on 25 February. She returned on 27 February with *Vasilissa Olga* escorting *Cleopatra*. On 1 March, *Kelvin*, *Vasilissa Olga*, *Dulverton*, *Pindos* and *Rockwood* sailed as escort for Convoy MW22 to Malta. The convoy contained several slow ships so was vulnerable to air attack, but these did not materialise until 5 March. The aircraft were picked up on *Kelvin's* Type 286P radar and the convoy was well prepared. Two aircraft attacked *Kelvin* but the rest concentrated on the tankers. However, unlike the convoys of old, no ships were damaged and one aircraft shot down with another damaged. The convoy arrived safely on 6 March.

Jervis had completed her boiler clean and with *Javelin* sailed as part of the escort for Convoy XT5. On 8 March *Javelin* almost collided with a floating mine and only an emergency turn saved her. The convoy arrived at Tripoli on

9 March where *Javelin* remained for Operation 'MH9', two convoys of empty merchant ships for Port Said and Alexandria. The first, Convoy TX3, sailed from Tripoli on 11 March. It was to rendezvous with Convoy ME19 from Malta which had sailed the previous day. The two convoys met at dusk on 11 March and sailed uneventfully to Alexandria. By now the enemy threat was much diminished but was still serious enough for continuous escort to be provided.

Javelin would sail for torpedo firing trials on 17 and 18 March whilst *Kelvin* and *Jervis* headed for Port Said to pick up *Orion* on the 17th. They escorted her to Alexandria and then on the 19th, joined by *Javelin* and *Isis*, escorted her to Malta, then took *Euryalus* in the other direction, arriving back at Alexandria on 23 March. On 24 March, there was yet another convoy to escort, XT8 to Tripoli. From Tripoli the convoy sailed for Malta to embark an infantry brigade destined for Alexandria. The escort throughout was *Jervis*, *Javelin*, *Kelvin*, *Nubian* and *Isis* but on reaching Malta, *Kelvin* and *Nubian* were replaced by *Aldenham* and *Rockwood* and sent to Benghazi on 1 April but recalled the next day to join the Malta striking force. *Kelvin* would remain in harbour until she was docked on 16 April. She would leave Malta on 21 April for Alexandria, arriving on the 23rd and remaining there as port ship for the next three days.

Javelin and *Kelvin* continued escorting convoys, taking Convoy XT8 from Alexandria to Tripoli between 12 and 16 April. On the 17 April *Jervis* headed back for Malta whilst *Javelin* remained at Tripoli to take Convoy TX8 back to Alexandria. She then sailed with *Llandovery Castle* and Convoy 'Heavy' to pick up captured prisoners of war, arriving at Alexandria on 24 April. By now both *Javelin* and *Kelvin* needed long refits and would shortly be heading for the United Kingdom. But before that, on 29 April both took part in Operation 'MJ8' which involved Convoy XT14 to Tripoli and Convoy MW27 to Malta. A Hurricane covering the convoy crashed nearby and *Javelin* rescued the pilot. Air cover was still needed as the escort fought off air attacks throughout the day but two ships from the convoy were sunk by torpedo bombers. *Javelin* and *Kelvin* left the convoy after dark on 3 May and returned to Alexandria for the next operation, 'MJ9', which involved empty ships returning to Port Said and Alexandria, keeping the two destroyers at sea until the 12th. With very little respite *Javelin* and *Kelvin* sailed on 15 May for their final Mediterranean operation, Operation 'MK1'. Firstly they escorted Convoy XT15 to Tripoli followed by Convoy MW28, which this time they saw through to Malta, arriving on 21 May. On the 22nd both ships sailed for the United Kingdom for their refits. By now it was safe for ships to sail through the Straits of Gibraltar and both ships took this route. *Javelin* arrived at Portsmouth on 7 June

and *Kelvin* arrived at Chatham on the 11th. Both would be out of action for the rest of the year.

JERVIS ALONE

Jervis, because of her position as flotilla leader, tended to get her repairs completed more promptly, enabling her to continue in service without the need for a major refit. After the departure of *Kelvin* and *Javelin* she was the only Kelly in the Mediterranean but was still the leader of the 14th Flotilla, which now included five of the 'P' class,[3] *Nubian* and *Vasilissa Olga*. Operating out of Malta, the 14th Flotilla was to interdict enemy shipping and on 2 May *Jervis*, *Nubian* and *Petard* sailed for a daylight sweep off the Sicilian Straits but saw nothing. Meanwhile, in Tunisia, the Afrika Korp's final defences were breached and their front collapsed. As there was a possibility of attempts being made to evacuate troops by sea, Operation 'Retribution' was initiated to prevent this. All available destroyers were to patrol off Cape Bon with coastal forces closer inshore. *Jervis*, *Paladin* and *Nubian* sailed on 6 and 8 May but found nothing. On the 8th they bombarded Keiliba. They were relieved on 10 May but on the way back came across an escaping group of Germans and Italians towing a rubber dinghy. The dinghy belonged to an RAF pilot who had been picked up by the escapees. The prisoners were taken on board and the force returned to Malta. They sailed again on 12 May and during a two-day patrol picked up another ninety-five prisoners, Keiliba being bombarded for a second time. The Germans also tried evacuation by air and both American and British planes were on hand to intercept the transports. Unfortunately, ship recognition was not a strong point and they

Nepal in an unusual camouflage scheme which consists of two colours, the nature of which are unknown. It was possibly symmetrical and was applied sometime in September 1942. How long it lasted is unknown but *Nepal* was repainted in the standard 7th Flotilla scheme by the end of 1942. Also visible in the photograph is her Type 281 installation located on her aft deckhouse. *Nepal* was the only Kelly to carry this particular type of radar and then only until October of that year.

(AUSTRALIAN WAR MEMORIAL: 041365)

occasionally attacked Royal Navy warships operating off the coast.[4] In an attempt to prevent this, the upper decks of warships were painted in red lead as a recognition signal. According to Pugsley, this was slow drying and sticky and not very popular.[5] Operation 'Retribution' was terminated on 13 May, a day after all organised resistance in Tunisia was overcome. *Jervis* returned to Malta on 15 May and then sailed with *Paladin* and *Nubian* again on 18 May, this time to patrol round the coast of Pantellaria. The patrol was uneventful apart from the investigation of a hospital ship.

Jervis next sailed from Malta in response to an intelligence report that there was an Italian convoy at sea, leaving Malta on 1 June with *Vasilissa Olga* for the east coast of Sicily. At 1.34am on the 2nd *Jervis*'s Type 286 radar picked up the convoy. The destroyers altered course to intercept and closed to within 2000 yards undetected. The convoy consisted of two freighters escorted by a torpedo boat, the *Castore* and another small escort, *X137*. The merchant vessels were seen first, and *Jervis* opened fire on a large merchant ship, hitting her with the first salvo and rapidly reducing her to a burning wreck. After eight salvoes she switched to the smaller

---

[3] *Penn, Petard, Pathfinder, Paladin* and *Panther*.

[4] In one incident, an RAF formation attacked a British force which was then rescued by German fighters who presumed the ships were theirs.
[5] A F Pugsley, *Destroyer Man*, p141.

merchant ship and hits were obtained.[6] They then fired on the escorts sinking *X137* first and then both engaging *Castore*. On fire, *Castore* turned towards the shore where she beached herself still under fire. During the engagement *Jervis* had only fired 65 SAP and 77 HEDA 4.7in shells, one torpedo and several rounds from her pom-pom and Oerlikons. Both ships withdrew quickly as they had reached the limit of their patrol. As they sped back to Malta, Captain Pugsley radioed their expected position at dawn and requested air cover. German aircraft could already be heard in the sky above waiting for dawn to make their attack. Malta sent out three Spitfires which drove the German bombers off but they could not stay as they were at the limit of their endurance. Then *Vasilissa Olga*'s boilers broke down. This took an hour to repair and it was 1.35pm on 2 June when the two ships finally arrived at Malta.

THE SICILIAN AND ITALIAN LANDINGS

Jervis did not remain in harbour long but sailed on 3 June to assist a force of nine LCTs which had run into bad weather. With the aid of the RAF, they were all located and directed to the North African port of Sousse. *Jervis* remained at sea and sailed for Tobruk to rendezvous with the cruiser *Mauritius*. However, the cruiser had run aground while leaving Alexandria and so *Jervis* entered Tobruk to refuel before sailing to participate in the assault on the island of Pantellaria. This took place on 11 June and the naval force which consisted of five cruisers, *Jervis* and seven other destroyers and the gunboat *Aphis* rapidly neutralised the island's defences. After reducing three outlying islands, *Jervis*

arrived back at Malta on 21 June. She was due to sail for the Sicily landings in July but before that escorted the battleships *Howe* and *King George V* into the Mediterranean leaving Gibraltar on 5 July for Algiers, arriving on the 8th.

The landings commenced on 10 July and *Jervis* continued escorting the battleships during the bombardments. She returned to Algiers on 13 July and picked up a force of four other destroyers with instructions to shell the coastal highway between Syracuse and Catania. On arrival on the 14th, they found the enemy in full retreat along the highway. The destroyers turned to starboard in succession and running roughly parallel to the highway opened up on the vehicles doing great damage over a mile-long stretch of road. The bombardments continued for several days, *Jervis* and her force returning to Malta on 22 July to refuel. She sailed the same day to patrol off Bizerte and Algiers, calling at the latter port to refuel on 26 July. On 30 July she was joined by *Pathfinder*, *Panther* and *Paladin* and sailed to Bône[7] to rendezvous with the cruisers *Euryalus*, *Sirius* and *Dido* for a bombardment of the River Olivo bridge.

The force left Bône at 8.00am and at 10.30pm *Euryalus* and *Pathfinder* were detached to bombard Vibo Valentia. An hour later the rest of the force arrived in the bombardment area where the destroyers were to illuminate the target by starshell, engage any enemy offering resistance and finally to engage the target. The cruisers would carry out the main bombardment. *Jervis* illuminated a tower north of the bridge as a reference point but the bridge itself proved to be difficult to locate until one of *Jervis*'s salvoes started an electrical fire clearly illuminating the bridge for a few min-

---

[6] The two merchant vessels sunk were *Vragnizzia* and *Postumia*.

[7] Now Annaba.

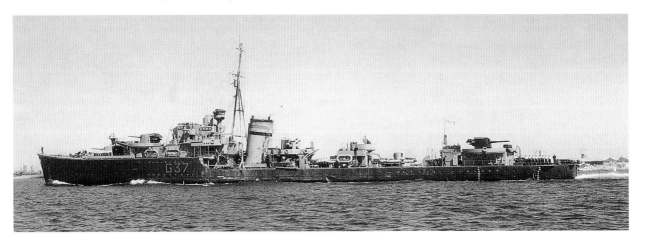

A very fine photograph of *Kelvin* returning to Alexandria in early 1943 showing the alterations to her during this period. Her colour scheme is interesting and is shown in greater detail in profile 11. She carries six Oerlikons, the barrels of the last two being visible behind the crewmembers lining the side. In front of No 1 mount can be seen the upper works of the French battleship *Lorraine* interned in Alexandria.

(COURTESY OF JOHN ROBERTS)

Jervis also sometime in 1943 with a 4in gun added. She also carries six Oerlikons, two of which are fitted on the roof of her aft deckhouse. She has also acquired a Type 285.   (IMPERIAL WAR MUSEUM: FL22386)

utes. *Jervis* and *Sirius* then fired at the bridge but had to stop when it was obscured by dust, switching targets to some electricity pylons but these were also obscured by dust. As there were no other targets the force retired to be rejoined by *Euryalus* and *Pathfinder*. The destroyers were ordered to Algiers but *Jervis* went to Bône first to refuel. The bridge, though, had been destroyed.

Jervis was next ordered to Bizerte and arrived on 6 August when she came under air attack but was undamaged. On 9 August. She sailed on Operation 'Annoyance', another bombardment mission involving four cruisers and three other destroyers. Once again it divided with *Jervis*, *Aurora*, *Penelope* and *Paladin* heading off to bombard troop concentrations at Castellamare whilst the other ships patrolled looking for enemy shipping. At 1.30am on 10 August the cruisers opened fire on a German camp and were rewarded with two explosions. *Jervis* and *Paladin* fired on a shore battery which returned fire and forced them to retire behind a smokescreen. The whole force arrived back at Bizerte later that day. The next bombardment was an attack on Vibo Valentia on 12 August where a warehouse bombed earlier was still burning and provided excellent illumination of the target. *Jervis* and *Paladin* then joined *Aurora* and *Penelope* in an apparently ineffective bombardment of Scala on the Italian mainland on the 16th.

Jervis then sailed from Bizerte to escort a convoy of five troopships on 2 September. She handed over the escort to destroyers from Malta on the 3rd and then sailed with her flotilla mates for Algiers arriving on 4 September, sailing the next day to bombard the coastal railway line from Taranto to Salerno. The line was to be cut where it ran through the Gulf of San Eufemia and when the destroyers arrived there was an ammunition train on the line. The plan had been to

bring the cliff wall down onto the line but as the train was there the destroyers engaged it, causing a spectacular explosion which also had the desired effect of bringing the cliff down, and the ships returned to Algiers satisfied, departing again on 7 September as the screen for *King George V*. Whilst at sea they received the news that Italy had surrendered and transported a small force of troops to seize the port of Taranto. The operation which was successful but the minelayer *Abdiel* was mined and sunk in the harbour on 10 September with heavy loss of life, *Jervis* making a high-speed dash to Malta with some of the seriously wounded the next day. She arrived early on the 13th and then sailed again on the 14th with other destroyers to support the landings at Salerno where a serious crisis had arisen.

Naval gunfire broke up a threatening German counteroffensive and enabled the troops to consolidate their foothold. The 14th Flotilla escorted the *Warspite*, which had been seriously damaged by a glider bomb, back to Malta arriving on the 19th, and then sailed to escort *Formidable* and *Illustrious* to Gibraltar, returning to invasion duties on 29 September. *Jervis* and *Petard* were detailed to sail ahead of the Allied advance looking for German shipping along the coast. They entered Brindisi on 1 October after it had fallen to the Eighth Army but *Petard* was ordered to the Aegean to take part in the occupation of Leros – a badly-planned operation which would cost the Royal Navy heavily. *Jervis* continued bombardment operations in support of the army with *Offa*. On 6 October they bombarded the town of Termoli before sailing to support the partisans in

Yugoslavia. Two days later *Jervis* was also ordered to Alexandria to support the Leros operation.

THE LEROS DEBACLE

After Italy's surrender German troops on the Greek islands had attacked the Italian garrisons there and in some cases overpowered them. British troops had been landed on some islands to stiffen the resolve of the Italians and fight the Germans. This brought a strong response from the Germans who themselves brought in reinforcements and using their local air superiority had been making things difficult. Already three destroyers had been lost and one cruiser badly damaged but stubbornly the British insisted on feeding in more troops and supplies despite the lack of air support. *Jervis* arrived at Alexandria on 11 October and sailed with *Penn*, *Hursley* and *Miaoulis* for her first supply operation to Leros on the 16th. She unloaded troops, guns and stores in Alinda Bay before sailing to Guvercinlik Bay on the 17th. There she and *Penn* were joined by *Hursley* and *Miaoulis* and sailed after dark to bombard the German-held port at Kalimno sinking *UJ2109* (formerly the British minesweeper *Widnes*[8]) and a merchant vessel. As they were leaving an aircraft dropped a flare which turned out to be a signal for a dive-bombing attack, *Jervis* being near-missed by a bomb that fell 50 yards off her port quarter. The destroyers retired in haste and on 18 October rendezvoused with *Aurora* and returned to Alexandria.

The next supply run took place on 21 October, this time *Jervis* and *Pathfinder* sailed together with *Hurworth* and *Adrias*. They rendezvoused with *Aurora* and *Miaoulis* at

Wear and tear affected camouflage schemes quite significantly as can be seen in this photograph of *Norman* in faded 7th Flotilla colours taken in 1943. Her TSDS looks to have been removed. Radar equipment is a Type 291 and Type 285. (AUSTRALIAN WAR MEMORIAL: 041429)

7.00pm when *Pathfinder*, *Hurworth* and *Adrias* departed to bombard Kalimno again. On their return all four ships anchored behind the Yedi Atala Islands. So unknown was this region that the only charts available were 105 years old. The four ships stayed in their anchorage for the whole of the 22nd before *Jervis* and *Pathfinder* sailed through the Kos Strait to unload their stores. *Jervis* had been specially equipped for unloading stores and so when the two destroyers arrived at Partheni was able to unload all her cargo in 40 minutes.[9] The two destroyers left shortly after midnight on 23 October and once again an aircraft dropped flares though this time no attacks followed. They then made their way back to Alexandria, arriving at 4.35pm.

Jervis remained at Alexandria for the rest of the month before entering dry dock between 1 and 14 November. She continued repairs until the 22nd, having her 4in gun reinstalled. During this period Leros was re-taken by the Germans and it was decided to withdraw the garrison on the smaller island of Kastellorizo and replace it by forty special service commandos to maintain the fiction that it was still garrisoned. This operation was christened 'Tiber' and got underway when *Jervis*, *Penn* and *Fury* sailed on 26 November. First they headed to Limassol where they moored alongside the Royal Fleet Auxiliary *Cherryleaf* and loaded up with life jackets and special Royal Engineer pontoons. *Jervis*, *Penn*

---

[8] *Widnes* had been damaged by air attack in Suda Bay on 20 May 1941 and beached. She was salvaged and repaired by the Germans who re-commissioned her as *UJ2109*.

[9] She unloaded five jeeps, five trailers, three 2pdr anti tank guns, 4 tons of diesel oil, 12 tons of ammunition, 4 tons of other stores and fifty-three troops.

and *Pathfinder*[10] each received two and *Fury* three. The ships arrived at Kastellorizo on 28 November and conveyed the garrison to Famagusta where they disembarked the troops. *Jervis* and *Penn* then returned to Limassol on 2 December. On the 3rd they returned to the Aegean Islands for Operation 'Tableland' to escort the Greek destroyer *Adrias*, which had been refloated after damage, back to Alexandria, arriving on 5 December. Then on 9 December, *Jervis* helped escort the cruisers *Penelope* and *London* to Malta. Winston Churchill was returning in *Penelope* from the Teheran and Cairo conferences.

Jervis, *Penn* and *Pathfinder* left Malta on 13 December to head for Bizerte and then Algiers, where they were joined by *Janus*. The two 'Js' and *Pathfinder* left Algiers on 17 December escorting Convoy NSF10 to Alexandria via Naples, arriving on the 22nd. *Janus* and *Jervis* remained at Alexandria until 29 December when they sailed to take part in the Anzio landings, arriving at Brindisi on the 31st.

PIROUN'S YEAR

At the end of 1942 *Piorun* had sailed with the Home Fleet to provide distant cover for Convoy RA51 bound for the United Kingdom and to intercept *Hipper* and *Lützow* after their encounter with Convoy JW51B, returning to Scapa on 3 January. *Piorun* next sailed on 11 January as part of a force of two cruisers and six destroyers in search of *Scharnhorst* and *Prinz Eugen* which were reported to be at sea but when the German force realised that they had been sighted, they cancelled their operation. This led to the British and Polish[11] ships being recalled to Scapa on the 12th. The Polish destroyer was still involved in convoy duties and her next convoy would be as part of the close escort rather than the distant escort.[12] On 16 January she left Scapa Flow with *Musketeer* to Seidis Fjord in Iceland where the escort for the Convoy JW52 was assembling, arrived on 18 January and sailing two days later with the others of the escort. They joined the convoy on 21 January and made good time in fair weather but were sighted by the enemy on the 23rd. Attacks followed the next day, from both aircraft and from U-boats. One bomber attacked *Piorun* but its bomb fell 200 yards in front of the ship. The experienced and skilful escort prevented the German submarines getting at the merchant ships, and the convoy arrived intact at Kola Inlet on the 27th.

After refuelling, the escort sailed on 29 January for the return trip with convoy RA52. This time the U-boats had more success and one merchant vessel was sunk. *Piorun*

and the rest of the escort left the convoy for Seidis Fjord on 5 February arrived at Scapa the next day. Convoy JW53 saw *Piorun* again part of the distant cover with the Home Fleet. They departed Scapa on 14 February but returned on the 17th due to a heavy storm. After a wait of a few days they were at sea again finally returning to Scapa on 26 January. Another patrol followed on 2 March but once again this was cut short due to heavy weather. On 8 March she sailed from Scapa, once more as part of the Home Fleet providing distant cover for a convoy, this time RA53 from the Soviet Union. However, the Battle of the Atlantic was reaching a crisis and all available escorts were needed there. *Piorun* was withdrawn from the Home Fleet and she formed part of the escort of an Atlantic convoy between 4 and 8 April. By then though the Mediterranean needed ships as well and so after this one convoy *Piorun* sailed for Plymouth to escort ships heading to and from Gibraltar. Her first task was to escort the battleship *Malaya* with *Meteor* and *Matchless* and the three destroyers departed Plymouth on 20 April. The three ships were due to meet *Malaya* on the 22nd April but the day before they picked up an asdic contact. *Piorun* made three attacks and *Matchless* and *Meteor* one each before breaking off but the official conclusion was that there was no evidence of a submarine. *Malaya* was met and safely handed over to other ships on 27 April and *Piorun* and her consorts returned to Plymouth. Her next battleship was *Valiant* which with *Wensleydale* and *Orkan* she escorted to the Clyde, returning to Plymouth once more on 7 May. After refuelling rapidly and dashed out to meet the incoming *Rodney*, home from Force H for a refit. She spent the rest of May at Devonport repairing weather damage.

Repairs completed, on 1 June *Piorun* escorted *Rodney* to Scapa Flow, then on 17 June she sailed from there with the battleship and her sister-ship *Nelson*, the aircraft carrier *Indomitable* and eight other destroyers for the Sicilian landings. They arrived at Gibraltar on 23 June where *Piorun* remained until the 28th and *Rodney* and *Nelson* rejoined Force H. *Piorun* then escorted *Formidable* and *Warspite* to Algiers arriving on 30 June and then sailed on to Mers-el-Kebir where she picked up the battleships *King George V* and *Howe* and escorted them to Gibraltar arriving on 3 July. On 6 July a massively-augmented Force H set sail from Gibraltar with *Piorun*[13] leading the capital ships and the rest of the destroyers on the flanks. South of Malta on 8 July, the screen was detached to the island to refuel and their place taken by the ships of the 12th Flotilla. The final element of Force H joined at 6.00am on the 9th when *Warspite*, *Valiant* and *Formidable* arrived ready for the invasion

---

[10] *Pathfinder* was already at Limassol awaiting the arrival of the other three ships.
[11] The force also included *Orkan*.
[12] *Piorun* had been 'arcticized' (converted for arctic service) to handle the extreme conditions on these convoys.

[13] *Piorun* was now attached to the 24th Destroyer Flotilla.

In 1943 *Piorun* joined the Italian invasions and was painted in this interesting two-colour scheme. She is shown at sea off Malta in late 1943.

(COURTESY OF JOHN ROBERTS)

on 10 July. Throughout the day Force H bombarded enemy positions and *Piorun* patrolled the invasion zone until 16 July, sailing to Malta whenever she needed refuelling. On the 16th the carrier *Indomitable* was hit by an Italian air dropped torpedo. She was escorted back to Malta by the battleship *Nelson* and several destroyers including *Piorun*. After arrival on the 17th *Piorun* joined the cruiser *Aurora* and seven other destroyers for a patrol in the Gulf of Squillace returning to Malta on the 20th. Interestingly, despite being in the vicinity of *Jervis*, there is no indication that the two ships worked together during this period. She refuelled and sailed to join Force H for a bombardment of Crotone on the Italian mainland returning to Malta afterwards. Until 16 August she was engaged in patrolling south of Sicily. She then reinforced MTBs operating off Augusta against Axis shipping between Sicily and Calabria for the next three days.

Piorun returned to Malta on 31 August and immediately rejoined Force H for the landings in Calabria, guarding the capital ships against E-boat and submarine attack, adopting the early war tactic of depth-charging any contact that resembled a submarine. This was successful, as if there were any submarines in the vicinity none of them were able to attack. On 9 September the Allied efforts moved to Salerno and this time *Piorun* was involved in providing fire support to the troops on shore. She patrolled between Augusta and Malta until the 23rd when she escorted the monitor *Roberts* to rendezvous with a convoy to Malta. *Piorun* then sailed with *Quilliam* on a patrol off Otranto and Corfu where she picked up the survivors of the Italian torpedo boat *Francesco Stocco* which had been sunk by German bombers. These patrols continued until 27 September when *Piorun* was ordered to escort the Italian cruiser *Scipione Africano* carrying the Italian King Victor Emanuel III and Marshall Badoglio from Brindisi to Malta for the formalisation of the Italian surrender.

Piorun was in need of a refit and so, following a series of patrols from Brindisi, Malta and Bari, she entered Malta Docks on 12 October staying until the 26th when she escorted *Nelson* and *Rodney* back to Gibraltar. Force H had

finally been disbanded as there was no longer a need for it and the battleships were sailing for other duties. *Piorun* remained at Gibraltar until 2 November and then sailed with *Tyrian*, *Tumult* and *Grenville* to Bizerta. On the way there the ships carried out an anti-submarine sweep which yielded no results. They arrived at Bizerta on 5 November and then sailed for Augusta the next day to take up a bombardment support role for the army. The first bombardment took place on the 8th when they fired on enemy positions in the Gulf of Gaeta, just north of Naples. A further bombardment followed on the 9th and this time a coastal battery responded. The four destroyers returned to Naples on 10 November and then *Piorun* and *Tumult* sailed for Oran, arriving on the 13th to escort the French battleship *Richelieu* to the United Kingdom.

Joined by *Inglefield*, the force sailed for Gibraltar and promptly ran into a heavy storm. *Piorun* was damaged and she had to put into Gibraltar on 14 November to refuel. She then rejoined the escort and they continued their voyage. On 17 November an unknown aircraft was spotted and *Piorun* immediately opened fire, her efficiency embarrassing the French gunners who were caught unawares. The aircraft turned out to be a Liberator and was undamaged though shaken. The escort left the battleship which was heading for Scapa and sailed to Plymouth to refuel. *Piorun* remained at Plymouth until 25 November before sailing for Greenock and the Clyde for a refit lasting until 31 March 1944.

THE FAR EAST

The Australian ships started 1943 with *Napier* refitting at Durban until 17 February. *Norman* had left Diégo Suarez on 1 January and arrived at Kilindini on the 3rd. She was joined a day later by *Nizam* which had just completed her refit and *Nepal*. It was On 13 January *Norman* and *Nepal* escorted *Illustrious* from Kilindini to Durban, arriving on 18 January. *Norman* departed on 23 January escorting NSIS[14] *Hong Siang* to Kilindini and arriving on 31 January, the same

---

[14] Naval Stores Issuing Ship.

day as *Nepal* which had proceeded directly from Durban. Shortly after, on 3 February the fleet sailed for Operation 'Pamphlet', covering a convoy of liners transporting an infantry division home from the Middle East. *Nizam*, *Norman* and *Nepal* all sailed with the fleet and remained at sea until 11 February when they put into Addu Atoll to refuel, finally returned to Kilindini on 20 February.

Norman sailed on 23 February for a refit at Simonstown, which would be completed on 22 April. *Nepal*, *Foxhound* and *Quilliam* sailed as the escort for *Warspite* on 11 March. The battleship was bound a short refit at Durban and the force arrived there on 16 March. Upon arrival *Nepal* was immediately lent to the South Atlantic command to assist in combating a new U-boat offensive in those waters. *Napier* took a bit longer than expected to complete her refit but she was finally ready at the end of February. *Norman*'s completion date was also put back to 6 May. Once *Napier* was operational she too was loaned to the South Atlantic command and spent her time patrolling the waters off the Cape.

Nizam remained at Kilindini from 20 February to 3 May when she sailed with *Quickmatch* escorting the battleship *Resolution* to Durban. She arrived on 9 May and joined *Norman* in patrolling South African waters. *Napier* had left Durban on 26 April with Convoy CM41 for Kilindini, arriving safely on 3 May just before *Nizam* sailed. *Napier* sailed for exercises with *Newcastle* on 8 June and the next day they were joined by *Raider*. On 15 June she sailed with the battleship *Revenge*, acting as her anti-submarine escort and then returning to Kilindini on 21 June. *Norman* arrived at Durban on 20 May after completion of her refit and on 25 May sailed for an anti submarine patrol. She returned on 31 May after an uneventful few days. On 30 May *Nizam* and *Fritillary* left Durban as the local anti-submarine escort for Convoy CM42 but encountered no trouble.

Norman left Durban on 25 June with *Quickmatch* and *Rotherham* as escort for Convoy WS29. She returned to Durban with *Relentless* as well as the other two destroyers but sailed again on 28 June to cover Convoy WS30 as far as the Comoro Islands. *Nizam* had also sailed on an anti-submarine search christened Operation 'Player' on 24 June. She sailed with *Relentless* and *Suffolk* to a point about 4-800 miles off the Madagascan coast to search the area for a U-boat supply ship which had been detected by D/F signals. In the event nothing was found and the operation was called off on 1 July

Nepal had completed her refit by 24 May when she arrived at Melbourne. She next sailed for Geraldton departing from that port on 1 June and sailing for Diego Garcia where she was due on 9 June. Her next port of call was the Seychelles on 13 June and whilst on passage she escorted the subma-

rine depot ship *Adamant* before putting into Victoria. On 20 June she joined the Armed Merchant Cruiser *Carthage* and the cruiser *Capetown* as anti-submarine escort for Convoy KR5. The convoy arrived at Colombo on 27 June and on 2 July *Nepal* and *Carthage* sailed with *Salween* for Kilindini, arriving on 9 July. On 17 July *Nepal*, *Napier*, *Rotherham* and *Racehorse* departed with the battleships *Resolution* and *Lorraine* and escorted them to Latitude 20° South where *Nepal* and *Racehorse* reversed course and returned to Kilindini. *Napier* and *Rotherham* continued on with the ships to Durban. *Nepal* and *Racehorse* arrived back in Kilindini on 22 July. *Nepal*'s next task was to escort the transport *Sibajak* to Durban. She left on 31 July and arrived on 6 August.

All the while the Australian destroyers were continuing to patrol South African waters without locating any German submarines. The only contact was with their victims. On 13 July *Nizam* picked up thirteen survivors from the *Sebastiano Cermeno*, which had been sunk on 27 June. Leaving Durban on 26 July she escorted Convoy CM43 to rendezvous with the cruiser *Suffolk* south of Mauritius. On 31 July she rescued six men from a lifeboat from the freighter *Cornish City* which had been sunk two days previously, landing them at Mauritius the next day. She then refuelled and headed for a refit at Geraldton in Australia. She would be refitting until 30 September when she would spend some time in Australian waters before returning to the Eastern Fleet in November.

Nepal sailed from Durban on 10 August with Convoy CM44. She then sailed to Diégo Suarez to refuel and escort the seaplane carrier *Albatross* to Durban. Both ships arrived on 23 August and *Nepal* docked for a refit which would last until 13 September. *Norman* continued her patrols and escort duties. On 28 August she left Durban with the cruiser *Hawkins* and the destroyers *Quiberon* and *Rapid* to escort Convoy WS32 to Kilindini via the Mozambique channel. The convoy arrived on 4 September and the destroyers sailed to meet *Emerald* and escort her to Kilindini as well. In an echo of what was normal for the Mediterranean, *Norman* and *Rapid* then sailed on 5 September back to Durban with Convoy MC9A (the cable layer, *Recorder*) arriving on 13 September. *Norman* docked for a boiler cleaning and when she returned to service on 24 September she rejoined the Eastern Fleet.

AT BOMBAY

On *Nepal*'s emergence from refit she joined Convoy CM45 to Kilindini which sailed 14 September. The convoy arrived on 21 September and on the 28th the two 'Ns' were joined by *Norman* which had left Durban on the 24th. The three ships left Kilindini the same day and escorted *Adamant* to Colombo, arriving on 8 October after a refuelling stop at the Seychelles. On the 9th they sailed for Bombay to take

up anti-submarine duties outside the harbour, arriving on 11 October. On 25 October, *Napier*, *Nepal* and *Frobisher* sailed for the Seychelles with the troopship *George Washington*, though *Napier* and *Nepal* only escorted the other two ships to the open ocean before returning to Bombay. On 27 October, *Napier* and *Nepal* together with the Armed Merchant Cruiser *Canton* sailed to the mid-Ocean meeting point[15] to rendezvous with the freighter *Lurline* and escort her in to Bombay. *Nizam* left Australian waters on 4 November and arrived at Colombo on the 17th. She would not join her sister-ships at Bombay but would await their return to Kilindini where she arrived on 26 November via the Seychelles. Meanwhile, *Norman* and *Nepal* joined the escort carrier *Battler* and *Rotherham* when they sailed from Bombay to rendezvous with Convoy AB20 on 11 November. The convoy arrived safely at Bombay on 17 November.

Napier departed Bombay on 16 November while *Norman* and *Nepal* remained at Bombay but on 26 November, *Nepal* escorted the Polish liner *Batory* to Hormuz. They arrived there on 29 November and the next day *Nepal* departed for Bombay escorting the troopship *Empire Pride*. *Norman* was the next 'N' to depart Bombay permanently. She sailed on 9 December escorting *Mooltan* to Colombo arriving on the 12th. She sailed the next day for Kilindini. *Nepal* sailed with *Battler*, *Rotherham* and *Penn* on 12 December to the rendezvous with Convoy AB24A. On the way they were joined by *Rotherham* out of Kilindini but rather than return to Bombay with the convoy, *Nepal* detached from it to escort *Arundel Castle* to Kilindini on 15 December. On arrival she sailed with Convoy MC10A for Durban arriving at the end of the year. *Napier* and *Nizam* sailed from Kilindini on 24 December to rendezvous with Convoy CM48. After the rendezvous they escorted the convoy to Aden arriving on 31 December. *Norman* also sailed for Aden on 28 December. With *Racehorse* and *Redoubt* she provided the escort for *Ramillies*.

---

[15] An area at sea normally designated for escorts to change over or escorts to meet charges.

Tjerk Hiddes arriving at Fremantle in 1943. Her aft tubes have been fitted and she carries six Oerlikons. At this time, searchlights were still carried.

(AUSTRALIAN WAR MEMORIAL: P0444/214/145)

THE DUTCH DESTROYERS IN AUSTRALIA

During their time at Fremantle both Dutch destroyers were attached to the 19th Destroyer Division, RAN. At the end of 1942 *Van Galen* had noticed problems with her rudder and put into Exmouth Bay on 2 January to have it examined. Surprisingly, it was found that during her short period of service the plating had rusted away exposing the wood filling, a great deal of which had disappeared, leaving just a frame with nothing filling the gaps. On 7 January *Van Galen* sailed back to Fremantle for repairs and a boiler clean arriving on 9 January. She re-entered service on 1 February when she was allocated the duties of meeting and escorting various liners and supply ships in and out of the port.

Tjerk Hiddes had already escorted *Île de France* once that year when she had rendezvoused with her on 2 January to escort the liner into Fremantle. The ships had arrived on 3 January and *Tjerk Hiddes* had remained in harbour carrying out maintenance when on the 7th one of her torpedoes exploded. This was due to a faulty air vessel, similar to the incident that led to the loss of *Khartoum* but this time the explosion did not have quite as drastic effects. Even so, three crew members were wounded and the ship would be out of action until 25 January. By the time she was back in service she was allocated to the same duties as *Van Galen*. These were punctuated with exercises with the other Dutch ships and various American submarines until May. From the 1 to 14 June *Tjerk Hiddes* cleaned her boilers, a necessary task for British-built destroyers if they were to remain able to steam at high speed. The two Dutch destroyers joined the cruiser *Suffolk* for an especially important convoy in August but continued with their normal duties. On 22 September *Tjerk Hiddes* joined HMAS *Shropshire* to search for a drifting vessel which had been reported earlier. After a fruitless

search *Tjerk Hiddes* returned to Fremantle, arriving on 24 September. There followed a series of exercises with *Van Galen* terminating on 9 November when *Van Galen* departed with the steamship *Koolinda* for a tour of Western Australian ports which took until 24 November. In December it was *Tjerk Hiddes*'s turn to escort *Koolinda* until the 24th when she arrived back at Fremantle.

JANUS IN HOME WATERS

On completion of her refit on the Tyne at the end of July 1943, *Janus* did not immediately rejoin the Mediterranean Fleet but remained in home waters for a considerable time. During the refit she had been converted to fire ten-charge patterns which meant doubling the number of throwers from two to four and fitting extra racks on her stern. She received a lattice mast at this time though the CAFO[16] for this was only issued on 3 June but *Janus* had been chosen to conduct trials with the new Type 293X radar. She landed her TSDS equipment when the enhanced depth charge armament was fitted but according to records was also fitted with bow paravanes with 5 tons of ballast to compensate. *Janus* completed trials on the Tyne and then sailed for Scapa Flow to continue working up on 24 August. Between 27 August and 4 September she carried out trials on the new radar set in the Pentland Firth. These indicated that the set needed further development before it could replace the Type 276. On completion *Janus* was fitted with a Type 276 along with her Type 285 and Type 242 IFF. She remained at Scapa Flow until 16 November but did not participate in any of the Arctic convoys.

Janus was at Scapa during early September when on the 13th she sailed from Hoxa Gate with *Rocket* and *Ripley* to investigate a submarine reported by the survey vessel *White Bear*. At 1.14pm one of *Janus*'s officers thought he saw a

Van Galen in August 1942 but showing her configuration in 1943 as well. The door to the director tower is open to allow cool air to flow through it, a feature seen in many destroyers. Her twin 0.5in machine gun tub can also clearly be seen as can her Type 285.

(AUSTRALIAN WAR MEMORIAL: A12923)

conning tower but visual contact was soon lost. *Rocket* obtained a asdic contact and attacked. *Janus* and *Ripley* turned to join her and at 3.19pm *Janus* attacked the contact with a ten-charge pattern. *Rocket* made three more attacks and *Ripley* one but although *Janus* made several runs she could not pick up the contact and did not attack. By 5.30pm it was considered that the target had stopped on the bottom and with a certain amount of confusion present *Rocket* left to obtain an accurate geographical fix. This enabled the destroyers to identify the contact as a non-submarine echo marked on the wreck chart. *Janus* made a short trip to Rosyth on 30 October but returned to Scapa the next day. However, she seems to have incurred some damage as she was under repair at Plymouth on 19 November.

She left Plymouth on 26 November with *Oribi* and *Athabaskan* to escort *Renown* back into Plymouth. On the 27th *Oribi* collided with another vessel and *Janus* took over the escort which rendezvoused with *Renown* on 29 November. On 1 December *Athabaskan* was detached from the fleet to investigate an aircraft report of a diving submarine. She had made two attacks on a contact when *Janus* joined her and made another three. The target was definitely thought to be a U-boat but it had escaped. *Janus* broke off the attack early on 2 December and, as she was running low on fuel, headed back to Plymouth. She sighted *Howe* at 5.30am and fell into company with the battleship, screening her into Plymouth and arriving at 8.45am. *Janus* left Plymouth and arrived at Falmouth on 9 December. She departed Falmouth the next day and sailed for Gibraltar. From there she sailed to Algiers where she joined *Jervis* and Convoy NSF10.

---

[16] CAFO 1161/43, 3 June 1943 also specified that where time did not permit the fitting of a lattice mast, radar Type 271Q(PF) was to be fitted in lieu of the searchlight.

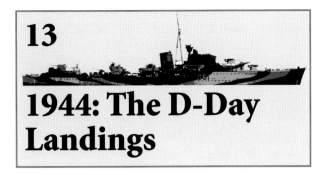

13
1944: The D-Day Landings

*J*ervis and *Janus* had seen the new year in at Brindisi and on 2 January sailed from the port for an anti-shipping patrol, during which they carried out a bombardment of Pesaro on 3 January, but no shipping was sighted and they returned to Brindisi. They carried out yet another patrol on 6 January but were relieved by *Tumult* and *Troubridge* and sailed for Naples. This voyage was slightly more successful as during the night of the 8th they sank three 40-ton schooners and damaged two trains. They also bombarded Civita Nova and a railway junction near Ancona and were fired on by shore batteries which stopped when *Janus* fired a torpedo which demolished a nearby pier. *Jervis* and *Janus* arrived in Naples on 9 January but were ordered to Malta arriving on the 11 January, returning to Naples on the 13th. On 18 and 19 January they were part of a shore bombardment force supporting the 10th Corps in the River Garigliano area before sailing to take part in the Anzio landings on 22 January.

Jervis and *Janus* were to guard the anchorage for the inva-sion fleet. On 23 January at 5.45pm both ships were sailing to take up their patrol positions at a speed of 6kts, with *Jervis* leading. An aircraft was heard which dropped a torpedo aimed at *Jervis*, which was able to avoid it but *Janus*, turning to port, was not so lucky and the torpedo hit No 2 magazine and set it off in a sheet of flame. It is also possible that the explosion set off No 1 magazine as well, blowing her bows off. The destroyer sank in about 8 minutes, her bows remaining afloat for some time after that. There were around ninety-four survivors. *Jervis* had no time to attempt a rescue as two more aircraft were heard off her port beam between 5.46 and 5.50pm. Two explosions were heard probably caused by Hs293 glider bombs and following these another aircraft was heard, and a Hs293 struck *Jervis* on the bows. The shock of the explosion blew the bows round to an angle of 75° and demolished all the superstructure of the ship in front of bulkhead No 9. The upper deck was split and distorted and there was extensive flooding. After picking up *Janus*'s survivors *Jervis* sailed for Naples at a speed of 7 knots. Without a flotilla leader Captain Henderson was in trouble. However, the flotilla leader *Grenville*[1] was also taking part in the landings under the command of Lieutenant Commander Roger Hill, who was ordered to swap ships with Henderson.[2] On 30 January, *Jervis* sailed to Gibraltar to have her bows replaced arriving on 5 February, remaining there until 31 March.

---

[1] *Grenville* was built as the leader for the 'U' class.
[2] For Hill's account of the change over see his book *Destroyer Captain*, pp225-35. He was none too pleased.

Javelin on 20 February 1944 on completion of her refit. Her appearance is much changed and her anti-aircraft outfit and radar equipment is heavily upgraded. She now carries both MF/DF and HF/DF, Types 285, 272 and 291 radars, the latter two mounted on a short lattice mast. Various IFF aerials are also visible and most of the radar equipment has been installed on a lattice mast. Eight Oerlikons have been fitted in four powered twin Mk V mounts and her aft set of tubes have been restored. She still retains her 44in searchlight but has lost her TSDS for a greatly enhanced depth charge outfit. *Javelin* wore this camouflage scheme for the 'Tungsten' operation but was re-painted for the Normandy landings later in the year.

(IMPERIAL WAR MUSEUM: FL10522)

RUN UP TO D-DAY

At the beginning of February the 'Js' and 'Ks' undergoing refit began to emerge for working up. *Piorun* was the first, and on 9 February she sailed for Scapa Flow and the Home Fleet. On 3 March she was allocated to the 17th Destroyer Flotilla and sailed with her flotilla for Plymouth the same day. After a stay of five days, the destroyers escorted a convoy up to Scapa, though *Piorun* was diverted into Greenock due to bad weather. On 15 March she joined *Marne* and *Onslaught* to escort *Richelieu* again. This time the battleship was bound for Africa and the destroyers stayed with her until the 18th when they were relieved. They then took over the escort of two troopships from Convoys KMS42 and SL151 and escorted them to Glasgow. *Piorun* and *Marne* left *Onslaught* with the two ships off Lough Foyle and arrived at Scapa on 22 March.

Kimberley was the next destroyer to finish her refit. On arrival in Bombay in 1942 her stern had been repaired but she had then been reduced to care and maintenance. With the need for destroyers it was decided to bring her back into service and work commenced on 19 November 1943. As she was located at Bombay, certain improvements could not be carried out and her updated radar suite was different to that of her sisters. The refit finished on 11 February but she remained at Bombay until mid-April when she sailed for the Mediterranean, arriving at Alexandria on 25 April. She remained with the Mediterranean Fleet and did not take part in the D-Day landings. *Javelin* completed her refit on 12 February and shortly afterwards sailed on a proving cruise to Horta in the Azores. She returned to Portsmouth on 19 February and spent the rest of the month on further repairs. On 6 March she sailed to Scapa and spent the rest of the month working-up.

OPERATION 'TUNGSTEN'

On 30 March, the Home Fleet left Scapa for Operations 'Tungsten' and 'FY', to cover Convoy JW58 to the Soviet Union. At the same time the convoy itself was cover for 'Tungsten', a carrier attack on the German battleship *Tirpitz*. *Piorun* and *Javelin* sailed with the main fleet (Force 1). The attack went in on 3 April and was successful in damaging *Tirpitz* but did not sink her. During this period *Piorun* and *Javelin* remained in the fleet screen but were later detached with *Ulysses* to escort the fleet tankers back to Scapa, arriving on 7 April. A second attack was agreed on, and *Piorun* (without *Javelin*) sailed on 13 April with four escort carriers for Operation 'Pitchbowl', but bad weather caused the operation to be cancelled and the force returned to Scapa Flow on 15 April.

During this time both *Jervis* and *Kelvin* had re-entered service. *Jervis* had completed her repairs on 31 March and on 17 April sailed for the United Kingdom, finally arriving at Scapa on the 24th. *Kelvin* arrived at Scapa on 3 April to begin her working up. On 21 April she joined another large force which included *Piorun* for Operation 'Planet', yet another attempt against the *Tirpitz*. Once again the weather prevented this and so an alternative plan, Operation 'Ridge' – a strike against Norwegian coastal shipping – was carried out instead. The force returned to harbour on 28 April. *Piorun* continued to participate in these operations whilst the other three Kellys concentrated on preparations for the invasion and training.

By late May destroyers began to leave the Home Fleet base and sail down to Plymouth and other south coast ports in preparation for the D-Day landings. *Piorun* and her consort *Blyskawica* left for Plymouth on 21 May, both being part of the 10th Flotilla for the operation. They arrived on 23 May. *Javelin* had completed her work-up on 10 May and on the 20th she had made her way down to Plymouth and the 10th Flotilla. *Jervis* joined the 25th Flotilla at Portsmouth and was attached to Force G ANCXF,[3] as a bombardment destroyer. *Kelvin* left Scapa with the 17th Flotilla[4] to which she was attached. She too would be a bombardment destroyer but would sail as part of Force S.

The ships of the 10th Flotilla were to take an anti shipping role and sailed for a flotilla work up followed by a full patrol on the night of 29/30 May. The force consisted of was *Blyskawica*, *Piorun*, *Eskimo* and *Javelin* and the main purpose of the patrol was to hunt E-boats but none were seen. *Piorun* and *Javelin* escorted the cruiser *Achilles* out of Plymouth on 3 June as she sailed to join the Eastern Fleet and then returned to carry out patrols until 5 June when they anchored at Plymouth once more. *Jervis*, meanwhile, had her 4.7in guns replaced whilst she was anchored at Spithead between 2 and 4 June. On 5 June the bombardment flotillas sailed for the landing areas.

GERMAN DESTROYERS AND PATROLS

For most of its patrols the 10th Flotilla would send out two or three destroyers in two Forces classified as Force 26 or Force 27 (though it did go up to four ships at times). The composition of these forces changed with the availability of ships and so did the patrol lines. The whole flotilla also sailed as frequently as possible, especially in the early days of the landings when it was likely that German destroyers would attempt to attack the invasion forces. On 8 June the flotilla[5] sailed from Plymouth to intercept a German attempt to

---

[3] Allied Naval Command Expeditionary Force.
[4] *Onslow* (D17), *Onslaught*, *Oribi*, *Scorpion* and *Scourge*.
[5] The flotilla comprised *Tartar* (D10), *Ashanti*, *Huron* and *Haida* (all 19th Division), *Blyskawica* (Divisional leader), *Eskimo*, *Piorun* and *Javelin*.

Piorun also around the time of 'Tungsten', March/April 1944. She seems to be camouflaged in a reverse of *Javelin*'s scheme and has also received an upgraded anti-aircraft and radar fit. This is similar to that of *Javelin* with some differences. *Piorun* does not have a lattice mast fitted and has a Type 271 radar lantern fitted on her searchlight platform. She also carries ten Oerlikons, retaining her two quarterdeck weapons in addition to the twin Mk V mountings she received.
(COURTESY OF MAREK TWARDOWSKI)

Piorun around May 1944 in an Admiralty Disruptive scheme which seems to be G10, G45 and B30. It is unknown exactly when she wore this scheme but she was repainted in the Admiralty Special Emergency Scheme shortly afterwards.

attack the invasion beaches. The German force consisted of *Z32*, *ZH1*, *Z24* (all 8th Destroyer Flotilla) and the torpedo boat *T24*. The two forces met about 30 miles south of Mounts Bay, the British being disposed in a staggered line ahead. The German ships had adopted a diamond formation which offered them no particular advantage. The British ships detected the German ships on radar at 1.16am on 9 June. The Germans had sighted the British as they closed and fired torpedoes except for *T24* which could not see the enemy. Up until then all was going well but *Blyskawica*'s next move altered the situation. As the Germans fired torpedoes, *Blyskawica* turned to starboard and her division followed her. None of the German torpedoes hit and a running fight developed as the German ships sought to escape.

Javelin had hauled out of line and increased to 24kts as soon as she sighted the enemy but was not bothered by the slow German fire.[6] However, once he saw *Blyskawica* turning *Javelin* followed her, assuming that this turn to starboard was to fire torpedoes, firing four as she turned. None hit. The 19th Division maintained contact and damaged *Z24* and sank *ZH1*. *Tartar* was damaged but the two Canadian ships

[6] Report of Proceedings 8/9 June 1944 Lieutenant Commander P B North-Lewis contained in PRO ADM 199/1644.

Javelin at speed taken from *Piorun* or *Blyskawica* on an offensive sweep in summer 1944. Her fore tubes are trained to starboard whilst the aft set are trained to port. (COURTESY OF MAREK TWARDOWSKI)

Jervis underway on 12 April 1944 after completion of the repairs to her bows following the damage by a glider bomb. Her searchlight has been replaced by a Type 271 and she also carries a Type 285 and Type 291. She is now under the command of Lieutenant Commander Hill and so has lost her leader band and carries her pennant number in white. Her flotilla bands also seem to be outlined in white. At the moment she retains her 4in gun and six single Oerlikons.

(IMPERIAL WAR MUSEUM: FL22387)

continued their pursuit and caught and stopped *Z32* before returning. *Piorun* had turned with the rest of her division but lost contact and slowed down to allow the rest of the division to find her. She had been the third ship in line but with *Javelin* hauling out had moved up to second. Unfortunately the other ships did not locate her and at 2.17am she turned north and a little later picked up a contact which she decided to close. This was *Blyskawica* which opened fire on *Piorun*. *Piorun* immediately switched her fighting lights on for 5-10 seconds and informed *Blyskawica* she was doing so. This had the desired effect and *Piorun* rejoined the division.

As they rejoined the 19th Division they came across the burning *Z32* and every ship in the division opened fire on it. Both *Piorun* and *Javelin* checked fire shortly afterwards, *Piorun* as there were already too many ships firing and *Javelin* because she did not want to wear out her guns. The flotilla set course for Plymouth at 5.30am and arrived there safely later in the day. The engagement was clearly a British victory and ended the German destroyer threat. However, in the Admiralty's view there was still room for improvement. The Canadian ships in particular had been profligate in their expenditure of ammunition though this was to some extent attributable to the fact that it was a night action. *Blyskawica* came in for particular criticism and it was thought that if she had not made the turn when she did, none of the German destroyers would have escaped and *Tartar* would not have been damaged.

Javelin and three other destroyers sailed for Operation 'Tunnel' on 10 June, to sweep along the French coast and sink any enemy merchant ships which might be trying to get to the French ports from the Bay of Biscay. Nothing was found and the force returned to Plymouth on 11 June. Later that day *Ashanti* and *Javelin* sailed to join Force 26 but once again the patrol was uneventful and they returned to port on the 12th.

Piorun sailed with *Ashanti* (Force 27) on 13 June to patrol the Île de Bas and Jersey area during the night. At 2.00am on the 14th they had reached Jersey when both *Piorun* and *Ashanti* picked up echoes on their radar. The warships increased speed and altered course to intercept and at 12.38am *Piorun* sighted several German 'M' class minesweepers. These were escorting a convoy and bravely turned to fight off the two destroyers. The subsequent fight was one-sided and *Piorun* fired five torpedoes, one of which hit. *Ashanti* and *Piorun* then damaged several of the minesweepers with gunfire. The only damage to the Allied ships was a hit in *Piorun*'s 4in ready-use locker which caused no real damage. At 12.52am *Ashanti* reported three more ships two miles away and these were engaged as well. The fight continued until both ships ran out of starshell and had to fire

blind. When they finally retired they claimed one minesweeper sunk by torpedo and three by gunfire. The Admiralty evaluation was different: one ship (*M343*) had been sunk and one damaged. In actual fact they had sunk two ships (*M83* was also sunk) and damaged five others which was a poor return for such a disparity of forces. *Ashanti* had disdained to use her torpedoes, deeming the 'M' class minesweeper not a suitable target and for this her captain was severely criticised both by C-in-C Plymouth and the Director of Trade and Staff Duties. Another relevant criticism of the action was that it had been conducted at too high a speed, 27kts, which had not allowed the destroyers to control the engagement.

Javelin's patrols during this period were all uneventful. At 5.40 am on 2 July she was in the Atlantic heading for Plymouth when she collided with *Eskimo*. Both ships were severely damaged and Force 26, *Tartar* and *Huron*, were ordered to take them in tow and return to Plymouth. Quite a force was assembled to escort them in, the entire 12th Escort Group and three ships of the 3rd Escort Group were despatched to provide an anti-submarine screen. Three tugs and a trawler also sailed but were not actually needed as *Javelin* was able to steam into harbour under her own power at 7.00pm with *Tartar*. *Eskimo* arrived the next day escorted by *Skeena* and *Saskatchewan*. *Javelin* had suffered three killed in the collision and she sailed for Liverpool the next day. She was under repair until 31 December 1944.

Piorun continued to patrol with others of the 10th Flotilla but after her encounter with the minesweepers she sighted nothing. She was engaged by German coastal artillery on 5 July but without damage. Between 17 and 29 July she underwent a short refit before emerging for Operation 'Kinetic', as part of a force including two cruisers and an aircraft carrier,[7] detailed to destroy enemy coastal shipping in the Bay of Biscay area. On 10 August *Piorun*, *Diadem* and *Onslow* sailed for a patrol in the La Rochelle area. Initially they exchanged fire with the coastal batteries in the area and on 11 August were attacked by an aircraft which launched an Hs293 which missed. The next day *Onslow* managed to shoot down a Liberator by mistake and *Diadem* picked up the crew of a Beaufighter which had had to ditch. From them they learned that the aircraft had been part of a force attacking two ships of which one had been damaged. The warships altered course to intercept and at 4.11pm sighted

---

[7] *Diadem*, *Bellona* and *Striker*. In addition to *Piorun*, the destroyers attached were *Tartar*, *Ashanti*, *Haida*, *Huron*, *Blyskawica*, *St Laurent*, *Chaudiere* and *Kootenay*.

Javelin in dry dock on 31 October 1944 after her collision with *Eskimo*. Her No 3 mount has been removed as has her depth charge outfit.
(IMPERIAL WAR MUSEUM: A26283)

the damaged vessel. She was the *Sauerland* (*Sperrbrecher 7*) and at 4.14pm the three ships opened fire on *Sauerland*. Cease-fire was ordered immediately afterwards and *Piorun* was ordered to finish her off with a torpedo, which missed, probably as a result of faulty locking gear. The warships then opened fire on her waterline until 4.34pm when *Piorun*'s second torpedo hit and sank her. There were about 100 survivors but the force did not stop to pick them up.

Kinetic was superseded by Operation 'Assault' on 19 August which focused on the area between the Gironde and Île D'Yeu. At St Gilles Sur Vie the three ships were fired on by a gun battery which was silenced by *Diadem*'s return fire. *Piorun* picked up two fishermen from Sable D'Olonne for interrogation about German troop strengths in the area. 'Assault' continued without any sightings of German naval activity. On 29 August the two fishermen were disembarked at Île D'Yeu and on the 30th the destroyers were investigating reports that the Germans were abandoning their defences. *Piorun* picked up seven Polish deserters from the German army, and more were picked up by *Blyskawica* on 4 September when she and *Piorun* patrolled in Audierne Bay along with an Air France captain and a Beaufighter pilot. The Polish authorities in exile had let it be known that Polish citizens impressed into the German army could desert and be rescued by destroyers.

About this time destroyer patrols also started landing supplies for the French Resistance. German shipping still proved elusive. A report might be received of a small cargo ship escorted by two 'M' class boats (as on 7 October) but by the time the destroyer force arrived it would have disappeared and many frustrating hours would be spent looking for it. On 9 October a Spanish fishing fleet of twenty-four trawlers was intercepted and ordered back to their home ports. The next day *Piorun* was in collision with SS *Greyvale* in Plymouth Harbour which caused only slight damage. *Piorun*'s major operation in October was an attempt to land diesel oil on Île D'Yeu but she was frustrated by bad weather until she finally succeeded on 22 October.

BOMBARDMENT DESTROYERS

There were two roles allocated to destroyers being used for bombardment, that of infantry support against various targets and patrolling off the beachhead. Both *Kelvin* and *Jervis* were in position on 6 June and joined in the general bombardment of the German defences. On the 8th *Kelvin* returned to Plymouth to refuel and take on more ammu-

Piorun with maintenance and re-painting work underway. She is camouflaged in one of the Special Emergency Fleet Schemes originally introduced in 1942. The anchors and anchor guards are clearly visible in this photograph as are the rudimentary safety precautions taken.
(COURTESY OF MAREK TWARDOWSKI)

On 12 June 1944 *Kelvin* transported the Prime Minister Winston Churchill across the Channel to visit the invasion beaches and this photograph is taken from a film of the event. *Kelvin* has lost her TSDS equipment and carries a Type 276 on her lattice mast. Her other radar consists of a Type 285 and Type 291. Oerlikon complement is the same as that of *Javelin*.   (IMPERIAL WAR MUSEUM: FLM3247)

nition, *Jervis* following a day later. When they returned, *Kelvin* and *Jervis* operated together until *Kelvin* had to return to the depot ship *Tyne* to have her salt water tank repaired. On 12 June she embarked Winston Churchill for a visit to the invasion beaches. Escorted by the destroyer *Scourge* she left at 8.30am and returned the same day. *Jervis* continued to patrol and bombard in the invasion area. Her initial bombardment had been good but naval staff considered that later ones were not particularly proficient. On 13 June she joined an endless chain patrol with several other destroyers and sailed to refuel and re-ammunition on 17 June, detonating six mines in her wake as she left the invasion area. The right-hand gun of No 3 mount was put out of action by the shock but as there were no spares available she returned to the invasion area with only five guns functional. On 19 June she was hit by a Liberty Ship which had broken free of its moorings during a storm. Her bows were badly buckled but could not be spared and remained in the invasion area until 21 June. *Fury* had been seriously damaged by a mine the same day and *Jervis* stood by her before sailing for Portsmouth.

Kelvin was also having problems. She had carried out the same type of duties as *Jervis* but on 27 June had to return to *Tyne* for repairs to her gun mountings. She was back on bombardment and patrol duties until 11 July when she needed repairs to her asdic equipment and then again on 19 July for even more repairs. *Jervis* remained at Portsmouth whilst repairs were carried out to her buckled stem, anti-submarine gear, hull, fuel oil pipes and gun mountings, returning to the invasion area on 26 June. By now German mines were a serious hindrance. The most serious threat was the 'Oyster Mine' which was activated by the pressure wave of a ship passing over it. The faster

the ship the greater the pressure and more chance of setting one off. As a countermeasure destroyers were restricted to slow speeds. *Jervis* remained in the invasion area until 4 July when she returned to Portsmouth to re-provision. Before she left the invasion area, she went alongside *Kelvin* and transferred her remaining HEDA ammunition to her. For the rest of July *Jervis* was either at Spithead or in the invasion area though no longer carrying out night patrols or bombardments. Between 22 and 25 July she was on anti-submarine patrol but only carried a total of twenty-six depth charges, less than five patterns.

CHANGING DUTIES

In August both *Kelvin* and *Jervis* moved to new duties as the need for destroyers at the beaches diminished. There were still considerable areas of France held by the Germans and *Kelvin* was despatched to join the others patrolling these waters and aiding the French Resistance. *Jervis* had her boilers cleaned between 25 July and 11 August. She then operated off the Channel Islands and was in frequent combat with shore batteries. During one of these engagements she slightly damaged by a near miss but was otherwise unaffected. After a short spell in the Western assault area she was ordered to test the defences on the Island of Cezembres on 27 August. These were active and none too welcoming and *Jervis* beat a quick retreat. The next day she was joined by *Samaurez* but once again was driven off by well-aimed fire from the coastal batteries. It was about this time that it was learnt that her turbines were in a very perilous state and could strip at any moment. Clearly she was in need of an urgent refit and so after another patrol in the western assault area she sailed for Belfast on 8 September. Her repairs would last until 4 May 1945.

Kelvin had joined Operation 'Assault' and was on patrol in the Bay of Biscay on 25 August. The destroyers investigated several innocent fishing boats off Île D'Yeu before *Iroquois* landed a party of French Canadians at the port. On 28 August *Kelvin* was detached to refuel, the other ships arriving in port a day later. *Kelvin* continued her patrols including some as part of Force 111 (with *Albrighton*). One of these had to be cancelled due to extremely bad weather but they were all uneventful until 6 September. During the morning *Kelvin* and *Haida* sighted two suspicious vessels west of the port. These attempted to escape but gunfire brought them to a stop. They turned out to be German armed naval vessels disguised as fishing vessels. Twenty-four prisoners were taken who were landed at Les Sables D'Olonne except for two officers and seven wounded ratings who were retained on board.

On their next patrol they were expected to carry a request from French fishermen that they be allowed to fish for tunny. They explored Audierne Bay on 21 September. The port was useable by vessels of up to 200 tons and was cluttered with scuttled German coastal vessels. Parties from the destroyers visited a large minesweeper and the trawler *V714* before the ships returned to Plymouth on 22 September. Another supply run followed on 28 September when *Kelvin* and *Urania* (Force 28) sailed with arms, ammunition and sixteen military personnel intended to aid the Resistance in mounting an assault on St Nazaire. They were disembarked at Les Sables D'Olonne. *Kelvin* would conduct another patrol this time with *Tartar* on 1 to 4 October before sailing for Chatham and a refit. This would last until 29 October and immediately on completion she would join the 3rd Destroyer on passage to the Mediterranean, arriving at Alexandria on the 10th.

In November *Piorun* transferred to the 8th Destroyer Flotilla and came under the administration of C-in-C Plymouth, being assigned to escorting important convoys and ships in and out of that port. *Piorun*, however, managed her second collision within a month, hitting *Tartar* in a heavy storm. Fortunately, the damage was slight and both ships were able to continue with their duty of escorting the liner *Queen Mary*. *Piorun* then sailed for Plymouth where she spent from 9 to 15 November making repairs. On the 18th she sailed for Milford Haven which was to be her base

of operations. She and *Eskimo* sailed on 25 November to escort *Queen Elizabeth* arriving from America but *Eskimo* had to withdraw when she damaged her rudder and left *Piorun* to return to Milford Haven by herself. She was called out on 1 December to go to the assistance of the Greek freighter *Taxiarchis* which had reported engine trouble. On 6 December it was *Piorun*'s turn to damage her rudder when she escorted *Pasteur* to the Irish Sea. On the way back she lost a man overboard in bad weather. German submarines were still active and on 18 December Convoy BTC10 was attacked. The freighter SS *Silver Laurel* was torpedoed and sunk by *U-486*. *Piorun* and *Impulsive* were detached to hunt the U-boat and sighted smoke from a snorkel on the 19th. They obtained a contact and made two attacks before they lost it. However, both ships remained in the area until an anti-submarine group arrived and took over the search after which they returned to Plymouth. *Piorun* now needed a boiler clean which commenced on 27 December and would last until 6 January 1945.

Tjerk Hiddes and *Van Galen* arrived in the United Kingdom in November from the Eastern Fleet. That part of their year will be covered later but the time they spent at Plymouth will be described here. *Tjerk Hiddes* was the first to arrive on 28 October when she was welcomed into Portsmouth by the Dutch naval representative. She would join *Piorun* as part of the 8th Flotilla but boiler problems meant she did not sail with *Van Galen* for Milford Haven until 11 December. Her final duties of the year were to escort Convoys MKF36A on 28 December and BTC21 on 29 December followed by *Empress* and the Landing Ship Dock *Eastway* on 30 December. *Van Galen* arrived at Portsmouth on 7 November. She and *Tjerk Hiddes* were due to be extensively refitted but until then were attached to the 8th Flotilla. As a result all *Van Galen* received was a full re-provisioning. Her first duty was to escort the US battleship *Texas* from Cherbourg to Barry Roads on 24 November, arriving on the 25th and *Van Galen* left for her new base at Plymouth the next day. On the 27th she sailed to calibrate her MF/DF and ensure that her degaussing was functioning effectively before sailing with a convoy of aircraft carriers bound for Gibraltar on the 29th. She joined her compatriot *Tjerk Hiddes* in escorting the various liners in and out of the Western Approaches. For the last few days of December *Van Galen* was escorting ships in and out of Liverpool, arrived back at Plymouth on the 30th.

KIMBERLEY IN THE MEDITERRANEAN
Initially *Kimberley* was allocated to convoy protection and offensive sweeps for German coastal shipping. These were uneventful and in June she transferred to Italian waters

being based mainly at Naples, escorting ships between the Italian and the French North African ports. In August she was allocated as part of the invasion force for Operation 'Dragoon', the landings in the south of France. On 15 August *Kimberley* embarked Winston Churchill who wanted to observe the landings, but he complained that *Kimberley*'s orders kept him too far out of the action. Conversely, the Chiefs of Staff felt that he had gone too near the coast. *Kimberley* returned to Naples on 18 August before sailing for Alexandria in September but quickly returned to Italian waters for most of the month. On 26 September she sailed for Malta for a boiler clean and short refit, leaving on 17 October for Alexandria. On 20 October she sailed to join *Sirius* and *Attacker* who were heading for the Aegean.

Considerable German forces had been tied down in Greece and on the Greek Islands and part of the aim of *Attacker*'s force was to keep them there whilst aiding the liberation of Greece. The force was based at Khios which was also to be the refuelling base. She patrolled with *Sirius* on 21 October but sighted only one ship which proved to be friendly and on 22 October joined *Attacker* as her escort until the 24th when they returned to Khios, arriving the next day. On 26 October she again escorted *Attacker* for flying operations off Lemnos and Mitylene. These were completed by 1.25pm and the ships anchored off Mitylene harbour before returning to Khios the next day. *Kimberley* remained at Khios and between 29 October and 2 November served as the W/T guard ship. The German hospital ship *Gradisca* arrived on the 29th but as there was no time to search her properly an armed guard was placed on board.

Between 2 and 4 November, *Kimberley* patrolled west of Kos and the Piscopi islands. The patrol was uneventful until 12.10am on 5 November when *Kimberley* sighted two enemy ships, a small escort and an F-lighter. *Kimberley* opened fire on the escort which broke in two and sank. The other ship returned fire and *Kimberley* opened the range before turning to re-engage. The ship's low silhouette and accurate return fire made it difficult for *Kimberley* to get within Bofors and pom-pom range but the result of the one-sided contest was never really in doubt and by 1.00am the craft was on fire and sinking from at least five hits. *Kimberley* searched for survivors but found none, though it was likely that any would have swum to a nearby beach. Shortly afterwards *Lookout* relieved *Kimberley* on patrol and the latter returned to Alexandria.

Kimberley was back at Khios on 8 November and on the 12th was called upon to bombard enemy targets on which she obtained eight hits. On 14 November she sank two assault landing craft in Livadia Bay. A reorganisation of Mediterranean Fleet destroyers took place on 17 November. Two specific functions were identified, general duties from Alexandria and an Aegean patrol and strike role. The Aegean force was designated Force 53 and consisted of four destroyers including *Kimberley*. Within the Aegean they were to be allocated on the basis of two destroyers patrolling between Kos and Rhodes to intercept inter-island traffic, one destroyer at Kos as a reserve and to assist the Commanding Officer Aegean Raiding Forces and one destroyer to be based at Khios to show the flag as requested by Commander Force 142. Force 54, operating from Alexandria on general duties would consist of *Kelvin* and three other destroyers. *Kimberley* was based at Kos and the rest of her year would be spent on uneventful patrols from that port until 23 December when she returned to Alexandria. On 29 December *Kimberley* was transferred to Kalamata and arrived there on the 31st.

Whilst Forces 53 and 54 had been constituted with designated ships the nature of naval operations soon meant that things changed. Shortly after the new arrangements had been implemented *Marne*, *Musketeer* and *Kelvin* found themselves at Khios and on 22 November *Kelvin* sank two enemy landing craft. On 27 November she was joined by *Meteor* in supporting a raid on Piscopi Island. The two destroyers escorted *MTB402*, *MTB403* and *ML1373* carrying troops on a nuisance raid. They also carried out a close reconnaissance of Livadia Bay and encountered some opposition. *Kelvin* then closed the shore and called upon the enemy to surrender but no reply was received and the coastal forces withdrew. *Kelvin* and her consorts continued to patrol from Khios until 5 December when she returned to Alexandria for repairs. These were completed on 13 December and the next day she sailed on escort duty to Port Said before returning to Khios on 19 December. On 24 December the 14th Destroyer Flotilla was re-formed consisting of *Kelvin* (Commander D14), *Kimberley*, *Lookout* and *Loyal*. The final act of *Kelvin*'s year was to relieve *Musketeer* on patrol in the Volos area on 30 December.

WITH THE EASTERN FLEET

At the beginning of 1944 there were four 'Ns' in the Eastern Fleet, *Napier*, *Nizam*, *Norman* and *Nepal*. On 1 January *Van Galen* and *Tjerk Hiddes* were re-allocated from Task Force 71 and the 19th Destroyer Division back to the Eastern Fleet to re-join the 7th Flotilla on fleet escort duties. Both Dutch ships sailing for the Indian Ocean via Geraldton on 1 February, arriving on the 14th. *Van Galen* arrived with leaking oil tanks which meant a voyage to Bombay dockyard for repairs and so she departed Colombo on 16 February, arriving in Bombay on the 19th. For her return journey on 4 March she joined *Redoubt* escorting a convoy to Colombo, arriving on 8 March. She continued escorting convoys in and out of coastal waters until 14 May. *Tjerk Hiddes* remained at Trincomalee until 21 February when she sailed as escort to *Illustrious*, being detached on the 23rd near Addu Atoll. She arrived there on 25 February and two days later departed to rendezvous with Convoy KR9. On 4 March the convoy split up and *Tjerk Hiddes* escorted two troopships into Colombo. She returned to Trincomalee on 14 March, rejoining *Van Galen*.

The Australian destroyers were dispersed. *Napier* and *Nizam* were at Aden and *Norman* was on her way to join them (arriving on 2 January). *Nepal* was at the other end of the ocean at Durban. This was all due to convoy escort work and would continue for most of the early part of 1944. *Norman* arrived back at Colombo on 21 January but only so she could escort another convoy up to Aden. Two days later, *Napier* and *Nizam* also sailed into Colombo and then headed for the main fleet base at Trincomalee. *Norman* returned to join them at the beginning of February. *Nepal* had returned to Durban on 3 February after escorting a convoy to Mauritius and would be under repair until the 22nd. The other three Australian 'Ns' continued to escort the busy convoy traffic with *Nizam* arriving at Bombay on 22 February and taking a coastal convoy to Chittagong on the 24th. *Nepal* completed her repairs and sailed for Addu Atoll then escorted a convoy to Trincomalee. On 8 March she sailed with *Renown*, *Valiant*, *Illustrious*, *Rotherham* and *Quickmatch* for a sweep of the Indian Ocean as a warm-up exercise for Operation 'Diplomat' but nothing was seen, the ships returning to harbour on 12 March.

Operation 'Diplomat'

This was the first major fleet operation of 1944. Convoy traffic had eased to some extent and so it was possible to assemble an adequate destroyer force. The aim was an offensive sweep along the Australia to India route hunting for German and Japanese surface raiders coupled with extensive fleet exercises. The fleet would also rendezvous with an American task force based around the aircraft carrier *Saratoga*. *Queen Elizabeth*, *Illustrious*, *London*, *Cumberland*, *Gambia* and *Ceylon* sailed on 21 March escorted by *Napier*, *Nepal*, *Norman*, *Van Galen*, *Tjerk Hiddes*, *Quilliam* and *Pathfinder*. *Nizam* remained at Colombo undergoing a short refit. On the 22nd they were joined by *Valiant* and her escort which had sailed from Colombo. *Tjerk Hiddes* was allotted to screen the fleet's three tankers. No raiders were located but *Saratoga* was met and escorted to Trincomalee. *Tjerk Hiddes* needed boiler repairs and was out of action between 5 and 24 April but on the 25th she suffered a burst boiler which necessitated more extensive repairs. On 1 May she

departed for Bombay at a speed of 20kts which was all she could manage on one boiler, arriving on 4 May. She would remain in dock until 10 August.

Norman was also in need of a refit and on 2 April she and *Van Galen* left Trincomalee for a sweep to the west before arriving at Addu Atoll on 4 April. Here *Norman* continued on to her refit in Sydney but *Van Galen* remained 6 April when she joined *Quilliam* in escorting a convoy to Colombo which arrived on the 9th. *Norman* would arrive in Sydney on 24 April and leave on 17 June. On 16 April the French battleship *Richelieu* joined the fleet for Operation 'Cockpit,' an attack on the Japanese base at Sabang which guarded the Malacca Straits, coinciding with landings in New Guinea. On the way out the fleet was divided into two forces, 69 and 70. Force 69 comprised the battleships whose screen included *Napier*, *Nepal*, *Norman* and *Van Galen*. The aircraft carriers were part of Force 70. When necessary the destroyers refuelled from the cruisers and battleships. The attack was a complete success and the fleet returned to Trincomalee on 2 April. *Van Galen* was cleaning her boilers until 29 April and on the 30th she sailed as part of the escort of a convoy of seven ships to Australia. On 3 May *Van Galen* and *Rotherham* were detached from the convoy to hunt a reported submarine but the search was terminated the next day and the destroyers returned to Trincomalee. *Napier*, *Queenborough* and *Quadrant* escorted *Richelieu* when she sailed for exercises on 3 and 4 May and *Nizam* had sailed to Madras escorting a convoy.

Saratoga was due to return to the United States for a refit but it was suggested that she first attack the oil installations at Surabaya and on 6 March the Eastern Fleet sailed for Operation 'Transom'. *Napier*, *Nepal* and *Van Galen* formed part of the anti-submarine screen for the battleships. Like the attack on Sabang this was also successful and later in the day the *Saratoga* departed for the United States. The Eastern Fleet finally returned to Trincomalee on 27 May. The next day *Napier*, *Nepal* and *Van Galen* sailed with *Richelieu* and *Queen Elizabeth* from Trincomalee to Colombo where the battleships' crews were being granted ten days of leave. *Napier* left Colombo on 31 May and *Van Galen* departed on 4 June to rendezvous with an American troop transport but experienced engine problems and had to divert to Trincomalee where she arrived on 7 June.

Throughout May *Nizam* had been busy on escort duties and on 12 June she and *Van Galen* sailed for Cochin to screen the carrier *Ameer* which was bound for Colombo to join the Eastern Fleet. *Napier*, meanwhile, was at Bombay, having arrived on 3 June. Throughout June escort duty would spread the 'Ns' widely, *Nepal* even re-visited Kilindini on 15 June but on 23 June all four 'Ns' concentrated together at Aden. On the 27th *Napier*, *Nizam*, *Nepal*, *Van Galen* together with *Rocket* sailed to the Red Sea to rendezvous with the aircraft carriers *Victorious* and *Indomitable* and escort them to join the Eastern Fleet. *Van Galen* experienced problems and was dry-docked at Bombay on 4 July to investigate a torn-away section of her starboard bilge keel. The rest of the force arrived at Colombo on 7 July. *Van Galen* then rushed across the Indian Ocean arriving at Trincomalee in time to moor alongside *Woolwich* and undergo a boiler clean until 19 July.

Napier, *Nepal* and *Nizam* spent most of July escorting fleet units as they sailed for various exercises. Once she completed her refit, *Norman* remained in Australian waters until 23 June and then finally set off to rejoin the Eastern Fleet. She arrived at Trincomalee on 19 July as *Napier* left for Australia and her refit which would last until 15 October. Shortly afterwards, *Nepal* followed her, entering Sydney docks on 18 August. She would not need as much attention as *Napier* and would leave on 2 October.

Until 30 July *Van Galen* escorted the escort carrier *Atheling* when she swapped to covering *Howe* in August. On 9 August she sailed to Madras to join *Nizam* and then returned to Trincomalee. *Norman* was also employed on escort duties and ranged from the Seychelles (3 August) to Aden (9 August). She also joined her sisters in Bombay on 15 August. On 19 August *Tjerk Hiddes* left Bombay after her refit. Not only had her boiler been replaced but also the cast-iron feet for both boilers. She returned to Trincomalee and escort duty for the rest of August and September. *Van Galen*, *Nizam* and *Norman* also continued their escort duties coupled with exercises and on 23 August had their first submarine report for a long time, but it was later determined that it was actually an Allied boat. Both Dutch ships spent extensive amount of time escorting *Richelieu*, *Van Galen* (with *Norman* and *Pathfinder*) on 7 and 23 August and *Tjerk Hiddes* on 7 September. Other major units escorted included *Victorious* (*Tjerk Hiddes* 11 September) and *Renown* and *Queen Elizabeth* (*Van Galen* 17 August). On 31 August, *Van Galen* arrived at Colombo with *Pathfinder* and *Nizam*. Whilst the other two ships rapidly sailed again, *Van Galen* entered Colombo docks for a refit which would be completed on the 30th. During this time her 4in gun would be removed and a set of quintuple torpedo tubes fitted in its place.

As the Allied advance in Europe continued, the Dutch authorities began to anticipate a speedy liberation of the Netherlands and they wanted to get the Dutch warships into British waters to participate. Consequently on 4 October it was decided that *Van Galen*, *Tjerk Hiddes* and *Willem*

Napier on completion of her refit in late 1944. Clearly visible is her Type 271 lantern which replaced her rangefinder tower. *Napier* was the only Kelly to have a Type 271 located in this position and the hut underneath it had to be raised 18in so the radar could clear the director in front. Despite not having a leader band on her funnel *Napier* does not carry her pennant numbers in line with leader practice.

(AUSTRALIAN WAR MEMORIAL: 301069)

van der Zaan should head for England. *Tjerk Hiddes* was the first to depart, arriving with a convoy at Aden on 13 October. On 15 October she sailed independently and arrived at Suez on 18 October. Ten days later she was in Plymouth. *Van Galen* remained in Eastern waters a little longer. On 15 October she departed with Force 63 for Operation 'Millet', a combined air and sea bombardment of the Andaman and Nicobar Islands intended as a diversion for the American landings in the Philippines. It was divided into three sections:

1. *Renown* (flag), *Quilliam*, *Queenborough* and *Quiberon*.
2. *London, Cumberland, Suffolk, Relentless, Raider, Norman* and *Van Galen*.
3. *Indomitable, Victorious, Phoebe, Whelp, Wakeful, Wessex* and *Wager*.

Van Galen and *Norman* refuelled from *Renown* on 16 October and on the 17th the warships arrived at a position 5 miles off Car Nicobar. The air strike was flown off at 6.00am and the warship bombardment started at 8.00am. *Norman* ceased fire at 9.58am having used up her allocation of 300 rounds. *Van Galen* opened fire later, at 8.15am, and engaged a light battery and a military barracks near Mus. The formation retired at 10.00am and though five enemy aircraft were seen there were no air attacks. The force cruised around for the rest of the day before embarking on the next stage of the operation, a night bombardment. *London, Norman* and *Van Galen* detached to feint along the northwest coast of Car Nicobar, covering the operations of the main body. Between 1.27am and 2.13am on 18 October *Van Galen* and *Norman* fired a quantity of starshell before the three ships turned and headed back to join the main force. Force 63 returned to Trincomalee on 19 October but the operation had had no effect on Japanese troop dispositions. On the 21st *Van Galen* sailed for England via Aden and Gibraltar, arriving in Portsmouth on 7 November.

The remaining 'Ns'

Nizam had not taken part in Operation 'Millet', continuing her escort duties. On 8 November *Napier* was at sea exercising with *Quiberon* when she came across two lifeboats from the freighter *Marion Moller* which had been sunk by a submarine which she towed to Trincomalee. *Napier* and *Nepal* had departed Fremantle together on 21 October and after a fast passage had arrived at Trincomalee on 1 November. *Napier*, which had been the flagship of Commodore (D) Eastern Fleet, reverted to the flotilla leader for the 7th Flotilla on 2 November. She was commanded by a Captain (D), in this case Captain Buchanan RAN whose appointment was initially in an acting role. On 20 November *Napier* and *Nepal* escorted *Victorious* to Bombay where they joined *Norman*. They returned to Trincomalee on 27 November and were followed three days later by *Norman. Norman* left Trincomalee for Diégo Suarez and Durban, arriving at the former on 14 December and the latter on 18 December.

Nizam in the meantime had departed for Australia and a long refit, arriving in Australia on 28 October. Her refit would last until 31 January 1945. *Napier* and *Nepal* left Trincomalee for Chittagong on 4 and 5 December respectively. Both ships were allocated to Operation 'Romulus', supporting the advance of the 15th Corps along the Arakan coast in Burma. Every three days or so they would return to Chittagong for fuel, ammunition and stores. *Napier* and *Nepal* arrived in the bombardment area on 13 December. *Napier* was the first to bombard, firing on an enemy position directed by an air observer. Initially she had difficulty hitting the target as the observer was passing spotting corrections not the positions of the bursts. Once this was clarified the shooting was satisfactory. *Nepal* also experienced problems with her bombardment until she allowed for a 60° error in the air observer's estimation of the line of fire. On 14 December both destroyers were in action again, with *Napier* firing on enemy gun emplacements and *Nepal* firing on a suspected enemy position followed by troop concentrations. This time her fall of shot was spotted by *ML1303*. She also fired several rounds of 2pdr LV, special low-velocity ammunition for her pom-pom embarked for bombardment work.

On the 15th *Napier* spotted her own fall of shot engaging a position on either side of a hill which proved very effective in clearing the crest of it. *Nepal* successfully prevented the destruction of a bridge across Kyaukpandu Chaung.[8] *Napier* was the only destroyer bombarding on the 16th when she fired on an enemy-occupied village. There then followed a break until the 18th when *Napier* carried out two separate bombardments. On 19 December, *Napier* and *Nepal* bombarded the enemy-held town of Rathedaung with the aid of an aerial observer. Another trip back to their base at Cox's Bazaar followed on the 20th but they were back at Rathedaung three days later. *Nepal*'s bombardment was limited to 30 minutes due to a risk of enemy air attack but she also increased the elevation of the guns by listing the ship by 8°. *Napier* did not bombard this time. No Japanese were killed during the whole operation and this was because they were withdrawing rather than attempting to stand and fight. *Norman* had remained at Durban since the 18th but would join the operations in the New Year.

---

[8] Chaung was the local name for a tidal creek.

14

The Last Months of the War

A T THE BEGINNING OF 1945 five Kellys remained in UK waters. *Jervis* was under repair at Belfast, *Javelin* had completed her repairs and was re-commissioning prior to beginning her work-up, and *Piorun*, *Van Galen* and *Tjerk Hiddes* were all based at Plymouth with the 8th Flotilla under the command of C-in-C Western Approaches. *Tjerk Hiddes* and *Van Galen* (from 10 January) continued to escort convoys until 16 January when *Tjerk Hiddes* sailed for Greenock escorting two freighters, remaining there for preliminary repairs until 17 March. *Van Galen* remained at Plymouth and on 18 January collided

with *Faulknor* as she was mooring alongside, but the repairs only took three days. The other 'N' in the 8th Flotilla, *Piorun*, patrolled with *Iroquois*, *Nubian* and *Eskimo* as far as Greenock Roads until 28 January. After escorting a convoy on 29 January she sailed to Pembroke Docks to begin a refit on 2 February and would be out of action until 21 April.[1]

Javelin continued her working-up exercises throughout January, sailing for the Mediterranean on 5 February, arriving at Alexandria on the 19th. However, on arrival she suffered a burst boiler and would be under repair until 30 April, when she rejoined the 14th Flotilla.

Van Galen arrived at Southampton on 8 February to begin her refit, which she would complete on 13 May, then being allocated to the British Pacific Fleet. *Tjerk Hiddes* arrived at Dundee on 4 April, going into Victoria Dock where she would begin extensive repairs lasting until 3 January 1946.

When *Piorun* completed her refit on 21 April she was the only operational Kelly in home waters. After initial work-

---

[1] A rumour circulated among her crew that this particular time was chosen to coincide with the Yalta talks and ensure that the Polish-manned ships would not take any desperate action.

As a result of damage received at Normandy, *Jervis* was refitted and this photograph was taken in June 1945 just before she sailed for the Mediterranean. She has lost her Type 271 but the searchlight has not been replaced. Twin powered Oerlikons have been added to the bridge wings but she has received hand operated twins on the platforms adjacent to the searchlight. She now sports a lattice mast with a Type 293, behind this is a Type 242 IFF and above an FM7 HF/DF aerial. The yardarm carries Type 87 TBS aerials. Her Type 291 has been moved to a pole mast on the rear deckhouse (where most other ships had their FM7s located) and she has an MF/DF aerial on the front of her bridge. The 4in gun has been removed and the quintuple tubes replaced. Also of interest are the rolled-up float nets and the fact that she carries both the flotilla leader's band and her pennant numbers which are reverse shaded. She did, of course, resume command of the 14th Flotilla when she returned to the Mediterranean.

(IMPERIAL WAR MUSEUM: FL16229)

ing-up trials she returned to Pembroke for further minor adjustments and repairs before joining the Home Fleet at Scapa, allocated to the 23rd Destroyer Flotilla. The war in Europe formally ended on 7 May. The day before *Piorun*, *Zest*, *Obdurate* and *Stord* had left Scapa to relieve the screen of the escort carriers operating off the coast of Norway but they were recalled on the 7th. On 26 May she left Rosyth for Oslo and arrived on the 28th. She then escorted the Norwegian *Bergensfjord*, carrying troops for Tromso, and the two ships arrived there on 7 June. *Piorun* and *Bergensfjord* returned to Rosyth and made two more trips to Norway and one to the Danish capital Copenhagen. On her return she was allocated to the 17th Destroyer Flotilla and remained with it until March 1946. Throughout July and August *Piorun* was involved in escorting convoys and repatriation runs for Polish nationals displaced by the war and those stranded in transit camps. She was so reliable that she was known as the 'Grey Funnel Line' after her repaint in overall light grey.

Her repatriation runs to the Scandinavian cities lasted until 20 October when she sailed for Leith and a refit which lasted until 20 November. On 24 November she arrived at Loch Ryan for Operation 'Deadlight', the scuttling of surrendered U-boats. *Piorun* was allocated to Group B to sink by gunfire any U-boats which for whatever reason could not be scuttled by opening their valves. On 29 November she sank *U-170* by gunfire as it had begun to sink whilst under tow. On 1 December *Piorun* and *Onslaught* sank three U-boats, *U-826*, *U-1061* and *U-1004*. The next three sailings[2] did not require *Piorun* to fire on any U-boats but on 20 December *U-149* broke its tow and was sunk by *Piorun's* gunfire, as was *U-318* the following day. Because the stormy weather precluded men boarding the boats to open the valves, *U-150*, *U-720* and *U-427* were all sunk by gunfire from *Piorun*, *Onslaught*, *Zetland* and *Fowey*.

Jervis completed her refit on 4 May just as the war in Europe was finishing. She remained at Belfast carrying out working-up trials until 3 June when she left for the Mediterranean. On passage she called at Lisbon to pick up some survivors from a scuttled German submarine who had been rescued by the Portuguese and continued to Gibraltar, arriving on 6 June. After landing the men *Jervis* sailed for Malta, arriving on 9 June, replacing *Kelvin* as Commander (D14).

Van Galen sailed for Southampton on 18 May to begin trials. She returned to Portsmouth for further adjustments which lasted until 24 June when she was finally ready for sea. With an all-new crew she underwent comprehensive working-up trials in the Solent before sailing for Rotter-

dam on 2 August. *Van Galen* remained in Rotterdam until 23 August before returning to Portsmouth for further adjustments to her guns. These were completed by 15 September and *Van Galen* rendezvoused with *Jacob van Heemskirk* for the nineteen-day voyage to Indonesia via Gibraltar, Port Said, Aden and Colombo, arriving on 3 October.

By now the pressure on warships had eased somewhat and *Van Galen* was able to spend twelve days in port before sailing for her first mission, a repatriation run. She left Tanjung Priok on 15 October and after a trip lasting two days arrived in Singapore where she embarked ninety-five men from the Dutch navy and army who had been held as prisoners of war. They were taken to Singkep and *Van Galen* returned to Tanjung Priok on 24 October. There were more serious challenges on the horizon though. When war ended many Indonesians, whilst delighted to be liberated from the Japanese, were not pleased to see the return of their former colonial masters and wanted the Dutch out. Some were prepared to take direct action and the situation began to deteriorate. On 18 November independence fighters shot dead a member of *Van Galen's* crew in Tanjong Priok, one of a number of incidents which let the Dutch know that they were no longer welcome. *Van Galen* left Tanjong Priok for exercises with *Piet Hein*[3] on 20 November and again two days later. She then sailed for Tanjong Pandan and patrolled the coastal waters there until 4 December. *Van Galen* sailed for exercises on 28 December but saw the New Year in at Sabang.

THE END OF THE WAR IN THE MEDITERRANEAN

At the start of 1945 *Kelvin* was patrolling off Volos and *Kimberley* was at Kalamata. *Kelvin* was relieved of her patrol duties by the *La Malouine* on 2 January and sailed to Patras to take over as Senior Officer, Destroyers at the port. *Kimberley* was employed on contraband control and intercepted several caïques on 2 January, all of which proved to be innocent. On 15 January she relieved *Kelvin* as the senior destroyer at Patras before the latter sailed for Malta. After her stint at Patras, *Kimberly* sailed for Alexandria. The Greek government and the communist insurgents had signed a peace agreement and units of the Royal Navy were to supervise the disarmament of the EAM[4] forces. *Kelvin* operated out of Piraeus between 29 January and 25 February. On 26 February she sailed to Kavalla to supervise the disarmament of ELAN[5] caïques and on 27 February ten caïques and three launches were disarmed. The following day it was dis-

---

[2] 6 December, 9 December and 14 December.

[3] Formerly *Serapis*.
[4] EAM: Ethnikón Apeleftherotikón Métopon (National Liberation Front), ELAS: Ethnikós Laïkós Apeleftherotikós Strátos (National Popular Liberation Army), ELAN: Ethnikó Laïkó Apeleftherotikó Naftikó (National Popular Liberation Navy).
[5] ELAN was the naval component of EAM, the communist Greek resistance movement, the military one being ELAS.

Kimberley at Devonport in July 1945 reducing to reserve. What is of interest are the prominent anti-guided bomb aerials on either side of her bridge. She was the only Kelly to carry these. She does not appear to have been fitted with an FM7 aerial. (COURTESY OF JOHN ROBERTS)

covered that ELAN and ELAS arms were stored together 2 miles from Kavalla jetty - a potentially difficult situation. On 3 March, *Kelvin* was still endeavouring to collect weapons, ELAS representatives being reluctant to give them up. She was relieved by *Kimberley* on 5 March and sailed with what she had collected for Piraeus.

Kimberly had left Alexandria on 15 February and sailed to Ras Ameer to relieve *Liddesdale*. On 18 February she headed for Tobruk to land a party of two officers and thirty men for Operation 'Forestall' but when she arrived on the 20th found she could not enter the harbour due to rough weather. The weather remained bad and *Kimberley* remained at sea throughout 21 February. Her port steering motor flooded and the starboard one burnt out and she abandoned the attempt to enter Tobruk and returned to Alexandria, but found she could not enter there either, once again due to bad weather. The weather moderated the next day and *Kimberley* was able to get in. After repairs she finally arrived at Tobruk on 1 March, sailing for Kavalla on 4 March. *Kimberley* stayed in Kavalla for four days until she herself was relieved by the cruiser *Sirius*. *Kimberley* then spent the rest of March visiting various Greek ports collecting arms and supporting the Greek government. She finished this cruise on 23 March when she arrived at Piraeus.

Kelvin, once relieved, had sailed to Alexandria for a boiler clean which lasted until the 16th. Two days later she had headed for Symi and, with the Greek escort destroyer *Themistocles*[6] and coastal craft, patrolled the Stampalla area in response to a reported German landing. This was the pattern for the rest of March and April as well, On 2 May *Kimberley*, *Catterick* and *Kriti*[7] covered a raid by several motor launches on Rhodes and Alimnia to eliminate German outposts, taking thirty prisoners. This proved to be the last wartime operation for the Kellys in the Mediterranean.

On 13 May *Kelvin*, *Salamis*[8] and *LCT357* sailed from Piraeus to re-occupy Crete, then *Kelvin* sailed that afternoon to Rhodes where she welcomed the Greek regent with a royal salute, returning to Suda Bay on 25 May to act as guardship. *Catterick* relieved her on 1 June and she sailed for Alexandria. *Kimberley* left Alexandria for Malta on 23 May, arriving on the 25th after a fast passage. She remained there until 15 June before sailing for the United Kingdom. On arrival she sailed to Dartmouth to begin preparations to join the reserve fleet, initially as Category B. She was the first of the Kellys to go into reserve. *Kelvin* continued in service longer, patrolling the Mediterranean until 27 June. She then sailed for the UK on 1 July via Malta and Gibraltar, arriving on the 11th. Like *Kimberley* she berthed at Dartmouth and began reducing to Category B reserve. This process would take several months and both ships would lose their camouflage, being repainted overall medium grey.

Javelin completed her repairs at the end of April and commenced another working-up period. She would mainly be based at Rhodes but on 17 June arrived in Scarpanto to hold a board of enquiry into an explosion on board *LCI(L)318*. A total of twelve people had been killed and fifty-one wounded. The cause of the explosion was traced to two boxes of ammunition being unloaded by the army and was almost certainly due to negligent packing before they were loaded at Rhodes. This completed, *Javelin* sailed for Haifa on 24 June to carry out staff college liaison duties until 1 July when she sailed for Famagusta. On 11 July she sailed for Piraeus to relieve *Liddesdale* as guard ship.

Jervis had remained at Malta until 9 July because Commander (D) initially preferred to carry out his work on shore. As a result of increasing trouble in Palestine *Jervis* transferred to Alexandria, arriving on 13 July. She remained there until the 26th when she sailed for Beirut and then Latakea

---

[6] Formerly the 'Hunt' class *Bramham*.
[7] Formerly the 'Hunt' class *Hursley*.
[8] Formerly *Boreas*.

Javelin at Grand Harbour, Malta on 5 November 1945. She has lost her searchlight and Type 272 which has been replaced by a Type 293. Her FM7 is located on the more usual position on the pole mast. Interestingly she retains her old-style aerial spreader. Her pennant number is in fact painted in B15 and she shows the new type flotilla marking on her funnel.

(COURTESY OF JOHN ROBERTS)

where she relieved *Musketeer* in providing security for the port. The first of the 'Ch' class destroyers which would eventually supersede the Kellys in the 14th Flotilla, *Chevron*, arrived on 10 August and followed in September by *Chaplet*. In the months up to September *Jervis* would continue to visit Middle Eastern ports and exercise with the fleet.

MUTINY ON *JAVELIN*

On 15 September, *Jervis* arrived at Rhodes to join *Javelin*. Commander D14 informed *Javelin*'s captain, Lieutenant Commander Marjoribanks, that he would inspect the ship on the 17th. Therefore *Javelin*'s first lieutenant, Lieutenant Bayne, decided that the crew should get up at 4.30am to clean the ship in preparation for the visit. The order however was not posted on the ship's notice board until 11.00pm on 16 September, after most men had gone to bed. When the call came to get up and fall in, several men remained below. After sending a petty officer to investigate Lieutenant Bayne sent another officer, Lieutenant Leech to see what was happening. Leech entered No 5 mess first and found some seamen sitting around doing nothing so he ordered them to fall in on the upper deck. They appeared to move and he went forward to No 1 mess were he found more seamen. Once again he repeated his orders but this time they ignored him. After repeating it another three times he warned the men about the consequences of their action and ordered a petty officer present to take their names.

Leech then left the mess and made his way back to the upper deck. As he passed through No 5 mess he came across another seaman who was not on deck. He ordered the seaman, Leading Seaman Leverett, a popular and well liked

individual to fall in on the upper deck. Leverett refused and Leech had his name added to the list. Once this was done he reported to Bayne and handed him the list. Bayne then took the list to the captain. Marjoribanks did two things, he ordered the hands piped to breakfast and Leverett arrested for incitement to mutiny. This was possibly the worst thing he could have done because, once the news of arrest of Leverett got out, the crew were even more incensed, especially as Leverett was innocent of the accusation. Once breakfast had finished, about 120 men locked the mess doors and refused to come out. Eight petty officers were also so disgusted that they held a meeting and refused to turn out for work. Bayne had to go and speak to the crew before they would return to work and all eight petty officers had their names taken. *Javelin* then sailed for Malta where the men who had had their names taken were placed in custody.

A board of enquiry was held and it recommended that eighteen seamen, one able seaman and the eight petty officers be tried for mutiny. The seamen tried to get a prominent Maltese lawyer to defend them but this was not allowed and they received an officer as the traditional 'accused's friend'. *Javelin*'s commission had not been a happy one, both the captain and first lieutenant being particularly disliked for their indifference to the men and their pettiness. *Javelin* was acknowledged as a clean and smart ship but this was only achieved at the expense of morale. The first lieutenant in particular was also given to unusual punishments. Another factor which affected the commission was that most of the men were hostilities-only seamen who were serving beyond their agreed time. Finally, the captain distrusted his petty officers and the feeling was reciprocated. This was recognised by both the Rear-Admiral Destroyers Rear-Admiral Dalrymple-Hamilton at Malta and the C-in-C Mediterranean Admiral Cunningham who both urged leniency.

Despite the lack of a proper lawyer, the court was more than inclined to show leniency. Lieutenant Bayne's evidence in particular was unreliable and he gave conflicting accounts in the two trials. The seamen were found not guilty of mutiny but guilty of failing to obey a direct order and were each given sixty days imprisonment. Leverett was found guilty of failure to obey an order and being absent from his place of duty. Once again the lenient sentence of sixty days was imposed. The eight petty officers were found guilty of mutiny without violence and imprisoned for one year with loss of all medals, privileges and rights. They were to be dismissed from the service on completion of the sentences.

There was a clear recognition that whilst the men had been guilty of disobeying orders, their officers had created the situation through their stupidity.[9] The affair created some concern in the UK with the MP Tom Driberg asking a question in the House and the *Daily Mail* devoting some coverage to it. The Admiralty was inclined to be even more lenient than the court. The seamen were released after serving thirty days each and Leverett's sentence was suspended without him serving a single day, although did lose his rank and good conduct badge. The petty officers were also released without serving their sentences but more importantly despite the sentences standing they were released from the service rather than being dismissed, allowing them to keep all the benefits earned during their service.

[9] The First Sea Lord, Admiral Cunningham used that very word when he commented on the file on 18 December 1945. He also pleaded for mitigation.

Nizam coming alongside *Victorious* in the Pacific. No 3 mount is trained forward almost up to the traverse stops. Visible on her searchlight platform is the barrel of a single Mk III Bofors. How many Bofors were carried by the ships of the Pacific Fleet is an unclear question and it is possible that another one is located just to the rear of the Oerlikon platforms. *Nepal* and *Nizam* carried at least one and possibly up to three whilst *Napier* seems to have carried three or possibly four. *Norman* does not seem to have carried any. Installing Bofors meant the removal of the aft tubes again. (IMPERIAL WAR MUSEUM: MH34063)

Marjoribanks was relieved of his command by Cunningham and sent back to the UK. The Admiralty made it clear that he would never command a destroyer again. Lieutenant Bayne was also relieved of his post and sent home. He was to be court-martialled for his unusual punishments. *Javelin* remained at Malta throughout the court martial proceedings and finally left for Algiers on 24 November.

Jervis continued to cruise and carry out exercises. On 12 November, she was replaced by the newly-arrived *Chequers* as the leader of the 14th Flotilla. The flotilla now had enough ships to form two divisions with the two 'Js' forming the 28th Division, with *Jervis* as leader. On 19 November she came across an abandoned freighter, *Jesse Billingsley*, which had hit a mine. A tug arrived from Trieste to tow the freighter into harbour. *Jervis* entered dry dock between 14 and 18 December for minor work. *Javelin* followed the same routine as *Jervis* visiting the North African ports in December and returning to Malta on 22 December. However, both ships were earmarked for the reserve fleet and instructions to that effect were issued on 10 December though they would not return until well into 1946.

OPERATIONS ALONG THE BURMA COASTLINE

With the completion of Operation 'Romulus' *Napier* and *Nepal* had enjoyed a respite at Cox's Bazaar. The operation had been a complete success and the 74th Indian Brigade had driven the Japanese out of the area. The next stage of the advance, a commando assault on Akyab itself, was brought forward from 18 February to the beginning of January. Operation 'Lightning' commenced on 2 January, when *Napier* and *Nepal* each loaded 420 troops from Teknaf Jetty in the Naaf River. A bombardment had been planned but was cancelled when it was learnt that the Japanese had already evacuated the island. The Australian destroyers then just unloaded their troops on 3 January and returned to Teknaf Jetty.

Norman left Durban on 1 January and sailed for Trincomalee via Diégo Suarez, where she was due to escort *Queen Elizabeth*. *Nepal* left for a short refit in Colombo leaving *Napier* the only 'N' in the area. She was serving as the headquarters ship for the naval forces in the region and with the cruiser *Phoebe* was the only heavy naval unit available for the next operation.

Five battalions of Japanese troops were retreating in the face of advancing West African troops and it was hoped to block their escape with a direct assault on the town of Myebon (Operation 'Pungent'). The same troops used for the Akyab operation were to be used but this time the commandos were embarked in two Royal Indian Navy sloops, *Narbada* and *Jumna*. *Napier* and *Phoebe* were to support

the sloops should they get into difficulties. The landing was successful but dogged Japanese defence enabled the retreating battalions to escape. *Napier* was not needed for bombardment and spent her time escorting *Phoebe* which was ferrying troops to the area. The last of these trips took place on 16 January after which they were detached to prepare for Operation 'Matador', the assault on Ramree Island. *Queen Elizabeth* escorted by *Norman* and *Pathfinder* sailed from Trincomalee on 18 January. *Napier* and *Phoebe* left Chittagong on the 20th to rendezvous with them and *Nepal* had sailed from Colombo the day before. Thus by the time the operation commenced on 21 January *Raider*, *Norman* and *Nepal* were screening *Queen Elizabeth* and *Napier* was acting as cover to *Phoebe*. The three aforementioned destroyers were available for bombardment duties as well and *Napier* carried the flag of Rear-Admiral Martin.

The bombardment began on 21 January and took the

A refuelling operation of various Pacific Fleet ships in progress. *Nepal* (left) has not yet received her Bofors and still retains the aft torpedo tubes. She carries a Type 271 on the searchlight platform, a Type 285 and Type 291. Once again No 3 mount is trained forwards.

(IMPERIAL WAR MUSEUM: AX164A)

defenders by surprise, they having anticipated an assault further to the south. As a result the landing force met with little opposition and once ashore was able to advance rapidly. Once she had completed her bombardment, *Queen Elizabeth* sailed for Trincomalee escorted by *Redpole* and *Napier*. *Napier* had bombarded gun positions on Georgina Point before retiring. As she left she transferred 'Matador' orders to *Norman*, which had previously transferred special operations charts to *Raider* on the 19th and then sailed to refuel at Akyab with *Pathfinder*. When she returned on 20th she also had orders for the carrier *Ameer*. *Norman* remained in the area, moored near Cheduba until 29 January when she sailed with *Raider* to support Operation 'Sankey', a landing on Sagu Island - the possession of which was essential for control of the waters inshore of Ramree. The landing was successful with the two destroyers' bombardment being particularly effective. *Norman* and *Raider* remained off the

island until 31 January when they sailed to support forces assaulting the heavily-defended Yanbauk Chaung.

Nepal had completed her repairs and sailed for Chittagong, arriving on 28 January and relieving *Rapid*. On 29 January she sailed with *Paladin* for Kyaukpyu and the next day *Nepal* supported minesweeping operations off Kaleindaung Chaung. The minesweepers came under fire but *Nepal*'s counterbattery fire silenced a Japanese gun. *Nepal* continued to support operations off Saga Kyun until 3 February. *Norman* had left Sagu and sailed for Kyaukpu on 1 February. For the next two days she supported the 71st Indian Brigade with *Paladin* before refuelling at Aykab on 4 February and then proceeding to Colombo. *Nepal* was designated as the support ship for Operation 'Mike', a landing on Kyaukpu, but there was no opposition and she did not open fire. *Nepal* and *Pathfinder* then sailed up the Kaleindaung River and *Nepal* took up a bombarding position off

Norman moored in Sydney Harbour in late 1945 with *Queenborough* behind. Her awnings are spread which makes it difficult to ascertain whether she retains her aft tubes. Her radar equipment is identical to that carried by *Nepal*.

(COURTESY OF JOHN ROBERTS)

Ramree Chaung. On 5 February she hit an uncharted rock in the river and ran aground, damaging her propeller. She had to be towed off by *Pathfinder* and refuelled at Akyab before returning to Kyaukypu. On 7 February she relieved *Paladin* supporting the 71st Indian Brigade but with the fall of Ramree town on the 8th returned to Kyaukypu. On 9 February she sailed to Akyab to refuel and also collect fuel and ammunition for *Pathfinder* and *Paladin* who were to remain in the area. This was transferred the next day and on 11 February *Nepal* sailed for Colombo and docking to repair her propeller. *Nepal*'s departure was the end of the 'Ns' role in the Burma campaign. Their bombardments had been effective but adverse comments were made about the appearance of both *Nepal* and *Norman*'s crews and they were contrasted very unfavourably with the smartness of the Indian troops used in the operation.

THE PACIFIC FLEET

Nizam had left Melbourne on 7 February, having completed her refit, and sailed to rejoin the Eastern Fleet. She called at Fremantle and on 11 February was twelve miles off Cape Leeuwin when she was hit by a freak wave which caused her to broach. Ten men were washed overboard and despite a search in appalling weather no trace of them could be found. *Nizam* righted herself but had to return to Fremantle for repairs.

Norman remained at Trincomalee, exercising and patrolling. *Napier* and *Nepal* were at Colombo and on 22 February *Napier* sailed for Trincomalee to pick up *Formidable* and escort her to Melbourne with *Urchin*. The three ships sailed on 23 February and arrived at Fremantle on 3 March. *Norman* and *Nepal* also left Trincomalee for Australia on 1 March to join *Napier*. All four 'Ns' of the 7th Flotilla were to transfer to the new British Pacific Fleet

(*Nizam* remained in Australia after her repairs). After a stop at Fremantle, *Formidable* and her escort sailed for Melbourne. On 7 March *Napier* had a similar experience to *Nizam*, being hit by a large wave and rolled on her side. She lost two men overboard and was unable to rendezvous with *Formidable* due to damage and shortage of fuel and sailed for Melbourne. *Napier* remained under repair until 28 March and on the 30th she sailed to join the other 'Ns' at Sydney.

Napier, *Nizam* and *Norman* departed Sydney to join the British Pacific Fleet at their base at Manus Island on 1 April, *Nepal* following a few days later. The Australian destroyers arrived in time for the second part of the Okinawa operation and were attached to Task Force 57. Before joining they escorted two convoys to Leyte Gulf in the Philippines, arrived on 13 and 15 April but *Nizam*'s main feed pumps broke down and she remained at Leyte for repairs when the other three ships headed back for Manus escorting a refuelling group TU112.2.5 to the carrier flying-off area. They remained with TF57 for the rest of April then escorted them back to Leyte to replenish. TF57 returned to the war zone on 1 May and throughout the month were escorted by *Napier*, *Nepal* and *Norman* among others. The destroyers provided an anti-submarine screen, anti-aircraft pickets and also acted as plane guard destroyers, picking up crashed pilots. *Nizam* had both her main feed pumps replaced but was suffered an outbreak of polio and was quarantined. On 12 May she escorted two tankers to TF57's replenishment area and then on the 15th escorted them back to Leyte. On 23 May she sailed for Sydney escorting the depot ship *Tyne*.

Norman replaced *Nizam* as tanker escort. *Napier* and *Nepal* remained with TF57 until 25 May when all ships sailed for Sydney to replenish. None of the four Australian destroyers would be attacked by kamikazes during their time with the Pacific Fleet.

Nizam entering Grand Harbour, Malta on her journey back to the United Kingdom. Her aft tubes have not been replaced and one Bofors gun is visible mounted on her searchlight platform. Either side are two twin powered Oerlikons with two singles on the bridge wings. Her radar outfit has been augmented with the addition of a Type 276 fitted to a bracket on the front of her foremast in place of the crows nest. She has reverted to her old pennant number.   (COURTESY OF JOHN ROBERTS)

Task Force 37[10] left Sydney on 28 June and sailed for Manus. They were due to join the American fleet in strikes on the Japanese homeland. The destroyers would mainly escort the carriers of TF37 though both *Norman* and *Nizam* worked with the American carrier *Shangri-La* at certain times throughout July. Between 12 and 27 July *Nepal* delivered mail, stores and messages to about seventy-eight ships. The first atomic bomb was dropped on Hiroshima on 6 August but the strikes continued, particularly against Northern Honshu and Hokkaido. The 3rd Fleet was due to withdraw from the battle zone for preparations for the invasion of the Japanese home islands but Admiral Halsey delayed this to pin down any Japanese aircraft which might be transferred to the Soviet front which had opened when the Soviet Union attacked the Japanese on 10 August. The second atomic bomb had been dropped on Nagasaki the day before and the end of the war was in sight.

Most of Task Force 37 had to withdraw from the battle zone for replenishment at this time but *Napier* and *Nizam* were among the ships that remained as a token force, *Norman* and *Nepal* sailing for Sydney with the fleet. The Second World War officially ended on 15 August 1945 with the surrender of Japan and on 23 August the two destroyers entered Japanese waters with the rest of the fleet. There was a wait until 29 August whilst minesweepers cleared the entrances and then at 8.30am *King George V* led *Quality*, *Nizam* and *Napier* to anchor in Tokyo Bay. They remained in harbour for the surrender on 2 September when *Nizam* was duty destroyer and anchored near the US flagship *Missouri*. *Napier* left Tokyo on 12 September and joined

Norman at Manus. *Nepal* had entered *AFD20*[11] for repairs on 26 August and did not sail for Tokyo until 10 September when she replaced *Napier*. She and *Nizam* remained there until the 19th when *Nizam* sailed for Wakayama to embark a group of Australian POWs. *Norman* arrived at Tokyo on 21 September and at the end of the month sailed for Okinawa. *Napier* meanwhile had sailed for Sydney and arrived on 21 September. *Nizam* followed on 24 September and then *Norman* from Okinawa on 11 October and finally *Nepal* left Tokyo on 16 October.

The Royal Australian Navy had decided to swap its 'N' class destroyers for three 'Q' class ships to allow them to operate a homogenous flotilla as they already had *Quiberon* and *Quickmatch*. On 11 November *Napier*, *Nizam* and *Norman* sailed from Fremantle for the UK where they were to join the reserve fleet. *Napier* and *Norman* reached Plymouth on 12 December. There they began to reduce to Category B reserve. *Nizam*, following a day later, berthed at Chatham and also began to reduce to the reserve. *Nepal* had left Sydney for the UK on 19 November. Her fate was different as she was intended to be converted to a minesweeping trials ship and relieve *Witch* at the mine warfare research establishment HMS *Vernon*, arriving at Portsmouth on 28 December.

---

[10] When Admiral Spruance commanded the naval forces it was designated the 5th Fleet and all Task Force numbers started with a 5. His command rotated with that of Admiral Halsey who commanded the 3rd Fleet. As a result the ships remained the same but the Task Force numbers now started with a 3. For the strikes in July and August Halsey was in command.

[11] Admiralty Floating Dock.

15

After the War

ON 5 JANUARY 1946 *Jervis* broke off exercises and sailed to Naples to embark the C-in-C Mediterranean, Admiral Sir John Cunningham, and take him to Malta, where *Jervis* moored at Hamilton Wharf on the 7th to re-ammunition but dragged her anchor in a squall and damaged one of her propellers. Repairs took until the 22nd. She then sailed for exercises with *Chequers*, *Chaplet* and *Chevron* and on their return the four destroyers were detailed to tow some MTBs purchased by the Egyptian Government from Malta to Alexandria. The commander of the 14th Flotilla asked for a postponement of the sailing due to bad weather but was refused and on 25 January the four destroyers set sail, each towing two boats with two seamen on board. *Jervis* was the guide ship for the operation which very rapidly ran into trouble with the MTBs becoming swamped and unmanageable. It being clear that the MTBs could not reach Alexandria, *Jervis* was ordered to sink them by gunfire after taking the seamen off. The last tow parted on 27 January and *Chaplet*, *Chequers* and *Chevron* returned to Malta whilst *Jervis* was detailed to help the Italian liner *Gradisca* which had run aground on Gavdo Island. The liner's crew had got out of hand and raided the liquor store so needed pacifying. If that was not enough, three tugs had been sent out to help but one, *Captive*, had herself run aground on the other side of the island. *Jervis* arrived at the island on the 29th and transferred some 3in portable pumps to the stranded liner. A landing party was disembarked in Potanos Bay and marched to the other side of the island to assist *Captive* in Kopki Bay, which unfortunately was beyond help but all but one of her crew were saved. Next she sent an armed boarding party to *Gradisca* to restore order and remain with the liner. *Jervis* took the crew of *Captive* to Alexandria and then returned to Gavdo and remained until 5 February but *Gradisca* eventually also had to be abandoned. Her next duty was to patrol off Haifa checking for contraband and refugee ships. During this time her Type 293 radar set broke down and then worked only intermittently. On 21 February she sailed to Beirut to help British army units deal with trouble between French soldiers and the locals, then returned to Haifa and resumed her patrol duties until 5 March. On 6 March, as *Jervis* sailed for exercises, her No 2 boiler broke down and she was restricted to 20kts.

Javelin had spent January at Malta throughout January but in February she sailed to join *Jervis* at Haifa. She also patrolled the coast of Palestine, relieving *Jervis* when she was at Alexandria. *Jervis* rarely exceeded 15kts during this time as any ship she intercepted was considerably slower than this. The rest of the month was much the same as before, a mixture of patrols, exercises and swinging around her buoy. Part of the reason for the later patrols was the interception of refugee ships carrying Jewish people fleeing from Europe to Palestine. Royal Navy vessels had to intercept and turn these ships back, a duty that was not popular. *Javelin* by now had returned to Malta and on 9 May departed for the UK and the reserve fleet. She arrived at Portsmouth on 17 May and began reducing to Category B. *Jervis* continued to patrol of Haifa and Palestine until 14 March. On that day she intercepted the badly overloaded refugee ship *Smyri*[1] and escorted her back to Haifa where she was impounded. *Jervis* remained at Haifa until 19 May

---

[1] *Smyri* had a displacement of 1662 tons and according to Connell was carrying 1760 passengers and 23 crew.

Jervis early in 1946 (for her final service scheme see profile 15). She now carries a divisional leader's band as per Admiralty SC7/46. Also visible are the prominent extensions to the rear of the gun shields to shelter the crews from the sun.

(COURTESY OF JOHN ROBERTS)

when it was time for her to return to the UK. Cheered by all the Mediterranean Fleet destroyers and escorted by *Chequers*, *Chaplet* and *Chevron*, she sailed for England, arriving at Chatham on 4 June where she paid off and began reducing to Category B.

PIORUN'S LAST DAYS

Piorun continued with Operation 'Deadlight' into 1946. She left Lisahally on 2 January with what would be her last group of U-boats. On reaching the scuttling area heavy weather forced her to sink two, *U-2502* and *U-764*, by gunfire. On her return to Lisahally, *Piorun* was replaced by *Garland* and sailed to Portland where she remained until 14 February. She then sailed for Rosyth and was under refit for a month. By now she was part of the 2nd DDiv, Polish Naval Command North, and on 4 April sailed for two days of exercises with other Polish ships, *Garland*, *Blyskawica* and *Conrad*. On 15 April the whole division sailed for Plymouth cruising along the east coast. The aim of this voyage was to bring together the separated Polish sailors of the Northern command and southern commands in Plymouth, where they arrived on 17 April and left nine days later for Rosyth. *Piorun* remained at Rosyth until 26 May when she sailed for Harwich. Once there she began reducing to Category B reserve. This was finally completed on 29 September, when the ship was returned to the Royal Navy. However, instead of assuming her old name, *Nerissa* she took the name formerly allocated to *Van Galen* and became *Noble*.[2]

THE DISPOSAL OF KHARTOUM

Of the three Kellys which had had the misfortune to be sunk in harbour *Jersey* had her stern blown off to clear the entrance to the Grand Harbour and the wreck was scrapped *in situ* after 1943. *Kingston*'s two halves had been welded together in 1943 and the wreck towed out to sea and sunk as a blockship, but *Khartoum* had been left where she had sunk in shallow water in Perim Harbour. When originally sunk, her No 2 mount, bridge and funnel remained above water but by 1948 the ship had sunk deeper into the mud. On 17 May 1948 a dhow had hit the wreck and sunk and her owner had made a claim for compensation. This was refused as the wreck was still visible but thoughts did turn to having it scrapped. Early in 1949 approaches were made to various salvage firms to see if they were interested, including the British India Salvage Corporation and Paul Fidale of Bombay. Neither were interested and in fact the only tender received was from a local firm. The firm offered Rs 400 which in the exchange rate of the time came to £30-0-0.

This was rejected as being far too low and the wreck remained where it was. By 1 June 1950 the wreck had sunk to the extent that only the foremast remained visible. Given that Perim Harbour was only used by dhows it was not considered a hazard to navigation and the wreck was formally abandoned.

THE RESERVE FLEET

The Reserve Fleet consisted of ships no longer needed for active service but too new to scrap or potentially still useful in case of another conflict. Ships in the reserve fleet belonged to three main categories, A, B and C.[3] Later Category B would be divided into BI and BII. Several ships would be grouped together and a skeleton crew allocated to look after the ships, living on one of them. *Kimberley* was one of those designated as such an accomodation ship. As time took its toll, ships would be moved from one Category to another, from B to C for example until they were finally allocated to Category Z, a list of all ships earmarked for disposal. Disposal usually took two forms, either scrapping the ship or expending it in tests. In 1947 a review[4] took place of fleet requirements and after satisfying the requirements of destroyers to be retained and those to be converted to anti-submarine frigates, ten ships remained for which no role could be found. They consisted of *Racehorse* which was beyond economical repair and the nine oldest ships remaining in the Reserve Fleet which included *Javelin*, *Jervis*, *Kelvin* and *Kimberley*, and they were all earmarked for disposal as soon as convenient.

EXPLOSIVE TESTS

Javelin, *Jervis*, *Kelvin* and *Kimberley* were all chosen to be expended in tests to examine the effects of underwater explosions on destroyer hulls (several other ships were used as well). Each ship was moored in Loch Striven close to the east bank of Brackley point in the deep-water berth and the relevant charge suspended beneath them. This was then detonated by remote control and once the effects of the explosion had subsided the results were evaluated. Once a trial was complete the ships were scrapped shortly afterwards.

Jervis was the first and was the subject of two trials, a preliminary one on 23 July 1948 followed by the main trial on 21 September. The first test did very little damage and so a second one was carried out, which ruptured her hull. The explosion also reduced the longitudinal strength of the ship with all longitudinals in the area of the hole being fractured from the fourth to the thirteenth longitudinal, damage which would have sunk her. Once evaluation of the effects was completed *Jervis* was towed to Port Ban-

---

[2] Several sources state that as *Noble* she remained in service. However, this is not correct and she was actually placed in reserve with the other British 'Ns'.

[3] The differences between these categories are explained in Appendix 7.
[4] See M 059872 of 6 October 1947. This was approved on 30 October 1947.

Explosive trials on *Jervis* on 21 September 1948.   (AUTHOR'S COLLECTION)

natyne where scrapping commenced on 21 January 1949.

Trials on the rest of the Kellys did not get going again until 1949 when *Kelvin* was prepared to represent a fully-loaded ship with her oil fuel and diesel fuel tanks filled to 95 per cent with salt water. At the same time all stores, ammunition, boats and gun barrels were removed but the torpedo tubes were left in place. A Mk XI depth charge was used and placed 70ft below the keel located under the centre of the boiler room, which resulted in some damage but this was not critical. *Kelvin* was towed to Troon for scrapping which would start on 6 June 1949. *Javelin*'s trial followed a month after *Kelvin*'s in April 1949. Once again all stores and ammunition were removed but the torpedo tubes and this time the main armament were left in place. Auxiliary machinery was also removed, the upper deck, beams and girders being cut away for this purpose and then roughly re-welded. The explosion damaged the bottom plating and fractured the re-welded deck. The effect of this explosion was adjudged nearly critical and on 17 June *Javelin* was also towed to Troon for breaking up.

The final Kelly to be used in this series of tests was *Kimberley* in June 1949 and she was prepared along similar lines

to *Kelvin*. After the explosion, both boiler rooms started to flood rapidly and both of the ships sides were buckled. The bottom plating was fractured in several places and both bilge keels severely distorted. Given this level of damage the ship would have sunk quite quickly and scrapping commenced very shortly afterwards at Troon. It should be understood that the trials on the four Kellys formed part of an extensive programme involving several ships. Whilst the trials indicated that a ship would not necessarily sink as the result of an underwater explosion they also showed that attention to certain features would improve survivability. For example, much greater attention was needed to the detail design of the connections between plating and to the attachment of fittings to the plating. Transverse bulkheads were also found to be very susceptible to these sort of explosions but dealing with the effects was not easy without radical changes in bulkhead design. However, these trials saw the end of the 'Js' and 'Ks' in British service. Four of the 'N' class still remained in reserve with a fifth, *Nepal* operating as a minesweeping trials vessel.

NEPAL AS A MINESWEEPING TRIALS VESSEL

Nepal had been detailed to be converted to a paravane ranging vessel/minesweeping trials vessel in 1945. Information is scarce between her return to the UK in January 1946 and when she actually took up her role in 1948. What is available indicates that she operated in the Channel as part of the shore station HMS *Vernon* until 1947 when she was transferred to Rosyth for training and sea trials. The conversion consisted of the removal of all her armament and the fitting of compensatory ballast. Also fitted were a large sweep winch and twin davits on her quarterdeck. For paravane ranging her crew was to be 127 officers and men and 131 for minesweeping trials. Her home base was Port Edgar near Rosyth and she re-commissioned on 14 October 1948. November was spent working-up before she conducted trials until 22 February 1949 with, anchoring either at Port Edgar or Rosyth. Then she sailed for Chatham for adjustments. Her trial programme continued into May 1949 when on the 7th she sailed for Devonport. The rest of May was spent conducting trials from Plymouth and Falmouth but at the end of the month *Nepal* sailed for Milford Haven.

Milford Haven was the base for an extensive series of trials which continued until 23 June when *Nepal* sailed to Pembroke Docks repairs. She returned to Milford Haven and continued her trials until 8 July when she returned to Plymouth remaining there until 17 July and then returning to Port Edgar. Once back, *Nepal* conducted a series of exercises and then a series of trials until mid-August when she returned south, this time to Portsmouth, arriving on 19 August. She commuted between Plymouth and the Scilly Isles until 26 September. Once again she returned to Port Edgar and continued the trial programme until 30 November. *Nepal* spent December at Port Edgar until the 5th and Rosyth until the

31st, this time undergoing a refit. In fact she did not sail again till 11 February 1950 and then only to Port Edgar. Towards the end of the month (21 February) there followed a short trip to Invergordon but the first main cruise of 1950 would not get under way until March. This was a tour of the Scottish coastal isles which included Oban, Torbermory, Lyness, Scapa Bay and Invergordon ending on 29 March.

More time was spent at Rosyth undergoing work to fit her for her next duty, conveying the First Sea Lord on a tour of Europe. *Nepal* sailed on 30 April with the First Sea Lord, Lord Fraser of North Cape, on passage to Oslo. One of her passengers the BBC correspondent, Mr Richard Sharp, was taken ill with an internal complaint and despite the efforts of the ship's doctors died. *Nepal* arrived at Oslo on 2 May and was visited by the C-in-C Royal Norwegian Navy and King Haakon of Norway. She next sailed for Copenhagen, arriving on 5 May and being visited by the Danish King and Queen. On 9 May she arrived at Brunsbüttel in Schleswig-Holstein for a short visit before sailing for Amsterdam where a cocktail party was held on 12 May. *Nepal* left Amsterdam on 14 May for her final stop, the Belgian port of Antwerp. She sailed for Harwich on 17 May and on arrival disembarked the First Sea Lord. After a short break at Harwich *Nepal* returned to Port Edgar.

Back at base, the trials continued and she mostly spent time at Port Edgar and Rosyth. Trips to Lerwick (11 August) and Scapa Flow (25 September) were the only times she travelled far during the rest of the year. Two fires in her galley were the only other events of note. With the need for *Nepal* as a trials ship coming to an end and the cost of a major refit looming it was decided to return her to the reserve. On 16

---

[5] Unfortunately, I have been unable to find any information on the exact nature of the minesweeping trials she carried out.

Nepal as a minesweeping trials vessel with all armament and radar removed. Visible are the paravanes and the large minesweeping winch on her quarterdeck. The photograph is taken at Plymouth which according to her log indicates it was taken in either May or September 1949.

(COURTESY OF JOHN ROBERTS)

Alternative Armament Proposals

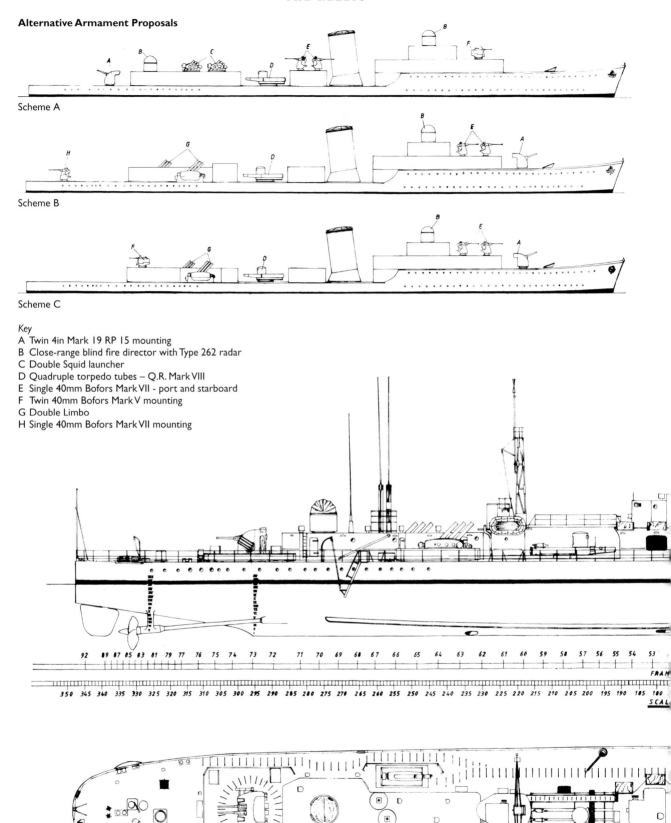

Scheme A

Scheme B

Scheme C

Key
A Twin 4in Mark 19 RP 15 mounting
B Close-range blind fire director with Type 262 radar
C Double Squid launcher
D Quadruple torpedo tubes – Q.R. Mark VIII
E Single 40mm Bofors Mark VII - port and starboard
F Twin 40mm Bofors Mark V mounting
G Double Limbo
H Single 40mm Bofors Mark VII mounting

November 1950 she sailed for Plymouth, arriving on the 18th, and there she was accepted into Category C reserve on 20 March 1951.[5] Like her sister-ships she would come under consideration for conversion to an anti-submarine frigate.

THE TYPE 18 ANTI-SUBMARINE FRIGATES

The new Soviet high-speed submarines were faster than most of the anti-submarine then in service. The wartime-built sloops and frigates not only too slow, they were also too small to accomodated the greatly improved sonar and radar that had been developed. However, a large number of comparatively new wartime-built fleet destroyers were available for conversion into fast anti-submarine frigates. Conversions took two forms, the Type 15 and the Type 16. The Type 15 was an expensive conversion costing £600,000 and taking about eighteen months on average to complete. The Type 16 was far less extensive, only costing £260,000 and taking about a year . Initially, the five 'Ns' in reserve were considered for conversion to Type 16s but it was decided to produce a different type of conversion, the Type 18. These ships would have had two primary purposes, firstly to protect convoys against

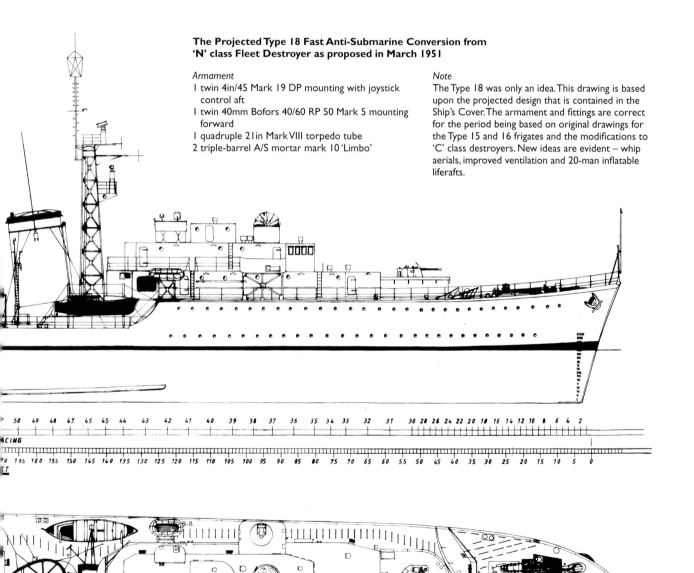

The Projected Type 18 Fast Anti-Submarine Conversion from 'N' class Fleet Destroyer as proposed in March 1951

Armament
1 twin 4in/45 Mark 19 DP mounting with joystick control aft
1 twin 40mm Bofors 40/60 RP 50 Mark 5 mounting forward
1 quadruple 21in Mark VIII torpedo tube
2 triple-barrel A/S mortar mark 10 'Limbo'

Note
The Type 18 was only an idea. This drawing is based upon the projected design that is contained in the Ship's Cover. The armament and fittings are correct for the period being based on original drawings for the Type 15 and 16 frigates and the modifications to 'C' class destroyers. New ideas are evident – whip aerials, improved ventilation and 20-man inflatable liferafts.

submarines and secondly a seek-and-destroy role, in co-operation with aircraft if necessary.

Three arrangements were considered, A, B and C with A being chosen as the basis for further work. Most of the conversion involved a new weapons suite but the bridge was to be removed and replaced by a totally new structure. A transmitter station was also to be built on top of the existing pom-pom platform. The main anti-submarine armament was to be a double Limbo mortar sited where the aft torpedo tubes had been with a reserve of twenty salvoes. The forward tubes were to be replaced by a quadruple mount equipped to fire anti-submarine torpedoes. No reloads were to be carried but in any case the torpedo proved to be a complete failure and never got beyond the development stage. The only other armament was a twin Bofors sited forward on a bandstand and a twin 4in RP51 AA mount on the quarterdeck controlled by a director located where No 3 mount had been. Asdic was to consist of Types 170 and 174 with Type 162 and 765 echo-location gear fitted. Radar was restricted to a Type 974 and a Type 293Q. Complement was to be 14 officers and 212 men which given the reduced armament would probably not have been too crowded.

On 29 June 1950, *Noble* was selected for conversion to the prototype frigate as an economy measure rather than just converting all the ships. However, it was *Norman* that was used for the preliminary inclining experiments. On 2 Novem-ber 1950 a meeting was held to discuss progress on the design and it was concluded that the 'Battle' and 'C' classes were more suitable for this conversion. Furthermore, converting the 'Ns' was not worth the expenditure as they were already halfway through their hull lives. Therefore they continued in reserve, all now listed as Category C. The five 'Ns' remained in reserve until 1955 when the decision was taken to scrap them and Table 11 shows where and when this occurred.

TABLE 11:
Scrapping of the 'N' class

Ship	Where scrapped	Date ship arrived for breaking up.
Napier	Briton Ferry	17 Jan 1956
Nepal	Briton Ferry	16 Jan 1956
Nizam	Grays	16 Nov 1955
Noble	Dunston	Dec 1955
Norman	Newport	1 Apr 1958

As can be seen *Norman* lingered a couple of years beyond her sisters and in fact would be the second-to-last 'N' to be scrapped. Of the 'Ns' only the Indonesian *Gadjah Mada* remained in existence after *Norman*.

16

The Dutch Destroyers Post-War

IN JANUARY 1946 *Van Galen* was based at Sabang in Indonesia, conducting patrols off Poeloe Weh and the north coast of Sumatra. Contrary to their expectations, the Dutch had not suppressed the Indonesian independence movement and the situation was still unsettled. On 13 February *Van Galen* was relieved by *Kortenaer*[1] and sailed for a refit at Trincomalee. Problems with the bearings on

one propeller shaft meant her stay in dry dock was extended and *Van Galen* finally left Trincomalee on 13 April, sailing for Sabang with *Evertsen*.[2] After arrival at Sabang on 16 April, *Van Galen* sailed for a patrol off Poeloe Weh and Aceh. The next day she had just stopped a boat at 7.40am when a republican battery situated near San Pedro Point opened fire on her. The destroyer withdrew out of range and returned fire with Nos 1 and 2 guns. After an hour she closed the shore and raked it with pom-pom fire for 10 minutes. It is not recorded if she was successful in disabling the battery though it did cease fire.

Van Galen returned to Sabang the same day to take the British crew who had helped bring *Evertsen* over to Singapore, where she picked an LCT and four HDMLs for transfer to the Dutch navy. The HDMLs made the passage under their own power but the LCT was towed by *Van Galen*. However, on 22 April *HDML1470* broke down and also had to be taken in tow. The small armada arrived at Tanjung Priok on 24 April, and he next day *Van Galen* sailed for a

---

[1] Formerly HMS *Scorpion*.

[2] Formerly HMS *Scourge*.

Van Galen arriving in the Dutch East Indies in the first half of 1946. Despite the fact that she carries a full radar outfit, she has only four single Oerlikons. Camouflage is also interesting, seeming to be some form of medium and light grey. The TSDS depressor paravane is not carried though the sweep paravanes are.

(COURTESY OF MARINEMUSEUM/DUTCH NAVY MUSEUM)

patrol along the coast with *HDML1260*. Two native boats were stopped and escorted into the anchorage where *Van Galen* remained until 29 April when she sailed to relieve the escort sloop *Van Kinsbergen*. From 30 April she was based at Pontianak supporting landings by the KNIL[3] along the coast of Borneo, accompanied by *HDML1260* and *RP101*. She then returned to Tanjung Priok for a short refit before relieving *Jacob van Heemskirk* on her patrol off Ketapang (on the west coast of Borneo) from 21 to 27 May when she returned to Pontianak to embark the Resident of West Borneo and the Sultan of Pontianak and transport them to Ketapang. On 29 May she sailed to support another landing by the KNIL, this one in Hitam Bay, Aceh. *Van Galen* was relieved by *Evertsen* on 31 May and sailed to Tangjung Priok to resupply, relieving *Evertsen* in turn on 3 June. She continued supporting the KNIL between 4 and 7 June then patrolled the south coast of Borneo until 11 June. During this patrol one of her crew was killed in a accident with a Lee Enfield rifle. On 13 June she was back in Hitam Bay ferrying soldiers to the recently-arrived sloop *Van Kinsbergen* before returning to Tanjung Priok. Throughout the rest of June, *Van Galen* patrolled the islands of Indonesia as the Dutch continued their futile attempts to re-assert their control over the population, leaving for Fremantle on 12 July for a refit. She would return to Tanjung Priok on 17 August. *Van Galen* did not remain in port for long but sailed with *Piet Hein*, *Kortenaer* and *Banckert*[4] for exercises until the 24th when *Van Galen* arrived at Semarang where she stayed for the next two days. A short patrol followed along the Javanese coast and round the Karimun Islands. On 28 August she was asked to illuminate the area around the Semarang coast with starshell in support of land forces. On 31 August two sections of her crew participated in a parade through Semarang. *Van Galen* then sailed for Surabaya for a short refit and docking until 16 September when she sailed for more exercises and patrols. This pattern continued through September until the 23rd when she sailed to meet *RP102* and *LV111* for a special mission, two 'protective landings' at Palau Kelapa on 24 and 25 September by a company from the Allied Military Affairs Administration Branch. The operations were successful and *Van Galen* returned the troops to Tanjung Priok on 25 September.

Van Galen arrived at Semarang on 27 September but before she could resume patrol duties was ordered to the assistance of the MS *Maros* whose engines had broken down. The destroyer located and stood by the stricken freighter during the night before escorting her into Semarang on the 28th. On 11 October she sailed to meet the Catalina flying boat carrying the Admiral commanding the Dutch East Indies naval forces and his staff, transferring them to the aircraft carrier *Karel Doorman*.[5] Both ships then sailed for Welcome Bay arriving on 13 October. *Karel Doorman* then sailed for Tanjung Priok and *Van Galen* for Singapore, arrived there on 15 October to replenish and on 19 October she sailed for Tanjung Priok to take part in the next stage of the Dutch re-occupation of their colonies. This was Operation 'Paling Baik', the occupation of Palembang and the handing over of jurisdiction by the British. *Van Galen's* role was to convey the troop commander and his staff and remain in support if needed. On 24 October she rendezvoused with the other units in the operation, principally the troopships MS *Boissevain* and SS *Plancius* together with the minelayer *Abraham Crynssen*. The force moored in the mouth of the River Moesi on 25 October and the next day the troops transferred to LCTs and LCIs for the landings. *Abraham Crynssen* accompanied them up the river but does not seem to have been needed. *Van Galen* did not sail up the river to Palembang until 29 October. The destroyer remained there until mid-December when she was relieved by *Piet Hein*.

Van Galen was due to return to the Netherlands and her journey home commenced on 3 January 1947 when she sailed from Tanjung Priok, arriving at Nieuw Waterweg in the Netherlands on 26 February when she embarked the C-in-C Royal Netherlands Navy and his staff at Berghaven Heights. She then conveyed them to IJmuden and sailed for Amsterdam. On 22 March she was laid up and would remain out of service until November 1947.

TJERK HIDDES ARRIVES IN INDONESIAN WATERS

Tjerk Hiddes had completed her refit by the beginning of January 1946 and began a long trials and working-up process, sailing for Rotterdam in March. *Tjerk Hiddes* remained there until 9 April when she sailed for Portsmouth but during the crossing serious vibrations were noticed in the starboard LP turbine. She had been due to depart for Indonesia but this delayed her and she remained at Portsmouth for two weeks before sailing for Amsterdam on 24 April where the problem was traced to the fact that the turbine was not properly balanced. It was also discovered that the vibration had cracked the deck plates which would need replacing. Spares were needed from England and these took a long time to arrive. *Tjerk Hiddes* finally departed Amsterdam on 2 June 1947 on an eventful voyage to Indonesia.

The first mishap occurred near Malta. As she approached the island the engine room started to flood. This was caused

---

[3] KNIL: Koninklijk Nederlands Indisch Leger – Netherlands East Indies Army.
[4] Formerly HMS *Quilliam*.
[5] Formerly HMS *Nairana*.

by a valve in the sluice flat which seems to have been opened by mistake. The destroyer was able to reach Malta safely and conduct repairs but whilst she was there was a security alert. An Israeli two-man submarine had been sighted outside the harbour and it was believed that she might have planted limpet mines. Ships were dragging their hulls with chains to try and dislodge them but it was all a false alarm. After leaving Malta, *Tjerk Hiddes* passed through the Suez Canal without incident and sailed to rendezvous with the troopship *Zuiderkruis*. She was sighted in the Red Sea and *Tjerk Hiddes* circled round her to take up station. Unfortunately the turn was a bit too sharp as the scuttles on the lower decks were still open. This would not have been a problem had wind scoops not been fitted, but they acted as perfect water scoops flooding the lower mess decks. This was the last incident of note and *Tjerk Hiddes* arrived at Tanjung Priok on 6 July.

She then sailed for a three-day patrol off Madura until 19 July. She then joined a landing operation at Pasirputih from 20-25 July. On the 26th she bombarded republican positions at Gresik and then joined the campaign to reimpose control on the area around the port of Tjilatjap[6] on 29 July. After three days' bombardment she landed a party on 5 August to demolish the town's defences. Charges were set using ammunition from the old Dutch battleship *Soerabaia* and all the fortifications were successfully destroyed. *Tjerk Hiddes* spent the next two months engaged in uneventful patrols of the waters around Java and Sumatra. At the beginning of November she sailed to Surabaya for a short refit but on 10 November was back on patrol. Patrols

continued into 1948 during which time she covered most of the seas off the main islands of the Indonesian Archipelago. In June 1948 she was joined by *Van Galen* for a cruise of East Indies waters before heading back for the Netherlands, arriving at Amsterdam on 1 October.

VAN GALEN'S LATER YEARS

After her long lay-up *Van Galen* departed for Indonesia again on 11 November 1947 arriving at Tanjung Priok on 12 December, and shortly afterwards sailed to her new station at Surabaya. There followed a long series of uneventful patrols. Information is sketchy during this period but *Van Galen* did visit the Netherlands Antilles with *Tjerk Hiddes* and cruise East Indies waters in June, and then probably resumed her patrol duties off Indonesia. The political situation had been quiet since July 1947 when the Dutch had in what is euphemistically called the 'First Police Action' imposed their idea of how Indonesia should be governed by force, but tensions continued until December 1948 when the Dutch decided another 'Police Action' was necessary. This began on 19 December and was disastrous for the Dutch, for not only did it unite the Indonesians against them but it also aroused American concern and the Dutch would be forced to give up their entire empire. *Van Galen* supported a landing by two battalions of marines near Glondong providing and would remain in Indonesian waters until the round-table agreement of 1949 when she was withdrawn to the Netherlands. On 30 January 1950 she arrived at Den

---

[6] Now Cilacap.

A rare photograph of *Gadjah Mada*, the Indonesian flagship. Her colours are shown in profile 16. According to Dutch sources her service life was brief and so this photograph was probably taken early in this career. (INSTITUUT VOOR MARITIEME HISTORIE)

Helder was refitting until 15 February 1952.[7] She would then join the United Nations forces in the Korean war.

Helder was refitting until 15 February 1952.[7] She would then join the United Nations forces in the Korean war.

Van Galen left on 16 March 1951 and would relieve *Evertsen* at Hong Kong on 16 April 1951, where she remained until 28 April when she sailed for Sasebo in Japan, finally sailing for the operational zone on 3 May to escort the aircraft carriers USS *Baatan* and HMS *Glory*. On 6 May she detached and sailed for Inchon where she commenced her first patrol. Patrol areas were named after British car manufacturers and *Van Galen* patrolled 'Austin' and 'Daimler'. On 14 May she investigated six junks but they all turned out to be genuine fishing vessels and she returned to Sasebo. She remained there until the 19th when she and HMAS *Warramunga* escorted *Baatan* back to the operational area. *Van Galen* then remained as screen to the aircraft carrier for the rest of the month. On 3 June they returned to Sasebo

Van Galen at the time of the Korean War. She appears to be in overall mid-grey and carries her pennant number in white on her bows. Noticeable changes include the life raft type and location, new boats and the removal of her TSDS equipment. (INSTITUUT VOOR MARITIEME HISTORIE)

and *Van Galen* departed for Kure and a short refit between 6 and 11 June. On her return she and *Warramunga* joined the escort carrier USS *Sicily*'s screen until the 19th when *Van Galen* again returned to Sasebo.

On 21 June *Van Galen* sailed for gunnery exercises with the cruiser *Kenya* and other British units. This involved a visit to Hong Kong but results of the exercises were poor and on 28 June *Van Galen* was again on her way to Sasebo. Unfortunately, when she arrived at the port on 1 July she had to remain outside the harbour as Typhoon Kate was in full flow. During this time No 1 boiler failed and had to be shut down due to leaks in at least ten of the superheater tubes on the port side and, once the storm had passed, *Van*

---

[7] I do not know if the refit took the whole year as once again records are not complete.

Galen put into harbour to repair them. Between 2 and 4 July all superheater tubes were re-rolled and tested. One was found to be leaking and once this was repaired the boiler was pronounced fit for service. *Van Galen* rejoined *Sicily's* screen on the 6th and remained with it until the 10th when *Sicily* departed for Sasebo. *Van Galen* escorted her part of the way but continued on to Kure. She remained at Kure until 8 August and then carried out a bombardment of Songjin on the 13th. Then on 3 September she left Sasebo for Hong Kong and a refit in the Royal Dockyard.

Her refit lasted until 7 October and the next day she sailed for Sasebo. On her arrival she remained in harbour until the 14th when she had to leave due to the approach of Typhoon Ruth. Whilst riding out the typhoon at sea she was also supposed to screen the aircraft carrier *Sydney*,[8] but she lost the carrier in the storm and for the next 36 hours had no idea where she was. Finally on the 15th she relocated *Sydney* and was able to escort her into Sasebo. After repairing storm damage *Van Galen* sailed on escort duty. Sasebo would be her base for the rest of the month and she patrolled the waters around the port. On 31 October she sailed in search of a reported enemy submarine and with the American destroyer *Swanson* searched the area around Wonsan, Sonjin and Chongjin but found nothing. On 18 November she took part in Operation 'Athenaeum', a combined air and sea assault on Hungnam. On 23 November she returned to her patrol duties around Sasebo with the occasional exercise thrown in as on 31 December when she carried out exercises with the destroyer HMS *Constance*.

The start of 1952 saw *Van Galen* employed on blockade duties along the west coast of North Korea and escort duty. When necessary she was also called upon for short bombardments mostly guided by shore observers or South Korean patrol boats. She was particularly busy on 5 January when she first fired on shore batteries which were engaging American minesweepers with spotting being provided by aircraft from *Sydney*. Later her fire was directed by the patrol boat *ROKN315*. The ability of warships to fire starshell was particularly welcomed by troops on shore as these provided very effective illumination. During the day *Van Galen* screened the carrier *Badoeng Strait* and continued her bombardments at night. When she finally left the operational area on 16 January she had fired 2775 HE shells and 117 starshell. She sailed for Sasebo arriving on 21 January and departed for Hong Kong on the 24 for another refit. During the last two months of the commission her commanding officer had been incapacitated by a broken leg and the ship had been commanded by the First Lieu-

tenant. Her overall commander, Vice-Admiral Russell, was very sorry to see her go as *Van Galen* had been a very worthy member of his force.

After the refit, *Van Galen* left Hong Kong on 2 March on her way back to the Netherlands but first making a two-month tour of South American ports, arriving back at Den Helder on 20 June. After a period of independent service she was allocated to Smaldeel (Squadron) 5 on 11 September. Between 14 February and 2 April 1953 Smaldeel 5 cruised off Las Palmas, Agadir, Gibraltar and Portland. On 18 April *Van Galen* sailed with the squadron on another cruise to Douarnenez, Penzance and Liverpool but returned to Den Helder on 21 April. She was decommissioned immediately she arrived and paid off into the reserve. In October 1956 *Van Galen* was stricken from the fleet and sold for scrap on 6 February 1957.

TJERK HIDDES'S LATER YEARS

Tjerk Hiddes did not return to Indonesia but instead sailed for the Netherlands Antilles in May 1949, arriving at the capital Willemstad on 5 June 1949. A month later firing exercises were held in Curaçao and the minelayer *Willem van der Zaan* and *Tjerk Hiddes* were ordered to join these on 13 July. Results were unsatisfactory and fresh exercises were held on the 15th. *Tjerk Hiddes* left Willemstad on 9 September and sailed for Rotterdam, arriving on 1 October 1949. She was inactive until 13 November 1950 when she formed Smaldeel 4 together with the cruiser *Jacob van Heemskirk* and the destroyer *Marnix*,[9] a special squadron for the King of Holland's visit to the UK. The three ships made their separate ways to Rotterdam on the 13th and on 20 November the king embarked on *Jacob van Heemskirk*. He disembarked at Dover but *Tjerk Hiddes* went on to Portsmouth.

On 23 November *Tjerk Hiddes* sailed to assist in an air-sea rescue search in the English Channel. *Jacob van Heemskirk* and *Marnix* returned to Rotterdam on 24 November but *Tjerk Hiddes* sailed separately for Den Helder once the search was over, where she remained until 11 July 1951 when she sailed for Indonesia. As part of the Round Table Conference Agreement of 2 November 1949 the Dutch had agreed to transfer warships for a new Indonesian navy. *Tjerk Hiddes* was to be the Indonesian flagship. She was officially transferred to the Indonesian Navy on 1 March 1951 and renamed *Gadjah Mada*.[10] According to Dutch sources, on her first voyage shortly afterwards she struck a reef and was declared a total loss. It is possible that she served as a stationary depot or training ship but sometime in 1961 she was scrapped. She was the last of the twenty-four Kellys to be broken up.

---

[8] Formerly HMS *Terrible*.

[9] Formerly HMS *Garland*.
[10] Some sources spell her name *Gadjah Madah*.

17

An Evaluation

LIKE ALL DESIGNS the Kellys were a compromise between various requirements, but in this case it was to prove to be one of the best wartime destroyer designs. A strong hull coupled with an effective armament made them formidable ships and the fact that the design formed the basis for most British wartime destroyer classes testifies to its effectiveness. Furthermore, the ability to take a lot of punishment ensured that several ships were able to survive incredible amounts of damage and still return to port – *Javelin*'s survival with her bows and stern blown off being particularly remarkable. The design also compared well with other nations' destroyers, including the later war-built classes. What follows is an evaluation of various aspects of the Kellys and a tentative comparison with several other types. I should stress that such a comparison is not intended to produce an overall 'winner', as navies built ships according their own service requirements, but just to show similarities and differences in these requirements.

TACTICS

Destroyers were unarmoured ships and as such the tactical appreciation of a combat situation and the numbers that could be brought to bear on that situation were more important than, for example, the number of guns or torpedoes carried. One can see this in the engagement of 29 November 1940 when the German destroyer commander summed up the situation better than Mountbatten who possessed the advantage of numbers but whose tactical appreciation was sadly lacking.

The ability to sum up a situation quickly was vital for a destroyer commander and as was the need to dictate the course of the action. The captain of *Janus* hesitated when faced with two French contre-torpilleurs in July 1941 and allowed them to seize the initiative by opening fire at a range greater than that he was accustomed to. This resulted in serious damage to his ship, which was only saved by the arrival of *Jackal* which provided cover until more destroyers could arrive and drive the French off. A later engagement between the two French ships and *Kimberley* showed the advantage of decisive action. Faced with the same situation her captain accelerated to full speed directly towards the French ships. They retired rather than face the British

destroyer. *Kimberley* had used this tactic successfully before when she sank the Italian destroyer *Francesco Nullo* but seems to have been a particularly efficient ship. A spirit of aggressiveness was cultivated in British destroyer captains which tended to work well but could create difficulties if over-indulged. Japanese destroyer captains were particularly prone to the 'attack no matter what' school of thought and suffered because of it. Japanese tactics differed from the British since like the Americans they emphasised the torpedo. Even British captains' enthusiasm sometimes got the better of them as was the case with *Kandahar* and *Kingston* when they were escorting Convoy GA15 on 29 April 1941, but in general the aggressive approach worked well. It was also suited to the close-range gunnery actions that British destroyer fighting instructions advocated.

Before the war the emphasis was on torpedoes with the guns being used to force a way into a suitable torpedo position. This continued to be the approach, particularly at night, when British destroyers would get as close to the enemy as they could and then open fire with all guns. During the war, however, the emphasis changed slightly and torpedoes were frequently held back to finish off ships already disabled by gunfire. American doctrine on the other hand favoured night attacks with torpedoes guided by radar but this was due more to the lack of a night-fighting doctrine at the start of the war and a preference for torpedoes as the weapon of offence. Each method could be devastatingly effective, for example the extermination of the *Tarigo* Convoy on 16 April 1941 by Captain Mack's 14th Flotilla and the victory at Vella Gulf on 6/7 August 1943 by ships of the US 12th and 15th Destroyer Divisions, the only difference being that the British tactics would perhaps be more likely to ensure complete extermination of an enemy force. Second World War torpedoes, despite the importance assigned to them, were inaccurate weapons which missed more than they hit, even with radar guidance. The Japanese 24in 'Long Lance' torpedo, despite being devastating when it hit, had to be fired in enormous numbers to achieve those hits. For example, at the battle of the Java Sea on 27 February 1942, 151 torpedoes were fired by the Japanese for 3 hits.

Despite this, the torpedo was a valued weapon as it allowed a destroyer to threaten larger ships. No cruiser or battleship captain could assume that a torpedo attack would miss and frequently the threat of a torpedo attack was enough to make a large ship turn away. The Second Battle of Sirte demonstrates this perfectly. The Italian fleet was hamstrung by the fear of a British torpedo attack, allowing an important convoy to escape. However, such attacks had to be judged carefully since to ensure a viable threat a destroyer had to approach quite close to an opponent which put the unarmoured ship at a significant risk. The 14th Flotilla at Sirte were aided by gradually worsening weather but even so *Kingston* took a 15in hit which temporarily put her out of action. Tactics in these cases were to hide behind smokescreens and dart out to threaten the enemy force as it attempted to work round the edge of the screen. Frequently the mere threat was enough to encourage caution but unless torpedoes were fired and hit or the weather intervened destroyers generally needed to count on the arrival of heavier support.

Apart from their strike role, the Kellys were also designed as fleet destroyers, intended to screen capital ships against the threat of submarine and destroyer attack. As a further string to their bows they were also given a restricted fleet minesweeping role using TSDS. This proved quite useful but as the war drew on became less and less relevant and by the end of the war no Kelly actually used its TSDS equipment. In several ships the equipment was removed and the weight gained used for extra depth charges and throwers enabling ships to fire a ten-charge pattern. This reflected the greater perceived threat from submarines and the allocation of the minesweeping role to specialist fleet minesweepers. By the end of the war in the Home and Mediterranean theatres even the anti-submarine role had receded somewhat though it was never to entirely disappear and the Kellys were mainly strike ships, looking for potential surface targets. In the Pacific the 'Ns' continued to screen fleet units and the fleet train though the submarine threat was by that time negligible.

When war broke out in 1939 the Royal Navy had the great new invention, asdic, which would it was believed solve the problem of submarines once and for all. Whilst asdic was very useful, it suffered from an inability to distinguish between contacts. Thus schools of fish, wrecks and even pockets of water of different density were identified as potential submarine contacts by inexperienced operators. These constant attacks did at least ensure if a submarine was present it would have to remain submerged until the destroyer had left. As a submarine's underwater speed was considerably lower than that of the fleet a destroyer would stay with a contact for up to several hours to ensure that the submarine lost contact, before returning to the fleet. This was also the case with convoys but as they were generally slower than fleet units a greater attempt would need to be made to destroy the submarine. Later in the war, as operators became more experienced, it was possible to identify many non-submarine echoes and indiscriminate depth-charging was reduced. This could have unfortunate consequences if a genuine submarine contact was misiden-

tified, as happened with *Jervis* in the sinking of the *Barham*.

Conditions in the Mediterranean were difficult for both submarines and hunters and offensive sweeps were initiated to hunt submarines. These invariably were failures, any submarine in an area being either long gone by the time a destroyer force arrived or having manoeuvred to a position from which it could counter attack. The problem for the hunters was that the submarine could use the different density layers of the water to hide from asdic and on occasions could attack without any warning, as in the loss of *Jaguar*. It was much easier for the submarines to be caught as they attempted an attack on a convoy or fleet, as when *Kipling* sank *U-75*.

In the Red Sea, it was more difficult for submarines to hide in the confined waters and the Royal Navy adopted a highly aggressive approach to convoy defence which totally overawed the opposition. Submarines were ruthlessly hunted by units of destroyers and sloops and the success of this approach can be judged by the fact that the Red Sea Destroyer Force did not lose a single ship from any of the convoys they escorted. The destroyers were also active in the minesweeping role, ensuring that the approaches to the British-held ports were kept clear but for this duty only one destroyer at a time would be employed and would lead the merchant ships in or out of harbour with their TSDS sweep on the low-speed setting. When escorting convoys two 'Ks' were generally stationed ahead as an anti-submarine screen to cover the convoy through the Red Sea. At first it was rare for one of the 'Ks' to escort a convoy all the way to Suez though this did start to happen late in 1940. When *Kimberley* sank *Francesco Nullo* she had been stationed astern of the convoy to counter any attack from that direction. When conducting anti-submarine sweeps it was found that a line of bearing was the most suitable formation with sloops and destroyers intermingled. If other ships were not available, a minimum force of a sloop and destroyer would be despatched together to hunt the reported submarine as soon as possible. Once again, as with surface warships, an aggressive approach was favoured.

Officially, Kellys were supposed to use a five-charge pattern but apart from the 'Ks' of the 5th Flotilla the 'Js' and 'Ns' tended to use a six-charge pattern and the 5th Flotilla eventually followed suit. By 1943, as ships were refitted, ten-charge patterns came into use but the 'Ns' never received this upgrade. Attack approach speeds varied but were generally between 20 and 25kts with two ships present, one holding the contact in her asdic. A single ship would attack at a slower speed to enable its asdic to monitor the contact as long as possible. Despite these tactics, fleet destroyers were not particularly good anti-submarine vessels, although

Kingston did well in sinking two submarines (*U-35* and *Luigi Toricelli*) and *Jupiter*'s performance against the Japanese submarine *I60* was also impressive. Balanced against these are the numerous submarines that were able to escape including one caught by *Kandahar* on the surface during Operation 'Cultivate' on 18 October 1941.

COMPARISONS

Comparisons with other destroyers are difficult as each nation built ships which conformed to the particular requirements of its own naval staff. These were affected by perceived threats from ships of other nations, the 'Tribal' class being a prime example. As has been seen earlier, the Kellys were also built with other ships in mind, particularly the Japanese *Fubuki* and the American *Porter* classes. The Royal Navy could not afford to be left behind in the race to build bigger destroyers. Another factor that is important to remember is that most sources quote ships' design speeds giving an exaggerated view of their performance. In service destroyers were generally not as fast nor did they have the range that the figures indicate. The maximum design speed of the Kellys was quoted as 36kts but this was only possible on a light displacement with a clean bottom. In service the maximum authorised speed was 33kts. This made them faster than some destroyers and slower than others – German destroyers were faster but their speed was only used for escaping, not to gain any tactical advantage. The speed a ship could adopt also depended heavily on sea conditions. To go too fast in rough weather was to risk damage.

German machinery was also unreliable. The Kriegsmarine had taken the decision to go for high pressure boilers for destroyers, which proved troublesome and prone to breakdowns. The United States Navy also followed this route but with considerably more success. Their boilers were efficient and reliable giving a far superior performance to the British boilers which remained at 300lbs per sq in. However, it should be noted that despite this, the American destroyers were both slower and had less endurance than their design levels. Only the French seem to have been able to achieve really high sustained speeds but at the price of reduced endurance and even these service speeds were less than trial speeds.

French destroyer development was an illustration of how a different set of requirements affected design. French destroyers and the larger contre-torpilleurs were designed for the Mediterranean and endurance was not considered as important as speed. Speed was expensive with the higher speeds costing more fuel and reducing endurance. Even the very efficient American destroyer machinery could not avert the fall in endurance as a ship's speed crept up. It was also more wearing on power plants, more maintenance being needed for boilers and turbines which ran constantly at high speed than at the economical levels. Here the Kellys also suffered from Royal Navy conservatism. Feed water for boilers left deposits. These could be cleaned up by chemical additives which had been used by the USN without problems and which greatly extended the time between boiler cleans.[1] However, the use of such additives was banned by the Engineer-in-Chief's Department until very late in the war. This ban meant that destroyers were either out of action more frequently for boiler cleaning or that they had to continue sailing with these deposits building up which affected performance. In the Mediterranean Admiral Cunningham tended to try to keep his destroyers at sea as much as possible and thought that they were in port far too frequently for boiler cleaning. This was probably true but there was nothing he could do about it. By the end of her commission in 1943 *Kelvin*'s machinery was seriously worn out and in dire need of a comprehensive refit. What is surprising is not that there were problems with the Kellys' machinery but that it performed as well as it did.

The Kellys were also vulnerable to their machinery being disabled by damage, having adopted a back-to-back arrangement for their boilers. This was a trade-off, the specification having called for a low silhouette which meant as short a ship as possible. Unit machinery was considered at the time but the extra length was seen to affect the silhouette and also to restrict manoeuvrability. The result was a very low-profile destroyer which could in certain conditions be unseen 2000 yards away. They were also very handy ships, for example, being far more manoeuvrable than the *Fletcher* class.[2] This manoeuvrability also served them well in the Mediterranean in particular when *Kipling* was able to evade attacks by forty aircraft whilst rescuing survivors from *Kelly* and *Kashmir*. With a responsive helm they turned quickly and had phenomenal acceleration, especially as Mountbatten had ensured that engineer officers attended a special course in increasing fuel flow as rapidly as possible. *Jackal* was able to survive a long engagement with two French contre-torpilleurs with only a minor hit on her stern and still pursue them when they retired.

The low silhouette proved especially useful in the night convoy battles in the Mediterranean when Kellys were able to get close to the enemy without being seen (though this could have been as much to do with poor lookout-keeping as anything else). With the advent of radar, the ability of

---

[1] D K Brown, *Nelson to Vanguard* gives a figure for RN boiler cleaning intervals of 750 hours and 2000 for the USN.
[2] Norman Friedman, *US Destroyers, An Illustrated Design History*, p118, states that the *Fletcher*'s turning circle was greater than that of an *Iowa* class battleship.

Kellys to locate their targets also increased. The engagement off Cromer on 7 December 1939 might well have turned out differently if *Jersey* or *Juno* had been fitted with radar but it did not reach the Kellys until the summer of 1940. Thereafter equipment was gradually upgraded but the restricted amount of space available did limit the number of sets these ships could carry and there was no need to fit an enormous radar suite to destroyers given their roles. Both the British and Americans made excellent use of radar in destroyer actions, something other navies lagged behind in. However, radar installations not only increased top weight but also needed accommodation to be found for their operators. In the case of the Type 271 set there were only a few places where it could be located, either on the bridge in place of the director or on the searchlight platform. The radar's power leads needed to be kept short to avoid a deterioration in performance. Most ships receiving 271s lost their 44in searchlights – which had been rendered superfluous – but *Napier* had her rangefinder replaced. This particular location cannot have been too successful as there were proposals to remove the set from it.

With the increase in radar equipment it also became necessary to replace the tripod mast with a lattice structure better able to take the weight. The USN, the only other major user of radar, also experienced similar problems and with the newly conceived radar picket role added legs to their destroyers' pole masts. Kellys were equipped with two different types of lattice mast but several ships did not receive this improvement, mainly those fitted with Type 271s. Once again this increased top weight but as careful attention was paid to stability it was not a problem.

More problematic was the increase in anti-aircraft armament as this involved finding stowage for ammunition and berthing space for extra crew besides the increase in weight from the installation of new guns. The larger destroyers were better in this respect as they had a bigger margin allowing them to absorb more weapons. This did not solve the overcrowding problems, however. The Kellys were overcrowded throughout the war but this was the case for all destroyers. American destroyers are frequently cited as being better but as Friedman demonstrates they were in fact just as badly off. German ships were probably the worst, with complements of well over 300 before any additions. There is no evidence that this factor had any effect on efficiency. During the war crewmen just accepted it though attitudes were different after 1945. In this respect the Kellys were no worse or better than other ships.

Another area where the Kellys are frequently criticised is in their main armament which is frequently seen as somehow inferior to other nations. This seems to be based on

two things, firstly that it was 4.7in calibre whilst other nations were 5in or more and that it did not possess a dual-purpose capability. The 4.7in was an effective weapon which fired a 50lb shell to a maximum range of 23,000 yards. This was more than adequate for the Royal Navy which favoured close action. It was also well in excess of the range at which *Janus*'s action with the contre-torpilleurs began and theoretically the British destroyer actually outranged the French ships. The important factor was the weight of shell, 50lbs, which enabled a reasonable rate of fire to be maintained whilst having sufficient hitting power. Japanese and Italian shells weights were the same, although American shells were heavier again and the rate of fire of the excellent 5in/38 gun was very good. French and German shells were significantly heavier but the trade-off was that the rate of fire was much lower. The standard rate of fire for Kellys was twelve rounds per minute whereas German and French ships could managed about four to six rounds a minute. This is especially surprising in respect of the French whose destroyer tactics were based on short, sharp engagements. The table below compares several features for destroyer guns.

TABLE 12:
Destroyer Main Armament

Gun	Maximum range (yards)	Rate of fire (rpm)	Weight of shell (lbs)
4.7in MK XII (UK)	23,000	12	50
5in/50 3rd Year (Japan)	21,800	8	50.7
4.7in (120mm)/50 (Italy)	24,068	6	51
5.1in (130mm) 1919 (Fr)	20,458	4	70.4
5.5in (138mm) 1929 (Fr)	21,880	12	88.4
5in (12.7cm) C/34 (Gr)	19,036	unknown	61.6
5.9in (15cm) C/36 (Gr)	24,700	unknown	99.7
5in/38 (US)	18,200	15	55

Later French guns were much better and theoretically able to maintain rates of fire of between twelve and fourteen rounds per minute. But they suffered from an overcomplicated design and were prone to breakdowns, meaning that in practice they were no faster than the earlier weapons.

The second criticism of the Kellys main armament is more valid. The guns could only elevate to 40° which gave them a limited capability against low flying aircraft and for barrage purposes. They could not tackle high- or medium-level bombers except at long range, and they certainly could not deal with dive bombing attacks. However, this was not quite the handicap that it might seem. Destroyers were very manoeuvrable and it was difficult for aircraft to hit them other than by dive bombing. They tended to be able to dodge attacks from high and medium level bombers and in fact the Kellys were manoeuvrable enough to evade the German glider bombs (some of the time!). However, it was more difficult for a Kelly to evade a dive bomber and her main armament could not elevate enough to deal with it. But even if it had been able to do so it would not have had the rate of fire to stop a determined attack. This was the case with the American 5in/38 as well. Thus the dual purpose role was not as serious a loss as might seem at first. The way to defeat the dive bomber was the use of plenty of light anti-aircraft weapons and for this purpose the 20mm Oerlikon was ideal.

The basic Oerlikon was improved with power operation and multiple barrels, the Royal Navy developing a highly-successful twin power-operated version (the Mk V) but the Kriegsmarine's four-barrelled version was truly formidable. The USN initially employed Oerlikons as a replacement for their 0.5in and 1.1in machine guns but with the advent of the kamikaze threat concentrated more on the 40mm Bofors, as the Oerlikon did not have the power to stop an aircraft which was intent on hitting the ship. When the 'N' class ships joined the British Pacific Fleet, they were fitted with single Bofors guns in place of their aft torpedo tubes. However, Bofors were in short supply and most ships had to make do with single army Mk III weapons. In the event, *Norman* not only does not seem to have received any Bofors but also to have retained her six single Oerlikons whilst her sisters received the twin mounts. By the end of the war the Kellys carried between six and ten Oerlikons which was a perfectly adequate close-range anti-aircraft armament. They also retained the four-barrelled 2pdr pom-pom mounting which had gradually developed into a reasonable weapon and which had a useful deterrent effect as well. The advantage of the pom-pom was that its shells exploded at the top of their trajectory which helped to deter kamikaze attacks. With the advent of the proximity fuse, the lack of dual-purpose main armament did become more glaring and if the 'Ns' had been rebuilt as Type 18 frigates they would have received dual-purpose guns.

SEAWORTHINESS AND SURVIVABILITY

The Kellys were very seaworthy ships but like many others suffered from some flaws as a result of the necessary compromises in their design. For example, their low silhouette and bluff bows caused spray problems with water reaching as high as No 2 mount. As has been discussed earlier the Royal Navy even approached the US representative Captain Lockwood to see if the USN had experienced similar problems and if so what they had done about it. Lockwood was a bit disingenuous in implying this was not a problem for the USN as all their destroyer classes were wet forward

and it was serious enough in the *Sumner* and *Gearing* classes to cause damage to No 1 mount in rough seas. German destroyers were worse, making firing the forward guns in any seaway very difficult. The French ships were better as their mounts were located further back. This could itself create other problems, as the French Nos 1 and 2 mounts were close enough together to be disabled by a single hit. Moving the bridge further back was also a solution to the problem but this was found to encourage captains to proceed at higher speeds than was safe, resulting in weather damage. Fully enclosed mounts would have made things a lot more comfortable for the gun crews but would have required a larger ship. The earlier US destroyers suffered quite seriously from being overweight and some classes had their rear mounts totally unshielded to compensate. When the 'L' and 'M' classes were completed with fully enclosed mounts, they were bigger and more expensive ships without any increase in firepower – in fact a reduction in capability as they carried two less torpedoes and no TSDS. The Royal Navy favoured the placement of as many guns as possible forward. This was as much to do with the tradition that Royal Navy ships were the ones meant to be attacking as anything else. This was why even the rear mount on the Kellys initially faced forwards and even after this had been changed to face to the rear, captains still insisted on training it forward to the limit of its stops. The option the Japanese used of fully-enclosed mounts with most guns aft was not even considered.

The open bridge was also considered vital as it gave an excellent view. It was ideal for spotting developing air attacks and for keeping close watch on a convoy or fleet formation. These advantages were considered to outweigh the disadvantages (cold and wet) and most navies did adopt some form of open bridge. However, with the development of increasingly capable radar, this advantage would disappear and with it the open bridge. The Kelly bridge layout proved to be the model for all wartime destroyers which adopted it without modification. Of the major nations, only the Italian and Japanese fleet destroyers kept enclosed bridges. The rangefinder and director tower were adequate though in later classes these would be combined into one. With the addition of radar they formed a very formidable fire control suite which was employed to great effect. Only the USN also combined radar and director control for its destroyers as effectively as the Royal Navy. Attempts had been made to link the rangefinder to the 4in HA gun but this was a failure and the Royal Navy did not develop an effective HA director before the end of the war.

The Kellys were very seaworthy vessels, as were all modern Royal Navy destroyers, none of which foundered due to inclement weather. Admiral Layton[3] thought that they handled very well in rough weather and in that respect were better than the *Southampton* class cruisers. Several ships from other navies did founder though, the Italian ships due to their light construction and poor design, French ships due to poor design and excessive top weight and American ships due to poor seamanship. The foundering of three American destroyers in a typhoon in December 1944 was generally taken to show that American destroyers were less stable than British ones. Certainly, two of the destroyers which foundered were from classes which were top heavy but to assume that this was due to design failings is misleading. Many of the older British destroyers were less stable than the American ones and the third ship lost, a *Fletcher*, was from a very stable class. The reason for this particular loss would seem to be poor seamanship and an inability to treat a violent storm with the caution it deserved. It was also the view among the Royal Navy that the American destroyer captains were not as good as the British ones when it came to seamanship. The captain of *Abdiel*, when the minelayer was serving with US forces in 1943, commented that they did not show the same ship-handling skills as RN destroyer captains and in many respects were positively timid. When Admiral Thebaud of the USN commented on the typhoon he also referred to the superior seamanship of the Royal Navy and did not think that this sort of disaster was likely to happen to the Royal Navy because of their greater experience with bad weather.

The Kellys had an initial problem with leaking in their forward crew spaces. This was solved, however, and other problems with their structure were dealt with by strengthening the relevant parts and by the end of 1940 they were very seaworthy ships. They were also very sturdy and able to survive significant amounts of damage. The Kellys had re-introduced longitudinal construction to Royal Navy destroyer design which was a radical step. Welding was not adopted due to the lack of knowledge on it and the difficulty in wielding D quality steel. Given the problems the Japanese, for example, had experienced with their welded ships this was a wise move. British industry was not up to welding at that time, the ship builders even having great trouble with longitudinal construction but the new method proved its worth and ensured several ships' survival. With longitudinal construction the Kellys were able to survive hits amidships on several occasions, the most notable being when *Kelly* herself had her bottom blown out by an E-boat torpedo. Where they were vulnerable was to torpedo hits in their magazines which generally finished the ship, both

Janus and *Jaguar* being lost in this way. But the biggest cause of sinking was air attack, particularly to multiple bomb hits or near misses. In the Mediterranean, the Kellys had to face very competent pilots who were able to deliver simultaneous attacks and hit their targets in succession. This was enough to sink the ships, frequently breaking them in two.

Even so, with more time, two ships could probably have been saved. Both *Kandahar* and *Nestor* though disabled were in no danger of sinking, but were just unfortunate to be in areas well away from air support which would have enabled them to be rescued and they had to be scuttled. What is impressive is not the number of Kellys sunk by air attack but the fact that so many survived. Not all air attacks were successful and even elite pilots could miss. I have already mentioned *Kipling*'s survival but other examples which stand out are *Kandahar* and *Kingston* which survived eleven and nineteen separate attacks respectively on 22 May 1941 whilst rescuing survivors from *Greyhound* and *Fiji*. Kellys were frequently and heavily bombed on the Tobruk runs but none were sunk, although *Nizam* was damaged. Several, however, were squandered on pointless operations. There was no need to order the 5th Flotilla to bombard Maleme airfield which could have had only a nuisance effect at best and the despatch of the 14th Flotilla to intercept an enemy convoy in waters dominated by enemy aircraft without cover was also one of the more foolish operations especially as the convoy that the force was due to intercept had already reached port. These two operations alone would lead to the loss of four Kellys. Later American experience would demonstrate that, using destroyers as radar pickets, air cover was necessary if a destroyer was to operate for a long period in waters dominated by the enemy.

After dive bombing, the next most frequent loss of Kellys was due to mines. That these destroyers could survive mining is demonstrated by *Kelly*, *Jervis* and *Jersey* but in the first two of these incidents the mines exploded after the ship had passed over them. When *Jersey* hit a mine in the entrance to Malta harbour she went down very quickly. *Jupiter* survived several hours before foundering and *Kandahar* could have been saved if there had been enough time. None of these ships had their TSDS streamed but there is no guarantee that this would have helped as the sweeps were streamed behind the ship and a mine could still be hit before the sweep reached it. TSDS was dispensed with when it was clear that the role was no longer appropriate and that it was not suitable for dealing with many types of mine. Interestingly the Australian 'Ns' retained their TSDS equipment longer than other ships though it is unlikely that they were using it by early 1945. The davits were removed on most ships which made it impossible to use the equipment

[3] Rear-Admiral Geoffrey Layton, commanding officer 18th Cruiser Squadron, letter of 27 February 1940 to Rear-Admiral Bruce Fraser, then Controller of the Navy.

207

anyway but the paravanes remained in place on most ships. Others such as *Kelvin* had landed TSDS much earlier, by 1943 in fact, for more depth charges and throwers.

The value placed on the Kellys is perhaps illustrated by the fact that they continued to be improved and updated. Several destroyers were declared constructive total losses and used as depot or base ships but Kellys continued to be repaired. For example, *Jervis* was repaired after she was mined off the Normandy beaches and *Javelin* was totally refitted after her collision with *Eskimo*. But by 1945, the winding-down of the war meant that there was no longer a need for such a large destroyer force and the Kellys went into reserve whilst the most up-to-date ships were kept in service. *Javelin* and *Jervis* lingered until 1946 and in fact improvements were still authorised in new Admiralty Fleet Orders. Once they were in reserve they were caught by the changing nature of sea warfare. The general-purpose destroyer was no longer a valid concept being replaced by ships which performed specific functions such as anti-submarine warfare. As has been discussed, serious consideration was given to reactivating the 'Ns' as anti-submarine frigates but this came to nothing. The 'Js' and 'Ks' had gone earlier and the 'Ns' were all scrapped. Activities after the war were limited to the Dutch navy who seem to have had trouble with the class and *Nepal's* minesweeping trials period. By the time they were scrapped there was no role for ships of this type.

The Kellys were a highly successful design. They formed the basis for future classes of fleet destroyer and proved to be sturdy and adaptable. Ships based on the original design were still in service in the 1970s long after the original destroyers had disappeared. A number of new features were introduced, all of which proved to be successful, such as longitudinal construction, low silhouette and high manoeuvrability although after the war there was a move towards larger ships and unit machinery. This should not be taken as a criticism of the Kellys: requirements change as do the needs of a navy. The Kellys could perhaps have introduced all-welded hulls as well but this would have been a very risky decision given the inability of British industry to use the technology at the time. On balance, the decision to stick with riveted hulls turned out to be correct. I have made several comparisons with other nations' ships, not to demonstrate that the Kellys were better but that they were among the best destroyers of the Second World War. Each nation built ships which served its own strategies and tactics and in the Kellys the Royal Navy were lucky in having three classes of ship which served theirs so well.

APPENDICES

Specifications

(Metric figures in brackets)

DIMENSIONS

LENGTH:

overall: 356ft 6in (108.6m).

between perpendiculars: 339ft 6in (103.4m).

waterline: 348ft (103.4m).

BEAM: 35ft 8in (10.8m).

DRAUGHT:

light: 11ft 6in (3.50m).

half load: 12ft 10in (3.91m).

full load: 13ft 8in (4.17m).

DISPLACEMENT (from inclining)

AS BUILT:

Jackal

light: 1724 tons (1751.58 tonnes).

deep: 2332 tons (2369 tonnes).

Jervis

light: 1770 tons (1798 tonnes).

half oil: 2135 tons (2169 tonnes).

deep: 2380 tons (2418 tonnes).

As equipment was added to the newly built 'Ns' they would be heavier.

Van Galen

light: 1760 tons (1788 tonnes).

half oil: 2155 tons (2189 tonnes).

deep: 2400 tons (2438 tonnes).

MACHINERY

MAIN:

Two Admiralty three-drum, water tube boilers with superheaters each generating 20,000shp.

Total No of tubes fitted

Generator: 8980

Superheater: 414

Working pressure: 300lbs/in²

Boiler temperature: 630°F

Superheat: 220°F

AUXILIARY:

One Spanner thimble tube type No. 1 with 192 tubes or one Clarkson boiler with 333 tubes. Each boiler drives one high-pressure and one low-pressure Parsons turbine connected in series. The turbines are connected to the shafts by a single reduction helical gearing situated in a separate gearing room aft of the main engine room.

OIL PRESSURE:

140 lbs/in²

ELECTRICAL:

2 × 155kW turbo generators

2 × 50kW diesel generators

supplying power at 220 volts

STEERING GEAR:

Electro-hydraulic system, employing two single-acting rams operating on a tiller. A hand pump is available for emergency use.

NO OF SHAFTS: 2

PROPELLERS: 2

Pitch: 13ft 2ins (4.01m).

Diameter: 10ft 6ins (3.20m).

Developed surface area 65ft² (18.12m²).

REVOLUTIONS:

deep: 340

half oil: 350

light: 360

'N' class had propellers with a pitch of 13ft 5ins (4.09m) which were retro-fitted to all 'Js' and 'Ks' and which gave 330rpm in deep condition.

PERFORMANCE

(see Appendix 8 for service speed and endurance)

AS DESIGNED:

Maximum design speed: 36kts.

Maximum speed in deep condition: 32kts.

FUEL CAPACITY:

484 tons (491.74 tonnes).

ENDURANCE:

5500 miles (8850 km) at 15kts with a clean bottom and 5 per cent reserve of fuel oil.

EQUIPMENT

SEARCHLIGHTS:

1 × 44in projector on platform between the torpedo tubes, remote controlled from the bridge, fitted with either Clark Chapman Special Reflectors or Bart Reflectors.

2 × 20in signal projectors on sponsons, one each side of the bridge.

2 × 6in signal lanterns.

TSDS:

2 × S Mk I* sweeping paravanes port and starboard.

2x D Mk I depressor paravane.

2 × permanent davits located on either side of the depth charge rail.

2 × Clarke Chapman port and starboard paravane winches.

WIRELESS TELEGRAPHY:

Leader

Type 49A in main office.

Type 60BLA (AC) or alternative in second office.

Type 51HA (AC) or alternative as fire control set.

Destroyer

Type 49A

Type 51HA (AC) or alternative as fire control set.

ANCHORS AND CABLES:

Anchors:

2 × 34cwt stockless anchors.

1 × 5cwt kedge anchor

Cables:

9 × lengths of 1in ⁵⁄₁₆ forged steel cable for starboard anchor.

5 × lengths of 1in ⁵⁄₁₆ forged steel cable for port anchor.

150 fathoms of 4in steel rope.

Capstan gear:

1 × double headed combined capstan and cable holder.

BOATS:

1 × 25ft fast motor boat.

1 × 27ft whaler.

1 × 25ft general service motor boat.

1 × 16ft planing dinghy.

6 × No. 20 pattern Carley floats (7 in leaders).

PROVISIONS:

3 months' supplies.

CENTRAL STORES:

4 months' supply of consumable stores.

COMPLEMENT (as designed)

Leader

228 officers and men

Destroyer

208 officers and men

ARMAMENT

MAIN:

6 × 4.7in Mk XII in three twin CP XIX high angle/low angle mountings with +40° elevation and -10° depression. The mountings were hand controlled, power worked by electro-hydraulic units situated near their respective mountings.

Arcs

No. 1 mount: 140° green and red.

No. 2 mount: 140° green and red.

No. 3 mount: 150° green and red.

Control:

1 × director control tower on bridge

1 × 12ft combined R/F – HA director

AMMUNITION:

'J' & 'K' class

250 rounds per gun made up of 190 Semi Armour Piercing, 50 High Explosive Time Fuse, 10 High Explosive Direct Action.

50 rounds of starshell per ship

195 practice low angle rounds per ship

69 high angle practice rounds per ship

Each of the three shell rooms contained 380 SAP, 20 HEDA, 100 HETF, 65 LA practice and 33 HA practice. The star shell was all stored in No. 2 shell room.

'N' class:

250 rounds per gun made up of 150 Semi Armour Piercing, 100 High Explosive Plugged.

50 rounds of starshell per ship.

TORPEDOES:

'J' & 'K' class

10 × 21in Mk IX or IX** mounted in two quintuple mounts PR Mk II.

10 × torpedo warheads stowed in warhead room.

10 × collision heads stowed in warhead room.

10 × blowing heads stowed in warhead room.

'N' class

5 × 21in Mk IX or IX** mounted in one pentad mount PR Mk II*.

5 × torpedo warheads stowed in warhead room.

DEPTH CHARGES:

'J' & 'K' class

30 Type D depth charges fired from

1 × Mk I depth charge rail

2 × Mk II depth charge throwers

10 charges stowed in the warhead room and 20 stowed on deck.

'N' class

45 Type D or Mk VII depth charges fired from

1 × Mk I depth charge rail

2 × Mk II depth charge throwers

25 charges stowed in the warhead room and 20 stowed on deck.

ANTI-AIRCRAFT:

1 × Mk VII 4-barrelled 2pdr pom-pom, 1800 rounds per barrel. Arcs from 36° starboard forward to 46° port forward with 80° elevation

2 × Mk III 4-barrelled 0.5in machine gun mounts, 2500 rounds per barrel. Arcs: 180° port and starboard with 80° elevation

'J' & 'K' class

4 × Lewis guns on twin mounts but could be mounted singly. 2000 solid, 500 tracer rounds per barrel.

'N' class

1 × 4in Mk V or Mk V* high angle on a Mk III** mount, 300 HETF, 34 star shell and 11 practice shells supplied. 96 shells stored in ready-use lockers and the balance in the magazine.

'N' Class (Nepal, Tjerk Hiddes and Van Galen)

4 × single Oerlikons Mk I or II (*Nepal* 6), 2400 rounds per gun made up of equal quantities of HE and Incendiary and stored in the QF magazine.

'N' Class (Tjerk Hiddes and Van Galen)

2 × 0.5in machine guns in Mk V twin power-operated mounting, 2400 rounds per gun stored in the QF magazine.

SMALL ARMS:

29 × No. 1 rifles.

2 × No. 2 rifles.

20 × pistols (Revolver No. 1).

10 × naval swords.

1 × 0.303in line-throwing rifle.

4 × Mk 3 signal pistols.

1 × strengthened No. 1 rifle.

'N' class

1 × tripod mounted Vickers 0.303in medium machine gun with 5000 rounds of ammunition.

2 × stripped Lewis guns.

APPENDIX 2

Flotilla Organisation 1939-1945

KEY:

¢ Captain D

§ Divisional Leader

7th Destroyer Flotilla, 3 October 1939*

P/No.	Name	
13TH DIVISION		
F00	*Jervis*¢	25th Sub-division
F72	*Jersey*	25th Sub-division
F61	*Javelin*	26th Sub-division
F34	*Jaguar*	26th Sub-division
14TH DIVISION		
F22	*Jackal*§	27th Sub-division
F53	*Janus*	27th Sub-division
F46	*Juno*	28th Sub-division
F85	*Jupiter*	28th Sub-division

* *Echo* (H23) had been a member of the flotilla prior to this date.

5th Destroyer Flotilla, 1 March 1940

P/No.	Name	
9TH DIVISION		
F01	*Kelly*¢	17th Sub-division
F50	*Kimberley*	17th Sub-division
F12	*Kashmir*	18th Sub-division
F37	*Kelvin*	18th Sub-division
10TH DIVISION		
F28	*Kandahar*§	19th Sub-division
F91	*Kipling*	19th Sub-division
F45	*Khartoum*	20th Sub-division
F64	*Kingston*	20th Sub-division

14th Destroyer Flotilla, 18 May 1940

P/No.	Name	
27TH DIVISION		
F53	*Janus*	53rd Sub-division
F46	*Juno*	53rd Sub-division
F36	*Nubian*¢	54th Sub-division
F31	*Mohawk*	54th Sub-division
28TH DIVISION		
F28	*Kandahar*§	55th Sub-division
F91	*Kipling*	55th Sub-division
F45	*Khartoum*	56th Sub-division
F64	*Kingston*	56th Sub-division

5th Destroyer Flotilla, 24 June 1940

P/No.	Name
9TH DIVISION	
G22	*Jackal*
G34	*Jaguar*
G61	*Javelin*
G85	*Jupiter*
10TH DIVISION	
G12	*Kashmir*
G37	*Kelvin*
G00	*Jervis*
F91	*Kipling*
G01	*Kelly*
G72	*Jersey*

Captain D administered the flotilla from ashore in Immingham. He went to sea in different ships of the flotilla on a rotating basis. *Jervis* was included in the flotilla as an administrative measure whilst she was repaired. As soon as she was ready she sailed for the Mediterranean. At this time, most of the ships listed in the 10th Division were in fact under repair and the effective strength of the flotilla was the 9th Division.

5th Destroyer Flotilla, 8 November 1940

P/No.	Name
9TH DIVISION	
G61	*Javelin*¢

P/No.	Name
G85	*Jupiter*
G37	*Kelvin*
G91	*Kipling*

10TH DIVISION

P/No.	Name
G22	*Jackal*§
G34	*Jaguar*
G12	*Kashmir*
G72	*Jersey*

The 5th Flotilla was based at Plymouth. During this time *Mashona* and *Punjabi* were both temporarily attached for periods of around two weeks each.

14th Destroyer Flotilla, 3 February 1941

P/No.	Name
27TH DIVISION
G00	*Jervis*¢
G46	*Juno*
G53	*Janus*
G34	*Jaguar*
G36	*Nubian*

28TH DIVISION

G05	*Greyhound*
H59	*Gallant*
H31	*Griffin*

7th Destroyer Flotilla (reconstituted), 7 March 1941

P/No.	Name
13TH DIVISION
G97	*Napier*¢
G38	*Nizam*
G02	*Nestor*

5th Destroyer Flotilla, 1 April 1941

P/No.	Name
G01	*Kelly*¢

9TH DIVISION
G37	*Kelvin*
G85	*Jupiter*
G22	*Jackal*
G61	*Javelin*

10TH DIVISION
G12	*Kashmir*§
G72	*Jersey*
G91	*Kipling*
	Isaac Sweers

Jupiter and *Javelin* were non-operational and *Isaac Sweers* did not join the 5th Flotilla when it sailed for the Mediterranean.

5th Destroyer Flotilla, 30 April 1941

P/No.	Name
9TH DIVISION
G01	*Kelly*¢
G91	*Kipling*
G12	*Kashmir*
G37	*Kelvin*

10TH DIVISION
| G22 | *Jackal*§ |
| G72 | *Jersey* |

14th Destroyer Flotilla, 5 May 1941

P/No.	Name
27TH DIVISION
G00	*Jervis*¢
G34	*Jaguar*
G53	*Janus*
G46	*Juno*
G36	*Nubian*
H31	*Griffin*
H05	*Greyhound*

28TH DIVISION
G28	*Kandahar*§
G64	*Kingston*
G50	*Kimberley*

7th Destroyer Flotilla 28th May 1941

P/No.	Name
13TH DIVISION
G97	*Napier*¢
G38	*Nizam*
G37	*Kelvin*
G91	*Kipling*
G22	*Jackal*

A division needed at least two ships to make it viable. Thus at this time the 7th Flotilla only had one division of five ships. As soon as another was allocated a 14th Division would be formed. This happened on 18 July when *Nestor* (G02) joined.

14th Destroyer Flotilla, 25 June 1941

P/No.	Name
27TH DIVISION
G00	*Jervis*¢
G34	*Jaguar*
G53	*Janus*
G36	*Nubian*

28TH DIVISION
G28	*Kandahar*§
G64	*Kingston*
H59	*Gallant*
H31	*Griffin*

14th Destroyer Flotilla, 23 July 1941

P/No.	Name
27TH DIVISION
G00	*Jervis*¢
G28	*Kandahar*
G64	*Kingston*
G50	*Kimberley*

28TH DIVISION
H31	*Griffin*§
G34	*Jaguar*
G53	*Janus*
G36	*Nubian*

Jupiter (G85) joined the 28th Division on 11 August.

7th Destroyer Flotilla, 31 August 1941

P/No.	Name
13TH DIVISION
G97	*Napier*¢

P/No.	Name
G02	*Nestor*
G38	*Nizam*
I69	*Vendetta*

14TH DIVISION
| G22 | *Jackal*§ |
| G91 | *Kipling* |

14th Destroyer Flotilla, 9 September 1941

P/No.	Name
27TH DIVISION
G00	*Jervis*¢
H31	*Griffin*
G34	*Jaguar*

28TH DIVISION
G28	*Kandahar*§
G50	*Kimberley*
G64	*Kingston*
G36	*Nubian*
G85	*Jupiter*

14th Destroyer Flotilla, 9 December 1941

P/No.	Name
27TH DIVISION
G00	*Jervis*¢
G34	*Jaguar*
G50	*Kimberley*
G64	*Kingston*

28TH DIVISION
G24	*Maori*§
G82	*Sikh*
G18	*Zulu*

14th Destroyer Flotilla, 21 February 1942

P/No.	Name
27TH DIVISION
G00	*Jervis*¢
G34	Jaguar
G22	*Jackal*
	Vasilissa Olga

28TH DIVISION
G28	*Kandahar*§
G64	*Kingston*
G37	*Kelvin*
G91	*Kipling*

7th Destroyer Flotilla, 23 February 1942

P/No.	Name
13TH DIVISION
G97	*Napier*¢
G38	*Nizam*
G02	*Nestor*
G49	*Norman*

14TH DIVISION
H27	*Electra*§
H10	*Encounter*
H61	*Express*
G85	*Jupiter*

This organisation lasted only a short time as *Electra*, *Encounter* and *Jupiter* - all due to join the 14th Division - were sunk in the Battle of the Java Sea. *Vampire* (I68) is also listed as part

of

of the 7th Flotilla on 2 March 1942.

7th Destroyer Flotilla, 15 August 1942
P/No.	Name
13TH DIVISION	
G97	*Napier¢*
G38	*Nizam*
G49	*Norman*
G25	*Nepal*
14TH DIVISION	
G16	*Tjerk Hiddes§*
G84	*Van Galen*

14th Destroyer Flotilla, 12 December 1942
P/No.	Name
G00	*Jervis¢*
G61	*Javelin*
G37	*Kelvin*
	Vasilissa Olga

14th Destroyer Flotilla, 23 April 1943
P/No.	Name
27TH DIVISION	
G00	*Jervis¢*
G61	*Javelin*
G37	*Kelvin*
I87	*Isis*
28TH DIVISION	
G36	*Nubian§*
G69	*Paladin*
G56	*Petard*
	Vasilissa Olga

14th Destroyer Flotilla, 5 September 1943
P/No.	Name
27TH DIVISION	
G00	*Jervis¢*

G69	*Paladin*
I67	*Wishart*
28TH DIVISION	
G10	*Pathfinder§*
G41	*Panther*
G77	*Penn*

7th Destroyer Flotilla, 1 October 1943
P/No.	Name
13TH DIVISION	
G97	*Napier¢*
G38	*Nizam*
14TH DIVISION	
G49	*Norman*
G25	*Nepal*

14th Destroyer Flotilla, 17 December 1943
P/No.	Name
G00	*Jervis¢*
G10	*Pathfinder*
X101	*Le Fantasque*

14th Destroyer Flotilla, 31 January 1944
P/No.	Name
13TH DIVISION	
G99	*Laforey¢*
G15	*Loyal*
G50	*Kimberley*
G61	*Javelin*
14TH DIVISION	
G37	*Kelvin*
G32	*Lookout*
G00	*Jervis*

This was purely administrative as *Kimberley* was not yet out of refit, *Javelin* and *Kelvin* were refitting in the UK and *Jervis* had just been damaged by a glider bomb.

14th Destroyer Flotilla, 11 December 1944
P/No.	Name
G37	*Kelvin¢*
G50	*Kimberley*
G32	*Lookout*
G15	*Loyal*

7th Destroyer Flotilla, 5 June 1945
P/No.	Name
D13	*Napier¢*
D14	*Nepal*
D15	*Nizam*
D16	*Norman*

14th Destroyer Flotilla, 2 July 1945
P/No.	Name
G00	*Jervis¢*
R51	*Chevron*
G37	*Kelvin*
G61	*Javelin*

14th Destroyer Flotilla, 7 December 1945
P/No.	Name
13TH DIVISION	
R61	*Chequers¢*
R52	*Chaplet*
R51	*Chevron*
14TH DIVISION	
G00	*Jervis§*
G61	*Javelin*

Notes:

1. The three main flotillas are detailed above but on several occasions a ship would be attached to a different flotilla whilst serving in another command or working-up. These are listed below:

Jervis: 25th Flotilla (22 May-30 October 1944).
Javelin: 49th Division, 25th Flotilla (10 March-10 April 1944); 23rd Flotilla (11 April - May 1944), 20th Division, 10th Flotilla (May -14 July 1944).
Jupiter: 40th Division, 20th Flotilla (2 May-18 June 1941); 12th Division, 6th Flotilla (19 June - 11 August 1941).
Kelvin: 23rd Flotilla (11 April-30 October 1944).
Nestor: 40th Division, 20th Flotilla (28 April - 5 May 1941); 12th Division, 6th Flotilla (6 May - 18 July 1941).
Tjerk Hiddes: 19th Destroyer Division Royal Australian Navy (4 January 1943 – 10 January 1944); 8th Flotilla (13 November – 23 March 1945).
Van Galen: 19th Destroyer Division Royal Australian Navy (4 January 1943 – 10 January 1944); 8th Flotilla (13 November 1944 – 8 February 1945).

2. Apart from two short periods *Piorun* did not serve with any of the three normal flotillas. Her units are as follows: 7th Flotilla (4 November – 9 December 1940); 10th Escort Group (10 December 1940 – 24 January 1941); 7th Flotilla (25 January – 22 February 1941); 10th Escort Group (23 February – 3 April 1941); 14th (Polish) Escort Group[1] (4th April – August 1941); 9th Escort Group (August 1941 – October 1941); 11th Escort Group (October – December 1941); 25th (Polish) Escort Group (December 1941 – March 1942); Escort Group B3 (March – 17 December 1942); 3rd Flotilla (18 December 1942 – 8 July 1943); 24th Flotilla (8 July – 19 November 1943); 3rd Flotilla (19 November 1943 – 2 March 1944); 17th Flotilla (3 March – 23 May 1944); 20th Division, 10th Flotilla (24 May – 9 November 1944); 8th Flotilla (10 November 1944 – March 1945); 23rd Flotilla (15 June – 2 August 1945); 17th Flotilla (3 August 1945 – January 1946); Unallocated (January – May 1946).

---
[1] Reclassified as "Special Escort Group" in June 1941.

3. Between 18 May and 1 June 1940, *Jackal*, *Javelin* and *Jaguar* were attached to the 1st Flotilla. This ended on 1 June when they were reallocated to the 5th Flotilla.

4. When the 7th Flotilla left the Mediterranean at the end of 1941 *Kipling*, *Kelvin* and *Jackal* remained. These ships remained unallocated until they all joined the 14th Flotilla in 1942.

5. No information can be found on *Janus*'s unit between July and December 1943. It is likely that she remained unallocated. This was also the case for several of the 'Ns' during their initial working up periods.

6. *Kandahar*, *Kingston*, *Khartoum* and *Kimberley* were initially allocated to the 28th Division of the 14th Flotilla. That remained the case until around July 1940 when the remaining three ship were reclassified as an independent unit known as the 'Red Sea Destroyer Force'. A new 28th Division was formed in the Mediterranean until April 1940 when *Kandahar*, *Kingston* and *Kimberley* rejoined the 14th Flotilla.

Alterations and Additions to Anti-Aircraft Armament

Jervis

As completed: 1 × 4-barrelled Mk VII 2pdr pom-pom, 2 × 4-barrelled Mk III 0.5in machine guns, 2 × twin 0.303in Lewis guns.

1st Alteration (by June 1940): 1 × 4in Mk V HA reportedly added.[2]

2nd Alteration (by ? 1940): 1 × 4in Mk V HA removed.

3rd Alteration (by April 1942): 4 × single 20mm Oerlikons added, two replacing 0.5in mgs on bridge wings, two added to front of the roof of the aft deck house.

4th Alteration (by June 1943): 1 × 4in Mk V HA added in place of aft torpedo tubes.

5th Alteration (by 5 June 1945): 1 × 4in Mk V HA removed. 2 × single 20mm Oerlikons on front of roof of aft deck house removed. 2 × single Oerlikons on bridge wings replaced by 2 × twin power-operated Mk V 20mm Oerlikon mounts. 2 × single 20mm Oerlikons adjacent to searchlight replaced by 2 × twin hand operated 20mm Oerlikons. This was *Jervis*'s final configuration.

Jackal

As completed: 1 × 4-barrelled Mk VII 2pdr pom-pom, 2 × 4-barrelled Mk III 0.5in machine guns, 2 × twin 0.303in Lewis guns.

1st Alteration (by August 1940): 1 × 4in Mk V HA added.

2nd Alteration (by April 1941): 2 × single 20mm Oerlikons added, on platforms adjacent to the searchlight. *Jackal* was in this configuration when lost.

Jaguar

As completed: 1 × 4-barrelled Mk VII 2pdr pom-pom, 2 × 4-barrelled Mk III 0.5in machine guns, 2 × twin 0.303in Lewis guns.

1st Alteration (by August 1940): 1 × 4in Mk V HA added.

2nd Alteration (by 8 January 1942): 2 × single 20mm Oerlikons added, on platforms adjacent to the searchlight. It is likely that *Jaguar* was in this configuration when lost.

Juno

As completed: 1 × 4-barrelled Mk VII 2pdr pom-pom, 2 × 4-barrelled Mk III 0.5in machine guns, 2 × twin 0.303in Lewis guns.

Juno received no alterations and was in this configuration when lost.

Janus

As completed: 1 × 4-barrelled Mk VII 2pdr pom-pom, 2 × 4-barrelled Mk III 0.5in machine guns, 2 × twin 0.303in Lewis guns.

1st Alteration (by 30 June 1942): 6 × single Oerlikons added, two located on bridge wings replacing 0.5in mgs, two on platforms adjacent to the searchlight and two located on the quarterdeck. It is likely that *Janus* was in this configuration when lost.

Javelin

As completed: 1 × 4-barrelled Mk VII 2pdr pom-pom, 2 × 4-barrelled Mk III 0.5in machine guns, 2 × twin 0.303in Lewis guns.

1st Alteration (by August 1940): 1 × 4in Mk V HA added.

2nd Alteration (by January 1942): 4 × single 20mm Oerlikons added, two replacing the 0.5in mgs on the bridge wings, two on platforms adjacent to the searchlight.

3rd Alteration (by 20 February 1944): 1 × 4in Mk V HA removed. 4 × twin power-operated Mk V 20mm Oerlikon mounts added, two replacing the two single Oerlikons on the bridge, two replacing the two single Oerlikons on platforms adjacent to the searchlight. This was *Javelin*'s final configuration.

Jersey

As completed: 1 × 4-barrelled Mk VII 2pdr pom-pom, 2 × 4-barrelled Mk III 0.5in machine guns, 2 × twin 0.303in Lewis guns.

1st Alteration (by September 1940): 1 × 4in Mk V HA added.

2nd Alteration (by April 1941): 2 × single 20mm Oerlikons added, on platforms adjacent to the searchlight. *Jersey* was in this configuration when lost.

Jupiter

As completed: 1 × 4-barrelled Mk VII 2pdr pom-pom, 2 × 4-barrelled Mk III 0.5in machine guns, 2 × twin 0.303in Lewis guns.

1st Alteration (by August 1940): 1 × 4in Mk V HA added.

2nd Alteration (by 23 May 1941): 2 × single 20mm Oerlikons added, on platforms adjacent to the searchlight. *Jupiter* was in this configuration when lost.

Kelly

As completed: 1 × 4-barrelled Mk VII 2pdr pom-pom, 2 × 4-barrelled Mk III 0.5in machine guns, 2 × twin 0.303in Lewis guns.

1st Alteration (by December 1940): 1 × 4in Mk V HA added.

2nd Alteration (by April 1941): 2 × single 20mm Oerlikons added, on platforms adjacent to the searchlight. *Kelly* was in this configuration when lost.

Kashmir

As completed: 1 × 4-barrelled Mk VII 2pdr pom-pom, 2 × 4-barrelled Mk III 0.5in machine guns, 2 × twin 0.303in Lewis guns.

1st Alteration (by August 1940): 1 × 4in Mk V HA added.

2nd Alteration (by April 1941): 2 × single 20mm Oerlikons added, on platforms adjacent to the searchlight. *Kashmir* was in this configuration when lost.

Kandahar

As completed: 1 × 4-barrelled Mk VII 2pdr pom-pom, 2 × 4-barrelled Mk III 0.5in machine guns, 2 × twin 0.303in Lewis guns.

1st Alteration (by 21st November 1941): 2 × single 20mm Oerlikons added, on platforms adjacent to the searchlight. *Kandahar* was in this configuration when lost.

Kelvin

As completed: 1 × 4-barrelled Mk VII 2pdr pom-pom, 2 × 4-barrelled Mk III 0.5in machine guns, 2 × twin 0.303in Lewis guns.

1st Alteration (by September 1940): 1 × 4in Mk V HA added.

2nd Alteration (by April 1941): 2 × single 20mm Oerlikons added, on platforms adjacent to the searchlight.

3rd Alteration (by February 1942): 2 × single 20mm Oerlikons added replacing 0.5in mgs on bridge wings.

4th Alteration (by 13th June 1942): 1 × 4in Mk V HA removed, 2 × single 20mm Oerlikons added to quarterdeck.

5th Alteration (by March 1944): 2 × single 20mm Oerlikons on quarterdeck removed. 4 × twin power-operated Mk V 20mm Oerlikon mounts added, two replacing the two single Oerlikons on the bridge, two replacing the two single Oerlikons on platforms adjacent to the searchlight. This was *Kelvin*'s final configuration.

Khartoum

As completed: 1 × 4-barrelled Mk VII 2pdr pom-pom, 2 × 4-barrelled Mk III 0.5in machine guns, 2 × twin 0.303in Lewis guns.

Khartoum received no alterations and was in this configuration when lost.

Kimberley

As completed: 1 × 4-barrelled Mk VII 2pdr pom-pom, 2 × 4-barrelled Mk III 0.5in machine guns, 2 × twin 0.303in Lewis guns.

1st Alteration (by late 1941): 1 × 4in Mk V HA added, 2 × single 20mm Oerlikons added, on

platforms adjacent to the searchlight.
2nd Alteration (by January 1942): 1 × single Oerlikon added on the centre of the quarterdeck.
3rd Alteration (by March 1944): 1 × 4in Mk V HA removed. *Kimberley* possibly carried 6 × single 20mm Oerlikons, two located on bridge wings replacing the 0.5 mgs, two on platforms adjacent to the searchlight and two on the quarterdeck.
4th Alteration (by November 1944): *Kimberley* carried at least one 40mm Bofors, location unknown.
Kimberley's final configuration unknown.

Kingston
As completed: 1 × 4-barrelled Mk VII 2pdr pom-pom, 2 × 4-barrelled Mk III 0.5in machine guns, 2 × twin 0.303in Lewis guns.
1st Alteration (by 25th December 1941): 1 × 4in Mk V HA added, 2 × single 20mm Oerlikons added, on platforms adjacent to the searchlight. *Kingston* was in this configuration when lost.

Kipling
As completed: 1 × 4-barrelled Mk VII 2pdr pom-pom, 2 × 4-barrelled Mk III 0.5in machine guns, 2 × twin 0.303in Lewis guns.
1st Alteration (July 1940): 1 × 4in Mk V HA added.
2nd Alteration (by May 1941): 2 × single Oerlikons added, on platforms adjacent to the searchlight.
3rd Alteration (by May 1942): 1 × single Oerlikon added on the centre of the quarterdeck. *Kipling* was in this configuration when lost.

Napier
As completed: 1 × 4in Mk V HA, 1 × 4-barrelled Mk VII 2pdr pom-pom, 2 × 4-barrelled Mk III 0.5in machine guns, 2 × twin 0.303in Lewis guns.
1st Alteration (by May 1942): 4 × single 20mm Oerlikons added, two on the bridge wings replacing the 0.5in mgs, two on platforms adjacent to the searchlight.
2nd Alteration (by 1943): 2 × single Oerlikons added on the front of the roof of the aft deck house.
3rd Alteration (by 23 June 1945): 2 × single Oerlikons on bridge wings replaced by 2 × twin power-operated Mk V 20mm Oerlikon mounts. Aft torpedo tubes replaced by 3 × 40mm Mk III Bofors, one on the searchlight platform, one on the port side of the searchlight platform, and one on the front of the roof of the aft deck house replacing the 2 × single Oerlikons located there.
4th Alteration (by November 1945): 3 × Bofors

removed. This was *Napier*'s final configuration.

Nestor
As completed: 1 × 4in Mk V HA, 1 × 4-barrelled Mk VII 2pdr pom-pom, 2 × 4-barrelled Mk III 0.5in machine guns, 2 × twin 0.303in Lewis guns.
1st Alteration (by 30 November 1941): 4 × single Oerlikons added, two on platforms adjacent to the searchlight, two replacing 0.5 mgs on the bridge wings. 1 × twin Mk V power-operated 0.5in machine gun tub added on quarterdeck between TSDS winches. *Nestor* was in this configuration when lost.

Tjerk Hiddes
As completed: 1 × 4in Mk V HA, 1 × 4-barrelled Mk VII 2pdr pom-pom 4 × single 20mm Oerlikons 1 × twin Mk V power-operated 0.5in machine gun tub.
1st Alteration (by 1943): 1 × 4in Mk V HA removed. Aft torpedo tubes replaced. 0.5in machine gun tub removed. 2 × single 20mm Oerlikons added on the quarterdeck.
2nd Alteration (by 1st July 1947): 2 × single 20mm Oerlikons removed from the quarterdeck. 2 × single Oerlikons on bridge wings replaced by 2 × twin power-operated Mk V 20mm Oerlikon mounts.
This was *Tjerk Hiddes*'s final configuration.

Nepal
As completed: 1 × 4in Mk V HA, 1 × 4-barrelled Mk VII 2pdr pom-pom, 6 × single 20mm Oerlikons.
1st Alteration: 1 × 4in Mk V HA removed.
2nd Alteration (by June 1945): 2 × single Oerlikons on bridge wings replaced by 2 × twin power-operated Mk V 20mm Oerlikon mounts. Aft torpedo tubes replaced by single Mk 3 40mm Bofors gun mounted to port just aft of searchlight platform.
3rd Alteration (by November 1945): Bofors removed.
4th Alteration (by December 1948): All anti-aircraft armament and radar removed.
This was *Nepal*'s final configuration.

Nizam
As completed: 1 × 4in Mk V HA, 1 × 4-barrelled Mk VII 2pdr pom-pom, 2 × 4-barrelled Mk III 0.5in machine guns, 2 × twin 0.303in Lewis guns.
1st Alteration (by May 1942): 4 × single Oerlikons added, two on the bridge wings replacing 0.5 mgs, two on platforms adjacent to the searchlight.
2nd Alteration (by September 19420: 2 × single Oerlikons added on the quarterdeck.

3rd Alteration (by 23 December 1942): 1 × 4in Mk V HA removed.
4th Alteration (by 9 February 1945): 2 × single Oerlikons on platform adjacent to the searchlight replaced by 2 × twin power-operated Mk V 20mm Oerlikon mounts. A single Mk 3 Bofors was mounted on the port side by the torpedo tube rings. It was later moved to the searchlight platform replacing the searchlight. Aft torpedo tubes removed. This was *Nizam*'s final configuration.

Norman
As completed: 1 × 4in Mk V HA, 1 × 4-barrelled Mk VII 2pdr pom-pom, 2 × 4-barrelled Mk III 0.5in machine guns, 2 × single Oerlikons.
1st Alteration (by February 1942): 4 single Oerlikons added, two on the bridge wings replacing the 0.5in mgs, two on the quarterdeck.
2nd Alteration: 1 × 4in Mk V HA removed.
3rd Alteration: 2 × single Oerlikons on quarterdeck removed. This was *Norman*'s final configuration.

Piorun
As completed: 1 × 4in Mk V HA, 1 × 4-barrelled Mk VII 2pdr pom-pom, 2 × 4-barrelled Mk III 0.5in machine guns, 2 × twin 0.303in Lewis guns.
1st Alteration (by November 1941): 4 × single 20mm Oerlikons added, two on the bridge wings replacing the 0.5in mgs, two on platforms adjacent to the searchlight.
2nd Alteration (by early 1944): 4 × twin power operated Mk V 20mm Oerlikon mounts added, two replacing the two single Oerlikons on the bridge, two replacing the twosingle Oerlikons on platforms adjacent to the searchlight. 2 × single 20mm Oerlikons added on quarterdeck. This was *Piorun*'s final configuration.

Van Galen
As completed: 1 × 4in Mk V HA, 1 × 4-barrelled Mk VII 2pdr pom-pom, 4 × single 20mm Oerlikons, 1 × twin Mk V power-operated 0.5in machine gun tub.
1st Alteration (by 1944): 1 × 4in Mk V HA removed. Aft torpedo tubes replaced. 2 × single 20mm Oerlikons added replacing the 0.5 mg tub.
2nd Alteration (by 1945): 2 × single Oerlikons on quarterdeck removed, 2 × twin power-operated Mk V Oerlikon mounts added to bridge wings replacing 2 × single Oerlikons. This was *Van Galen*'s final configuration.

Commanding Officers

Abbreviations

DSC	Distinguished Service Cross
DSO	Distinguished Service Order
GCVO	Knight Cross of the Royal Victorian Order
Lt Commander	Lieutenant Commander
MVO	Member of the Royal Victorian Order
OBE	Order of the British Empire
RAN	Royal Australian Navy
RN	Royal Navy

Jervis

Captain P J Mack	12 Mar 1939 – 20 Mar 1940.
Lt Commander A M McKillop	19 Jun – 14 Jul 1940.
Captain P J Mack	14 Jul 1940 – 1 Feb 1942.
Captain A L Poland	1 Feb 1942 – 8 Jan 1943.
Captain A F Pugsley	8 Jan – 21 Jun 1943.
Captain J S Crawford	21 Jun – 16 Nov 1943.
Captain H P Henderson	16 Nov 1943 – 28 Jan 1944.
Lt Commander R P Hill DSO, DSC	28 Jan – 17 Sep 1944.
Commander G Ransome DSC	1 Feb – 1 Mar 1945.
Commander C A Williamson	1 Mar – Sep 1945.
Commander D H Maitland-Makgill-Chrichton DSO	Sep 1945 – 4 Jun 1946.

Jackal

Commander T M Napier	14 Mar 1939 – 27 Aug 1940.
Commander C L Firth MVO	27 Aug 1940 – 11 Mar 1941.
Lt Commander R Mc P Jonas	11 Mar – Dec 1941.
Commander C M Leitaigne DSC	Dec 1941 – 12 May 1942.

Jaguar

Lt Commander J F W Hine	1 Aug 1939 – 1 Dec 1941.
Lt P Cole	1 Dec 1941 – Jan 1942.
Lt Commander L R K Tyrwhitt DSC	Jan – 26 Mar 1942.

Janus

Commander J A W Tothill	5 Aug 1939 – 16 May 1940.
Captain P J Mack	16 May – 18 May 1940.
Commander J A W Tothill	18 May 1940 – Jul 1941.
Lt Commander J M Alliston	Aug – Dec 1942.
Lt Commander W B R Morrison	16 Jun 1943 – 23 Jan 1944.

Javelin

Commander A F Pugsley	8 Jun 1939 – 29 Nov 1940.
Lt Commander H C Simms	8 Jan – 30 Sep 1942.
Lt Commander W F N Gregory-Smith	30 Sep – Dec 1942.
Lt Commander J M Alliston DSC	Dec 1942 – 16 Jun 1943.
Lt Commander P B North-Lewis DSC	26 Nov 1943 – 14 Nov 1944.
Lt Commander J B Majoribanks	14 Nov 1944 – 17 Nov 1945.
Lt Commander H Hutchinson	17 Nov 1945 – May 1946.

Jersey

Lt Commander A M McKillop	28 Apr – 15 Nov 1939.
Lt Commander W Evershed	31 Aug 1940 – 8 Jan 1941.
Lt Commander A F Burnell-Nugent	8 Jan – 2 May 1941.

Juno

Commander W E Wilson	16 Aug 1939 – 31 Oct 1940.
Commander St J R J Tyrwhitt	31 Oct 1940 – 21 May 1941.

Jupiter

Lt Commander D B Wyburd	16 May 1939 – 28 Oct 1940.
Lt Commander N V J T Thew	28 Oct 1940 – 28 Feb 1942.

Kelly

Captain Lord Louis Mountbatten GCVO	27 Jun 1939 – 23 May 1941.

Kandahar

Commander W G A Robson	31 Aug 1939 – 20 Dec 1941.

Kashmir

Commander H A King	11 Sep 1939 – 23 May 1941.

Kelvin

Lt Commander J L Machin	26 Oct 1939 – 23 Jun 1940.
Lt Commander J H Allison	26 Jun 1940 – 24 Apr 1942.
Commander M S Townsend OBE, DSO	24 Apr 1942 – 24 Mar 1943.
Lt Commander J T B Birch DSO, DSC	24 Mar – 30 Jun 1943.
Lt Commander R M W MacFarlan	7 Feb 1944 – 13 Jul 1945.

Khartoum

Commander D T Dowler	15 Sep 1939 – 23 Jun 1940.

Kimberley

Lt Commander R G K Knowling	20 Nov 1939 – 1 May 1940.
Lt Commander J S M Richardson	1 May 1940 – 3 May 1942.
Lt Commander J W Rylands	30 Aug 1942 – 10 Mar 1945.
Lt Commander E F Baines DSO	10 Mar – 22 Jun 1945.

Kingston

Lt Commander P Sommerville	22 Jul 1939 – 11 Apr 1942.

Kipling

Commander A St Clair-Ford	15 Nov 1939 – 11 May 1942.

Napier

Captain S H T Arliss RN	16 Sep 1940 – Oct 1942.
Lt Commander A H Green DSC, RAN	Oct 1942 – 2 Nov 1944.
Captain H J Buchanan DSO, RAN	2 Nov – Aug 1945.
Commander G S Stewart RAN	Aug – Nov 1945.

Nepal

Commander F B Morris RAN	11 May 1942 – Dec 1943.
Lt Commander J Plunkett-Cole RAN	Dec 1943 – 8 Oct 1944.
Lt Commander C J Stephenson RAN	8 Oct 1944 – Jan 1946.
Lt Commander W J Taylor	1 July – Dec 1946.
Lt Commander B S Pemberton	Dec 1946 – May 1947.
Lt Commander J A Eardley-Wilmot	7 Aug 1947 – Jun 1948.

As a Minesweeping Trials Vessel:

Lt Commander G H Evans	28 Aug 1948 – 25 Nov 1949.
Lt Commander T P Baillie-Grohman OBE, DSC	25 Nov 1949 – 1 Feb 1951.

Nestor

Commander G S Stewart RAN	31 Dec 1940 – 14 May 1941.
Lt Commander C B Alers-Hankey DSC, RN	14 May – 26 May 1941.
Commander A S Rosenthal RAN	26 May – 16 Jun 1942.

Nizam

Lt Commander J M Clark RAN	19 Dec 1940 – 26 Jan 1943.
Commander C H Brooks RAN	26 Jan 1943 – Nov 1944.
Acting Lt Commander W F Cook RAN	1 Feb – Nov 1945.

Norman

Commander H M Burrell RAN	20 May 1941 – 23 Jun 1943.
Commander H J Buchanan RAN	23 Jun 1943 – 2 Nov 1944.
Lt Commander J Plunkett Cole RAN	2 Nov 1944 – Aug 1945.
Lt Commander A H Green DSC, RAN	Aug – Nov 1945.

Piorun

Commander E Ptawski	4 Nov 1940 – 2 Aug 1941.
Commander S Hryniewiecki	2 Aug – 21 Aug 1941.
Commander E Ptawski	21 Aug – 14 Nov 1941.
Commander S Hryniewiecki	20 Jan – 22 May 1942.
Commander T Gorazdowski	22 May 1942 – 16 Apr 1943.
Commander S Dzienisiewicz	16 Apr 1943 – 7 Jan 1944.
Commander T Gorazdowski	7 Jan 1944 – 6 Jan 1945.
Commander J Tchórznicki	6 Jan – 21 Nov 1945.
Captain W Maracewicz	21 Nov 1945 – 17 Apr 1946.

Tjerk Hiddes

W J Kruys	27 May 1942 – 21 Jan 1944.
J W Caspers	21 Jan – 14 Feb 1944.
G A Cox	14 Feb – 25 Apr 1944.
N W Sluijter	25 Apr 1944 – 1 Aug 1945.
J A Feith	1 Aug – 14 Nov 1945.
F Th Burghard	14 Nov 1945 – 25 Feb 1946.
A W Kruk	25 Feb 1946 – 16 May 1947.
C Hendrikse	16 May 1947 – 1 May 1948.
W A Montanus	1 May 1948 – 22 Apr 1949.
H S J Coumou	22 Apr – 8 Oct 1949.

F Bruyn	8 Oct – 12 Dec 1949.
J F G Haentjes	23 Oct 1950 – 26 Feb 1951.

Van Galen

F Th. Burghard	11 Feb 1942 – 19 Feb 1945.
F L Capel	19 Feb – 20 Apr 1945.
Ltz 1e Kl Mulock van der Vlies Bik PA	20 Apr 1945 – 7 Sep 1946.
Ltz 1e Kl J W Caspers	7 Sep 1946 – 21 Jun 1947.
Mzn W Wader	21 Jun – 2 Sep 1947.
G A Cox	2 Sep 1947 – 1 Nov 1948.
B Poortman	1 Nov 1948 – 4 Apr 1949.
L M van Geen	4 Apr 1949 – 17 Feb 1950.
A M Valkenburg	12 Feb – 15 Oct 1951.
R M Elbers	15 Oct 1951 – 15 Feb 1952.
A M Valkenburg	15 Feb – 27 Jun 1952.
H D B Beudeker	27 Jun – 27 Sep 1952.
W P Salm	27 Sep – 22 Oct 1952.
H D B Beudeker	22 Oct 1952 – 5 Feb 1953.
P W C de Vos	5 Feb – 2 Apr 1953.
W P Salm	2 Apr – 21 Apr 1953.

Notes

1. Commanding officers were frequently appointed before a ship was commissioned so they could supervise the final stages of the commissioning.

2. I have only listed the commanding officers of the ships during their service lives. They often had a commanding officer listed during refits (usually a lieutenant) but he would not take the ship to sea.

3. Commanding officers' decorations and ranks are as for when they were first appointed. I have not included any promotions or decorations earned whilst the officer was in charge of a particular ship. For example Lt Commander Philip Sommerville was promoted to Commander and awarded both the DSC and DSO during his period with *Kingston*.

4. I do not have details of all the Dutch ranks for *Van Galen* or *Tjerk Hiddes*. Where I have these, they have been included.

APPENDIX 5
Launch and Commissioning

Ship	Keel laid down	Launched	Commissioned	Ship	Keel laid down	Launched	Commissioned
Jervis	26 Aug 1937	9 Sep 1938	12 May 1939	Khartoum	27 Oct 1937	6 Feb 1939	6 Nov 1939
Jackal	24 Sep 1937	25 Oct 1938	13 Apr 1939	Kimberley	Jan 1938	1 Jun 1939	21 Dec 1939
Jaguar	Nov 1937	22 Nov 1938	12 Dec 1939	Kingston	6 Oct 1937	9 Jan 1939	14 Sep 1939
Janus	29 Sep 1937	10 Nov 1938	5 Aug 1939	Kipling	20 Oct 1937	19 Jan 1939	20 Dec 1939
Javelin	11 Oct 1937	21 Dec 1938	8 Jun 1939	Napier	26 Jul 1939	22 May 1940	28 Nov 1940
Jersey	28 Sep 1937	26 Sep 1938	28 Apr 1939	Nepal	9 Sep 1939	4 Dec 1941	1 May 1942
Juno	5 Oct 1937	8 Dec 1938	25 Aug 1939	Nestor	26 Jul 1939	9 Jul 1940	3 Feb 1941
Jupiter	20 Sep 1937	27 Oct 1938	22 Jun 1939	Nizam	27 Jul 1939	4 Jul 1940	8 Jan 1941
Kelly	26 Aug 1937	25 Oct 1938	23 Aug 1939	Norman	27 Jul 1939	30 Oct 1940	15 Sep 1941
Kandahar	Jan 1938	21 Mar 1939	10 Oct 1939	Piorun	26 Jul 1939	7 May 1940	4 Nov 1940
Kashmir	Oct 1937	4 Apr 1939	24 Oct 1939	Tjerk Hiddes	27 Jul 1939	25 Jun 1941	6 May 1942
Kelvin	5 Oct 1937	19 Jan 1939	27 Nov 1939	Van Galen	27 Jul 1939	17 Apr 1941	23 Feb 1942

Repairs and Refits carried out at the Humber Ports to 31 December 1939

Minor problems needing attention affected the availability of destroyers during the initial months of the war. Mostly records of these have not survived but Nore Command initiated a report to assess their destroyer availability. Concentrating on Hull and Immingham it listed all destroyers which were docked, the length of the docking and sometimes the reasons for the docking. I have extracted the 'Js' from this list to demonstrate just how frequently destroyers could be put out of action.

Hull

Name in hand	Date taken completed	Date	Remarks
Jackal	7 Nov 1939	21 Nov 1939	Refit
Jackal	11 Dec 1939	19 Dec 1939	Repairs to shaft brushes
Jervis	23 Nov 1939	9 Dec 1939	Refit
Jupiter	16 Dec 1939	3 Jan 1940	Refit

Immingham

Name in hand	Date taken completed	Date	Remarks
Jupiter	2 Nov 1939	3 Nov 1939	Minor repairs
Janus	3 Nov 1939	17 Nov 1939	
Jaguar	8 Nov 1939	8 Nov 1939	
Jupiter	10 Nov 1939	10 Nov 1939	
Jersey	9 Nov 1939	19 Nov 1939	
Jaguar	20 Nov 1939	21 Nov 1939	
Jupiter	21 Nov 1939	22 Nov 1939	
Jersey	25 Nov 1939	4 Dec 1939	
Jersey	7 Dec 1939	7 Jan 1940	Major repairs to damage caused by enemy action.[3]

Reserve Categories

Category A	Operational Reserve	Ships fit for full operational service, all of which will be required for service within three months of mobilization. Normal notice for service for these ships to be considered as fourteen days but see note 1.
Category B	Supplementary Reserve	Ships required for operational service but which will not normally be commissioned until after those in Category A. The normal notice for service for ships in this category should be three months.
Category C	Extended Reserve	Ships required to be preserved for future employment. They will not be commissioned until after post-mobilization expansion takes effect.
Category Z	Disposal List	Ships no longer required for service.

Notes

1. The mobilization of ships in Category A will be spread over three months. Due to defects and lack of manpower a proportion will be at longer notice than fourteen days but this should be kept to a minimum. Peacetime reliefs will be taken as far as possible from this category.

2. Flag Officer Commanding Reserve Fleet will forward to the Admiralty a quarterly 'state of readiness' of ships in Categories A and B for use with mobilizing lists

3. All ships in Categories A and B are required to be refitted and docked at the standard intervals. Those in Category C should be docked as necessary for preservation and given such limited refits as the refitting capacity allows.

4. Ships which have been dehumidified will have a 'star' after their reserve category (B*). This will generally apply to ships in Categories B and C only.

5. The numbers and classes of ships required in each category will be decided by the Naval Staff, Flag Officer Commanding Reserve Fleet, in consultation with the Naval Staff, will exchange ships in these categories if defects or other reasons make it necessary.

Categories BI and BII

Category B was split into two new categories BI and BII. With BII ships were on extended notice and could not be brought forward without a refit. The maintenance routine was every four to six weeks unlike BI where it was every week. Ships in Category BII were based at Harwich in groups of twenty-four and were cared for by a working group of fifty-one officers and ratings and fifty-six watchkeepers. All Kellys in the reserve fleet were reduced to Category BII in November 1946.

APPENDIX 8

Endurance and fuel consumption

Endurance and fuel consumption for 'J', 'K' and 'N' class under war conditions (extracted from Home Fleet Tactical Instructions 1 June 1943).

Speed (kts)	Consumption Tons/hour	% per day	Endurance Hours	Miles
8	1.65	8.55	267	2140
9	1.68	8.70	263	2360
10	1.72	8.90	256	2560
11	1.80	9.32	245	2700
12	1.90	9.84	232	2780
13	2.02	10.46	218	2840
14	2.18	11.30	202	2830
15	2.38	12.33	185	2780
16	2.60	13.45	169	2710
17	2.88	14.90	153	2600
18	3.16	16.35	139	2510
19	3.50	18.10	126	2390
20	3.85	19.90	114	2290
21	4.28	22.15	103	2160
22	4.75	24.55	92.8	2040
23	5.27	27.20	83.8	1930
24	5.82	30.10	75.8	1820
25	6.44	33.30	68.5	1710
26	7.05	36.50	62.6	1630
27	7.77	40.30	56.7	1530
28	8.57	44.40	51.5	1440
29	9.50	49.20	46.4	1350
30	10.55	54.70	41.8	1250
31	11.84	61.40	37.2	1150
32	13.60	70.40	32.5	1040
33	14.70	76.20	30.0	990

Notes:
(a) Machinery in units.
(b) Half hour's notice for full steam.
(c) All steam dynamos running.
(d) Hydraulic engines as required for third degree of readiness (where applicable) and allowing for 5 per cent fuel remaining, ship six months out of dock and paravanes not in use.

Admiralty cruising orders with endurance

	Kts	Tons/hour	Endurance (miles)
Full authorised power	33.0	14.70	990
With all despatch – 9/10	31.5	12.60	1100
With despatch – 3/5	28.0	8.57	1440
With all convenient despatch – 2/5	24.5	6.10	1770
With moderate despatch – 1/5	20.0	3.85	2290
Economical	13.0	2.02	2840

Note: With full normal stowage of 464 tons and 5 per cent reserve

[2] See Connell, Mediterranean Maelstrom.

[3] These were initial repairs to enable the ship to arrive safely at Hull. She would be out of action for much longer.

Sources

PRIMARY

Ships' covers

These are a useful source of information covering the design process of a particular class of ship and are held at the National Maritime Museum. They can also contain some service information but they are not the whole story. For example the covers for the 'Js' and 'Ks' do not contain any mention of Mountbatten's role in the designprocess. The following were consulted:

Nos. 565 and 565a   'J' and 'K' class destroyers.
No. 609   'N' class destroyers.
No. 810   Type 18 anti-submarine frigates.

Ships' contracts

Also held at the National Maritime Museum these form a detailed specification of all the requirements and standards needed to build a Kelly. Each consists of a hardback book about 6in thick and the contracts for the 'N' class contain amendments in ink. The following were consulted:

Contract for 'J' class
Contract for *Kingston*
Contract for *Nepal*

'As built' drawings

Held at the National Maritime Museum these need to be treated with caution as they do not necessarily show the actual configuration of the ship. For example, the drawing for *Kipling* shows a tripod mast with a DF aerial installed on the rear deckhouse, but this was never actually installed. Also consulted were the class modification drawings which showed the changes authorised during the ships' service lives. The following were consulted:

Modification drawings for the 'J', 'K' and 'N' class
General drawings for the 'J' and 'K' class leader
Drawings for *Kandahar*, *Kashmir*, *Kelvin*, *Khartoum*, *Kimberley*, *Kingston*, *Kipling*.
Drawings for *Jackal*, *Jaguar*, *Janus*, *Javelin*, *Jersey*, *Juno* and *Jupiter*.
Drawings for *Napier*, *Nepal*, *Nestor*, *Nizam*, *Norman*, *Piorun*, *Tjerk Hiddes* and *Van Galen*.

Builders' drawings

For the drawings in the book, copies of builders' drawings were purchased. These are accurate and do show the ships as they were actually built. Of interest was the re-use of several drawings for *Juno* in the drawings for the leader of the 'N' class, *Napier*.

Drawings used were:
From Fairfield Archives: *Napier* and *Kelvin*.
From John Brown Archives: *Jackal*.

Ships' logs

Held at the Public Record Office, Kew, these are incomplete in many ways. Firstly, at the end of the war most wartime destroyer logs were destroyed and only a few of these and several of the pre-war period survive. Secondly, they can either be detailed and useful or perfunctory, just giving a course and a statement like 'escorting convoy'. The logs for the 'J' class were fairly complete and extended from the start of a ship's commission to December 1939 or January 1940. Only four logs for the

'K' class survive and one post-war one for *Nepal*. They are all held in the ADM53 series. The following were consulted:

Jervis	ADM53/109400 to 109407	May to December 1939
	ADM53/121581	December 1945 to January 1946
	ADM53/123060 to 123062	January to June 1946
Jackal	ADM53/109350 to 109358	April to December 1939
	ADM53/112487 to 112488	January to February 1940
Jaguar	ADM53/109363 to 109366	September to December 1939
	ADM53/112491	January 1940
Janus	ADM53/109367 to 109371	August to December 1939
	ADM53/112492	January 1940
Javelin	ADM53/109384 to 109386	August to October 1939
	ADM53/116101 to 116106	January to August 1942
	ADM53/117686 to 117688	February to June 1943
Jersey	ADM53/109394 to 109399	June to December 1939
	ADM53/112496	January 1940
Juno	ADM53/109411 to 109413	August to October 1939
Jupiter	ADM53109414 to 109420	June to December 1939
	ADM53/112505	January 1940
Kelly	ADM53/109433 to 109437	August to December 1939
	ADM53/112518	January 1940
Kelvin	ADM53/109447	November to December 1939
	ADM53/112519 to 112520	January to February 1940
Kimberley	ADM53/109471	December 1939
	ADM53/112540	January 1940
Kipling	ADM53/109487	December 1939
	ADM53/112552	January 1940
Nepal	ADM53/124960 to 124962	October to December 1948
	ADM53/126503 to 126514	January to December 1949
	ADM53/128548 to 128559	January to December 1950
	ADM53/130854 to 130856	January to March 1951

Admiralty Fleet Orders and Confidential Admiralty Fleet Orders

Held at the Public Record Office, Kew, these detail service alterations and modifications. The ordinary Admiralty range deal with such modifications as hull changes and main armament. The confidential series deals with such matters as radar, anti aircraft weapons and camouflage.

The Admiralty Fleet Orders for January 1939 to December 1945 are to be found in the range ADM182/99 to ADM182/124. The Confidential Admiralty Fleet Orders for January 1939 to December 1945 are found in the range ADM182/125 to ADM182/142.

'Pink Lists'

Held at the Public Record Office, Kew, these documents give details of ship location, refits and flotillas. They also – up to 1944 – gave fairly detailed equipment fits for ships including radar. Compiled weekly, they are sometimes out of date and the information contained in them can be inaccurate. Used with caution though they are very useful and are very good on flotilla organisation. The Pink Lists for the whole war are found in the series ADM187/1 to ADM187/55.

Damage reports

Held at the Public Record Office, Kew. These give very detailed accounts of what damage a ship received on a particular occasion. Several are missing but some can be found in other series such as the ADM199 and the ADM234 series. They do not cover collision damage. However, most are to be found in the ADM267 series which also contains several interesting analyses.

War diaries
Held at the Public Record Office, Kew in the ADM199 series. These are also patchy but frequently give good information on the location of ships and why they sailed. Accidents and collisions are also mentioned as are operations and patrol lines. A useful starting point and frequently the only source of information on a particular operation. Those consulted included the diaries for the Home Fleet, Mediterranean Stations, Red Sea Command, Plymouth Command, Nore Command, East Indies Command and all the Scottish commands early during the war. The war diary for the Dartmouth station was written by a genuine wit and is a joy to read.

Reports of operations
Held at the Public Record Office, Kew. Mostly concentrated in the ADM199 range, these consist of a summary of an operation, the orders for it and frequently individual ships' reports of proceedings attached to it. However, Korean war reports are held in the ADM116 range as ADM199 deals exclusively with Second World War history. The complete history for the Syrian Campaign is held in ADM199/679 'Operations in the Mediterranean' though *Janus*'s damage report appears elsewhere. The plans for Operation 'Catherine' appear in the range ADM116/6289 to ADM116/6292.

Individual ship's Reports of Proceedings
Held at the Public Record Office, Kew. These are scattered all over the place but mostly concentrated in ADM199 with several in the ADM1 range as well. Some are attached to operational reports, others to war diaries and yet others are just by themselves. A report of proceedings could cover a passage from one port to another or it could be an account of a major engagement. What is also clear is that some have been chosen as a representative sample and many will have been destroyed. For example *Kelly*'s report on an abortive submarine hunt survives (ADM1/20029) as does a report on convoy escort from Rosyth in appalling weather by members of the 'J' class in January 1940 (ADM1/10539).

Aircraft engagement reports
Held at the Public Record Office, Kew. When a warship was attacked by an enemy aircraft a report was made. These are concentrated in ADM199/99 for ships in the Mediterranean. They include the time, date, location, type of aircraft, type of attack, and the response together with the weapons fired. Some include mention of damage and if a group of destroyers was attacked they frequently all filed a report making it easy to reconstruct the action.

Anti-submarine reports
Held at the Public Record Office, Kew. Early in the war a pro forma was devised for every time a depth charge was dropped. These were sent to the Admiralty, collated and assessed. If the report was interesting enough and led to the sinking of an enemy submarine it could appear as a full account in the Monthly Anti-Submarine reports. Extensive examples of all these stages exist in the ADM199 range. The attacks are concentrated in the ranges ADM199/126 to ADM199/133 and ADM199/2032 to ADM199/2036. Assessments appear in the range ADM199/121 to 1123. I should stress that these ranges only cover 1939 and 1940. Finally *Jupiter*'s sinking of the Japanese submarine *I60* is recounted in one of the Monthly Anti-Submarine reports which is preserved as ADM199/2059.

Convoy reports
Held at the Public Record Office, Kew. These records are extensive but confusingly organised (something one can say about the whole ADM199 range). Several documents exist for each convoy but care is needed to find the details of the escort. Frequently, escort commanders filed a report of proceedings but these have not necessarily survived. Coastal convoys are the worst documented but I was able to find reasonable details for the times the 'J' class were used as a strike force. Also useful were the BN and BS Red Sea series convoy reports (ADM199/19) and the Mediterranean daily state which listed the convoys being escorted. The war diaries helped in this respect.

Reports on the loss of ships
Held at the Public Record Office, Kew. Several have not survived but those that have seem to have been concentrated in ADM1 and ADM199. Particularly interesting are those which cover Boards of Inquiry into losses. *Khartoum*'s loss is covered in considerable detail in ADM1/11210 and likewise the loss of *Neptune* and *Kandahar* appears in ADM1/11947. ADM199/2067 contains the loss of *Jupiter* and ADM199/2068 the loss of *Nestor*. Others are not covered in so much detail.

Arrangements for the 'N' class
Held at the Public Record Office, Kew. These are concentrated in ADM1 and ADM116. ADM1/11141 concerns the five Australian 'N' class, ADM1/11154 the sale of *Noble* and *Nonpareil* to the Dutch and the transfer of *Piorun* is to be found in ADM116/4098.

Weapons and tactics
Held at the Public Record Office, Kew, some in the ADM234 range which includes damage reports as well. ADM234/192 is the gunnery manual for the Mk XII 4.7in and ADM234/511 is the paravane drill book. Others are held in the ADM186 range, particularly ADM186/533 for depth charge drill and ADM186/355 for the 0.5in quadruple machine gun mounting. Extensive information on weaponry and tactics are also to be found in the Destroyer Fighting Instructions (ADM239/132) and the Mediterranean (ADM199/1084), Eastern (ADM199/1085) and Home Fleet (ADM199/1082) Tactical Instructions.

Director of Naval Construction's correspondence and diaries
Held at the Public Record Office, Kew and at the British Library. The relevant correspondence is held in the ADM299 range particularly ADM299/11 to ADM299/14. Mr Stanley Goodall's diaries are held at the British Library under the reference Add 52785 to Add 52792 with the relevant diary being Add 52789. Several entries are of particular interest in particular, those for 10 March 1939, 11 March 1939, 1 March 1940 and 5 April 1940.

Miscellaneous
There are many references in the ADM1 range at the Public Record Office to the Kellys. ADM1/22541 for example covers the funnel markings for destroyers introduced in 1945. Reserve categories are detailed in ADM1/19815 and the potential salvage of *Khartoum* in ADM121289. Another relevant reference was ADM280/407 which covered the trials on the remaining 'Js' and 'Ks' in 1949. The information on the *Javelin* mutiny is contained in provisional references ADM116/6420 and 6421.

Commanding Officers
The main source for the list of commanding officers was the Navy Lists which are held in various places. I consulted the copies held on open shelves in the Public Record Office at Kew. These listed the commanding officer of each ship in service during the war and were published on a quarterly basis during the war. Post war they were published twice yearly. They do contain one or two gaps and here the reports of proceedings are most useful especially if a commanding officer changes after the list is published and the ship is then sunk before the new list appears. Ships which had been lost did not appear in the lists.

PUBLISHED

Books

Anon, *Male Monografie 3, Niszczyciel Klasy J, K, N ORP Piorun* (GPM)

Carl Boyd and Akihiko Yoshida, *The Japanese Submarine Force and World War II* (Airlife Publishing 1996)

David Brown (ed), *The British Pacific and East Indies Fleets* (Brodie Publishing Ltd 1995)

D K Brown RCNC, *Nelson to Vanguard, Warship Design and Development 1923-1945* (London 2000)

J Campbell, *Naval Weapons of World War II* (London 1985)

Ronald Careless, *Battleship Nelson, The Story of HMS Nelson* (Arms and Armour Press, 1985)

G G Connell, *Mediterranean Maelstrom, HMS Jervis and the 14th Flotilla* (London 1987)

Jean Labayle Couhat, *French Warships of World War II* (Ian Allan, 1978)

Viscount Cunningham of Hyndhope, *A Sailor's Odyssey* (Hutchinson & Co, 1951)

A D Divine, *Destroyer's War* (John Murray, 1943)

Aldo Fraccaroli, *Italian Warships of World War II* (Ian Allan, 1978)

Norman Friedman, *US Destroyers, An Illustrated Design History* (Annapolis 1982)

Jack Green and Alessandro Massignani, *The Naval War in the Mediterranean 1940-1943* (London 1998)

Captain Russell Grenfell, *The Bismarck Episode* (Faber and Faber, 1948)

Roger Hill, *Destroyer Captain, Memoirs of the War at Sea 1942-1945* (Grafton Books, 1986)

David Holmes, *G64, The Last Trip* (Merlin Books Ltd, 1994)

Richard Hough, *Bless our Ship, Mountbatten and the Kelly* (Hodder and Stoughton, 1991)

H T Lenton and J J Colledge, *Warships of World War II* (Ian Allan, 1980)

L J Lind and M A Payne, *N Class* (The Naval Historical Society of Australia, 1993)

Captain Donald Macintyre, *Narvik* (Pan Books, 1962)

Edgar March, *British Destroyers* (Seeley Service, 1966)

Ministry of Information, *Ark Royal, The Admiralty Account of her Achievement* (HMSO, 1942)

Ministry of Information, *East of Malta, West of Suez, The Admiralty Account of the Naval War in the Eastern Mediterranean: September 1939 to March 1941* (HMSO, 1943)

Ministry of Information, *The Mediterranean Fleet, Greece to Tripoli, The Admiralty Account of Naval Operations: April 1941 to January 1943* (HMSO, 1944)

F C Van Oosten, *The Battle of the Java Sea* (Ian Allan, 1976)

S W C Pack, *The Battle of Matapan* (Pan Books, 1968)

S W C Pack, *The Battle of Sirte* (Ian Allan, 1975)

Ian Parsons (Editor), *The Encyclopaedia of Sea Warfare* (Salamander, 1975)

Kenneth Poolman, *HMS Kelly* (New English Library, 1974)

Rear Admiral A F Pugsley, *Destroyer Man* (Wiedenfeld and Nicolson, 1957)

Rene Sarnet and Eric Le Vaillant, *Richelieu* (Marines Edition, 1997)

Peter C Smith, *Eagles War, The War Diary of an Aircraft Carrier* (Crécy Books, 1995)

David Thomas, *Battle of the Java Sea* (Andre Deutsch Ltd, 1968)

David A Thomas, *Crete 1941, The Battle at Sea* (New English Library 1975)

Ben Warlow & Sydney Goodman, *The Royal Navy in Focus in World War II* (Maritime Books, 1994)

A J Watts, *Japanese Warships of World War II* (Ian Allan, 1978)

M J Whitley, *Destroyer! German Destroyers in World War II* (Arms and Armour Press, 1983)

M J Whitley, *Destroyers of World War Two, An International Encyclopaedia* (Cassell & Co, 2000)

M J Whitley, *German Capital Ships of World War Two* (Arms and Armour Press, 2000)

John Winton, *Carrier Glorious* (Arrow Books, 1989)

John Winton, *Cunningham, The Greatest Admiral since Nelson* (John Murray, 1998)

Richard Woodman, *Arctic Convoys* (John Murray, 1996)

Philip Ziegler, *Mountbatten* (Collins, 1985)

Articles

D K Brown, 'The Great Pacific Typhoon', *The Naval Architect* (September 1985)

D K Brown, 'Stability of RN destroyers during World War II', *Warship Technology*

Robert Dumas, 'The Last Super Destroyers? *Mogador* & *Kléber* Classes', *Warship 30* (April 1984)

'The Launch of HMS *Jersey*', *Jersey Evening Post* (27 September 1938)

'HMS *Jersey* Arrives', *Jersey Evening Post* (10 July 1939)

Donald L Kindell, 'The 5th Destroyer Flotilla, Autumn 1940, *Warship 16* (October 1980)

Alan Payne, 'The Origin of the J Class Destroyers', *Warship 15* (July 1980)

'Kingston Has a 1,600 tons Godchild', *The Surrey Comet* (10 January 1939)

UNPUBLISHED RESEARCH

Anon, *Service History of HMS Kingston* (Kingston Local History Studies Centre)

Anon, *Service History of Hr.Ms Tjerk Hiddes* (Marinemuseum, Netherlands)

Anon, *Service History of Hr.Ms Van Galen* (Marinemuseum, Netherlands)

Marek Twardowski, *Service History of ORP Piorun*

Admiralty

Anon, *The Camouflage of Ships at Sea* (CB 3098 (45) R)

Videos

The Naval Video Time Capsule series, *Episodes of the Royal Navy* contains several film sequences of Kellys. Parts Two, Three, Four and Nine contain some good shots of 'J' and 'K' class ships, the sequence involving *Kelvin* in Part Nine being particularly lengthy and good. 'N' class ships can be seen in Parts Four, Ten and Eleven.

INDEX

Page numbers in *italic* refer to illustrations, in **bold** to tables.
All ships are Royal Navy unless otherwise indicated. Kellys' names are in **bold**.
For individual operations see under 'Operations', for individual destroyer flotilla see under 'flotillas'.

Abbreviations

Adm = Admiral; Capt = Captain; Cdr = Commander; GB = British merchant ship; Ger = Germany;
Ind = Indonesia; It = Italy; Jpn = Japan; Lt = Lieutenant; Lt-Cdr = Lieutenant-Commander;
Neths = Netherlands; Pol = Poland; R/A = Rear-Admiral; Swe = Sweden